EX LIBRIS
XXXIII.
Wayne Harburn
IL MENEGHELLO · MILANO

THE STUMP JUMPERS

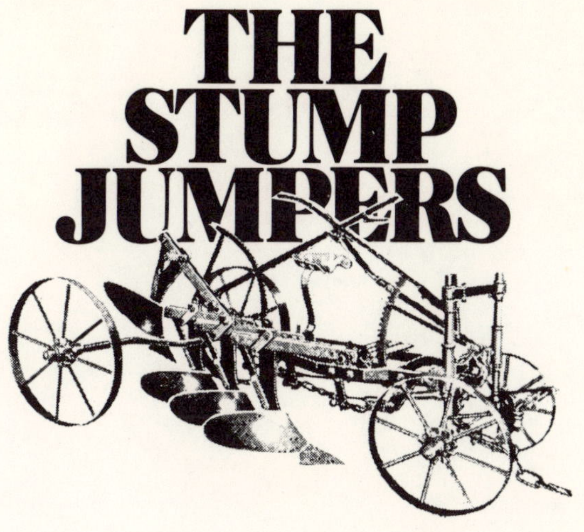

Stump-jumper /stʌmp-dʒʌmpə/, *n.* (*f. Aust. colloq.* stump-jump plough) **1.** One who or that which jumps stumps, i.e. overcomes obstacles by innovation and independence, to attain high achievement. **2.** A self-made, resilient Australian achiever of vision. (As in, *You little . . .*)

THE STUMP JUMPERS

A new breed of Australians

Neil Lawrence
&
Steve Bunk

Hale & Iremonger

Typeset, printed & bound by
Southwood Press Pty Limited
80–92 Chapel Street, Marrickville, NSW

For the publisher
Hale & Iremonger Pty Limited
GPO Box 2552, Sydney, NSW

National Library of Australia Catalogue Card no. and
ISBN 0 86806 222 7

Contents

Foreword

This book began as something slightly other than what it has become. Neil Lawrence's original intention was to assemble a collection of contemporary life stories of pacesetting Australian business people, as told in those Stump-Jumpers' own words. However, in talking with many successful Australians from virtually all walks of life, he soon became aware that stump-jumping is a peculiarly Australian way of looking at the world and its challenges. This unique view embraces not only business but sport, entertainment, art, personal relationships — in fact, every aspect of experience in this promising, albeit occasionally frustrating, country.

The stump-jumper, Neil reasoned, is a symbol of and a precursor to Australia's future. The attributes of the stump-jumpers and the lessons learnt from their successful struggles against the odds of geographic isolation, bureaucracy, and a nagging national self-doubt are tools that can bridge the gap between Australia's pioneering heritage and the demands of years yet to come. We'll tell you more of what we mean by that.

Australians know that this country was built on innovation, by people who often had no choice but to improvise if they were to forge ahead in a frontier where 'traditional' ways and means were not only far-off but sometimes inappropriate as solutions to the challenges posed by this rugged continent. That the pioneers met such challenges was central to the development of the Australian character and is a source of our quiet pride today in the nation they founded. It is no accident that Australia has produced one of the world's highest numbers of inventors per capita of any country — more than either England or that often-praised incubator of innovation, the United States.

Then came World War I and, with it, a loss of many young Australian men of promise. World War II brought an influx of people from other cultures and a heightening of the new age of mechanisation. This country was ill-prepared, by the very isolation that fostered her lateral-thinking style, to deal with the demands of manufacturing and exporting products and services. As a result, she has relied heavily on imports in the post-war years to maintain what has become one of the most enviable living standards on earth. The danger in this is that Australia's pioneering ethic, the ability to make the best of whatever is at hand, is slowly being strangled by the cheap convenience of goods and services mass-produced abroad. Australia, a nation of creative thinkers, is now threatened with becoming a colourless second cousin to that doyen of Western marketing, America.

Australia today is poised on the outside edge of a constricting globe and is faced with the newest, perhaps biggest, challenge of all: to consolidate her status in the world culture and economy that have emerged in the post-industrial age, the age of instant communication and frequent travel. In order to do that, she must turn back to her greatest natural resource, the ingenuity of her own populace. This is why the contemporary stump-jumper is much more than simply one who excels. He or she represents a spirit and a method of leading Australia into tomorrow via this country's traditional strength in fostering the pioneer ethic.

This isn't to say that the people whose stories are told herein have exclusive licence to the title of stump-jumper. Not by a long shot. The interviewees have specialised skills and are among the best in their respective fields but, as such, they represent only a cross-section of Australia's virtually untapped reserves of non-academic expertise. Each of them is self-made, each has displayed the burning determination to achieve that makes a mockery of the 'she'll be right' Australian stereotype. But there are many others like them, both sung and unsung by the media. The wisdom they offer is largely the wisdom of the real world, in which Australia must become more competitive if she is to retain her individuality as a nation.

The combination of famous and relatively unknown names is important in our mix of interviewees, because creativity and accomplishment run neither in tandem with nor contrary to renown. There are more men than women on our list because, let's face it, until recently it has been exceedingly difficult for Australian women to excel outside the constraints of the home, as the women in this volume convincingly attest. There are first-generation immigrants here and people whose Australian ancestry goes back to the First Fleet, there are old achievers and relatively young ones. There are even stump-jumping feats chronicled here that some might consider to be less significant than other deeds done by Australians in these pages or outside them, because stump-jumping *is* a common occurrence at all social levels of this country. The fact is that stump-jumping, the vision to conceive and the perseverance to reach the goal no matter what the complications, is a too-often overlooked way of Australian life. It demands attention because in the act of stump-jumping lies the hope for Australia's future.

The people in this volume have earned fortunes in pursuit of their visions but, somewhat surprisingly, they don't tend to equate money directly with success. The responsibility of wealth and how they use it to improve both their own lot and that of many other Australians are among the points of interest in this book which illuminate the nature of stump-jumping as a blueprint for personal fulfilment. These and other characteristics, as depicted in the concluding chapter, are common to far more Australians than our often self-effacing countrymen might expect.

In individual cases and in the life of the nation, such a blueprint cannot be drawn up without changes, additions and deletions, for the essence of stump-jumping is the ability to remain uncowed by setbacks and to find, by hard work, courage and native 'nous', a way of turning adversity to advantage. The attitudes and opinions expressed herein are individualistic, highly provocative, even inflammatory at times, because these people have learnt well the lesson that sheer luck has run out for the Lucky Country. Their dealings with the Japanese, Europeans and Americans are recounted here as valuable source material on what Australia offers the world today and what the world can give to Australia. Similarly, the personal lives of these stump-jumpers reflect the peaks and pitfalls of matter-of-course, calculated risk-taking.

Although our interviewees are helping to lead the resurgence of patriotism that Australia enjoys these days, their optimism about this country's future is far from unqualified. They realise that a pat on the nation's back, all the recent talk about the forging of a national identity, simply aren't enough. Because of that realisation, this book does not draw a bed-of-roses picture. People who see Australia and the world as they really are can't possibly be content with the status quo; for beyond complacency, ruin awaits. What the people in this volume are doing is actively changing the status quo for the better, before it's too late.

By allowing the interviewees to put their stories in the first person, the authors hope to have acted as conduits to the messages these experts bring — uncluttered messages which in many ways are remarkably like-thinking. It's as if by totally different approaches in their many endeavours, these Australians have come upon certain truths others amongst us have yet to grasp. Despite often frenetic working lives, they are only too happy, even eager, to pass on this knowledge. Stump-jumping is a hands-on experience, which is why, in an effort to encourage active involvement, we have included a Stump-Jumper's Quiz for honest self-evaluation in this book.

Why did we choose the title, *The Stump-Jumpers*? Because it expresses success under Australian conditions, a success which may be relative to each individual's challenges and restraints but which has the common characteristic of being achieved by and for Australians. We also chose it because, based on an invaluable Australian invention, the stump-jump plough, 'stump-jumper' is a new word, our own little innovation. Australia already has her battlers and tall poppies, her cultural cringe and tyranny of distance, her mateship and multiculturalism. We can think of no more positive outcome of this work than if 'stump-jumper' were to enter the Australian lexicon.

Neil Lawrence, Steve Bunk
Sydney, 1985

Introduction

Neil Lawrence marched into a supermarket in downtown Manhattan and broke his last ten dollar note on the biggest bunch of flowers he could find. Then he strode purposefully across the street and took the elevator directly to the executive suite atop the New York Post building.

At reception he asked for Mr Rupert Murdoch's private secretary. A young woman dressed for success duly appeared and Lawrence jumped into action.

'These are for you,' he said, thrusting the flowers at her. 'I've travelled halfway around the world to see Mr Murdoch and I know you won't disappoint me. I'm prepared to wait as long as it takes but I must see him.'

The secretary was overwhelmed, amused, and sympathetic. The ploy — a classic stump-jumper technique — would have worked but for one thing: Murdoch was in Los Angeles stitching up the Fox deal and wouldn't be back for a week!

For Lawrence, who had been busting down the doors of the rich and famous for over two years, it was a rare and hopefully temporary defeat. As this book goes to press negotiations are proceeding for the inclusion of Rupert Murdoch in *Stump-Jumpers II*. But if Murdoch is missing from this collection, then remember that a number of influential and successful interviewees are already in the bag for No. II.

Armed with a tape recorder, a lot of energy and a hide as thick as a rhinoceros, marketing man and former theology student Lawrence has put together a formidable collection of interviews in which notable Australians disclose the secrets of their success and shed some light on the uniquely Australian style of getting ahead which Lawrence calls 'stump-jumping'.

When this immense labour of love began, Neil Lawrence was, by his own admission, anything but a stump-jumper. His approach to his career was rigidly conformist, although he had arrived in marketing via an interesting and circuitous route. Born in England 33 years ago, Lawrence got his first taste of the communications industry writing for a Belgian sporting newspaper. The job proved to be so interesting that Lawrence delayed his return to England and consequently missed out on admission to most of the university faculties open to him. Undeterred, he applied for such obscure courses as Egyptology, Theology, and Chinese ceramics. Theology won him, and he went down to Kings College, London, with not a thought in the world of ever reversing his collar.

'Oddly enough,' Lawrence recalls, 'theology was great preparation for the work I would eventually do. It is, after all, the motivation for millions of people all around the world, and if you understand that motivation you understand a lot about the people you meet.'

Lawrence drifted to Australia in search of new opportunities some six years ago, dabbled in marketing and helped a friend establish a company. But, gripped by the travel bug, he continued on to the United States. In New York he signed on as a senior partner in a marketing consultancy, advising such major corporations as Johnson and Johnson and Westinghouse, and enjoyed the work so much that he stayed three years before returning to Australia.

Settling in Sydney, Lawrence established his own marketing and public relations consultancy. During this period he was approached by a training and development company. 'Put together a program for me through which we can work less and earn more,' the principal asked. Lawrence considered the nature of this assignment and decided it was less difficult than finding the fountain of youth — but only marginally so. However, he had observed with increasing interest the rapid climb up the best seller lists of such books as *In Search of Excellence* and *The One Minute Manager*, and it thus occurred to him that the logical way to gather information on the subject of business success was to go and ask the successful how they did it. Furthermore, the success of books on just this subject alerted Lawrence's marketing senses to the commercial possibilities of such information.

What began as a program for a training and development consultancy soon became an obsession. Lawrence put together an outline for a book on Australian success stories in business and a variety of other fields of endeavour, bought a cheap tape recorder and started interviewing.

His early choice of subjects proved to be fortunate. Paul Hogan was first on the list. Lawrence visited him at home in Belrose, NSW, turned the tape recorder on and Hogan, a natural raconteur, did the rest. Next came Dame Joan Sutherland, of whom Lawrence, a long-time opera buff, was deeply in awe. He felt strangely nervous when he shared a cab with La Stupenda, but Dame Joan put him immediately at ease when the interview began in a tiny dressing room at the Sydney Opera House. She chatted and laughed as though she were spending an afternoon with an old friend.

This was to be the form for many of the interviews. Lawrence found that once he had pinned his subject down, the conversations tended to go way past the allotted time, so enthusiastic did they become. As well, Lawrence discovered that the information they supplied helped him to formulate his interviewing approach for the next person on his list. He became, in effect, a walking encyclopaedia of business acumen.

At this point he approached advertising executive Jacqueline Huie, who had just been named Businesswoman of the Year, to co-author the book. Initially interested, Huie eventually passed because she felt that Lawrence's intention to cover successes in many different areas of endeavour took the work beyond her company's sphere of interest. However, Huie's associate Constant Behrens thought the idea a winner, followed through on the association with Lawrence and became a sounding board and ideas man on the project.

Convinced he now had the basic ingredients for a successful book, Lawrence contracted freelance journalists and editors Phil Jarratt and Neil Jamieson to help him prepare a test chapter and synopsis. Bypassing the literary agents — he had already learned that stump-jumpers eliminate the middle-men whenever possible — Lawrence went direct to the publishing houses, eventually settling on Hale and Iremonger, where Sylvia Hale expressed her confidence in the project not only by agreeing to publish the work but by writing a cheque for an advance.

This injection of funds enabled Lawrence to devote more time to the project, but he soon found that his book had a voracious appetite for cash. For one thing, the people he needed to interview were not all conveniently located in Sydney. They were as far afield as the Great Barrier Reef, London, New York and Alaska! Having exhausted his own financial resources, he turned to contacts in the travel industry and received generous support from TAA and Pan American. At the same time Lawrence secured the services of expatriate American writer Steve Bunk and secretary Barbara Wuthrich to work as his team in Sydney, transcribing and editing the interviews as he brought them home.

Thus early in 1985 — some 18 months after he had begun work on the project — Lawrence dropped all other work and began a global orgy of interviewing. A master of the foot-in-the-door technique, he often announced his presence from a phone in the airline terminal and arrived by cab at the subject's office five minutes later. Such enthusiasm was usually rewarded by extraordinarily frank and revealing interviews.

During this period, Lawrence, a workaholic, made every second count. On one occasion he completed an interview in the VIP room at Sydney International Airport, caught a cab around to the domestic terminals, flew to Coolangatta, rented a car and drove back across the border for an interview in Mullumbimby. The next morning he was up at dawn to drive to an interview in Surfers Paradise, then on to Brisbane where he interviewed a giant of the pastoral and primary industries, followed by a drive north of Brisbane to another interview at Buderim, finally arriving back in Brisbane at three in the morning, where he was able to snatch a couple of hours sleep before racing to Toowoomba for a daybreak interview with a living legend of the Outback. Next came a Grand Prix exit out of the Toowoomba Ranges to Brisbane Airport, where he caught a plane to Proserpine, connecting with a private plane to Hamilton Island in time to interview its owner, Keith Williams.

The constant battle against the clock and the budget for the book continued when Lawrence took his interviewing show abroad. He flew direct to London, showered in the Heathrow terminal and arrived 45 minutes late for his interview with director Fred Schepisi, not because of jet lag or plane delays, but because of the inefficiency of the London taxi service. In New York, having successfully completed interviews with one of the world's most high-powered financial brokers and with the current guru in the USA of the telecommunications industry (the millionaire self-styled 'apostle of success'), Lawrence bolted for Kennedy Airport to catch a flight to San Francisco in order to connect for Alaska. However, United Airlines' workers had timed a strike to coincide with the start of the school holidays and every seat on every Pan Am plane headed west was taken. Flying standby, Lawrence was bumped from flight after flight. Just as he reached the point of exasperation he was called for a Los Angeles flight.

He had just buckled into his seat when a flight attendant apologised and explained that he had been called incorrectly. There was no seat for him. Lawrence then hid at the back of the cabin until the plane began to taxi. The attendants had no alternative but to find him a seat and he was on his way west.

Often the interview subjects were as strapped for time as was Lawrence. The interview with Bob Ansett, for example, was conducted in the Budget boss's car as he drove to and from a court appearance. Wine merchant Richard Holden was also interviewed in a car — this time at a scenic rest stop overlooking one of Alaska's most spectacular ski resorts. The interview with Keith Williams began over dinner at Hamilton Island and finished at one in the morning beside the pool. As Lawrence interviewed celebrity hairdresser Stefan Ackerie in the garden of his Surfers Paradise canal-front home, he was intrigued by a boatload of people who waved frantically as they passed. As Stefan did not seem to know them Lawrence deduced that they must have been waving to him and waved back. Only later did he realise that they were paying customers on a 'see the homes of stars' tour.

As he travelled the world in search of the rich and famous, Lawrence was constantly made aware of the gap between their lifestyles and his. He moved cautiously at first, then confidently from appointments in the finest restaurants and hotels in the world to the realities of his own bargain basement life on the run, sleeping in airline terminals or at the homes of supportive friends. But as he learned more about the people he interviewed, he discovered that underneath the trappings of success they were mere mortals, obliging and friendly. He found that the elements common in all of their life stories were these — hard work, self-confidence, and the vision and guts to be nonconformist.

'It was a wonderful learning experience,' Lawrence says. 'Seeing how stump-jumpers operate has changed my whole approach to doing things. I think I'm more inclined to jump in at the deep end now.'

As *Stump-Jumpers* the book reached a state of preparedness, Lawrence enlisted the services of world renowned caricaturist Pascual Locanto to illustrate the people whose interviews Steve Bunk had honed down to immensely entertaining and informative chapters. The book was in the home straight, but Lawrence had so much good material and so many ideas which had sprung from his experience, that he was already planning extensions of the project to encompass television and reader participation. He contracted sculptor Ian Mackay to fashion Stump-Jumper award trophies and began talking to television executives whose immediate response was positive.

The first *Stump-Jumpers* book was all but complete and it would have been reasonable to expect Lawrence to have a rest. But he had become an apprentice stump-jumper: for him the project was just starting . . .

Robert Bowyer Smith

The original Stump-Jumper

Robert Bowyer Smith had a problem. He was tilling his scrub land on Yorke's Peninsula, South Australia, and came slap upon the farmer's curse, a stump. One blade broke, but, to his satisfaction, the plough now jumped over succeeding stumps and still worked. This set Smith thinking.

What if the plough's blades were made to work independently, by weights and balances, so they could jump a stump and keep plowing? Smith knew a great deal about machinery, had formerly made farm implements over by Mt Barker, and had even become foreman of the company. And his brother Clarence Herbert was a blacksmith. Robert did some more thinking, made some drawings, and Clarence forged the first stump-jump plough. It was 1876. Robert dubbed his creation 'Vixen'. In a way, he wasn't far wrong.

He demonstrated the plough, and it worked all right, but most people didn't like it. Some thought it slovenly farming to jump over stumps instead of digging them out, but they overlooked the time, effort and money that could be saved by the new way. Smith's friends and relatives ridiculed him and mistook his zeal for craziness. His brother also lost faith in him, refusing to help build another, better plough.

Robert went to Mt Barker for funding and got the second plough built anyway. He took out a patent for it, too. This new model was a single-furrow instead of three-furrow design and he displayed it at the agricultural show. Nobody cared. Meanwhile, a farmer at Maitland had ploughed 25 acres with Robert's Vixen and was delighted by it. Smith ran out of money, a year went by, and he allowed the provisional patent to lapse. The implement makers pounced, and soon all kinds of new, improved stump-jump ploughs were rewarding someone else.

Robert wrote to a friend: 'My invention has cost me some money, some anxiety, and condemned my little ones to all the miseries of poverty and banishment to the bush. If I had been a successful cricketer, a good bowler or a rifle shooter, without pluck, a Blondin or an acrobat, I and mine would have escaped these ills.'

The stump-jump plough, however, was doing fine. People in high places were saying it had opened up vistas in farming — and indeed, the plough broke new ground in agriculture throughout the world. It was not only acknowledged as a main reason behind the opening up, to cultivation, of 500,000 acres of Australian scrub land in the 1870s, allowing new towns to spring up as a result of the explosion in pioneer farming, but it was also later adapted for use by American farmers on the sagebrush-littered plains of the western United States.

When someone proposed a government bonus of 500 pounds for the inventor, it straightaway became apparent that everybody and his dog was willing to take the credit. One fellow even published a pamphlet claiming he had invented the principle but couldn't get funding for it. Having had his fill of misfortune, Smith was determined that no one should claim credit for his brainstorm. There was an intense debate in Parliament about what to do with the reward, but in the end Smith received the award, along with a gold medal and a square mile of land. It was 1882 and Smith's battle was won. He and some partners patented a new model of the plough that same year. Robert's brother Clarence saw the error of his ways and started manufacturing the plough as part of his own implement-making business. Clarence added some improvements and his sons carried on the tradition.

Robert Smith moved to Western Australia, where he used part of the prize money to set up shop and was soon managing a company that produced his stump-jump ploughs. He never was the successful cricketer that he knew would have made life easier but, in the end, Robert Bowyer Smith went out like a first class batsman — on 81, unbeaten.

THE
STUMP
JUMPERS

Locanto

Paul Hogan

When Paul Hogan first burst onto Australian television screens a dozen years ago, no-one believed his story. No-one. It simply wasn't feasible that a rigger could climb down from an arch of the Sydney Harbour Bridge after a hard day's work and head straight for the television studio, still in his work clobber, to impart there his wit and wisdom in front of the cameras. No, it had to be a put-up job. This was a professional actor playing the part of an ordinary, whimsical ocker. How else could he appear so relaxed, so natural?

But Paul Hogan, then just into his 30s and a knockabout lad from Sydney's Western suburbs, was very much the real thing. He was an ordinary bloke and, in a quite extraordinary way, he gave television back to the masses. Within a couple of years his 'soft ocker' image had become an industry and Hogan himself had emerged as a champion of the underdog and proof positive that proud Australians still could laugh at themselves. This was the key to Hogan's acceptance by the viewers, even as the critics' brickbats landed all around. Hoges was a man of the people. You laughed with him, not at him.

With partner John Cornell (Strop of the series), Hogan has built a highly successful production company which rakes in most of the profits from Hogan shows seen around the world. Starting with little more than the right attitude, the duo has, in less than a decade, changed the rules for independent television production in Australia.

But Hogan's success can be measured in ways other than financial. At 44, he is his own man, relaxed, happy and supremely confident that, given a bit of help from the government, he can cure Australia's unemployment within two years.

I came into the entertainment business with one great advantage over almost everybody else. For the first 30 years of my life, I was a viewer who had no vested interest in television or entertainment. In those 30 years, I knew just what entertained me. When I joined the television industry, I found many people who were too close to the business. They didn't actually watch television, they read ratings and listened to each other's opinions. They sat and analysed rather than being entertained by a show. In my mind, I'm still an outsider. I came into the game without prejudices and I think I've been lucky enough to maintain that attitude.

One of the traps of being an entertainer is forgetting what you really are. You're only a court jester. Three hundred years ago, your ancestor wore a pointy cap and bells and did somersaults. We're only modern versions of him. Unfortunately, there are entertainers who lose sight of that and start to take themselves and what they do too seriously. You've got to guard against that.

The reality of this business is that there are numerous television actors and celebrities who have been household names one day and working in supermarkets the next. The reason for that is that they never made any money. Those people weren't getting paid any more than a good cameraman. A good technician behind a camera can stay in the business for almost as long as he wants, whereas the poor buggers in front of the camera usually get two or three years before they disappear. While they're on top, they're expected to wear expensive clothes and turn up for first nights in Rolls Royces. No wonder they've got no money!

We looked at this situation and saw that the only people making the real money out of television were the producers and the people who owned the channels. And that's why we formed our own production company rather than going to the ABC or Reg Grundy and taking a salary.

By 'we' I'm referring to John Cornell (manager and partner) and myself. We've been friends almost from the time I started in television.

Of course, we got all the advice in the world about how foolish it was to go it alone, but when we looked closely at it, it wasn't all that terrifying. It was, however, a bit strange for two guys who didn't even know what a production company was or did to say, 'All right, we'll form our own'.

But by then we knew that the Hogan shows were the success they were because of Hogan on camera and the scripts that Hoges wrote. We reasoned that no one could make a Hogan show without the scripts and the performer. So, we figured that all those people who supply the mysteries of production shouldn't be making the money. By trial and error, Cornell negotiated the deals with the channels, we wrote and performed and we became a production company. If there were any profits to be made, *we* made them. We also retained all rights to the programs and were given unlimited repeats. It's been that way for 12 years, and in that time the Hogan specials have been the longest-running and highest-rating comedy shows in Australian television, seen in the United States, England, France, Spain and Italy, and have been dubbed into numerous foreign languages. And in so doing, the series has made a pot of money for its producers.

It's brought me to the stage where money is not important any more. But in a way it's been like that for most of my life, anyway. Because I never had it, it wasn't important. I've never been a two-bob snob; I never wanted a slightly better car than the guy next door — I either wanted a Rolls with a chauffeur or I'd prefer to stick with my 1964 Holden. It was never a case of wanting a brick veneer house in the next best street — it was a home of my choice in the suburb of my choice.

Money was never much of a motive for me except at the very start, when I thought, 'Jeez, they're gonna pay me all that money just for a day's work!' But I soon discovered that if you like what you're doing and you do it well, then you make money anyway.

Actually, money can be a lousy motive because it can make you think, 'What are they paying me? A thousand dollars! Next door they'll pay me $10,000 but I'm not going to be 10 times funnier. And what happens if you do it for charity? Does that mean you won't be funny at all?'

It took me some time to accept that I had made the transition from being a bloke who worked on the Sydney Harbour Bridge to someone who could earn a full-time living in television. Now my life is terrific. I love it. I wouldn't swap jobs with anyone. I've found a job I like and I'm pretty good at it. My job is to make people happy. That's better than being a prime minister or president, who are usually in the business of making people miserable.

Before Hoges started bobbing up on television screens, I was pretty frustrated with my life and work. Like so many others, I was a bloke who had a lot of energy and ideas but I didn't have an outlet. I'd had plenty of jobs, but none of them provided a way to use what I had up top.

I was a child of the suburbs. I had a brother and a sister and my dad was a professional soldier. I suppose we were a lower middle-income family. I was bright but I hated school, and I left at 15 to enter the workforce and a phase of my life that saw me through 40 jobs in 10 years. You name it, I've worked in it. They were all basically unskilled jobs, starting as an apprentice moulder in an iron foundry. I did four nights a week metallurgy at tech and found it worse than school. I was working like two slaves and it was a dirty, filthy job. An iron foundry is the pits of the world but I stuck it out for 18 months. I don't know why. The only things it did for me were to give me hard muscles and lots of dirt in my lungs.

The period that followed could be classified as a career drift. I worked summers as an attendant at Parramatta and Granville Olympic swimming pools and had jobs as a builder's labourer, wharfie, truck driver, sock salesman, on the railways, on the Water Board, in the Department of Main Roads and in the abattoirs. Eventually I drifted into the building industry and acquired rigger's, scaffolder's and dogman's tickets in order to chase the good money. When the buildings went beyond 15 storeys or so, the money got pretty good.

The building industry period coincided with my marriage and the start of our family. Suddenly, I was 23 with three kids, no money, no prospects and a few minor debts. I'd been living all over the Western suburbs by this stage but had finally settled into a Housing Commission place at Chullora. I was looking for a bit of security and found it as a rigger on the Harbour Bridge. That proved to be a stabilising point because, unlike other buildings which require little maintenance once they're finished, the bridge provides ongoing work. But it still seemed a dead-end job.

I liked to talk, so I became a shop steward. I was offered a job as a union organiser with the Federated Ironworkers' Association. Going around negotiating stoppages, confabbing with Bob Hawke and 'Bruvver' (John) Ducker appealed to me but they preferred to use me as a small debts collector rather than to make me national secretary. So, I went back to the bridge.

I had a reputation as a bit of a smart arse. I was a sarcastic type, always quick with the smart response and very good at insulting someone or dropping the bucket. Not a very nice bloke, but that was probably due to frustration more than anything. I had no inclination whatsoever towards show business, and what's more I had no family background in that line of work. My old man might have fancied himself a bit because I remember him singing at parties. He was a good bloke but a terrible singer.

My only grounding in public performance was that as a kid I was a fair sort of 'diver' and used to give exhibitions with the State troupe. I was a worse than average light welterweight boxer who fought a couple of professional fights, beat a few people who couldn't fight, but lost the ones that counted. That was the nearest I'd been to show business. I never entered talent quests, I didn't sing and didn't tell jokes at parties.

During 1971 and 1972, we used to sit around at work and talk about this new television show, *New Faces*. It was an extremely popular form of entertainment: all those poor, untalented people appearing and being persecuted by equally untalented judges, who'd tell these poor souls just why they'd never be a star in 'our' business. We used to get annoyed at these supercilious judges and someone would always say, 'Someone should go on and take the mickey out of those bastards for making all those poor kids burst into tears'.

Now, as a kid I'd acquired a habit whereby if somebody said, 'Someone should set fire to that building or someone should ride his bike through there', I tended to see it as a challenge and therefore do it. So, I volunteered to go on TV and take the mickey out of the judges. My mates said, 'Yeah, all right, go on; but what are you gonna do?' I said, 'I dunno, but I'll take the mickey out of 'em'.

My first problem was how to get on the show without waiting nine months while they worked through all the other applicants. So, when I wrote my letter to the producer, I told him that I was a former shearer and trapeze artist and I had this act that combined tap dancing and knife-throwing and I'd love to appear on the show. I knew they couldn't resist a letter like that, because I knew what they were looking for.

Sure enough, within two weeks I'd been invited to appear despite the fact that I'm a tap dancing knife-thrower who can neither tap dance nor throw knives with any great accuracy. The carpentry shop at work produced a set of great big knives and I turned up with a handful of them, plus a garbage bin to put over my head as a blindfold

and a great big pair of gumboots for tap dancing. Other than those props I had no plan, except to walk on that show and get stuck into those dinner-suited talent judges and tell them what was wrong with them and how they could improve their act.

Not surprisingly the judges didn't find it hilarious, but the great Australian public saw the funny side of this guy who was doing just what everybody else had longed to do. I didn't win the quest but the producer invited me to appear again. He said I'd receive $25 or so for my troubles and I thought, 'Oh well, something different to do on Saturday', and went on.

Being nervous never occured to me, but when I was at the studio I started thinking, 'What are you doing? You're going to make an absolute fool of yourself in front of thousands of people, because you've got no background in entertainment whatsoever.' But the act before me was yet another poor tap dancing kid, a 16-year-old who'd been dancing for 10 years or so. The judges dropped buckets on her and she burst into tears.

'I'm not going to burst into tears,' I thought. 'I'm champion of the underdog. They can't hurt me, they can't embarrass me, they can't do anything to me, because I don't care.'

The tap dancing, knife-throwing act couldn't be repeated, so for my second appearance I was billed as a shovel player. The trick was to bang a couple of shovels together at the end of a song. Pure nonsense. And so I continued on to the grand final, where I was beaten by a 15-year-old cello player. I thought that was wonderful because it showed what those shows are all about. What sort of future in show business has a cello player got? He's not going to have his own show, is he?

As far as I was concerned that was the end of my brief television career. But during the same period Mike Willesee had launched *A Current Affair*, which was to appear five nights a week. Mike sent Tony Ward out to interview this bloke who worked on top of the Harbour Bridge who was also a part-time comedian. I automatically started sending the interviewer up by talking at a hundred miles an hour and making a farce of it all.

By coincidence they'd been looking for someone to provide the comic element for the program, and as my interview went over rather well they asked me if I'd do it.

I was an amateur and refused to waste too much time on all this but I decided to do it. I used to wander into the studio at four o'clock after working on the bridge, stand in front of the camera and talk for four or five minutes about something that was topical or had been in the newspapers that day. There was no script and I refused to rehearse, but somebody liked it enough to make it a key part of the program. That segment got more fan mail than the rest of the show. It also got more complaints and protests from people who wanted me off.

It was from that ordinary down-to-earth, know-all Aussie who appeared on the Willesee program that Jim Walpole and his team at Hertz, Walpole, Campbell, Ewald Advertising Agency devised the character for the Winfield cigarette commercials, back in the good old days before smoking became a health hazard. It was a strange period because although I was a nationally-known figure, I was still working on the bridge, still catching the train to and from work each day and still had no money. However, the saturation coverage provided by the Winfield campaign brought Hoges to everybody, including all those people who hadn't seen him on the Willesee show. Suddenly, I was a national celebrity, star, entertainer or whatever. Offers to do concerts, make club appearances and do more commercials were coming from everywhere.

Perhaps the most important decision I made during that time was letting John Cornell manage me on a hobby basis. Cornell was producing the Melbourne end of the Willesee show and he realised that Hoges could do a lot more than just the little bits that appeared on a current affairs show. It was then that we formed our little company and decided to make comedy shows. Instead of doing five-minute segments on other people's shows, we would do the *Paul Hogan Show*.

To a certain extent, we were flying blind. *Mavis Bramston* had been the last great Australian television comedy show but that was a long time ago. So there were no mentors, old pros or sources we could approach to learn how to do it. We had to do it ourselves. We formed the company and became the producers. I wrote, Cornell produced it and a guy called Jimmy Fishburn, who was a great variety producer, helped fill in what we didn't know.

You could probably only get away with that in Australia, which is great but it also makes it very hard. In England and America you would go to Thames Television or Mary Tyler Moore, people who turn out variety shows and sitcoms, and if they thought you were worth it they'd assemble the necessary people and build the show around them. But in Australia there was nobody to go to, no comedy packagers, no experienced comedy directors, hardly any writers, no producers. We had to make it up as we went and take the risk of hiring people who hadn't done that sort of work before. It was a crash learning process.

Selling the show was a different problem altogether. We had to sell them one at a time, because although Channel Nine wanted the first show, they didn't want the second. They said it was too expensive. Instead, Channel Seven bought it and said they'd like another. By the time we put our fourth show to air they were really starting to rate, so we made a deal with Channel Seven to do a series on a yearly basis.

Cornell had been in the media, particularly television, much longer than I had, but to both of us the whole experience was pretty new. I later learned that my wife was more unsettled by it all than she let on. The world of entertainment and show business was foreign to us. We knew what we read in the papers and, like most others, believed that the entertainment industry was full of con artists. That's partly true. As far as the kids were concerned, they were more impressed when their dad worked on the Harbour Bridge.

There was the added pressure of the media critics. The press hated me from the word go. Australian television was a world of Roger Climpsons and Stuart Wagstaffs, blokes who spoke nicely and dressed in dinner suits. In the naive world of Australian TV, that made them sophisticated. The media critics never saw me as a bright new star. For the first couple of years they rubbished me, which I didn't mind because it gave me a coat of armour and the knowledge that what they say doesn't really matter.

Because of that and the fact that people resented an overnight success who hadn't paid his dues in the industry, the first couple of years were shaky. People kept saying, 'He'll disappear next week', but that didn't worry me because the big advantage I had was that it didn't matter to me. It took me three years to take it seriously; three years before I understood that this was a profession that was more fun than crawling around the Harbour Bridge. Before that, I wouldn't have cared if the public had gone sour on me overnight and it all ended. At that stage, I thought it was fun while it lasted. But after three years I began to realise that what we had could last.

Cornell was different. He'd always thought from the word go that Hogan could last as long as he wanted to last — as long as he tried hard, as long as he didn't take it for granted, as long as he tried to make each show better than the last one.

Cornell was not a comedy writer, but as a trained journalist he was a good writer. More importantly, he was a good judge of comedy. I tended to be a bit lazy but he constantly rejected things I wrote so that

I'd be spurred on to do better. He cracked the whip and we really worked. We taught ourselves and helped each other; after a while, I saw that the faith he had in the show was justified.

There were plenty of pitfalls, the most obvious being that Hoges, as the one ocker character, was extremely limited. The first three or four shows were like that but we recognised just where that would lead unless we started introducing more characters. However, rather than going for wholesale alterations, we introduced gradual changes. Those critics who hadn't been following it closely enough were still claiming in 1977 that Hogan was doing the same old material, but they were wrong.

The new characters were drawn from real people. Unlike Dick Emery, who devised five or six characters and stuck with them for most of his career, I'd only give my characters five or six sketches before I'd abandon them. I figured if I was sick of them, so were the viewers. I destroyed Luigi and Smithy, and let Nigel die.

Instead, I started doing real people like Don Lane, Tony Barber and Mike Willesee. After working through recognisable Australian and American TV stars, I started looking for other ways and other things to do with them. That device provided a great source and variety of material and is one of the reasons why the show has lasted so long and rated so well. It's been 12 years undefeated. Occasionally, a show in Sydney might outrate us, but we'll still get up in the other capital cities. I might get a couple of my repeats knocked off, but as a general rule our first run shows win the time slot, no matter what you put up against them.

Despite Cornell's optimism, there were no plans to take the show overseas. The early shows were designed solely for local consumption. They were very ethnic, based around the ocker and what was happening in Australia during that time. But as the show changed and came to depend less on that character, we started receiving comments and letters from overseas visitors who liked what they saw and were certain that there were elements of the show that would work outside Australia. I have always been my greatest critic, but by that stage I knew there were some elements of the show that were superior to, or at least funnier than, the imported comedy.

Through 1979 and 1980, I deliberately started to broaden the show so that the material comprised 20 per cent for purely Australian consumption and 80 per cent that involved lots of colour and movement and was so international in theme that it could be understood almost anywhere. By the end of 1980, I had enough material from all the old shows to cut them up and make 26 half-hour shows that I figured would work just about everywhere in the world. Richard Price, who is an international distributor based in England, sold them in the United Kingdom and America, and eventually they were dubbed into six or seven different languages and sold in 40 countries.

The critics thought that Hogan's humour could never travel, and they would have been right if I'd left the shows full of jokes about Gough Whitlam, Toongabbie, and meat pies. If the critics had watched the show with any real insight, they would have observed that there were elements which were just plain funny. It had nothing to do with being Australian.

I was not the least bit mystified by our overseas success. You see, most of those shows were cut to visual unity. For instance, a wino wandering down the street doesn't even talk. He doesn't have to be in Australia to do the things he does. It's a sight gag, just like Charlie Chaplin did. They laugh at that in Spain, Japan or wherever. They don't put Hogan on in other countries because he used to work on the Harbour Bridge and is therefore a bit of a legend; they put him on because he's funny. And it's got nothing to do with whether they like Aussies or not. Those punters couldn't care less where it came from, as long as it's funny.

The attitude reeks a bit of the old inferiority complex. You know, 'They're made in Australia so therefore they can't really be funny like Benny Hill or Mary Tyler Moore'. Of course we can be as good as them! In fact, we can be funnier than them and sell in a whole lot more countries than they can. That Australian inferiority complex is diminishing but there are still those who say, 'Oh, what will they think overseas when they see Hogan? It's an awful, uncouth race!' What are they going to think when they see Norman Gunston, for God's sake? That we're all retarded nitwits? They're not. They're going to think that we've got a sense of humour. If you're an unsophisticated dunce, you can't write comedy. You might be able to write drama but if you want to write comedy, then first of all you've got to grow up in order to laugh at your own shortcomings. Look at the English. They're the greatest bunch of self-knockers in the world but England is virtually the home of comedy. If the English didn't invent comedy, then they must have invented satire. In Australia we were incapable of it, because we took ourselves too seriously. When I first started, people were hostile about having their shortcomings revealed. If there was one area in which we had to do some heavy pioneering, it was in getting people to laugh at themselves.

With comedy, people either think it's funny or it's boring. But we were getting another reaction. I used to generate a fair bit of passion from people who hated having our shortcomings satirised. They thought people would think that we're all like that. We should be so lucky! Better to be like that than a pale imitation of a Pom or a copy of a Yank minus his self-confidence.

In England they take their comedy very seriously. They like to analyse it, and I noted that they ended up finding things in my work that I never even knew were there. I'd say, 'A bloke fell off a ladder'. How is that supposed to represent the downtrodden masses rising up against the bureaucracy? There are a lot of students of comedy in England and they told me that the reason the show works over there is because Hogan has a point of view and a lot of the English comics don't; they merely come out and do slapstick. If you do have a point of view and if there are strong characteristics that emerge in your comedy, then the English tend to take you seriously. The only problem there is that the more you analyse comedy, the less funny it becomes.

I never took the time to analyse it. In fact, I didn't even see comedy as a career until I went out to work live in the clubs. Television is such a mechanical industry and involves so much visual trickery that, within reason, you can make almost anyone funny. I'd had this short-but-limited career on television and I thought I should go out and do some live work to find just what in the hell they were laughing at. The clubs were my way of putting myself on trial. I did it and found it terrific. It's like an instant rating to say something funny with 1,200 people in a room and to make them all laugh.

After my national clubs and pubs tour of 1973, I came home and realised I was in this business for good. I thought, now I'm a profes-sional, I don't have to keep my rigger's and scaffolder's ticket up to date. So I resigned from the Federated Ironworkers Association. It gave me the faith to achieve what I once might have thought impossible.

By having enough gall, we put ourselves in the position of owning everything I ever did on television. Whenever we signed a contract, we made sure the package included world rights. We didn't have a hard time getting them because, as the TV moguls would say, 'It's an Australian show; where are you going to sell it, New Zealand?'

We had nothing to lose but it was a matter of getting off our bums and doing it. We went to America with the project under our arms, had lunch with the distributors and tried to do deals but didn't get anywhere. Eventually we cracked a distributor, and by going through the normal route with people getting their little backhanders along the way, we were able to place programs in the right places. The show worked there and eventually we were able to sell it to the rest of the world.

From a business point of view, what we did was genuine pioneering. Normal practice was to go to a channel and work for a package system. At first, the networks were mystified and some were a bit reluctant about our approach. But we found that if they wanted the product badly enough, they'd generally come around to our way of thinking. They'd say, 'We don't normally do business this way but you're rating the house down, so we'll try it'.

We broke some rules, including changing channels when everybody told us that if you change channels, you die. But we went from Nine to Seven and back to Nine again. Since about 1976, I've had a handshake deal with Kerry Packer, and in that time there never has been any editorial or artistic interference from Channel Nine. The only interference I get is their requests to make more than one or three shows a year. But the arrangement has provided the time to pursue other ideas, such as the Australian tourism project.

The last great initiative I took was to talk the government into backing the tourist campaign. Alan Johnson, who is the 'Jo' in the Mojo advertising agency, has been a friend ever since I did the Winfield ads with his firm. We were discussing what products we'd most like to sell and we both said we'd like to sell Australia as a tourist destination. We made a half-baked attempt to get in touch with the Minister for Tourism when the Liberal Party was in power but they were not prepared to spend any money. When Labor came to power, the new minister, John Brown, talked about doubling the tourist intake and just how important tourism was as an industry. He pointed out that tourism employs 370,000 people. John Cornell asked Mojo to approach John Brown, so we set up a meeting, told him what we had in mind, and he approached Cabinet for the money.

To show him that we were fair dinkum, I offered my services free of charge to help get the campaign off the ground. My fee for an international campaign of that size would have been in seven figures. If we'd gone to the Government and asked for $4 million to promote Australia, with $1 million of that going to Hoges, they would have thought this was just another cheap agency trying to line its pockets.

We said we weren't interested in doing a $2 million campaign. I wouldn't even do it if they gave me half. We said, 'Let's spend $4 million or $5 million and eventually $20 million. Hoges will do it for nothing until it gets off the ground and starts making money.' The Government accepted our advice and the campaign went on American television and produced brilliant results. In just five weeks, Australia went from being number 49 on the 'Most Desired Destination' list to number one. It was the most successful tourist commercial in America in 10 years. It was a case of marketing success being achieved by having the right product at the right time and the right person selling it.

Now it's up to the Government to keep shovelling in the money. If they really want to double the tourist intake, they will. It sounds too easy to be true but that should just about cure unemployment in Australia. The average tourist stays for two weeks and leaves behind $1,500. That's instant capital straight into hotels, shops, and the service industry. It's better than finding gold in the ground, because it's instant capital. The first tourists who were stirred by those ads arrived in Australian within a week of the campaign's launch.

I'm not a super brainwasher and I'd never accept an amount of money to sell champagne or caviar or Rolls Royces. It doesn't fit the Hogan image and the viewers wouldn't really believe I'd know anything about those products. But I sell Fosters Lager on British TV and the viewers know that this Hogan bloke does drink the product, likes it, knows his beer and seems like the kind of fellow you could have a drink with in the pub. So, they like the ad and they buy the beer.

That campaign came from us, not an advertising agency. In fact, the agency wrote an awful campaign that would have embarrassed the hell out of every Aussie who saw it. It was the full hat-and-corks bit. With the blessing of Fosters Australia, we rewrote the campaign on the premise that first, you've got to like the person selling the product.

I receive 30 or 40 offers a year to do commercials and most of them would be very lucrative if I accepted. People tell me I should strike while the iron is hot. At this point, I could do a Tonight Show five nights a week but I wouldn't want to see me on television every night and bobbing up in every commercial break as well. So, I take breaks as I go and I avoid too much exposure.

When I take a rest, I make sure I don't touch anything to do with entertainment. I bludge, play tennis, mow the lawn, play touch football, go fishing with the kids or read. I take great periods in which I have no endeavours, but eventually I sit down and do some solid writing. Making television shows is easy, but to sit down and write them is pure labour. I don't see my profession as a trial, however. I avoid the meaningless trappings of this business, as I've never been carried away by the idea of being a first-nighter or running around with a showgirl on my arm. That's pure ego but too many people fall for it.

Job satisfaction is my big motivator. That's what everyone should aim for. Some time in life everybody has to work, and if you hate your job, as I did for many years, it means you're throwing away a third of every day of your life. Australia is a country of great inventors: people who saw our isolation as a challenge rather than a handicap. The ratio of inventions that come out of Australia would be about 10 to one compared with any other country. The first film industry was founded here but died out, and I have this burning ambition to make a bloody good movie, capable of grossing more than $100 million and being enjoyed by people all over the world. I'm inspired by that sort of challenge.

Lang Hancock

Lang Hancock likes nothing better than to stand on top of a Pilbara mountain, gouge out a piece of iron ore beneath his feet, hold it aloft and declare: 'This is Australia's future. All we need is the guts to develop it'.

In Hancock's lexicon, the 'guts to develop it' includes the use of hydrogen bombs detonated deep below the surface to crumble the ore. Since 1952, when he flew through the mushroom cloud above the British atomic test at Montebello Island and lived to tell the tale, he has been an outspoken advocate of nuclear mining. But this is not the only reason controversy has stalked the 76-year-old prospector all his life.

Hancock also believes in virtually unlimited foreign investment to enable the development of our mineral resources, the prospector's right to stake his claim to unused land regardless of the consequences, and the complete elimination of bureacracy. In short, he believes in the survival of the fittest and, if fitness can be measured in terms of wealth and power, he is very fit indeed. Since Hamersley Iron began mining the Hancock-discovered Tom Price deposits in 1966, he has received a two-and-a-half per cent royalty on every tonne taken from the ground: an estimated $30,000 a day.

Such wealth has enabled him to pursue a dream which many have called impossible — to develop the Pilbara with his own mines and on his own terms. To this end, he has spent millions on ore prospecting and on lobbying for foreign capital to finance a mine, port and linking railway that would dwarf Hamersley's massive network. He envisages ore carriers 26 times the size of the *Queen Mary* berthing at the world's deepest port to carry away ever-increasing quantities of the ore that make up so much of his beloved Pilbara.

And it *is* his 'beloved' Pilbara, despite his earnest desire to
dig it up and sell chunks of it. Born in Perth on 10 June 1909,
Hancock was raised in the north-west on his family's station,
'Mulga Downs'. There he grew up with Aborigines who
taught him to hunt and fish and, as a result, he knows and
loves every inch of the Hamersley and Chichester Ranges.
This prehistoric landscape is his domain and, to him, using
some of it to ensure his country's future prosperity is as
natural as skewering a goanna on a stick and roasting it over
a fire.

Lang Hancock has canvassed his dreams all over the world
for many years now. To celebrate his 70th birthday, he
chartered a jumbo jet and flew people of influence around
the country, pointing out our mineral resources and his ideas
for exploiting them. He brought Edward Teller, the father of
the hydrogen bomb, to Australia in an abortive attempt to
convince people that there was absolute safety in a nuclear
future. As a result of his efforts, Hancock has been ridiculed
often in Parliament, in the stock exchanges and many of the
corporate boardrooms — a fact that worries him not the least.

Now, however, it seems that Lang Hancock may have the
last laugh. Although it was greeted with scepticism in some
financial quarters, in April 1985 he and Western Australian
Premier Brian Burke announced the signing of a billion-
dollar barter deal in which Pilbara iron ore would be
exported to communist Romania for an initial period of 15
years in return for advance payments in Romanian heavy
machinery. In other words, the Romanians would finance
Hancock's dream without receiving any equity. 'Father
Christmas has come to town,' commented the delighted
Hancock.

My grandson is a seventh generation Western Australian, so that makes this family as West Australian as you can get. My father was one of the very first white children born in the north-west, in a stone hut his parents had built and called 'Woodstock'. My mother was also from the west but I'm not sure how far she goes back. The Hancocks pioneered the north-west, going up there with a few sheep and settling on a lot of ground at a place called Cossack, where there still is a monument to them, although that's now a ghost town.

I came down to Perth to be educated when I was eight. Prior to that, I'd spent my entire young life on a very isolated station. One neighbour was 80 kilometres away and the nearest on the eastern side was almost 200 kilometres away, so there wasn't much communication. There were no white children, of course. I played with the blacks. Then I came to Perth and went to Howell's School before going back to our station, 'Mulga Downs', which was where I stayed until I became interested in minerals.

I was better than average at school and I made the first teams at cricket and football. My father wanted me to go on to university and become a mathematics professor, but luckily I elected to go back to the bush. For a few packets of lollies you can buy a professor to work for you, so I'm very glad I didn't waste my time at university.

When I was 26 my father retired and I took over management of the station, where we had up to 40,000 sheep. It was during this period that I found blue asbestos near our property and sent a sample down to the mines department in Perth. They said it was worth about 18 pounds a tonne and the freight was about 30, so you couldn't make much money that way. I used a block of it as a doorstop at 'Mulga Downs' and had given up on the idea of making any money out of it, even though I knew there were huge deposits in the gorges right through the Hamersley Ranges. Then a fellow from an asbestos company in England passed through the station — I don't remember why now — and he expressed great interest in the doorstop. I told him the sad story and he shook his head and said, 'It's worth 70 pounds a tonne'. I suggested to him that he was talking rubbish, and then he said *he'd* pay me 70 pounds a tonne! Of course, I pegged out the best of it and went into asbestos mining.

At the time, the only known commercial blue asbestos deposits outside Russia were in South Africa and here. The South Africans had an army of black fellows who would chip away at the stuff with hammers and put it in bags — very painstaking work indeed — and this was the recognised method of mining asbestos, and the way it started in Western Australia. It was rather like a gold rush, with men chipping away for so much a bag, but I could see that we weren't going to get very far that way, so I managed to construct a sort of Heath Robinson affair in the workshop at Mulga Downs. It could crush, screen and bag the asbestos, which was a much better arrangement, but I still could sell only about 960 pounds worth each month. Of course, I thought that was a fortune at the time, but I felt that if I involved a company with some capital, things would move much faster. CSR, the sugar company, came in and formed a new company called Australian Blue Asbestos, of which they owned 51 per cent. I was foolish enough to believe that gave them 51 per cent of the say and me 49 per cent, but of course they had 100 per cent. I was disillusioned, so I got out. As it turned out they ran the mine at a loss for many years, then closed it and moved into iron ore.

I then became interested in various minerals. I started up a white asbestos mine and used that as a headquarters, and I was overseeing a copper operation and a lead mine, all of which were several hundred kilometres apart. The drives between the sites took days, so I became interested in flying to overcome the time problem. The old fellow who founded WA Airlines had a single-engine plane for sale, so I made a deal to buy it provided he taught me how to fly. Since then I've owned more aeroplanes than motor cars, and without the planes I doubt that I would have found iron ore. Flying changed everything around.

In 1937, Peter Wright, whom I had known for some time, came up to 'Mulga Downs' for a holiday. He was run down and asked if he could come up and rest for a few weeks. Well, he saw this Heath Robinson affair of mine and the way it was churning out money and he wanted to be my partner by hook or by crook. We went into white asbestos together, and later into copper, tin and lead. We put managers into all of these operations and I would fly around in my little plane and supervise them.

The white asbestos mine was in a very narrow gorge and, if you stayed there until the height of the rainy season, you'd never get out,

Above, Lang Hancock's grandfather, and below, his father

so I used to close the mine down and the workers would go off until the wet ended. We'd pay them all off, then a few weeks later my wife and I would hop in the plane and come down to Perth.

On one of these occasions, in November 1952, I'd left it later than usual to get out and I had to fly over the Hamersley Ranges in thick cloud in a single-engined aircraft. This is some of the roughest country on earth, and the clouds got lower and lower. I didn't have the instruments or the power to get up through the top of them, so I had to follow them down and I found a creek flowing through one of the gorges. I was about 25 feet above the treetops but well below the walls of the gorge. Still, I knew if water could get out, I could. It was then that I noticed the walls looked to be solid iron ore, but I also knew that Australia was supposed to have very little worthwhile iron, so I assumed it was low grade and of no use. But next winter I went back for a look. I found the same spot and I followed the ore along for about 70 miles and there was so much of it, I thought that even if it was very low grade, you had to be able to upgrade the stuff with metallurgy.

I landed in the spinifex, walked around and took some samples, which I had assayed. To my great surprise, the stuff was two per cent higher than the standard blast furnace feed of the greatest industrial nation on earth, the United States. I thought, if it's good enough for them, it's good enough for me. I knew then that the find was not only big but also very valuable.

At that time, as I said, iron ore was thought to be very scarce in Australia. The Australian government had an embargo on exporting it and the Western Australian government was refusing titles to it, so we had to sit on the find for a number of years. When the embargo was lifted in 1960, our next move was to try to get capital into the project.

This wasn't easy, because I still didn't have title to the site. You'd approach big international companies like the United States Steel Corporation and they'd say, 'Well, where is it?' I couldn't tell them, because I didn't have title. They all thought it was fairy tale stuff. The way I got them involved in the end was to tell them I didn't want any of their money, I didn't want shares, all I wanted was a royalty on what they mined. That meant if they didn't make money, I didn't make money.

But before I got a deal, I tried to interest many people. I tried the Australian firms first and, when they weren't interested, I went to 30 different overseas concerns. Eventually I got the risk capital involved, on the strength of orders from the Japanese. I brought a Japanese fellow out to Hamersley Station, which was my headquarters at the time, flew him around and showed him the iron ore. He got very excited and wanted me to fly him all the way to Port Hedland immediately, so he could head for home. I asked what the hurry was, and he said he didn't want anyone else to see it before his people had a chance to buy! He was the chap who induced the first Japanese steel mission to come out here. The steel companies there all banded together so as not to compete price-wise, and they sent out this mission. I flew them around and showed them everything, and from there they issued their orders and Hamersley Iron got the first.

Riotinto in London had been the first people to take me up on the iron and, through their Australian company, they formed an offshoot called Hamersley Iron. So it was Riotinto who got the orders from the Japanese and passed them down the line. Then in came the banks, but of course they never would have come in on their own.

That's a problem in this country. Australia is not a land of entrepreneurs. Socialism is embedded right through the school system and there seems to be an attitude that 'the world owes me a living'. When people talk about things they believe are wrong in our society, they always say 'the government ought to do this or that'. They don't seem to realise that they're the ones who have to make things happen. There's also this idea that all people are equal. When they say that to me I say, 'Yes, socialism makes them equally poor'. The idea seems to be that all people should be cut down to the same financial level. Anyone with any brains can see where that would lead.

Anyway, this had been the case, this lack of spirit, when we tried to get the iron ore moving, but once it began everything changed. Australia went from being a theoretical importer of iron ore to becoming the world's number one exporter, capturing 47 per cent of the Japanese market. The effect on the Australian economy was quite staggering because, prior to that, we had been a one-industry economy, living on the sheep's back.

For me, the iron ore industry in the Pilbara meant that as Hamersley grew, so did the size of my royalty cheque, and it enabled me to spend time chasing around the area discovering other large deposits. With those I was able, after four special acts of parliament had been introduced, to secure prospector's rights to some billions of tonnes which I'd discovered. Then, of course, it was a matter of trying to exploit the sites and get them into production. In this I haven't been very successful up to now, even though I've involved some very big people.

Before CRA became involved, before any of the iron ore mines, ports or railroads were built in the Pilbara and when they were having trouble nailing the contracts down, I got the world's richest man, D. K. Ludwig, to come out. I flew him around and sold him on the idea of one central railway and one giant port. He took this up with the Western Australian government and put a proposal to them. The deal was that he would build and finance one railway and a port which was capable of servicing ships three times the size of the iron ships in existence at that time. In fact he had on order the *Iron Trader*, which could move 166,000 tonnes, whereas the next biggest capacity was 50,000 tonnes. That would have lowered transport costs to such an extent that Europe and America would have been able to import iron ore at much the same price as Japan. So, instead of just having 47 per cent of the Japanese market, we could have had 40 to 50 per cent of the world market, which is about eight times the size of what we had.

Well, the Western Australian government turned him down. We've never known why — due to Cabinet solidarity — and, in my opinion, that was the greatest opportunity this country has ever had. Ludwig's money went into Brazil, which is now the world's leading exporter of iron ore.

It was a very frustrating period for me, because I'd put a lot of effort into getting Ludwig interested in our ore. When Hamersley Iron was getting off the ground and Kaiser Steel was involved, a man named Dick Barber was out here supervising Kaiser's involvement. Well, he got a bit frustrated at the way the thing was shaping up and we got to talking one day about the other iron ore deposits I knew of and how to develop them. He suggested I talk to Ludwig, so I went to New York and arranged a meeting where I told him all about it and asked him to come out and have a look. Ludwig said, 'Put it all down on paper and I'll have a look at it'. Then he pressed a button and a guy called Cameron came in. He told Cameron to give us an office and set us to work, Wright and myself. We worked all weekend on it, because Cameron had told us, 'For Christ's sake, get it all on one page, because he won't read more than that'. Try as we might, we couldn't condense it beyond three pages.

On the Monday, we went in to see Ludwig again and gave him this thing. Cameron started reading it to him and he listened for about half a page, then he said he'd have to get a friend to have a look at it. So he got this fellow, Tom Reid, to come down. Reid was a vice president of the United States Steel Corporation, and it used to be said about him that the American President always had to ring Reid to see how much steel he could get before he got involved in a war. Well, Reid had a look and he was impressed, so Ludwig got him to come out and have a look. He said if Reid thought it was worthwhile, then he'd come out later. And that's precisely what happened, until the Western Australian government slapped him in the face.

Since that opportunity was missed, mining has become stationary in this country. In 1964, four big new mines sprang up — Hamersley, Newman, Goldsworthy and Robe River — but very little has happened since then. This is because the government has clamped down with rules and regulations which have made development impossible. I hope that these stupid things are not going to get in my way now, with the Romanian deal.

This is a deal in which CRA is my 50 per cent partner. We're going to get Marandoo deposits, on the basis that CRA takes five million tonnes of the ore to blend with their Hamersley stuff and I take five million tonnes to sell where I like. My five million is a private deal I've negotiated with the Romanian government, which works like this: three years ahead, they supply me with enough equipment to start the mine, build the railway link and expand the port. With that done, I churn out the iron ore to pay them back. This is only possible because the Romanians have built a canal from a Black Sea port to the Danube River. It is bigger than the Suez or Panama Canal and it opens up all those countries in eastern Europe that currently consume 98 million tonnes of iron ore a year, while the Japanese consume 100 to 110 million tonnes. Not one scrap of Australian iron ore has ever been sold in this market, so we have penetrated a brand new market which is almost as large as the Japanese. The other part of the deal is that I have to expand their port facilities from being able to unload 50,000-tonne ships to being able to handle 150,000-tonne ships. We have to freight it in big ships or the freight cost will become enormous.

Of course, this sort of barter agreement has been going on for some time now in Brazil, and we silly buggers have sat back and watched. The Romanians build rail carts for Brazil in return for ore and so on. I've been looking at eastern Europe and other markets for some time now, wondering what could be done. There's potential in Russia, for example. There's potential in China, although that's a bit dicey, and there's the Middle East market, where they have finally awakened to the fact that when the oil runs out, they'll be left with nothing but sand. So they've decided to use their gas for industrial purposes and they are building steel mills, so another market opens up. There are plenty of them, but the problem is we now are competing with Brazil, whereas we could have had it on our own.

Once we get this Romanian canal going, I believe the day is not far away when we will be selling iron ore to the USSR, just as we now sell them wheat. They can't get their iron ore quickly enough over that shonky railway from Siberia. They're having huge problems, because they need the steel for their armament-building program.

What happens to the Chinese market depends very much on whether the government of the day stays the way it is. They've decided to turn to free enterprise just as fast as we in Australia are turning to socialism. As a measure of security, so that one bloke can't grab central power in a *coup d'etat*, they've diffused power into the provinces. Now there are 110 steel mills in China and if there's not a central power handling them, you have to get around the provinces, which is not easy but can still be done.

I think one of the things that we have to do now to encourage development is to make Australia north of the 26th parallel an income tax-free zone with a compulsory reinvestment clause of 40 per cent applicable to capital only. The blokes who work up there, the engineers, surveyors and so on, would see the benefit of that in their first pay packet. The people who put the money into the projects wouldn't see the benefit until later on but when they did, it would flow in. The government, of course, would get its cut through indirect taxation, payroll tax and sales tax, and from the money saved on dole payments because so many more men would be in the work force. The entire area where these riches — the iron ore and the uranium — are would boom, and everyone would be better off. All this would cost the taxpayer nothing, because the tax on nothing is nothing. The government would be giving away nothing and gaining a hell of a lot.

I believe a strong, populated north of Australia is essential for our survival and also the key to our defence because, at the moment, Australia is defenceless. If you put the army, navy and air force together, they could defend a total of 12 miles of coast and Western Australia has 4,400 miles of it. There is no way 15 million people can defend a coastline like ours, but I believe the solution lies in our mineral wealth. The western superpowers need to be reminded that they are sitting on a minerals bubble that could burst at any moment. They are all reliant on South Africa for their strategic minerals. If South Africa goes, western civilisation goes, so wouldn't it be wise for them to develop an alternative supply? As it is, Japan is dependent on Australia for iron ore and wheat and many other things, so they can't

*Lang Hancock, geological pick in hand, with daughter Gina
and iron ore at Wittenoom*

afford to see us go down. If we were just as indispensable to other major nations, our defence position would be secure.

Australia and the United States, linked together, have total defence. Some years ago the Americans took my daughter and me out in a nuclear submarine observation vessel, and they explained how it was capable of firing missiles which had a range of 2,000 miles, accuracy within a few yards, and could unleash more destructive power in two hours than was unleashed by both sides in World War II. They had 55 of those subs, so I suggested to them that they consider the north-west of Australia as an alternative mineral source to South Africa. I said that they should lend us just three of these submarines in exchange for us supplying all the strategic minerals they needed. As I told them, you can have all the armies in the world but they're no good to you unless you have the minerals to make the equipment they need to fight. Everything comes from the earth. You either grow it or you mine it, and you can't even till the soil until you've made the plough. It all gets back to these holes in the ground that people so despise.

Now, if we got these subs from the Americans, they could patrol around North West Cape and, with a range of 2,000 miles, we'd have a complete defence umbrella. But of course people are very funny about the word 'nuclear'.

I don't know anyone of even average intelligence who is anti-nuclear. That's a lot of claptrap put about by the press and by these people who wouldn't even be able to feed themselves if the government didn't hand it to them. Anything constructive seems to be unpopular these days. You get a whole lot of people howling like hell if a cocky knocks over a tree to grow a bit of corn to feed some people. It's quite ridiculous.

I've never had any pre-determined ambitions in my life, I take things as they come. If there's an opportunity to do something, I'll do my best to take it. Of course, I've developed plenty of ambitions as I've gone along. Things like a tax-free north and its industrial development, as well as the downhill railway, which I hope one day will take iron ore out of the Pilbara to a huge port facility at Cape Ronsard, where it will be loaded onto huge ships and sent at competitive freight costs to Europe. That, to me, is an absolute must.

I'd like to see Australia nuclear-dependent so that it could be entirely self-sufficient and have the cheapest and safest power in the world. I'd like to see an east-west railway linking the Queensland coalfields and the Pilbara ore mines, with a heavy steel industry at both ends. I'd like to try to harness the tidal power in the Kimberley region.

With one installation there, you could generate six times the power currently generated in Australia by all other means. The power is just sitting there and it will be with us as long as the moon lasts. To me, it's remarkable that all these things just sit there and nothing is being done with them.

Most of my life people have regarded me as an idiot. Whether that's a good thing or a bad thing, I don't know. But more than anything, success has meant that people now have to listen to me.

Of course, I've had my share of setbacks. The biggest, no doubt, would be the trouble I've had trying to get this giant port going since 1964. Seeing Ludwig turned away was a huge setback, because he then went across to the eastern states and bought up a coal mine and became the largest producer of coal in Australia. Then he turned around and sold that to BP for around $460 million and then invested a billion dollars in Brazil which could have come here. If you add it all up, it was a pretty shocking mistake. But you can't stop a wheel when it's spinning, and I've always bounced back from setbacks.

I think there is a recipe for success in the world today. I'd take a little bit of character from Sir Joh Bjelke-Petersen, I'd take a pinch of Lee Kuan Yew for political effectiveness, a bit of commercial nouse from D. K. Ludwig, and the scientific brain of Dr Edward Teller. Then you'd have the cream of the world.

I think Australia is heading downhill fast, and there seems to be no way of stopping it. We've gone from being the country with the fourth highest standard of living on earth to the 24th. We are becoming the poor relation of the Pacific Basin. It wouldn't do any harm for people to realise that the elected representatives of the people are not really the government. A lot of money is spent on elections and they are completely ineffective. The real government has four arms. The first and most powerful is the bureaucracy, which expands according to Parkinson's Law; the second is the trade union movement; the third is the press in all its forms, because no parliamentarian will do anything until he's read all the newspapers; and the fourth is the people with their hands in the till, the ones collecting handouts and subsidies and so on.

Before anything changes in this country, people have to realise that this is the mess we're in.

Rosemary Moore

'Like sports trophies, you wonder why you bother dusting them,' says an unassuming Rosemary Moore of the numerous business and sales awards she has won. National and international sales records, Australian Salesman of the Year in 1974, a nominee for the *Bulletin* Businesswoman of the Year, winner of the Zondervan Corporation's prestigious International Territory Award — her achievements would fill a catalogue in their own right. It might be said that nothing less would have been expected of someone whose lineage depicts a long history of pioneering achievers, but Rosemary Moore is different.

At age 40 she resigned or, in her own words, was sacked from her career as full-time mother. Unqualified and afraid, Mrs Moore, housewife in Sydney, carted her career hopes into the often cruel world of direct selling. There, after a slow start, she found a friend and business partner in Diana Rose. As a team, with Rosemary in the sales seat, they shattered national and international sales records for World Book Encyclopaedia. When professional pride deemed it necessary that they quit World Book, the Moore-Rose combination founded their own Australian company, based on the direct sales of Christian home and educational products. At the time it appeared a risky move for the two women, who had not only co-held the post of national sales director for World Book, but were celebrated as Australia's highest-paid female executives.

The cynics, however, didn't allow for the refreshingly personal style Moore brought to sales and the training of her sales team. Imbued with a powerful Christian ethic to help others, Moore and Rose recruited yet more people to their dedicated sales force. By negotiating contracts with international publishers, notably the Zondervan Corporation of the United States, they made available a new range of Christian publications and educational items.

As a sales executive and entrepreneur, Rosemary Moore proved to be an inspiration to her sales force. The company has recruited the disadvantaged, the young and unemployed, and others wishing to supplement their income and support a Christian product. Her code is equality of opportunity. The results have been nothing less than spectacular. Not only has the company expanded its operations overseas, but the Moore sales, training, and motivation techniques are in demand in other markets. With one of the world's best direct sales records, Moore and company are primed to enlarge their international influence, to strengthen the reach of their three Australian companies, and to move seriously into the export business.

Perhaps the most singularly stunning detail about the Rosemary Moore success story is that it is little more than a decade since the housewife swapped her apron for a sales kit. In that period, her iron will, compassion, endeavour and courage became evident, as she helped revolutionise an industry that had acquired a less-than-savoury reputation. If Rosemary Moore's single greatest achievement was to help give a decent image to direct sales, then she would have succeeded where many had failed. But she has given much, much more than that.

I'll tell you what changed my life: a crazy little thing. I was standing in the kitchen the day my son Julian went to Sydney University, to play in the university football team. He stood at the door and said, 'Mum, do you have to come? Everybody else has a girlfriend. Would you bring your dark glasses and a scarf?' I couldn't believe it. I thought, he doesn't want me, and he's been my life. I cried all Saturday afternoon but by Sunday, I was furious. How dare he speak like that to his mother. On Monday, I thought, I'm not going to spend my life feeling this way. I'm going to find a job.

I wasn't qualified in any way but I'd always wanted to teach and, in fact, had enrolled at teachers' college at 18, but cancelled out in favour of matrimony. However, it was to the teachers' column in the Positions Vacant section of the *Sydney Morning Herald* that I turned on Monday morning. Maybe there would be something for a pathetic woman who wanted to teach. I found Alan Robins' advertisement, which read: 'Teachers or women ambitious to teach'. Wow, I thought, that's me. For six months, I tried to negotiate an interview. Mr Robins assured me that he was planning training in my area and when I finally got my interview, I found that the job was to sell encyclopaedias. I came home and explained to my husband Michael, 'I have to go into training'. I didn't tell him what the training was for, fearing his reaction. My self-esteem was rock-bottom. The only job I'd ever had was to serve voluntarily in the school tuckshop, and now I felt I was sacked from being a mother.

On my return from training class, I revealed the awful truth. Almost in unison, the family reacted: 'You've been conned. You can't do that — anything but that. No-one will ever pay you. Encyclopaedia companies are dishonest.' Michael didn't see the need for me to work. He supplied a good income and we had the things we needed, if not everything we wanted. But I had a need to do something with my life.

The class trainer, Margaret Christensen, didn't 'con' me. As I saw it, she showed me beautiful books and talked about the need for children to have a home library, with which I agreed. She enabled me to feel I could find a home within the company. I decided to have a go. If that was all I could do, then I was going to try. I had gone to a school that had encouraged you to think for yourself, even if wrongly! Some years later, with the aid of my manager Diana Rose and others, we helped to change the encyclopaedia marketplace. We got to the top of it. We made a fortune, made good investment decisions and contributed to the product's acceptance in the marketplace.

An encyclopaedia is a needed product, but it has suffered from an unsavoury reputation, often unjustified. We began to realise that here were excellent products which needed a new image in the marketplace. In the end, I did set a new Australasian and world sales record. This gave me confidence. In 1974, Tony Street, then Minister for Employment and Industrial Relations, presented me with the sales award of the year at Ron Tacchi's Australian Sales Congress. He said something to me then which I still remember: 'Rosemary, thank you for not sitting home and playing bridge, but instead going out and helping the Australian economy.' I did that? I hadn't thought of my work in that way. Thus inspired, I went to women everywhere, offered them a job opportunity and said, 'Go out and do something for yourself, your family, and above all, your country. If I did it, you can.' And many did. That was exciting. They were great people and we were privileged to work with them. Many are our lifelong friends. Diana and I built one of the biggest sales teams that World Book or, I think, any encyclopaedia company has achieved, and we became national directors of the company.

It was March of 1972 and I was 40 years old when I went for that first interview. I must have the distinction of being one of the few people who ever failed an encyclopaedia class. Yet because of my inane questions, I think, Mrs Christensen asked me to come again. I doubt that she actually would have let me go, because you don't let people go out of an encyclopaedia sales class. Nevertheless, I was saying to myself as I drove home, 'You can't even sell encyclopaedias'. Michael contributed by saying, 'The whole thing's ridiculous, you shouldn't take it on'. But something in me replied, 'Just a moment dear, I'm going to do something and it has to be this, because there's nothing else.' Had Michael said, 'Run along, Rosemary, you'll be fine', I probably wouldn't have continued. But because he doubted my ability to be successful, I felt challenged and said, 'I *will* do it. At least my mother will buy one!' She always has supported me.

Finally, I received this precious piece of paper, which was a contract that authorised me to sell encylopaedias. Like a lot of women, I had no reason to imagine I could do anything other than perform domestic and social functions, but I believe I felt a basic resentment that my family didn't seem to trust my judgement. Today, Michael is one of our greatest supporters. He, too, needed to learn that most encyclopaedia companies are honest, and the fact that they sell directly to the public is a benefit to the public.

Diana Rose was a district manager and I was allocated to her team. Still apprehensive, to say the least, I thought, here I go. Michael says I can't do it, my mother says I shouldn't do it, the boys say I won't have time, but just the same, I'm going to do it.

I went to a couple of dear friends of mine and stuttered through my sales presentation. One of them said, 'Darling, put all that away, would you mind? If you say I should have it, I'll take it.' That discouraged me. I had the sale but I felt like a failure, because I'd misassessed the customer. My first confidence-building experience came when a friend said, 'I don't buy anything unless it's good, and I'm not buying anything from you unless you can convince me that I need it.' Together we went through the presentation and she bought the World Book Encyclopaedia. For the first time, I felt I'd contributed.

However, the critical environment proved too strong, and for my first year, I hardly sold at all. I could not see myself as an encyclopaedia salesman, I was too deeply prejudiced against them. Finally, Diana suggested that I do her service calls. This entailed calling on families which had already purchased books from her and teaching the children to use them. She said, 'I'll give you $4 for each family you teach'. I could see that I could earn $50 a week, so I started doing service calls, making appointments, and teaching the children. What fun it was!

One day, a customer said, 'Mrs Moore, when Mrs Rose was here, she showed us dictionaries. We decided against them at the time but we've since decided to buy them.' I had forgotten how to write up an order. What a struggle it was. When I got back to the car, I began to see myself as I really was, a total coward. I was doing all the service calls but didn't have the guts to do the hard part. I saw myself as a hypocrite, spoilt, snobby, and protected. I saw myself as I really was, and I didn't like what I saw.

I went back to Diana and said, 'I must stay on and I'll have to change my character and attitude. I don't like myself. How can I start again?' She replied, 'You could knock on a door'. That was too much, too soon. Surely I was an educational consultant, not a door-to-door salesman. I said, 'I don't think I could do that', and she smiled. 'No my dear,' she said, 'I don't think you could, either.' I thought she meant that she recognised I would be above that sort of thing.

I said goodbye, went to my car, sat and thought. What did she mean, she didn't think I could do that sort of thing? It struck me like a thunderbolt. It wasn't that she thought I wouldn't, she thought I couldn't. There were 70 steps up to her front door at that time. I got out of my car and ran up them two at a time. 'What do you mean, you don't think I could do it?' I asked indignantly. Years afterwards, she told me she had realised a salesman was born that day. 'Isn't there anything I can do to be successful?' I bleated pathetically. Diana turned around at the window and said, 'If you can learn to knock on doors and sell encyclopaedias, then in the end there's nothing in the world you can't do.' I hung onto those words for a long time. Well, if I was going to make a fool of myself, it would be where nobody would know me. After driving around and around, miles from home, I got out and approached the first door in sight, feeling I would surely fall into the hydrangeas with fright. The door opened and an elderly housewife, sensing my stress, said, 'My dear, you look hot and tired. Would you like to come in and have a cup of tea?' Unqualified kindness at the door; it was new to me, and a humbling experience. Since then, I've visited every nation under the sun, I've made friends, and I've learnt to adjust. I've learnt that not all people have the priorities and problems that I faced. I began to get my own problems into perspective. Gradually, I learned many things that my life, lived within narrow confines, hadn't taught me. I changed.

I'm proud to be a sixth-generation Australian. My ancestors on my father's side were Irish landowners, and our original settler, Samuel Pratt Winter, left Ireland at the age of 14. He cut his way through 20 miles of forest between Portland and the Wannon River in Victoria, found the valley, and settled there. He never married, because I don't think there was anyone to marry, although he travelled widely and brought beautiful antiques to the homestead that he built. His brothers came from Ireland to join him. They were visionary people. When I get time, I'd like to write their story. They built one of the most beautiful homes in the country — named Murndal, an Aboriginal word for 'spring' — after the permanent water supply beside which it was built. Samuel Winter Cooke, who was the nephew of our first settler, became a member of the first Australian Federal Parliament.

The family on my mother's side were Scots, who migrated to New South Wales. One of them became the first Premier of New South

Left, Rosemary Winter-Cooke, aged 6. Below, 'Murndal', the Winter-Cooke family home in Hamilton, Victoria, 1918. Herbert Pybus Cooke and great uncle Sam Winter-Cooke play croquet with two unidentified ladies

Wales, Sir John Robertson, so we're connected with politics on both sides. Old Sir John Robertson had long white hair. When haircuts went up to four pennies, he swore he'd never have his hair cut again, and he didn't. They were real characters. They all had dozens of children and I came from one of them. I think they always honoured achievement.

My father's contribution was definitely on the battlefront. He was at Gallipoli and in France and much-decorated, but he was badly injured and never completely recovered. Of the 25 boys in his class at Geelong Grammar, only two returned from the war. To use a cliche, they really were the cream of the country's manhood, those sons and grandsons of our pioneers.

Nurtured as individuals in an uncompromising environment, they didn't need to learn to handle excuses — they didn't make any. It was a tragedy that our country lost them in the excitement of being involved in a war that wasn't even our own. I don't think Australian history has properly assessed the calibre of the men sacrificed to European ambition and fears. It's not commonly known that Australia lost more men per head of population in World War I than any other country in the world. Those of us who followed the pioneers were deprived of their influence. They were innovators, initiators, improvisers — we lost what we could ill-afford to lose.

My mother was English, although as I said, her ancestors were Australian. Strangely, every one of the Winter Cookes of Murndal returned to England to find wives, even my younger brother Sam. My mother's father, John Geddes, was a true entrepreneur, and I think my favourite ancestor. He brought refrigeration to Australia. He threw a party at the Australia Hotel in Sydney and invited everybody who was important. Although nobody backed him, he was responsible for the first ship carrying meat from England. During this big party at the hotel, English lamb was served. Everybody was enjoying it and at the end, he rose, lifted his glass and said, 'Ladies and gentlemen, you have just eaten English lamb'. Horrified at the thought, each of them went outside and retched.

He died of cancer at 52. His wife, being English, packed her bags and took her four sons and two daughters back to London. So my mother grew up in an English environment, and met and became engaged to an Australian soldier, who was blown to bits in France. Her would-be in-laws invited her to Australia to meet them, and she met my father on the Lane Cove ferry. She had made up her mind to marry an Australian.

I have three sisters and one brother: Elizabeth, Ann, Caroline and Samuel — the last two are twins. We had a happy childhood: ponies, picnics and governesses, and then the girls went to boarding school at Clyde Woodend, Victoria. I wanted to go on to university but my parents didn't think it necessary for girls, and sent me instead to be 'finished' in England, on the debutante circuit. 'Finished' is the right word. Having been finished, the only acceptable future is up the aisle.

In fact, I didn't ever go to finishing school, but I did perform the all-important curtsy to the Queen at Buckingham Palace, as well as Ascot, the Derby, and Henley. It was fun, but totally restrictive, and it nurtured priorities which are inappropriate in today's world. I had gone to a girls' school which aimed to produce, in the headmistress's words, 'good country girls with character'. We didn't need to bother our heads with an excess of Greek and Latin. You married the boy on a neighbouring property and you did your thing in the country. It was somewhat nonconformist to take another path. We had a few clever girls; Rupert Murdoch's sister, Helen, was dux of the school. I became engaged and married young — I was 18 when I accepted Michael's proposal. We were married at St Margaret's Westminster in London, the church where my mother was christened.

Michael was among the many young people who visited our country home. He was intelligent and intellectually stimulating, and we've been very happy. We had three sons and a good life. We had to work very hard, but that's good for young people. Michael was an engineer on a salary of 500 pounds per year. We had no capital, so everything we have, we've achieved ourselves, except for a small loan from my father. The family estate was left, by tradition, to the eldest son. Just the same I never contemplated working, and saw my role as wife and mother. My life's direction was dictated by our sons' activities. I think I can say they are achievers. We value that. Julian was very good at sport, captain of the football team, and athletics champion. My job, as I indicated earlier, was packing the picnic lunch and arriving at the match — until it all came to an abrupt end.

The children were generally supportive — they tend to be entre-preneurial. Julian outgrew the embarrassment of having his mother and father watch him play sport. Two months later he was inviting us back, but I didn't have time then. He left Australia six years ago and has been most successful with an American computer company, Paris/London-based. I hope he'll come home one day.

The children started giving me encouragement, especially Alastair. He graduated in Arts Law, a career which is suited to his individual personality. It was Alastair who said to me, 'Go on, Mum, get out and show them you can do something. I know you can. Do something with your life.' It was timely encouragement — he was my motivator. He never cared what people thought.

Nicholas, at nine years old, was too young at the time. He was apprehensive that I might go to see his friends' parents. I must have been a disgrace to him in the early days. If anyone suffered, it was my third son Nicholas. I wasn't there to encourage his school activities. But he has turned out to be the most goal-oriented and self-reliant. Early on, he learned that if he wanted to go to Scouts on Monday nights, he'd have to prepare his uniform on Sunday. He learned that if he was to pass his exams well, he would have to get books from the library himself. I fetched them for the other two boys. The result was that when he reached Sydney University, he was accustomed to controlling every aspect of his activities, and he outshone them all. Each of the boys was captain of his house at Cranbrook. We were proud of that. To me, Nicholas' achievement was a special relief. Every working mother fears the consequences of her absence from the home front.

When I received an international award, Michael and I went out to dinner to celebrate. I said, 'It can't have been easy for you. When you were so discouraging to me in the beginning, you couldn't have felt that you were part of what I was finally able to achieve.' I'll always remember his reply: 'I figured either I would have you that way or not at all. You would have been bored. You had to have something to do. But promise me, wherever you go, for however long, come home.' That was special. But then, he is a special person.

Some of my friends avoided me. A couple of them made comments such as, 'What's happened to Michael, dear? Has he lost his job or something?' and, 'Selling encyclopaedias? Oh, I couldn't do that.' Some were most disparaging. I lost friends, but I had to handle that. This chemistry, a combination of encouragement and discouragement, insults and innuendo, faith and hope, acted as a spur, and somehow I got across the river. I made it with help where many drowned. How gratifying it was, though, when finally some of those same friends, with whom I had had no contact for years, acknowledged my success and came to me to ask about the possibility of joining the company. They are among my dear friends today. I understood that they would have to go through what I went through, and I tried to provide the support I had received from Diana Rose and Margaret Christensen.

I asked my father, 'Do you think I should not sell encyclopaedias?' He said, 'There are only two worthwhile considerations, your God and then your own opinion. Don't be directed by anyone else's opinion in life. What exactly are you doing?' I said, 'I'm knocking on doors', giving him the very worst picture of it. I can still remember him smoking his old pipe and replying, 'Well, your ancestors knocked on the door of this continent. I don't see any reason why you shouldn't knock on doors, if what you do when you get inside is good for the people, and not just good for you.'

My father was a grazier but he should have worked with people, not sheep and cattle. He had a vision for people, or rather more accurately, for men. He was a man's man. The sad thing was, he had four daughters and only one son.

Everyone who is going to achieve anything must learn not to listen to the 'don't-doers'. If you want a 'give-up' decision made for you, they'll make it. Like flies, the don't-doers are everywhere. When Walt Disney had a new idea, he'd ask his friends whether or not he should go ahead with it. If enough of them said 'For goodness' sake, don't do that', he concluded he was on a winner and did it. I always thought that was inspiring. We women especially worry about what people think, but then in Hamlet, Shakespeare gave Polonius these words: 'This above all: to thine own self be true . . . thou canst not then be false to any man.' This is the criterion by which to live.

Diana Rose, my manager in World Book, my partner and my friend, has that rare combination of administrative and people skills. She should be the one sitting here because she is one of the greats in Australian sales management. At our peak, there were over 3,000 sales agents selling World Book and Childcraft in our team. The company sold nearly 1,000 sets a week. We hired and trained salespeople who cared about the customers' children. We disapproved of the hit-and-run marketing concept, preferring to develop a representative who lived in the area, was known and respected, and who would handle sales service calls, back-up and follow-through. This builds a company's reputation and the representative's confidence in his perceived role.

In Zondervan we have a smaller market, but we stretch over three countries: Australia, New Zealand and Canada. Our main product, the *Book Of Life*, a Bible programme helping families to know and understand their Bible better, is now in thousands of homes throughout these countries. Everybody needs good books — reading is of paramount importance. We live and work in an exciting environment.

With time, Michael became more supportive. Eventually, I was making more money than he was, and Michael had a different character on his hands. The fact that we survived all that is entirely to his credit. He approached the problem calmly and intelligently. He adjusted, where most men feel threatened. I have seen so many men wittingly or unwittingly take steps to remove the competition, to the destruction of their wives' careers. Michael saw the benefits, where others could see only themselves. We had more financial security and our conversation was infinitely more interesting. What had happened to the boys' socks in the washing machine was no longer the major day's preoccupation. While I began to climb and succeed in World Book, Michael was climbing to the top through the ranks of his company, NEI John Thompson Australia Pty Ltd, so he had an understanding of the processes which are usually accelerated in the direct selling industry. We came to the crossroads but finally travelled along the same road. He came to understand and change his opinion of sales people. A company, indeed even the world, depends on sales people selling products. Not until someone sells something to someone are jobs created.

You must forgive me if I show prejudice towards sales people; I have loved them for a long time. Often maligned, they carry a tremendous national responsibility. I have never known a successful salesman who does not have courage, persistence, integrity, empathy, self-discipline and humour, with varying emphasis. Often these qualities need to be developed, but long-term salesmen will not succeed without them, and it is with people of this calibre that I want to spend my life.

The government should establish chairs of salesmanship in every university. It should be a degree course. The curriculum should cover attitude, qualifying, prospecting, approaches, objections, closing, sales management and psychology, time management and goal-setting.

It is so truly said that:
>'A man who works with his hands is a labourer.
>A man who works with his hands and brain is a craftsman.
>A man who works with his hands and brain and heart is an artist.
>But a man who works with his hands and brain and heart and feet is a salesman.'

Yet, instead of being the most qualified profession, we are among the least qualified. If all those on Social Security were obliged to attend

Above, the Winter-Cooke family at 'Murndal', 1937. Between mother, Marcia, and father, William, are Caroline, Rosemary, Elizabeth, Ann and Samuel. Left, Alastair, Michael, Rosemary and Nicholas Moore, 1985. Julian lives in Europe

sales training programs, the government would decrease expenditure and increase productivity. If only they could be made aware of this truth. This is my belief.

Of course, it wasn't all smooth sailing for Diana and me. I haven't told you why we left World Book. Changes were made in the international division which we could not support. Basically, we lost trust and confidence in the company's decision-making capacity. The changes discriminated against our sex, and on behalf of women everywhere we decided they were unacceptable. Sometimes in life you have to stand up for the things in which you believe, at other times you have to stand against the things in which you don't believe. This was one of those times. A belief that men are more successful motivators than women was one of the reasons for the changes. This is a legitimate and understandable point of view, but motivation is not just a 'whoop-up'. If you lift people up, you need to be there when they come down, you need to be there in the morning as well as in the evening. We figured the way to handle the situation was to leave the company and let the results speak for us. We did — and they did. But no-one should look back. Cut, forget, and go on. That's our philosophy. No-one's ever irreplaceable, and I believe the company, now under new management, is bounding ahead as it deserves to do.

After we resigned I went to the Direct Selling Association's headquarters in Washington. All ethical and established direct selling companies register there. Direct selling is a huge industry which makes a valuable contribution, providing a flexible environment for people everywhere to supplement the family income within the confines of their commitments. I thought I'd go and see if there was a new product we could take to Australia. I wasn't looking for something to sell — I was looking for something that it was important for people to have. The Zondervan Corporation's new *Book Of Life* had just been published. The sample hadn't even arrived, the DSA could only give me a brochure. They also gave me information on hundreds of other companies whose products didn't appeal to us. Education and books had been our world. The mission-oriented *Book Of Life* attracted us both. We had the privilege of breakfasting with the editor, Dr Gilbert Beers, in Chicago, and this publishing masterpiece won our support. We had sought worthwhile products and found them in this beautiful series of Bible stories. Christianity is one of the major forces for peace in the world, and we could see that this inspiring material could be a contributor. We were delighted with the 20th Century approach to the Bible stories that the *Book Of Life* presented. We felt grateful for the opportunity to work to bring families together, to share time and fellowship, and to gain a knowledge of the historic narrative of the Bible. In a society which solicits disunity, we felt we could find many others who would support such a product. I believe that Jesus Christ was a direct salesman, and look how he influenced the world. Perhaps in some small way we could contribute our sales experience to the greatest cause of all.

On returning to Australia, Peter Dinsdale, to whom a lot of our success is due, became a partner. We are privileged to work with this master sales manager and dear friend. Together we started a second company designed to sell Christian home and educational products, to extend an opportunity to people whose expertise and preference was to sell low-ticket items. The *Book Of Life* will always be our major product, but we have expanded considerably since then and are about to offer our customers the full range of Zondervan productions. We had worked up to a turnover of $1.5 million by the end of the second financial year, and we have moved on from there. Because of our success in Australia, the Zondervan Corporation in America granted us the distribution rights for New Zealand and Canada too, and we are grateful for this recognition of our ability to get the job done. Originally, we knew nothing about forming companies, budgets and cash flow, so we went to the best lawyers and accountants who, of course, are very expensive. The paperwork and set-up costs were $120,000. Now, because of the dollar plunge, we are planning to market sales services to the Asian and North American markets.

Each of us in Australia must be aware of the imbalance of exports. We have made tapes, and I'm just finishing my book, *You Can Learn To Sell!* The tapes were originally made for our people but I'm transcribing them for the open market. I took a sample to the North American continent last trip and made 28 sales, but we didn't have much time as we were hiring and training in every Canadian province, excluding the northern territories. We have to work more in this area in the coming year.

Sales people should find a product in which they can believe enthusiastically, then become committed and aim high. Too many people say, 'Oh, I'll try this and I'll try that', and they end up where there's most competition: at the bottom of everything. Start by finding one thing, doing it well, and then build on that. Diversify later, where it's less competitive. To lift your standard of living, set financial goals — the first $100,000 is the hardest. Money gets progressively easier to accumulate. We are now in a position to take risks, and that's why we're moving to other areas. We plan to take our sales package beyond Australia. If people with the opportunity don't try, and people who can afford to lose don't care, there is no progress. You must always be flexible in the marketplace. I don't think the drop in the dollar is temporary. We must change our thinking.

I went to see Charles Jamieson, who is the Australian Trade Commissioner in Toronto. He told me that when he was in Canberra, they had a phone call from Arabia asking for sales expertise. Evidently, confidence in Australian expertise has been built through our agricultural connections with Arabia. They told the caller that Australia had no-one they could recommend. I told him that we were putting together a sales package, and he said, 'Well, start with Arabia'. I'm bearing that in mind, hoping to be successful in taking an Australian product, a package of sales training programs, overseas. Time is the challenge. Could you imagine us teaching handling excuses and closing the sale in a harem? That would be different.

Many prominent people started out by selling door-to-door. Everyone benefits from the experience. Did you know that Robert Morley sold Electrolux vacuum cleaners? Since we appeared on television as probably the highest paid women in Australia, a judge and all sorts of eminent people rang to say that when they were at university and needed extra money, they sold door-to-door, and how much they had benefited from the experience. You are forced to delve deep within yourself to find the resources with which to cope. This develops initiative, because there's nowhere to run: you can't very well back down the path.

We have had the privilege of working with people of many races. My biggest mistake was when I put two Arab salesmen under a Jewish manager. That decision set off an 'international' incident in the office. I asked, 'Why don't you want to work for a Jew?', and the Arabs replied, black eyes flashing, 'Because he's a Jew'. I asked them if they wanted to work for an organisation where achievement and results were not the criteria upon which promotion was based. I talked to them from my heart. Isn't this what's so wrong with our world? Should we not honour achievement above race in a sales organisation? My Jewish friend had more units of sales than anyone at that time. I asked them how they would feel if the position were reversed. I left them in the office and asked them to write and suggest company policies under which all nations could work happily. I've always found it successful to hand decisions back to the complainant, like this: 'I appreciate the fact that you feel free to come and tell me what you really feel, but if you were sitting at my desk what would you decide would be the fairest for everybody?' They agreed to work for the Jewish manager. Finally, they beat him on the score sheet and one of them took the promotion himself. I believe today that they are all good friends. They took pride, in the end, in the fact that they were part of building a company where different beliefs were respected, but achievement was honoured. Lord Justice Hewitt once said, 'Justice must not only be done, but be seen to be done'. Every sales manager should commit those words to heart.

In their specialist area, direct sales companies make a significant contribution to international understanding. We've had thousands of sales people over the years, and we are in a position to weld them together with a common goal. Isn't that an exciting environment? Names such as Angelakos, Galati, Pantelic, Lopez, Garcia, Ng, Mansour, Desaureaux, Sotiropolous, Hussein, Chong, Stravinsky, Cwikel, Ammerlaan, Jeyarathnam, Engelbrecht, Yeshim, Schize-rotto, Punnyakanthi, Riquelme, Redenbach and Andrijesavich are among the sales people with whom we have worked. What a privilege it is to strive with these people, who joined with those of us of British origins to support common educational or Christian goals. We are a mini-United Nations.

Another area in which we believe our company has made a valuable contribution is that of building bridges between church denominations. A pastor stood up at a Brisbane meeting and stated, 'Zondervan of Australasia is achieving something that churches often have failed to achieve. They are bringing people of all denominations together to work to support the Christian cause.' We have representatives from the Pentecostal Churches, Roman Catholic, Greek Orthodox, Anglican, the Alliance Church, the Church of the Nazarene, Apostolic, Seventh Day Adventist, Presbyterian, Methodist, Baptist and Uniting Churches, the Church of Christ, Christadelphian and others, and we come together at our meetings with common goals, presuming to interpret nothing, but simply presenting the historic narrative of the Bible. We share sales training, fun, fellowship and a better knowledge and understanding of the Bible.

Sales people need to have quality sales material and first-class sales training. When they meet the inevitable triumphs and disasters of the sales environment, their training and sales material support them. We give them 12- or 15-hour sales training courses, followed, where possible, by ongoing classes. That's the practical plan, although it isn't always possible when you have an agent out at Cobar. The job of management is to make decisions which create an environment where the sales representatives can be successful, and this is different for different people. At World Book, we had an outstanding deaf and dumb salesman. Among our sales agents in Melbourne we have a blind man, and in Adelaide an inspiring lady with cerebral palsy. We rejoice to be in a position to bring an interest and an opportunity of achievement to these courageous people. Then again, environments change. What motivates one person has the reverse effect on another. Most people, but certainly not everyone, are motivated by money and trips. Each year, we take our top seven achievers to the Zondervan Conference in America. This year we will be including a Canadian contingent. Last year Canada's top salesman was a naturalised Philippino. We send an Australasian manager to manage Canada for three months a year. These trip winners are very precious people. It's a privilege to work with sales people such as our champion, John Smart, a previous Baptist pastor.

Involvement in the import-export business in three countries has meant we have to watch the money markets on a daily basis. We are concerned with international currencies. Diana, Peter and I attended the ANZ Bank seminar on finance at the invitation of our bank manager, John Lyons. John is an entrepreneurial bank manager who encourages women, and we have benefited from his enlightened attitude.

You ask about enthusiasm. Enthusiasm can be ignorance-based. I'd rather use the word 'attitude', because it suggests a greater permanency. I've seen many people come into direct selling who attempt things with tremendous enthusiasm, which can be wasted on the rocks with great speed unless it is carefully protected. Knowledge arms it. The last four letters of enthusiasm, 'i a s m', (I am sold myself), clarify enthusiasm. It is such a precious little flower, but it's the responsibility of management to not plant it where it will shrivel and die, and a sales manager himself must acknowledge responsibility for his own mental attitude. I remember the day I realised I must look within and not without for my own motivation; that was the day I was set free. Many a time I've counselled sales people in this way: 'Listen, dear, what you are saying is all true, but forget the lot. It isn't going to do you any good. Remember this instead: you're responsible for your own attitude. If you can accept that and activate that thinking, then you are half-way to your goal.'

Henry Ford said, 'Failure is simply an opportunity to start again more intelligently'. Failure is a clarifying process, it really is. Every successful person has learned valuable lessons through failure. What will work is revealed through experience of what won't work. If you don't know failure, then you run on a very narrow road. I have never met anyone I really admired who hadn't experienced and overcome adversity, even if it was self-inflicted, which it often is.

I'm a dedicated Australian. I feel we should all realise 'I'm only one, but I am one'. With this attitude, we'll build a better nation. No observer of the Australasian national character could conclude, in the main, that we have the right attitude. Too many of us want to take more and more and give less and less. Nothing is achieved without action. We must work, plan our work, and work our plan.

We may believe that mateship is part of our national character, but I think in the last decade we tended to think more of ourselves than the other person. In a sales environment, success depends on forgetting yourself and helping the other person achieve his goals. I am convinced that in terms of human nature, people make the mistake of concentrating on personal ambition. Forget yourself, and work for the things you believe in: your product, your company, your manager, your family, or your country. Then, and only then, can other things come through for you.

Stamina is important too. If people don't have stamina of character and physical stamina, they can't take pressure and they retreat to failure. Character is the resolve to keep going long after the desire to do so has passed. It's commonly thought that self-confidence is vital, but it isn't in the sales environment. It grows. It is necessary when you begin to teach others to succeed. If you say, 'This is how you do it', you must have confidence in your own opinion. I love the words, 'You cannot teach what you do not know, and you cannot lead where you will not go'.

A survey was conducted in America to discover what qualities were common to achievers. Many professions and callings were assessed. You might think that the qualities we are discussing would all be found in successful people in varying degrees, but the results showed that only one single quality was common to all achievers. Some of them had courage, some didn't; some showed tenacity, some didn't; some had stamina, some didn't. But what do you think was the one trait they all shared? It was *self-discipline*.

Another contributor to achievement is goal-setting. In our company, Diana and Peter are our experts. Their concentration is better than mine. I fragment too easily but I do have ideas. They issue the goals, I like to chase them. I'm very aware of goals. Goals can be a contentious subject — some people like high ones, some like low ones. I like attainable goals that are not too high. This might be surprising, but I'll tell you why. We are in a business of building people, building their ability to achieve, and often we are working with people whose experience of life hasn't given them faith in their own ability to achieve. I feel my greatest contribution has been with people, especially women, who have never had a successful opportunity to reach out to their potential. I feel strongly that we should stretch and strain, but not crack, that potential. I have seen companies crack their sales people, but sales management should challenge, not defeat; accompany, not defy; give wings, not chains to people's potential.

I look for self-motivators. I believe I am a self-motivator. In the beginning, at meetings, when I should have been concentrating on what was being said, I'd find myself thinking, I'm going to beat Betty. And I found that I could. Then I set out to beat the boys. I found I could. I set out after the state record, and following that the national record. I found they were attainable. One day I thought, I'm Australian, but why can't I have a crack at those American records? This was more difficult because, being American products, they sold in America at a much reduced price. However, with the support of Margaret Christensen, Diana Rose and my family, I did it in 1974. Zone manager Jim Bleth wrote from the USA to confirm my new world sales record.

Winning is important but it should be conditional. I learned that the hard way, on my eleventh birthday. My Godfather had given me a magnificent chestnut thoroughbred, Trixie. How excited I was. My sister's horse, Wendy, had long been the fastest horse on our property, but when Trixie arrived I determined we would be a winning combination. I challenged my elder sister. We rode down to the river flats. Anyone who has ridden horses in the country will know that when you turn your horse in the direction of home, he doesn't need to hear, 'Ready, set, go' before he's off. Wendy was a powerful horse who had galloped the flats many times. My hands were new to Trixie and so was the terrain. Perhaps her nervousness contributed, perhaps my urging helped, but slowly Trixie started to surge ahead. Sensing the competition, both horses were bolting. Determination to win prevented both Bid and me from reining them in in time. The attitude of 'win at all costs' and a fear that the other would claim the victory directed our actions. Suddenly, the heavy wooden gate loomed ahead. It was just like going over Niagara Falls. We were heading into a closed gate at about 35 miles per hour. I still remember desperately trying to lift Trixie's head and adjust her vision. (Today I would say,

'Change your attitude, you have a new goal'.) Maybe she could jump — I didn't know. In those last seconds she took off into the air, and we might have cleared it only the heavier Wendy, two feet behind, smashed into the solid structure. It broke from its hinges and crashed into Trixie's suspended forelegs. For one terrifying second she reeled sideways, then reared up in fear on her hind legs. I recall a blinding flash as I was suddenly looking at the sun, then I fell and fell. From the ground, I watched with relief as Wendy bolted up the lane towards the hill where I knew Bid, expert rider that she was, would rein her in. I lay there in the dust. I had won, but the price had been too high. I was bleeding and aching and filled with remorse. My beloved Trixie, would she ever trust my guiding hands again? The gate lay in smithereens around me; my parents' wrath lay ahead; my world was broken. I felt more fear than pain. It was all my fault — the race had been my idea.

We need to have these experiences and learn from them. I learned that winning must be conditional, and not achieved at the cost of things of permanent value. In a sales environment that is usually represented by the personal relationships dearest to us, our own reputations, and the reputations of the institutions and organisations to which we owe loyalties. Damage to either of these lasts longer than the taste of victory. However, and this is important, too often people use this as a justification of mediocrity. This is discernible in statements such as, 'My family comes first, not like Sally, who neglects hers — no wonder she wins.' Or, 'All he wants is to look important. I don't need to do that.' Unfortunately this attitude, the enemy of achievement, is more prevalent than the 'win at any price' attitude. The secret of success is to find the balance. After the horse race, when my father came to find me, he taught me another lesson. He lifted me up from where I had been sitting, magnifying my aches and pains. I was hoping his anger would dissolve into sympathy, but he said, 'The only thing that matters is that Bid and you are all right. Trixie is all right, she's cut a bit and frightened, but she came home. Bid and Wendy are fine, too. Come along, Trixie needs you.' What a lesson in love. Today, when my boys ring to say they've pranged my car, I always remember his words and say, 'The only thing that matters is, are you all right?' But I must say, I was tested the day one of the boys put a third dent in my new BMW. I was guilty of saying, '*First*, tell me are you all right', but a few other comments of an uncomplimentary nature did follow!

Salesmanship is a challenging profession. It's never dull unless you let it be. There are always mountains to climb and crevasses beneath your feet. How you cope makes you what you become. Experience changes you. Men and women react differently to situations, even allowing for personalities. Vive la difference! I would handle a sales presentation with a male prospect very differently from one with a female prospect. As a starter, when I arrived, I'd make a point of sitting some distance from a man. If a woman seats herself too near a male prospect, he feels his territory is invaded, and resents it. He prefers to dictate the terms of the interview, and to be impressed professionally and challenged mentally. With a female prospect, I tend to move closer and show more friendliness. She looks for trust and genuine care. The variety is a constant stimulus.

My time in sales management has convinced me that the Australian character, which tends to be entrepreneurial and disrespectful of authority, could demonstrate leadership in many areas not yet attempted. We have a creditable record in medicine, sport and music, but perhaps because of distance our service industries don't play a significant role. So much sunshine, health, wealth and opportunity have been invested in us that I feel we should be obligated to take calculated risks and share the benefits. We should feel responsibility for national goals.

In Canada and New Zealand, where we have established our companies, we have found many unexpected bonuses. I believe there are few Canadian companies run by Australians, and we had endless hassles with authorities who discouraged 'foreign' businesses. However we seem to have overcome most of them, and the Canadians, if surprised, have proved welcoming. 'Who are these Australians with a New Zealand manager, an American product, and a Canadian company?' they ask. I tell them we've come to get to know them. 'Who on earth are you two women with such strange voices?' one job applicant asked. I replied, 'I'm not going to tell you now, but by the end of the training class, I hope you'll know'. At the end of the day, he took my hands across the table and said, 'I thank God you came to us'. Wasn't that a precious compliment? Diana, Peter and I have trained around Canada, knee-deep in snow, in almost every province from Vancouver to St John's in Newfoundland. We even trained a Canadian Indian and a Mountie in full uniform, who brought two revolvers to class in New Brunswick. I got a real kick out of that. In Newfoundland there was a man who brought a bag of fish to class. It's all been an adventure. We built a sales team of approximately 300 people, and made many friends. It's been a privilege to work in Canada, and in the incomparably beautiful New Zealand. We were invited as guest

*Rosemary Moore addressing a sales motivation conference
at Miami Beach, Florida*

speakers at seminars in two other leading direct selling companies in Toronto. I hope we helped them.

An article in a French national paper recently said that Australia was the 'winningest' country in the world. It listed all sorts of achievements, some unknown to me. That excited me, because another country was recognising our contribution. Every company in a position to do so should try to start overseas, because in that way we contribute to world understanding. I have always felt proud to be an Australian, proud of Morris West's contribution to literature, and proud of others who have brought international recognition. As we travelled in North America we found it was Alan Bond, not Captain Cook, who put Australia on the map.

Conversely, Australia can learn much from other countries. We have a lot to learn about the promotion of free enterprise. Our government is guilty of creating an environment restrictive to free enterprise. This tends to penalise endeavour, reward failure, encourage the mediocre, and establish comfort zones for the undeserving. The government should encourage more small businesses who are activating work for Australians. In my opinion young people are not helped by free handouts, they are taught dependency. I think it's appalling that Social Security, in many cases, offers a viable, alternative lifestyle. People shouldn't be allowed to leave jobs and go on the dole at will. In Canada, you are eligible for the dole for only six months of your life. In North America, it is common for people to have two or three jobs, but in Australia there is no incentive to do so. Small businesses are handicapped here, and yet they employ 60 per cent of the workforce. What you 'stroke' is what you get, and we 'stroke' mediocrity. People who show initiative should be encouraged in taking their next steps. But as soon as they get off the ground, the government wants to whip everything from them, strip them back, and fill their hearts with despair. Those who are proving themselves capable of carrying the responsibility for this country are often dictated to by those who have proven nothing. The cost of government is too high, and who wants so much anyway? At my age I don't have as much personal ambition — well, yes, maybe I do — but I'd like to contribute, in some way, to an Australian endeavour.

Parents have a responsibility to set an example. I talk about boys because I have a male-dominated family, and I have always tried to influence their direction in life, as I think a parent should. But we have only 15 years in which to do so. After that, the peer group takes over as the major influence. I believe successful parenting stems from making constant small correct decisions, on a daily basis, rather than a couple of major, about-face decisions.

You asked me what quality I feel has contributed to my success. I think it would be courage, and I think I've always shown that in life situations. I've always been prepared to take a risk, but I fragment dangerously if I'm not kept on the track. Diana, Peter and I have made right moves, we have made wrong moves, but we have moved! Pat Zondervan, founder of the Zondervan Corporation (which had a $100 million turnover last year) has had considerable influence on our thinking. He's nearly 80, yet he comes out here for our conferences and handles an incredibly tough schedule, taking in the capital cities in seven days. He always has a cheerful smile, an encouraging comment, and a Bible quotation for each of us. His favourite is from Matthew 6:33: 'But seek ye first the kingdom of God, and his righteousness: and all these things shall be added unto you.' The world needs more such men — and women.

Another quality I admire is the ability to make quick, accurate decisions. It's important to be a decision-maker and to practice it from a young age. Parents should teach children to make their own decisions, and handle the consequences. Ethical decision-makers are much needed in the business world. People who have been exposed to failure and to success and to a variety of life's experiences are more likely to make valuable decisions. Too many people drift on the tide of circumstance without making things happen.

Goal-setting is important too. You cannot know the joy of arriving if you never aim to go anywhere. Our goals are to increase sales, to generally see our companies more established, and to offer a work environment to more people. I'd like to make a contribution to the release of women from the bondage of traditional thinking. Elsie Shealy, when she was promoted to vice president of World Book in America, was warned that women had to be twice as good as men to hold high positions. Said Elsie, 'So where's the problem?'

On the subject of recognising opportunities, did you ever hear the saying that opportunity knocks and you should listen? It's not true. Opportunity doesn't knock at all. Usually it rushes past you in the dark, and if you put out your hand you feel the wind. Most times, that's as close as it ever will come. You do the rest. You have to feel the wind, put out your hand and grab it, and having grabbed it, even then, it might be nebulous. You have to make it into something.

When one of our sales managers, Katy Patterson, was a little girl, she broke her back in 15 places. She was in hospital for years and they didn't think she would walk again. But she has a vast reserve of courage. When she decided to take up a sales career with World Book, Katy was disadvantaged by constant pain, but she didn't see herself as a loser. Katy made a brilliant sales manager, and she was always talking encouragement to others. The finest moment of my sales career was in Chicago, when she was announced as the top international sales manager of the year at divisional level. I still weep when I remember that. She got up and came across to me and said, 'Rosemary, I owe it to you'. It wasn't true, she did it herself. Someone once asked me, 'How did you make money?' I think the answer is, 'By doing the right thing in the right place at the right time'. That's salesmanship in a nutshell. There are two ways of making money. One way is to go out and bring it in: inflow. The other way, you don't spend it: restrict its outflow. We did both.

Somebody once said, 'To become a millionaire, if that's important, (and I don't say it is) you need to have the capacity to borrow'. I think it was Sir Frank Beaurepaire of Melbourne who, as a young man, went to his bank manager because he wanted to start a tyre company. The bank manager refused the loan request. In such a case most people fade out the door, but Beaurepaire was annoyed and told the bank manager to keep his money, he would do it anyhow. He was as good as his word, but he was an exceptional man. I think it was Baron von Rothschild who put his finger on the crux of the matter when he said, 'Put all your pieces of paper in the bin (referring to qualifications), give me someone who can handle people, and I will make him a millionaire.'

Success breeds success, failure breeds failure. So it's important to be successful from the beginning, then it becomes a habit. I believe that optimism is the child of courage. No matter what trouble comes up, if you acknowledge but don't accept it, if you just go right on, you'll pick up in the face of anything. Peter Dinsdale exemplifies this attitude, which is courage-based.

Self-discipline is a major contributor to success. With it, you can make yourself do the things that need to be done, though you don't really want to do them at all. Things such as getting out of bed an hour earlier in the morning, or writing that letter instead of relaxing. Accomplishing unpleasant tasks is terribly important to a successful career, because we are all swamped every day with things we don't want to do. There's an ingredient of chance in any success, but I believe the ability to get things done is a crucial factor in any goal-oriented endeavour.

Basically though, success starts, is maintained, and ends, with attitude — a creative and activity-producing attitude — and an
acknowledgement that life does not owe us anything. Life was here
first! To be successful you need to have a dream, make it a goal, then
chase that goal for all you're worth. Keep your eyes on that goal at all
times, because obstacles are the things you see when you take your
eyes off your goal. Then, when you have achieved it, take stock of how
best you can share it.

For me, entrepreneurial thinking is clarified in those inspiring
words that have long been among my favourites:

'Some men see things as they are, and say "why?"

I dream things that never were, and say "why not?" '

Keith Williams

When fire raged through Keith Williams's spanking new Hamilton Island luxury resort on the Great Barrier Reef in April of 1985, his response — to rebuild — was so swift that it left no time for remorse. This counter-punching instinct, the absolute and final refusal to be deterred, is one big reason why a Williams plan usually ends up as a Williams project.

The quintessential self-made man, Keith Williams quit school and started work at age 13. At 55, he still thrives on competition, making no distinction between work and enjoyment. An early love of motor-cycles led to the establishment of a nationwide manufacturing and service company, his first big coup in business. Likewise, the former champion water-skier saw potential for setting up a school and showground for the sport near Surfers Paradise, and he did so despite tremendous early opposition to the proposal. Later, a fascination with cars prompted him to construct a successful motor racing circuit in Queensland.

Williams moved onto the centre stage of commerce with the establishment of Sea World, now Australia's most popular man-made attraction. Again, it grew from his love of boats, the sea and the animals in it. When he sold Sea World in 1984, it was because Hamilton Island was proving to be a job worthy of his undivided attention. His private villa on the island's best spot is a miracle of Italian marble, with sweeping views even from the one-way mirror in the spa. There's a rifle range, a huge motorcycle collection, his own helicopter and hangar, and a jet that once belonged to Jordan's King Hussein.

The resort itself, over which his 240 workmen were still swarming when we spoke to him, was only half-jokingly described by Dent Island neighbour Bill Wallace as 'the way God would have made it if he had the money'. Even George Harrison has given the resort his seal of approval by building a private villa there.

It's not hard to see why Keith Williams is a magnate's magnate. He's a perfectionist who does what he sets out to do. Don't let the monocle he uses for reading fool you; this man's vision is true.

An old friend, Archie Spooner, who used to own Tom Piper Foods and more recently Mercury Outboard Motors, said to me one day, 'Keith, the most difficult part of any job is to take off your coat, roll up your sleeves, and say you've started'. I often think today how true that is, because you'll look at a project and think, 'Jesus, it is enormous. Where do I start, how do I start?' But the moment you get into it, everything falls into place. What appears to be the impossible suddenly becomes easy. And that's what it's all about, taking off your coat, rolling up your sleeves, and getting stuck into it.

Sure, having the fire go through Hamilton Island was a hell of a blow. I hate looking out there and thinking that beautiful building isn't there anymore. But what the hell are you going to do about it? Sit down and cry, whinge on people's shoulders? That isn't going to get the thing rebuilt. So as soon as my daughter rang up and said, 'Dad, the place is burning down', my only thought was to get on the aeroplane, get up here, and start rebuilding, because there was nothing else to do. We started that day. We started tearing down the burnt timber on one building that could be salvaged, and we started rebuilding it. Today, there are conventions being held in it and that's less than a week later. We've now got most of the major materials re-ordered for the new building, and the challenge is how to get it up in double-quick time, how to make it better than it was. Outwardly, I don't think we could improve on it. There was nothing I didn't like about it, but some of the technical things — in the kitchen, layouts of toilet areas, back-up systems for bars and such — I may change.

I can develop this island because I've adopted the policy of keeping my borrowings pretty low by comparison with my asset values. I don't ever want to see a situation occur where you can lose everything. I've seen a lot of friends who are multi-millionaires today and broke tomorrow. That happens through borrowing too high in relationship to your assets. You see people who have built up businesses suddenly out on their ear, because they became public companies in order to finance their projects. Gradually, somebody else gets control of the shares and out they go. It certainly won't happen here, because I'll never go public.

I develop things by the seat of my pants. So many people have said over the years, 'I suppose you have a great master plan'. I see what I'm going to do in my brain and I change it once a day. Anybody who says they can master-plan something like this or like Sea World is quite crazy. The public tell you how things are going to be developed. You can develop something and think you are on the right track, then suddenly find that you are not because the public don't go to it. That's what it's all about: being flexible enough to change the designs to suit the demands of the public.

You need to be tenacious in this world to get anywhere. You've got to decide that you are going to get the job done and go out and do it. If the game gets tough, you kick it into shape and make it work. There were plenty of things that didn't work, but I usually got out and made the bloody things work. Put enough effort in, you'll make it work.

I never let the setbacks affect my thinking. When I opened the Surfers Paradise motor racing circuit, our first year was the greatest disaster in history. I had grandiose ideas of how many people were going to go to a race. I brought Jack Brabham to Australia for the first time since he was world champion, set up an enormous program of racing, and lost my socks. Same with the Touring Water-Ski Show. That was a disaster financially, though I must admit it was a lot of fun — the laugh of my life. But the idea is to cut your losses, get out and get on with the next thing, and always learn from what you did wrong. The other thing is, you have got to go into everything with great confidence. If you're thinking, Christ, it mightn't work, don't do it.

I think the great satisfaction you get out of business is the people that you associate with in the course of your business, and also the people that you become attached to on your staff. I've always tried to keep very much in touch with everybody in the organisation. It is easy to be remote from your staff and remote from what's happening, but that's the way to lose touch with your own business and finally, you'll find it will fail. I think the other thing people need to remember is who they are, where they came from, what they've done, and remember how to converse with everybody. There are too many people who will try to become the high and mighty overnight and they forget about the people who helped along the way. I get a great kick out of my staff. I hate losing people, but you can't try and twist everybody's arm to stay. Some stay for years and years, though, and I keep an interest in what they are doing.

Of course, the other thing is I'm a hard task-master, I want everything done perfectly. My favourite expression is, 'Trifles make perfection; perfection is no trifle'. I believe you can be demanding and tough, providing at all times you are totally fair to everybody. I guess the old story is right, you get smarter as you get older. You learn to be a bit more tolerant and you also learn to assess things better. I am now a lot more tolerant than I used to be, although I'm not more tolerant of incompetence, nor am I ever likely to be. I accept that people make mistakes, but I try and make them have a feeling that they will have to take a more responsible attitude.

I always try and say, 'Now, if I were the other fellow, what would I think?' The same is true if I write a letter — I explain everything in great detail. You've got to *be* the person receiving the letter and say, do I know what he's talking about? I can assure you, if you ever receive a letter from me, you won't have to ask what it means.

I'm a second generation Australian on my mother's side and third generation on my father's. My mother is now 94, and until she was well over 90 she was still making all the clown clothes and the ballet skirts for the girls in my Water-Ski Show. When I started in the leather goods business, at a very early age, she was an enormous help to me.

My father died at the age of about 76. He had started his working life as a paper merchant. He joined the public service before the Great Depression as a temporary public servant but lost his job. He had some rather funny principles. He wouldn't take work as a charity through any of his relations or my mother's relations, and consequently he just about held the record for being out of work. I think it was for seven years straight. So most of my school days were spent getting by with the barest essentials: no such thing as shoes for school, it was a barefoot job. Luckily the school was only 100 yards up the road, and all the books in those days were supplied by the government to anybody whose parents were out of work. That was in Hawthorne, in Brisbane. I was born and bred in Brisbane, and have, in fact, never lived outside Queensland.

I didn't enjoy school at all, from the day I started until the day I finished. I couldn't really see the need for English and I couldn't see the need for most other subjects, except mathematics. I was particularly good at that and always have been. I used to have a reputation for backing away from school and turning up at home, which wasn't far away. Even when I left school I left on rather short notice, because the teachers had found out that I'd been taking a day off school, one day a week, for about 12 months. I thought I'd better disappear before they had time to punish me for it. I was 13 at the time and of course the war was on, in 1942. I went straight to the Commonwealth Employment Office, because there was nowhere else to go, and saw a job for a bowser boy at Howard Motors, Adelaide Street, right in the heart of Brisbane. Those were the days when bowsers were out on the footpath and there was no such thing as electric fuel pumps in Queensland. It was a case of put the lever up to six gallons and pump it up by hand.

Then I sat for the Public Service examination, because my father, having been put out of work as a temporary public servant, had said the only way to be sure of a job was to be a permanent public servant. My sister, who is five years older than I am, went into the Public Service and I followed in the family footsteps, getting a job as a telegram messenger. I remained as a messenger for a couple of years, then moved around the Public Service a bit, went to the Department of Immigration when it was first formed, then got a transfer to the drafting section of the engineering branch of the Post Office. That came about because I always had a bit of a talent for printing and mechanical drawing, so I finished up as a cadet draftsman.

I stayed there until I was about 18. In the meantime, I'd bought my first motorbike when I had turned 16. I borrowed 30 pounds off my sister, since my salary at that stage was only about two pounds a week. I was always mechanically inclined, and I took to pulling down engines and doing them up, then got into buying and selling motorbikes. I used to buy ex-Army motorbikes for 76 pounds and do them up, chromium-plate the tanks and get them re-painted. There was no such thing as paint remover in those days, so to get the paint off I used to fill my mother's copper with caustic soda and hot water, boil it up, and fit the small parts in that. The larger parts of the motorbike I would put in one end first, then swap them around. It was great lengths of trouble but the result was good, and I was selling the bikes for about 125 pounds, mostly to another fellow in Sydney who in turn was reselling them. By a strange coincidence, we turned out to be lifelong friends. That's Arnold Glass, who owned Capitol Motors in Sydney. Arnold was up here only a couple of weeks ago with Sir David Brown of Tractor and Aston Martin fame.

All these Army motorbikes had been allowed to stand out in paddocks and the seats had rotted off them, so I had to do something about that. I had some knowledge of leather, because my grandfather on my mother's side was a shoe manufacturer. At least my mother was able to tell me where to buy leather. I went down to Jolly and Bachelor and said, 'I want to buy three square feet of leather'. The fellow said, 'I'm terribly sorry, you don't buy it by the square foot, you buy it by the side. You see, a side of leather was tailored very nicely to fit a cow, but it wasn't tailored very nicely for anything else. There's a lot of waste in it.' The cost of the side was 30 shillings, about a week's wage for me. To recoup that, I made a seat not only for my own motorbike but for several others, and I found a ready market with some of my friends who had the same problem. I went into making quite a lot of these seats and enjoyed doing it, so I went on to making other items out of leather.

I was still in the Public Service, but I did have a fair bit of time on my hands because I did a lot of shift-work. I figured I was about the next best thing to a millionaire at that age and I thought, now that I'm so wealthy, I might as well do what the wealthy people do. So I went down to the races. For about four weeks, I think I lost every cent I'd earned, and I was just starting to get the message that this wasn't a pretty good deal. I'll never forget my last day at the races. I backed a horse called Sweet Romance in the last race, and won back about 75 per cent of what I'd lost in the previous four weeks. That was it, I walked off the track vowing never to go back again. I suppose I could count on both hands the number of times I've been to the race track since then, but I enjoy it if I go along socially.

Anyhow, I kept buying more and more leather and making more and more goods. When I started selling to shops rather than to individuals, I found that I wasn't getting paid straight away. One day, when I was buying more leather from Jolly and Bachelor, the fellow said to me, 'You're such a regular customer, you should open an account'. I said, 'What's an account?' and he said, 'You take the leather now but don't pay for it until the end of next month'. I said, 'Christ, how long has this been going on?' That was a change in my lifestyle, when I discovered there is a thing called credit.

At that stage, I decided to quit the Public Service. It was a bit like the day I quit school. I went home and said, 'Mum, I've quit my job, I'm going to work for myself'. She said, 'Son, what will you do if you fail?' Knowing my father's attitude, I said, 'I'm not game to fail'. I didn't have to be too smart to realise that if you work harder than any-body else, you can't possibly fail. And I was prepared to work harder than everybody else.

Long hours became quite a thing with me. I was still doing up the odd motorbike, making the accessories for it, and selling it. I used to hand-stitch everything. All I had was a needle, a punch, and a lot of kangaroo hide binding. As I moved to more and more production, that was where my mother came in handy. She was always a great machinist — she'd been a milliner, so she'd spent half her life at a sewing machine. Suddenly, I found I was earning quite a sizeable sum and I was able to buy an industrial machine and keep improving my situation. The highest wage I ever earned in my life was three pounds, 19 shillings and sixpence (the equivalent of $7.95) before I left.

We lived in an old house up on stumps, like most Queensland houses were. We had one power point in the whole house and into that you plugged every electrical appliance you had, which in our house was one, an electric iron. I bored a hole in the floor and put a lead in and dropped it downstairs. I had so many double adaptors and leads that it looked like a spider's web. As I bought more and more machines, I just kept working on one power point. Of course, the fuse didn't go too well, so I put something in that looked like a piece of fencing wire and we carried on regardless.

Then I got into a partnership with a fellow, which didn't work out too well. He was making industrial polishing mops with a leather core, so it happened that we got associated. It went the way of all partnerships. He was much older than I was, so I had to get out. I vowed and declared that I would never have another partnership as long as I lived.

I walked out of the business thinking I was getting nothing, but some friends of mine said go and see a solicitor. I didn't really know what a solicitor was all about — I thought they were Shylocks who took your money — but I found a solicitor whom I liked very much. He was very kind to me, taught me a lot, and without very much effort at all he got me what I considered to be a very generous settlement out of the partnership arrangement. It enabled me to get going again, and in fact I got too big for our house. In those days, still early after the war, you couldn't get most building materials, so I decided the only way I was going to expand was to build a factory for myself.

I went and bought a hammer, saw, chisel, axe and a few other things (no electrical tools, didn't know anything about that) and I had a go. Because you had to have a permit to buy timber, obtaining same without a permit was a bit like boot-legging; I used to go out to a sawmill in the country at night with a struck I'd borrowed, load the timber, and get back without anybody seeing me. I bought a piece of land at Bulimba, which didn't cost too much, and I built a factory with my own hammer and nails and a bit of determination. I didn't know anything about building, except through commonsense. If I was stuck on how to do the next part of the job, I'd rush around the street and find a house half-built and work it out from there. One of the great challenges was putting up the roof. The building was about 50 feet wide and I had timber trusses which I'd fabricated, but there was no such thing as hiring cranes in those days. So I made a gin pole, went and borrowed a block and tackle and endless chain from the local garage, put some guy ropes on the gin pole and got the roof up. This factory grew into a very large business in manufacturing motorcycle accessories. I suppose I was successful at it because I gave a service that the people had never had before.

I sold all round Australia. When I took my first trip to Sydney and saw the big city, I quickly learned that there is a lot to how you market a product, how you present it, how you package it, and consistency in being able to deliver on time. I could quickly see that these were the secrets. I did a deal with Ansett, ANA in those days, and they gave me back-loading rates (which I'd never heard of either) to get my stuff down cheaply. I used to guarantee my customers that if I received their order by nine o'clock in the morning, I would have the goods to them the next day, regardless of whether the customers were in Sydney, Melbourne or Adelaide. I used to air freight their orders out every night, even to Western Australia, although that took an extra day or two.

The motorcycle business fell to bits some years later, because the first new cars came onto the market, about 1949 if I remember correctly. I didn't wait around. I kept on manufacturing motorcycle goods but I also moved into other goods. I finished up by chance in children's playwear. Then I got the licence to manufacture Hop-a-long Cassidy cowboy suits in Australia. I was cheeky enough to say, 'Look, I like your products but your boxing is lousy. I'll show you how I'd box it.' Of course, that upset them, because they thought they were top marketers in that area. Then I got the franchise to manufacture under licence to the Walt Disney organisation. I made Davey Crockett apparel, Mickey Mouse Club material, Zorro, and all sorts of things.

Then I went into ladies' and mens' belts, both the fashion end and the mass production end; I also went into travel goods and a lot of goods in general, so I converted the factory over. I still held a great interest in motorbikes, and in fact even now I have probably the best collection of motorbikes in Australia up on the hill here. But I devoted most of my time to the factory, even though as a kid I also loved boats,

Above, Keith Williams, wife Thea, mother Louise, and sister Joyce celebrating Louise Williams's 80th birthday, October 1971. Right, Keith Williams skiing at Surfers Paradise Ski Gardens

and built my first canoe years ago with galvanised iron. I always loved sailing but I didn't get much of a chance because my business became an all-consuming thing.

At about this time, I decided that I wanted to buy a piece of land up on Currumbin Hill (on the Gold Coast). Never having bought anything other than a second-hand motorbike, I approached the fellow in much the same way. We haggled a bit and ended up with a price of 350 pounds. I pulled the 350 out of my pocket and said, 'Well, here's the money'. He said, 'You don't buy land that way, you've got to sign a contract and go to the solicitors'. Anyhow, I was a bit lucky, because no sooner had I bought it than all my friends said, 'You're a fool, it's up on top of a hill and there's no road, no way to get into it', but by sheer luck, about six months later some fellow bought all the land up the side of the hill right to the boundary of my property. He put in a complete sub-division and a road. I said, 'Do you mind going the further 50 yards and I'll pay "x" amount?', and he did, so I had a piece of land with access to it. I cut that up into three pieces and sold the cheapest part of it for 1,350 pounds. I intended to build there at the time, because my sister had gotten married and was living down the road and I enjoyed that area, but I guess I was tempted by money and I ended up selling.

Then in 1954-1955, which would have made me around 26 or 27, I took up water-skiing as a sport. I guess I've always been either right into something or right out of it. I took up competitive water-skiing and won the Queensland championship in trick skiing in 1957-58-59-60, I think it was — four years in a row. I won the Australian overall championship in 1959 for trick skiing, slalom and ski-jumping. The overall title was awarded to the skier who gained the highest number of points over the three events.

In 1954 I shifted to the Gold Coast to live, and a couple of years after that I started out to establish a Water-Ski Show and a school for water-skiing, while still retaining my business in Brisbane. By then I had a manager and about 40 employees up there at the factory, so we were going okay.

I was anxious to buy land in a good position on the Nerang River to start this school. An old friend of mine, Viv Birt, who used to own a lot of property in the area, was such an enthusiast for Surfers Paradise that he would do anything to help anybody who took an interest in the place. He insisted that I buy a certain piece of land. I said, 'Look, I can't afford it', but he said, 'I don't care. Give me 100 pounds and pay the rest when you can'. The price was 3,500 pounds, with a 100-pound deposit.

Then I applied to the Harbours and Marine Department and the Council to set up this water-skiing facility. Their attitude was that there wasn't any water-skiing when Captain Cook sailed up the coast, and they didn't see why there should be any now. So I fiddled around and tried to work out where they would allow me to ski, and I was such a pest that I think they finished up trying to get rid of me. They said, 'You can ski further up the river if you can find a site up there'. I found a site about three miles downstream from Nerang, where the ferry used to cross the river, at Carrara, but as soon as there was talk about me setting up a water-skiing facility, all 22 of the landowners between there and Nerang signed a petition opposing water skiing on the Nerang River.

Back at the Harbours and Marine Department, one particular fellow, thinking he would be rather funny said, 'We'll give you permission to ski up there if you can get the written permission of every land-owner'. I wasn't perturbed by that. I grabbed a bundle of books, literature on water-skiing, particularly good photographs of Cypress Gardens in Florida, United States of America, to show what I had in mind, and off I went. I finished up getting all but two to sign. I went back to the Harbours and Marine Department, who said that was no good, I had to get the whole lot.

So I went back and really talked. One bloke said, 'I really would like to sign but I gave my word to my mate across the creek'. His mate was worried that skiing would upset the fishing. I said, 'I'll give my word, I'll close the thing down if it upsets your fishing. At least give me a trial period of six months.' Of course, when one said yes, the other said yes, so I got my permission for the Ski Gardens.

One councillor, Bill Birmingham, was a great old character but he was dead against my water-skiing plans. But the Albert Shire Council had a different attitude and they sent a fellow along, who was a bit of a lad in those days, called Russ Hinze. He and Sammy Andrews were the two councillors that I took for a ride in the speedboat to see the water-skiing, and they said, 'We can't see anything wrong with this, we think it's a bloody good thing'. So they convinced the Council, even though Bill Birmingham was still dead against it. Birmingham had five sons. I taught them all to water-ski and three of them became Australian champions. I got more kick in those days out of training the Queensland water-ski team than I did from skiing in it, because whilst I was training the team they had quite a lot of success. But I was a hard task-master, got them out every morning at daybreak, and trained the hell out of them.

I guess the council and government's attitude really started me on the road to success, because earlier they'd knocked me back for the use of my land at Surfers Paradise for the Ski Gardens. I had to do something with that land — this was just the time when Surfers Paradise started to take off — and my friend Vic Birt, who was in land development, advised me to sub-divide it. This land was a very odd shape and it had some land attached to it on the end of the peninsula that wasn't mine. It had built up like a sand bank. I was reading through the Lands Act and I found a passage that said: 'Land which is built up through gradual and imperceptible accretion, and to which there is no convenient access other than through adjoining freehold land, may be claimed by the owner of the adjoining freehold land'. I thought, that's me. I can claim that bit of land.

I went to the Lands Department and they threw me out the door. They said, 'Don't be silly, nobody has ever done that'. I kept coming back and coming back, until finally a new section of the Act came about. That's how all land today is arranged for sub-division where you're developing tidal lands, and the whole procedure is now simple, but in those days there wasn't any procedure. I was the first to obtain land in that way. In the process of developing that land, it grew from about seven acres to 13 acres because of the accretion, and I built the first canal in Surfers Paradise. It was also the first sub-division in Surfers to have full-width bitumen roads, kerbs, and water channelling.

I cut that land up into 49 blocks, if I remember rightly, but I had no money to develop it. So I went along to a mate of mine and said, 'I've got no money and I need some sand pumped up, but if you pump up "x" amount of sand, I'll give you a block of land'. He said, 'That'll do me'. Then I went to a fellow who could make the road. Same deal, no money but a block of land. That's how the sub-division came about. I finally sold it and made quite a substantial profit on it, which in turn enabled me to develop the Ski Gardens further.

When I bought the land for the water-skiing, I only wanted about 28 acres, but the farmer wouldn't sell the property unless he sold all of it. There was a limited amount between the road and the water, which was what I wanted. The land on the other side of the road was a big, flat area and I was trying to think what I could do with it. I decided to build a motor racing circuit. I was always keen on motor racing, and at that stage they'd just decided to build the Warwick Farm Motor

Racing Circuit in Sydney. I thought, 'Well, a motor racing circuit here would be great'. Back in 1953, they held a Grand Prix at Southport on public roads. By coincidence, the fellow who organised it, Bill Pickett, is my secretary's husband, and Bill has been working for me now for 28 years. I can remember at the time the headlines in the paper: '65,000 to Grand Prix at Southport, biggest crowd ever in Australia'. I thought, this will do me, I'll get into the racing business.

Unfortunately, I found out that when you do it in an organised manner on an organised track, you don't get anything like those crowds. I don't know that we ever got any more than about 10,000 people to the track, but that's a hell of a big crowd when they are all paying money to go through the gate. So apart from running the Ski Gardens, which I began in 1959, I started building the racing track in 1965.

Going back a bit, in the course of developing the ski shows at the Surfers Paradise Gardens, I decided to close down the manufacturing business in Brisbane and shift it to the Gold Coast. That is, I used the same plant and machinery but went into aquatic sporting equipment. I started making water-skis, wet suits, life jackets, ski ropes — everything you'd use in aquatic sports in those days — and applied sound marketing techniques, which had never before been applied to that type of equipment. Again, we graduated very quickly to gaining a lion's share of the Australian market in all those areas.

So we had quite a nice operation going. All the skis were manufactured under the name of Surfers Paradise Gardens Skis, and we used the names of all the champions we had there, which helped to sell the gear. It wasn't a novel idea, because Cypress Gardens in Florida, which had been a model for my development, manufactured on their premises as well.

I had never been to the United States, though, until 1964. So I had been operating for six years before I'd ever seen Cypress Gardens, in the same way that I'd developed my entire leather goods factory before I'd ever walked into someone else's. When I did, I got a hell of a shock, because I thought most of their ideas were pretty old-fashioned.

Then came the big go: I applied to run the World Water-Ski Championships in 1965. That was the one thing that I probably got more satisfaction out of than anything else I'd ever done, because everything went so smoothly. We had a terribly big team out here from the American Broadcasting Corporation. The *Wide World of Sports* program sent about 20 men out and we got world coverage. I must say there was a bit of luck involved in that event, because the weather was perfect. Every day for about eight days there wasn't a breath of wind, and the water was like glass.

That project was what caused me to make my first trip overseas. I went around to all of the countries who were going to take part and negotiated with them. It was like running a small Olympic Games. We had something like 200 competitors from 22 countries speaking 12 different languages, and we provided complete hospitality, all accommodation and meals for a week, and paid 50 per cent of their airfares. I had to raise the money, of course, and that was a bit of a trick. Every other country who had ever run it had government subsidies for it and the airlines of the country had chipped in, but not here. So I had to find some sponsors. We found them: BP, Rothmans, Mercury Outboard Motors and Caribbean Boats.

The year before, I decided to take a Water-Ski Show on a tour of Australia, so I packed up like Barnum & Bailey's Circus: three semi-trailers, a six-ton truck, eight station wagons, six speedboats, 2,000 grandstand seats, and enough flood lights to light about half-a-mile of river. Of course, all those shows happened at night. In Victoria and South Australia, you couldn't hold an exhibition on a Sunday.

I could fill a book just talking about the funny things that happened on that tour, but in the process we met some great people. One of them was Reg Fogarty, who later became Sir Reginald Fogarty. He ran Carlton & United Breweries like a great dictator. He's a legend, old Sir Reginald, but I found him to be a hell of a good bloke and a character. I liked his straightforward, dictatorial manner. He came up to visit when we were getting ready for the World Water-Ski Championships and asked how I was going to pay for it. I said, 'It's going to cost us initially about 40,000 pounds, and I hope to get maybe 30,000 back at the gate. To cover it, we are looking at about 20,000 pounds in sponsorship.' He said, 'I'll take it', just like that. I was shocked. I said, 'That's very generous and I really appreciate that, but I've already got three sponsors at 5,000 pounds each. If you would like to be a quarter sponsor at 5,000 pounds, that would be really great.' He said, 'The lot or nothing. If you are going to be a dog, be a bloody Alsatian.' I got the fourth sponsorship from someone else, but he was so generous as a result of that talk that he put on functions and did all sorts of extras to help. In fact, I would say he helped us to a much greater degree than the 5,000 pounds would have anyhow. He died not long after that, but he was a character that I thought the world of because I liked his forthright manner.

The Surfers Paradise Gardens went from strength to strength. I had begun with one show a day on Sundays, which was pretty comical. I was the clown on water-skis, commonly known as Bo Bo. The last clown act was about three acts from the finish of the show, so it allowed me time to rush up, wipe my make-up off, run over to the cafe and start making milk shakes, ready for the onslaught after the show. So I was jack-of-all-trades, involved in the catering and everything else.

We got one of the first licensed restaurants in Queensland. The next year, I opened the Surfers Paradise International Raceway as part of the overall property. We put on daily water-ski shows and built the Ski Gardens up — a nice swimming pool and nice grounds. I became very interested in tropical flowering trees, because I'd bought 20 to 30 acres of cow paddock without any trees on it, and I planted all sorts of flowering trees.

At the motor circuit we started Speed Week, which became quite well known. In conjunction with that was the Concor Elegance, which became a popular social night on the Gold Coast for 13 or 14 years. Eventually, we intend to re-introduce it on Hamilton Island. It's a prize for the best combination of gown and automobile. The car is driven up on the stage and the girl hops out and parades the garment. That was enormously successful and was always booked out 12 months ahead.

In 1964, just before I took the Water-Ski Show on tour, Thea, my new bride, decided she had to go with us. I tried to explain it wasn't really the place for a new bride. For our first show, we went straight from Queensland to Tasmania and it was a disaster. The advance guard had forgotten to ask about tides and didn't realise that the tide went up and down about 25 feet at Devonport. We got to the site, I looked out and said, 'Christ, where's the water?' He said, 'Gee, it wasn't like this when I saw it'. Then I woke up that he'd seen it at high tide, and I borrowed ladders from the fire brigade to get down over this great sea wall to our pontoons.

This caused a bit of a panic and finally, when we all rushed out of the hotel, Thea got left behind. At that stage, she burst into tears and decided to go home to her mother for a while. So we started off with a bit of a rough deal but we survived all that very happily.

My wife has devoted herself to looking after the children and to efficiently running the home, and she's done a hell of a good job of it. Rebecca is now 20 and Ben is 12. As far as business is concerned, Thea is not inclined that way, but she's a very busy person and takes interest in a lot of things. She's an exercise crank and gets up and rows with me early in the morning. She paddles the surf ski around the lake, I row a scull, and my son does the same. We all get up at six o'clock and exercise for half an hour to an hour. During the day she's involved in certain fund-raising organisations and fashion parades.

Bo Bo the clown, aka Keith Williams, Surfers Paradise Ski Gardens

She did modelling for many years and still does the odd job. I joke about trying to catch her at home, saying Thea is a very appropriate name: 'Now you Thea, now you don't'.

Those next years rolled along, from the Water-Ski Championships in 1965 to the opening of the motor racing circuit in 1966, and then I could see problems staring us in the face. In fact, I had seen them for years in my hassles with the Harbours and Marine Department back in the early days. I had told them then, 'This site really isn't going to be a good one. It's all right today because there isn't a lot of traffic on the Nerang River, but everything is going to build up and eventually I'll be trying to run a private show on a public thoroughfare, and I believe a problem will occur.' When I started, there were five houses on the road between Broadbeach and Nerang, but our development attracted a lot of homes into the area.

Boats became popular. Instead of seeing one boat a week coming up the river, we were seeing 100 boats a day. The river silted up as a result of the development downstream. Also, the tide couldn't move as well, so high tide became about a foot lower and low tide became about a foot higher. So I could see the problems staring me in the face. In about 1964 I applied to the government to get some land on the spit at Southport. Today, people say, 'You've been lucky, the government has been good to you, you're mates with the Premier', and all that sort of rot — absolute garbage. I had never even met the Premier in those days. I was reminded of it the other night, when I met a fellow who was the secretary to the Premier. He had introduced me to the Premier back in about 1968, so for four or five years I'd been applying to get this land on the spit.

Finally, I did my block and insisted on seeing the Premier, whom I'd never met. Russ Hinze organised it for me through the Premier's private secretary. The Premier listened to my story and said this sort of thing shouldn't happen, you've been messed around a lot. He intervened and arranged for the land to be put up for public tender, so even though I had been applying for five years, I still had to tender for it. I got it. Nobody else tendered for it because the conditions were so severe, and I had to negotiate the conditions. But that was the only way to go. Then I started to develop what, today, is Sea World.

We caught our own dolphins for Sea World, and in the first five years there was never a dolphin expedition that I wasn't on. By this time I had a big boat, which was essential to the Sea World operation. Through moving around in those boats I learnt a hell of a lot about the sea and the animals in it. The greatest thing about catching dolphins was their natural affinity for man. Any animal you have cornered is going to attack you. It doesn't matter whether it is an ant or an elephant, sooner or later it is going to turn and try to do you damage. The only animal that I can think of that doesn't do that is a dolphin.

When we netted dolphins in Moreton Bay, we never netted more than we had men to handle. There would be six dolphins and you've run the net around them, then suddenly they'll all hit the net at once. They'll wrap themselves up in it and they can drown. So what you have to do is net a dolphin in shallow water only. We'd put all our men in rubber boats, and I'd never allow them to wear anything other than a pair of swimming trunks — no knives on legs and all this sort of thing — because the biggest danger is getting yourself caught in the net. If you have anything on your body, it will get caught in the net and you'll drown.

So we'd move around the dolphins in rubber boats, and the minute they went for the net, one man got dropped off at every dolphin. Most of them were up at the surface. If any were down a couple of feet, you'd grab the dolphin, lift it to the surface, take a fistful of net, put it over the boat and hold the dolphin up there so it could breathe easily. Meanwhile, you'd unwrap the net. We'd inspect the dolphins and immediately free any that were too old or badly marked or not what we wanted.

When you unwrapped the net you'd have to open the dolphin's mouth, and in in many cases you'd put your hand in to get the net off its teeth. They have got a pretty fair sort of a jaw and a fair set of teeth, and there's not much doubt that they could take your hand off without trouble. Yet you could open its mouth and put your arm in, and it would never attempt to bite you, never even put pressure on you, nothing. Some oceanariums have to calm them down with tranquilisers, but the best way to calm down a dolphin is to pat it and talk to it, just like you would a dog. Straight from the wild, their compatibility with man is unbelievable. You'd take them back and be hand-feeding them in a couple of days at most, and sometimes in a couple of hours.

We saw a great example of a similar compatibility with a whale one time. I was at Sea World in the early days, and a fellow rang up and said that there was a whale in close to the shore. I said, 'That's not of much interest to me, but I'm driving down to Surfers Paradise and I'll have a look at it on the way'. I got into my car and saw this whale coming up the coast; it was about a 40-foot humpback. This whale was coming up close to the shore and I saw him go past a buoy, then I saw the bouy moving. I thought, Christ, the whale has got caught in the shark net. Most whales are too smart to get caught in the shark net, but I watched for a while and could see he wasn't going to get out of it. So I rushed straight back and grabbed one of our competitors in those days, a good fellow named Johnny Reynolds from Marineland. I said, 'Forget our differences of opinion at the moment. Let's get in the boat and go rescue the whale.'

So he took two of his blokes, I took two of mine, and out we went. I stayed in the boat, because somebody had to man it, and the others went over the side to cut the net away from the whale. There was a hell of a westerly wind blowing that day, and I was about 30 or 40 metres away and couldn't see exactly what they were doing. They stopped cutting and sat on the whale's back to have a rest and the whale didn't move. Finally, I shouted, 'Haven't you fellows finished yet? What the hell is the whale sitting there for? He must be caught up somewhere.' They checked and said, 'Nope, he's free'. They stood up on his back and were waving and acting the goat, then they dived off the whale's back and swam to the boat. As soon as they dived off, the whale moved slowly out to sea. He stayed on the surface and went out a couple of hundred yards before he dived. There is an actual affinity between man and the cone-toothed whales.

Once I had Sea World developed, we changed the water-ski show from the old Ski Gardens across to Sea World. I think that was in 1970-71. Of course, Sea World has risen from being a lowly water-ski show to being Australia's largest man-made tourist attraction, taking in something like 750,000 people a year.

Also back in about 1971, I felt that motor racing in Australia needed a good change. We needed to introduce oval track racing on a bitumen surface track, as they have in American racing under what they call NASCAR rules (National Automotive Stock Car Racing). I tried to get permission to build tracks in Sydney, Melbourne and Adelaide as well as the one I had in Surfers Paradise. That was the prime purpose: to introduce this new type of motor racing.

For two years or more I searched for properties in Sydney and Melbourne, and there were so many hassles with councils and conservationists that trying to build a motor racing circuit became a nightmare. Governments' attitudes in those states made it absolutely impossible so I gave it a miss, but in the process I had bought some land in Adelaide and gotten permission there, by sheer fluke I think, to build the track. Even so the whole thing had failed, really, because I didn't have the two major areas, so to introduce this new type of racing wasn't on.

I had lots of arguments with Bob Jane, who had the Calder Motor Raceway. Bob saw me as a great competitor if I was going to build out in his direction and introduce this new type of racing. Also, I felt that we had to make some drastic changes in the controlling body of the motor sport. Even though Bob and I used to argue over motor racing, we were very good friends in an odd-ball sort of way, and we became closer as the years rolled on. Today, I'd say we are very close friends. I finally sold him the Adelaide Raceway some years ago and now he's saying to me, 'Well, all the things you said should have happened about 15 years ago, I'm going to try and make happen now'. He's building a big oval track in Melbourne, exactly as I wanted to do 15 years ago. Oval tracks will come to Australia, because they are more appropriate to our type of racing.

I was always at loggerheads with the Confederation of Australian Motor Sport, because I felt they were a bunch of amateurs trying to tell professionals how to run motor racing. The professionals, of course, were the drivers and the owners of the circuits. One day, when we were talking about speed differentials and how tracks should be built and safety arrangements and so on, one of these officials said, 'What the hell would you know about motor racing circuits? You've never driven a racing car.' He did happen to drive a racing car, so it was like a red rag to a bull. I bought myself a racing car and took great pleasure in bowling him off the track in about five seconds flat.

I always joke that only two people I know have taken up a motor racing career at 40, Fangio and myself, and Fangio did a better job because he won five world championships. But I raced in Monaros, both sprint races and long distance racing, and competed in three of the 12-hour events we held in Surfers Paradise. I enjoyed motor racing enormously, as I enjoy anything competitive. I also took up speed boat racing for a while, about that same time or a bit earlier.

Not long after I started my own business, I took up flying. It began when a friend called Don Dixon and I bought our first motorbikes at the same time. We tried to out-motorbike each other for years, he bought a bike, I bought one better, and so it went on. Finally, he bought a Vincent HRD, which was the top motorbike of its day, and I thought, 'That's the bloody end of it, I've got to do something else'. So I bought a motor car. Then he bought a better motor car than mine and this went on until finally, I bought a Ferrari and he bought a Lamborghini. Anyway, I got the last say in the motor cars, because I bought one of these Lagondas, which was the most expensive motor car in the world. Never drove the damn thing, I sold it again. Oh well.

Then Don and I took up flying. We went out to the Royal Queensland Aero Club and learned to fly in Tiger Moths. That would have been about 1949 or 1950. He took his flying seriously, went on to become an airline pilot, and only a few months ago retired as a captain with SwissAir. He recently came out and had a holiday with me; we've kept in close touch. So all these years I've flown various types of aeroplanes. Six years ago I took up flying helicopters, and since then I've never been much interested in flying a fixed wing. I fly helicopters very regularly.

I've always had a great love of anything competitive. I reckon the spirit of competition is the greatest thing anyone can have. I don't believe all this garbage about going into a sport for the sake of the sport, and it doesn't matter if you win or lose. I believe that's bullshit, you go into sport to win. If you're not going in it to bloody well win, you shouldn't go in it at all. Where you draw the line between a good and a bad sportsman is that the good sportsman doesn't complain if he loses. I'm a great believer in that attitude and I'm happy to say that both my son and daughter have the same spirit. My daughter just had her entry at the Royal Sydney Show in horse riding and she got a first and three seconds on her first go. My son has just got the competitive feeling at the age of 12. He's sculling now and he went into the Queensland under-14 championship. He's also gone into sailing at school, he's playing football, and he's looking forward to next year when he can get into the big rowing teams, the fours, and later the eights.

I talk to my children a lot about the spirit of competition. The other thing I talk a lot about to them, and to everybody when I get the chance, is that we should encourage young people to take pride in achievement, to develop pride in what they do. You should get enjoyment out of everything you do. I don't think it matters whether you are the garbage man or the Prime Minister, so long as whatever you are doing, you try and do it to the best of your ability. If you do that, you'll find that you get great enjoyment out of it. There is nothing I've ever done that I haven't enjoyed, nothing, because I apply myself to it and try and do a good job on it. That's the thing that annoys me about the media in this country. They have this 'chop down the tall poppy' syndrome, when in a country like Australia what we should be doing is developing heroes, in everything we do. We need heroes in sport, in commerce, in everything. We should be building up our heroes so that our children will realise there is something worthwhile to aim for. Otherwise, they will be totally devoid of ambition. What is there in life if there isn't something to aim for? We don't spend enough time making sure that our children understand this, and to me the media have not helped at all in this country in building up people who strive to do well, and who *do* do well. They are only interested in trying to tear them apart.

The United States has a whole different attitude. For American children, it seems to be in-built that they want to do well. They seem to have more ambition and they have more drive to get there. In an address I heard somebody give, he was saying, for instance: a man drove down the street in a Rolls Royce and people in Australia made smart remarks, but then he drove down the street another day and a little Italian newsboy came out and said, 'Gee, mister, I'm going to work real hard and I'm going to own a car like that one day'. That's the attitude we should be encouraging. If you want something, you work for it.

A slogan I've lived by I take credit for having invented in the heat of the moment, because I wanted to be particularly nasty to somebody. We were having lunch one day and somebody said, 'You've been lucky'. Of the entire group who used to meet for lunch, he was the only one who didn't work for himself. He was always having a little dig at everybody else for what they had or what they'd done, and when he said to me, 'You've been lucky', I said, 'Yes, the harder I work, the luckier I get'. That's the way I see it.

I think we really need to change our attitude in this country. Patriotism is another thing that we don't encourage enough. We should be a nation of flag-wavers and take pride in our country, because so many different benefits will then accrue. It seems to have become fashionable not to salute the flag at school and not to be a patriot. To me, that's a totally wrong attitude.

Hamilton Island has something to do with all that. In the course of my Sea World work, I'd been going up and down the Barrier Reef quite a lot. I've always had a great love of islands and boats, and I always wanted to build a resort on an island. In fact, about 20 years ago, I approached the government to lease Pea Island in Moreton Bay. They had given me permission but we had a disagreement over the conditions. I wanted to do virtually what I'm doing here at Hamilton Island, have a combination of apartments or privately-owned residences as well as the hotel to make the whole thing viable. They wouldn't agree with that, so I said I'd rather not do it because I didn't think it would be successful otherwise.

In about 1974, I met a fellow called Bryan Burt. He and I became close friends through motor racing, and he was the biggest Ford dealer in Queensland. We did a lot of boating together and we happened to be sailing past this island on a beautiful, sunny day. I had only seen the western side of Hamilton Island, which wasn't that attractive because it had a big shallow bay that dried out at low tide. This day we saw the northern side of the island, and I thought, that's a great sight, I didn't even know about it. By coincidence, the very next Sunday there was an article in the *Sunday Mail*, talking about 'An island paradise for sale, parents want better education for their daughter'. So I rang up Bryan and said, 'What do you reckon? That island is for sale, do you want to try and buy it?' He said, 'Yeah, let's do that', so I rang them up, haggled a bit, and bought Hamilton Island. We were happy to buy it as a grazing property — we didn't think we'd have much chance of doing anything else — because the lease specifically stated that it was not to be used for any tourist purposes. But we got mixed up with a helicopter pilot from New Zealand who had been involved in deer farming, so we got the idea of turning the island into a deer farm. It really started off in that way; we put deer on the island with permission of the National Parks and Wildlife. Unfortunately, not long after that, Bryan discovered he had cancer. I spent quite a lot of time travelling around the world with him, and he even got to a stage, when all else had failed, of going to the faith healers in the Philippines, which is a dreadful confidence trick in my opinion. Anyhow, after Bryan died I pushed on with the development of the island. I think more than anything else I became a bit sick and tired of hearing about what was going to happen at Yeppoon (on the Queensland coast), and how it was supposed to bring a new dimension to Australian tourism. I said, 'Hell, we don't need to have overseas people develop these tourist resorts in Australia'.

So I applied to the government and rattled off all the things that I wanted to do. It was an all-encompassing proposal and I thought the government would say yes to only about half of it. I pointed out to them that I was a local and not a foreign company, all my business interests were in Queensland and that was the way I intended to keep it, and they said yes to my proposal.

Once I had the permission, I could see that the only way to do it was to have a combination of hotels and apartments, because that was the way the Gold Coast had developed. It never would have developed the way it did if there hadn't been a lot of additional capital put into it by people with comparatively small investments, because the way our tax situation is in Australia, you can't get a sufficient return on your invested capital to pay the high interest rates and still keep a reasonable relationship between your borrowings and your assets. So I developed this idea of how to go about it and it worked.

Gradually, I divorced myself from other interests. I sold out the Adelaide Raceway, I took over my old competitor Marineland, changed it into Birdlife Park, then sold that and it became Andalucia Park. I had a big property at Nerang where I was going to develop another fauna park, on a bigger scale, and I sold that. I sold Marineland Tweed Heads, finally sold the Surfers Paradise Raceway, and also sold the old Ski Gardens. All this happened over a period of years, and of course last year I sold Sea World. That's only because, as I said, I get joy out of doing things, out of being a hands-on developer. I'm not one for sitting in boardrooms and discussing take-overs. I could do that, sure, I could work the financial markets the same way as Alan Bond and (Robert) Holmes à Court, but that's not what I get enjoyment out of. If you don't enjoy what you are doing, you shouldn't be doing it. I've always gotten my kick out of Sea World by having someone come up and say, 'This is a great place'. That makes it all worthwhile. In the same way I get an enormous thrill out of people coming up here and saying, 'This is beautiful, this is the best resort we've seen in the world'. That kind of thing gives you great joy, great pride in what you've done.

Of course, I was finding great difficulty in keeping my hands on both projects. I couldn't keep my hands on Sea World and here too, because I'd spend time up here, then I'd race back to Sea World and only have a few days. By the time I'd picked up the threads and saw what was happening at Sea World, it would be time to leave for Hamilton Island again. So I thought Hamilton Island, to me, had greater potential. One of the things that made me decide was that I had taken this interest in tropical flowering trees. I love beautifying things and I wanted to personally position every tree on this island. We're planting trees throughout the whole island now, through the hills and along the sides of the roads.

It always annoyed me that at Sea World I could never get great tropical gardens growing. Because you have all that salt air content blowing in from the sea you'd never get them growing on the spit, but here I could see that for the next 20 or 30 years I could keep on doing something that would give me satisfaction. For many years to come, I could also be developing better styles of buildings, catering to different markets. Even though I believe the existing hotel to be the most up-market resort in Australia by a long, long way, I consider this to be only a step in the right direction. What I really want is a top hotel, which is equal to, if not better than, the best in the world. I'll get my kick out of doing that. Everything will evolve here on Hamilton Island.

Of course, it has had the advantage of allowing me to play around with the harbour, and I love everything to do with boats, so I have developed several atmospheres here. There's the harbour itself, and around it I have developed in an early colonial-style of architecture. The next building to go in will be the administration building, like an early colonial executive building, with a couple of cannons out front, old-style verandahs, and so on. That's where my office and the administration for the whole island will be, as separate from the administration for this resort, because over the years we'll see this particular resort become only one of three or four. The others will be built on different parts of the island.

Around the harbour we already have the Mariner's Inn, with a great restaurant up the top and the Barefoot Bar downstairs. We have the general store, and the Verandah next door, which is a huge colonial-style meeting room for conventions and functions. Across the road is the Italian restaurant, next to that is the Chinese restaurant, and around the corner we've built the Yacht Charter Base, with a bakery next door to that. An ice factory goes next to that, a big disco called Durty Nellie's, a barber shop and laundromats, all built in colonial style. The whole harbour will be developed that way, with shops and art galleries. Up in the hills is the Fauna Park, where we have kangaroos, wallabies, emus, koalas and deer. From the earlier days when we had the deer farm here, we now have hundreds of deer running around, not only in the Fauna Park but wild, all over the island. We also have wild kangaroos on the island.

By 1986 we'll have an oceanarium with dolphin shows and reef tank displays and so on. For the outer Barrier Reef we've built a big floating catamaran, a ship actually. It will do a regular cruise out of Hamilton Island, leaving in the early hours of Monday morning and be out on the reef in time for breakfast. It will stay in the reef area until Saturday night, when it will return to dock by 6 p.m. It has 20 cabins, all self-contained. We have helicopter services connecting us to pontoons on the outer reef, where we have all sorts of facilities. So the whole island is an endless project. I jokingly say that when I was a kid I liked playing with plasticine, and this is like a great big lump of plasticine: you can shape and mould it and do what you want with it.

The more people tell me I can't do something, the more I enjoy doing it. When I told the first engineers that I was going to build an airstrip across Crab Bay, they said I wouldn't be able to do it, I'd have to excavate all the mud. One engineer said, 'You'll never get all that mud out of there', and I asked, 'Why? I'm just going to push it out. How do you get toothpaste out of a tube?' He said, 'Squeeze it out', and I said, 'That's what I'm going to do with the bloody mud. If I put hard material in, it will squeeze the mud out.' So that's the way we built it. Nothing has ever moved, it is perfect.

You always find the academic theorists who tell you it can't be done, and most of them never do get any job done. Academics! I have a story about two fellows who went up in a balloon. The weather closed in and they didn't know where the hell they were. Finally, there was a break in the clouds and they got down to about 20 feet off the ground. A fellow was standing in a paddock and they yelled, 'Hey, where are we?' This fellow looked up at them and said, 'You're up in a balloon'. One fellow in the balloon said to his mate, 'That man is an academic'. His mate asked, 'How do you know that?' He said, 'Because what he told us is correct, absolutely precise, but of no bloody use to anyone'.

When you do get the job done and it's a success, the reward is in personal satisfaction. I don't think I've missed out on a damn thing. I've always been able to make my hobby a business or vice versa. When I went out in the boat catching groper or something for Sea World, I got fun out of it, that was my enjoyment, what else did I need? When I got involved with motor racing, that was my sport and business at the same time. So I'm doing my share of enjoying life as I go along, building what I want to build.

Probably the greatest cost of my success is not being able to spend as much time with the children as I'd like, but I do make a point of spending as much time as possible with them, and fortunately this is on the increase. I've just had my family up here for a couple of weeks and I get back to see my daughter all the time. Even now, when I'm putting in a lot of time and effort here because of the fire, I'll still slip back to the coast on the weekend to spend time with my son and daughter. I just pick the days that I can afford to get away.

I don't have any holidays but what the hell do I want them for? I get more fun out of being here. If I go overseas for a holiday, I think, what the hell am I doing here? I like it better back home. If I do go away, I spend my entire time assessing where I am, what it's all about, what they are doing right and wrong, picking up ideas. My wife thinks it's a joke, she goes off to visit all sorts of things and I'm running around with a camera, taking photographs of rubbish bins. Anything I see that I think is good, I photograph and copy it.

A lot of the things we develop in Australia, we develop along similar lines to the United States. I'm not infatuated with America, it's just that their lifestyle is almost ours to a 'T'. You go to Europe or Japan and it's not the same. What succeeds in America probably succeeds here, the whole idea of theme parks, the types of resorts, the sorts of facilities. I like to pick the best ideas out of anywhere. If I see anything that is brilliant anywhere else, I'll take it. In the type of business that I'm in, you need to have the ability to look at something, assess its potential, imagine it in Australia, and then alter it to suit our situation and the likes and dislikes of the average Australian. I think that Australians are inclined to be a little more impatient than Americans. They don't take as kindly to standing in a queue as the Americans would, for example, so you have to vary things here and there. It's just having the ability to adapt what you see to our local conditions.

I think our main appeal to American tourists is to take them back into history a bit, to the days when this was more of a pioneering country, a more vibrant country, a country in which there was more escape for the individual. That's the way they perceive it to be. I'm not saying that's entirely correct, but many perceive it as being an enormous country with a small population, and they see roads and highways of a standard which existed in the United States 50 years ago. Australia is not a step back in time, because I believe in most things we are right up with the rest of the world, and in some cases we're ahead of them, but it is a giant country with a small population and with enormous potential to be developed, in much the same way America was in the early part of this century.

When I developed this resort, people often asked what percentage of the tourists did I expect to get from overseas, and I said that by the end of three years I'd expect about 30 per cent. Today, with the value of the Australian dollar, there will more likely be 50 per cent after three years. That's a combination of Americans, Asians of all descriptions, Europeans and New Zealanders, of course, if it's still a foreign country.

What Australians do I admire the most? All the goers, including some of the people I mentioned earlier. I always was a great admirer of Sir Joh Bjelke-Petersen, only because he's a straightforward person who doesn't change course in midstream. He decides what has to be

Sea World, April 1981. Keith Williams rides the newly-opened water slide

done and gets on with the job. But over a period of time, there have been great leaders of all colours. As far as industry is concerned, I think Rupert Murdoch has done a great job, and likewise Alan Bond has been very tenacious, which is to be admired. I always had rather a liking for Alan Greenaway, who has done a lot for Australia. It is a great pity to see him living in America, because he did a hell of a lot of good with the Travelodge chain, and he did a lot of work in his 10 years as chairman of the Australian Tourist Commission.

There are people who do similar things to what I've done, put a similar amount of effort into their work, but I don't believe they enjoy it because they seem to look upon life differently. They work because it is a means of making money, yet I've a total disregard for money. Any idiot can develop a business that loses money, that's not a challenge, so the measure of whether or not the business is successful does depend on whether or not it makes money, but that money is only a tool to improve the business or do something else. Compared to, say, a foreign-owned or big public company, my situation is very different, because the money that I make goes back into this business to create more employment. Nothing disappears, nothing goes overseas, nothing goes out to the hands of shareholders. This is why the government's attitude to tax is wrong. A private company is taxed more heavily than a public company, which to me is the greatest disincentive to development in this country. There's got to be a better system.

Japan is well-disciplined and has strong leadership. It's always going to be a very successful country. Too many of the Western nations are governed by the whingeing minorities and not by the majority. I am a great believer in the idea that democracy is a self-destructive form of government. We are going to go through a cycle in this country the same as most of the Western countries. Gradually, over a period of 50, 100, maybe 200 years, we will change our forms of government and lifestyle many times. This has happened right through history. Great nations and great empires only last for so long, because of wishy-washy government. In a democracy, politicians must try to hold favour through give-aways and not through strong, responsible government, but there's a limit to how much you can give. All of a sudden, you get into trouble.

This country is in trouble now because it has given away too much. We can't afford a 38-hour working week, we can't afford four weeks annual leave a year, we can't afford a 17½ per cent loading, we can't afford the ridiculous superannuation schemes and the various pensions you've got for every bloody thing you can think of. And most important of all, we certainly can't afford any government that does not have the ability to curtail its own expenditure and doesn't have the guts to drastically cut the size of the parasitic bureaucracy. You wonder why the Australian dollar is down to 60 cents? It is, very simply, because the average Australian workman, in productivity, is worth 60 per cent of the American workman. Don't think I am decrying the Australian workman. He's equal to anybody in the world, providing he is directed properly and given some incentive, and some pride in what he does. But our taxation, wages and awards systems have tried to bring everybody down to the lowest common denominator. Take the awards system away, because it is the greatest deterrent to ambition there is. A man who picks up a hammer and drives a nail through a piece of timber has got to be paid exactly the same wage as a man who has done a five-year carpenter's apprenticeship. If that isn't bloody ludicrous, what is? Where is the initiative and where is the ambition to do the thing properly, to learn a trade and to learn to be efficient? Those sort of things have to change in this country and they have to change very quickly.

•

Locanto

Bob Ansett

'No Job For Bob' was the headline that greeted the disenfranchised heir to Australia's largest independent transport company upon his 1965 return from America to his homeland. Bob Ansett, at 32, had reason to believe that his family connections and position as the son of Sir Reginald Ansett might ensure him some foothold in the Australian business community. But Australian-born, United States-educated Bob discovered that family genes meant more to carving his name in the Australian paddock than did family connections.

Bob Ansett found more than a job. Not only did he move into the business area in a managerial sense, but he chose to tread his father's path in the transport industry. While Budget Rent A Car was an international entity before Ansett's involvement in it, he gave the company a particularly antipodean style. From a management capacity, he moved into independent operation by virtue of his aggressive and powerful personal identification with the service. Ansett became inextricably linked with the Budget name, and together they grew to dominate the Australian car rental business.

The perfect expression of his attitude toward the competition was Ansett's renunciation of his American citizenship in the early 1980s. At that time, both Hertz and Avis brought Americans out to head their Australian operations. When Ansett retaliated by reclaiming the citizenship of his childhood, it was a statement with more than one meaning.

Although most of his life has been spent in Australia, his many years in America have not only given Ansett unique insight into how the two countries' systems compare, but have also helped him to hone a fine

competitive edge in business. Under his guidance,
Budget has already expanded into more than 15 other
South Pacific and Asian countries in an ever-widening
spiral that includes seven outlets in that most challenging of foreign markets, Japan. Generally Ansett wants
Budget to grow without relying on takeovers or mergers,
because above all he intends for it to remain an entrepreneur's company. His goal: to turn Budget into Australia's number one firm, within a decade.

If an entrepreneur comes up with a great idea, he must then find the funds to be able to produce a product or offer a service, and that's very hard to do in Australia. Assuming that he gets started, the next thing that he has to deal with is government regulations, government interference at every conceivable level. He has to deal with an industrial system that doesn't recognise profitability when it awards wages. If he's able to get through all those things, he then has to pay for that success, because he can't capitalise his business. Many entrepreneurs, such as Dick Smith or Arnold Glass, sell out at the peak of their business lives, because you cannot accumulate wealth in Australia. I can't accumulate wealth. No matter how successful I am, the government gets their 60 per cent. In addition, my company has an insatiable appetite for capital, so whatever profits are left go into the company.

The only time I can benefit from the business that I have created is when I sell it and get a tax-free capital gain. That's all backwards. It should be the other way round, so that a person who builds a business can accumulate sufficient wealth to help him fund his business. The current system induces people to sell out at the peak of their careers, and we lose talent which this country can ill afford to lose.

An investor is far better putting his money into an interest-bearing fund of some sort than into a business that has to face up to all the difficulties of the labour problems, the funding problems, the government interference and regulations, the marketplace, and competitors. We have to understand in Australia that we need an environment which encourages achievement instead of discouraging it.

If the government were to say that a tax on capital would be introduced, but to off-set that personal income tax would be reduced down from the maximum of 60 per cent to 30 per cent, then I would agree with that idea wholeheartedly, because it reverses the cycle. You could then accumulate some wealth, which you do need if you're building a business, and you wouldn't have any motivation to worry about selling it at the most appropriate time. Unfortunately this never will happen, because the thrust of all governments is to create an egalitarian society. The principle is great but unfortunately the only way you can have that in practice is to bring people down to the lowest common denominator and to discourage achievement, because there's no incentive to achieve. Right now, America really is worth looking at. Despite all its problems, in the last decade it has created 13 million jobs. Japan, with its record growth in the last decade, created only five million jobs. The reason America did so well is because it's less fettered by government interference. The capitalist system is very finely balanced and when you start to interfere with it, it gets out of sync. The serious repercussions which result can minimize future economic growth.

Yet despite those negatives I've gained great personal satisfaction from Budget's success. I now have an image whereby I'm still seen to be a fighter and an underdog in Australia. That's important. I must always be in touch with the public and I do this in many ways, such as working in the rental office regularly, serving customers, and answering every letter that comes to me, whether it's a letter of commendation or of complaint. I'm also available to travel all over Australia for Budget, to participate in the team runs, give speeches and so forth.

I find it very hard to disassociate business and my private life, because the business is such a very important part of my life and I get such satisfaction and enjoyment out of it. Everything is related to Budget, although the company does open doors for me to do many other things. In the last couple of years I've started to take a great interest in art, and have accumulated some very fine Australian art which has given me great pleasure. I do a lot of running and I enjoy playing tennis. I enjoy theatre as well, although lately there hasn't been much time for that. My type of holiday is not to sit in the sun, but to go somewhere like a game park in South Africa and spend a week seeing all the wonderful wild animals in their natural habitat, or climbing to the base camp of Mount Everest, or cycling through Japan.

The quality of time I spend on my private life is very important. I was married and had three children in the United States. We came to Australia and my lifestyle changed dramatically. In the first couple of years the changes were gradual, but by 1967 I had become a different person. I have different sorts of disciplines imposed on me now than I had in America.

My first marriage broke up about 1967, and I think in about 1968 or 1969 I met Josie on a flight. She was a hostess on what was then called MMA, operating in Western Australia. It was an Ansett airline.

I was with an American friend, we were flying to Darwin, she was on a couple of legs of the flight, we met one another, and it was six or seven months later when I saw her again. She had gone to Europe, then later moved to Sydney and joined the company as our first sales girl in Sydney. We were seeing one another quite regularly at that time, although I was living in Melbourne. Josie moved to Melbourne and took on a national sales and PR position with the company. We finally got married on 1 January 1975, and my three children moved in with us and have lived with us ever since, although one is now in Perth as our West Australian manager. My daughter married about a year ago and lives just around the corner from us, and my younger son still lives at home. He has finished university and has joined the company in our administrative area.

Of course, one's childhood can offer clues as to how one has developed as an adult. In that respect perhaps I should touch on my own upbringing. When I was born in Hamilton, Victoria, on 8 August 1933, my father, who was later to become Sir Reginald Ansett, had a bus line and a hire car service operating in the Western Districts of Victoria. He was about to move into aviation around the time of my birth. My mother's maiden name was Nichol and her father was the town clerk of Maryborough. The Nichol family was from Maryborough and my father's family came from Inglewood, Victoria. I don't have strong recollections of early childhood other than during the period we were living in Hamilton. I was probably three or four when I was taken for my first aircraft flight. I also remember driving with my father on some of his rounds. It wasn't actually a bus line at that stage — he had Studebaker hire cars which carried about 12 people each. During the summer holidays or when I was not at school I would ride with him, and I thought he was the fastest driver that had ever set foot on the earth. He scared hell out of me.

Later we moved to Mount Eliza, which is on the Mornington Peninsula in Victoria, and my father, in his early 30s, bought 100 acres of uncleared land with about a mile-and-a-half of coastline at Mount Eliza. It was an incredible acquisition for someone who had started without any financial support, had built up his business, and was able to afford a place of that magnitude at the age of about 32.

I went to boarding school at Westley College, where I stayed until I was about 11. Then my mother and father split up and divorced, at a time when divorces weren't common in Australia. Because my father was an up-and-coming businessman and building a reputation for himself, the divorce generated much notoriety. Not long after the divorce my mother married an American and we moved to the United States. I was 11 then and my brother was nine. My step-father was an engineer with Lockheed and was on assignment in Australia at the start of World War II. He was recalled to America and we went with him. I was enrolled into a military academy, which was a boarding school. The academy offered a military-type existence and had a very strong academic discipline. The academy was in a place called Canoga Park, which is about 50 kilometres from Los Angeles. My parents lived in West Hollywood at the time.

I never really understood why I was sent to a military academy and not a conventional school. For me it was hell. I had led a charmed life until then, but that was a period of perhaps two or three years that I detested, although I did conform to the establishment. As in the army, you gained rank. I became a sergeant but I really didn't like it at all. My brother was there with me.

At the end of the war my step-father quit Lockheed and bought an avocado ranch in a place called Vista, California, which is about 120 kilometres south of Los Angeles, near·San Diego. I was about to start high school and it was a great period for me. It was a small town with a population of about 10,000, and I really enjoyed my high school education there. I played most sports, became a pretty good football player, and got my high school diploma.

My parents split up whilst I was in high school. Although we continued to live on the avocado ranch, it was becoming increasingly clear that it wasn't paying sufficient income to support my mother and her two children. She later sold it and we moved into town for my last year of high school. My brother returned to Australia to live with my father whilst I finished school.

I had the chance to go to university on a football scholarship, but I chose to go with a friend to Anchorage, Alaska, where I hoped to have a bit of adventure. I was 17. We drove up there and proceeded to spend the next two years in Alaska, working on all sorts of projects mainly as labourers, building an underground tunnel for a hydro-electric plant and driving taxis. It was a tough living but a great adventure. This was a very important period of my life, because I became totally self-supporting at 17.

Then I was drafted into the United States Army because I was an American resident. After basic straining near San Francisco I volunteered for the paratroopers, because they were paid an extra $50 a month. From there I was to be assigned to the 187th Airborne Division, fighting in the Korean War. However our flight went via Tokyo, where General Maxwell Taylor, who was the Armed Forces Chief of Command in the South Pacific and South-East Asia, was building an army football team. They pulled me off the plane and I spent the next two years playing football in Tokyo and Yokohama, all over Japan and Korea. So I had a great time in the army and probably would have stayed there, except that Maxwell Taylor was re-assigned to the United States and the emphasis went off Special Services, such as playing football.

I finished my service and was given automatic American citizenship for serving in the Army. I had an option of about a half-dozen football scholarships to universities in America, and chose the University of Utah for two reasons. One reason was the coach there was exceptionally good and I wanted to play for him. The second reason was the scholarship was more lucrative than the other offers. They paid my books and tuition, room and board, and gave me $15 a week in spending money.

I was about 21 and older than almost everyone else at the university. Having spent four years on my own, roughing it either in Alaska or throughout Asia, playing football for the army, I found it very difficult to readjust to school life. I didn't have very much in common with my so-called peers, because I was three to four years older than them, so after the first year I pulled out and went back to California to start work.

My first job was with Carnation Milk. Later I joined a specialty bread company. At the age of 30 I was still with the bread company. I decided to return to Australia. I'd had a good life, was making good money, was married with three children, had a nice house in suburbia, a boat and a couple of cars, and I was very, very comfortable, with lots of very good and close friends. But there was something missing. I didn't really know what it was but I felt that, firstly, home was always Australia and I wanted to go home, and secondly, I wanted a challenge which I wasn't getting in California. I knew if I stayed there much longer I would accept forever this very pleasant lifestyle, and I needed more than that.

I knew I had done well in all my jobs, but I had never really tested myself in a business of my own. It would have been very difficult to do that in America, because I would have needed to break away from the social lifestyle and from people that I had grown up with. The other thing was that I got deeply involved in the Presidential campaign of 1964. Barry Goldwater was the Republican candidate and I worked very hard for him in California. I made a public statement that if

Goldwater lost the election, I would return to Australia. So I used that as the key mechanism, although it really wasn't the reason. I was disappointed. I thought America was moving more toward a welfare state than I thought was good for it, so I used that as a final excuse to make the decision to return.

I arrived with an American friend who was previously in the construction business in the United States, and we thought that we might do something together. He was a pilot also and he later went to work for a light aircraft company in South Australia. But I really had no preconceived ideas of what I was going to do. In the correspondence I had with my father before returning, he had made it pretty clear that it wouldn't be in either of our interests for me to work for his company, although nine years earlier, when I had gotten out of the army, he wanted me to learn about the bus business, because he thought that there was a specialised area in that business which I might be interested in. This suggestion didn't suit me at the time, and as it turned out it was good that it didn't happen.

Because I had spent my formative years 16,000 kilometres away from my father, my awareness of his career prior to 1965 was very limited, but I think genetically there are similarities between him and me. In no way have I patterned myself after him, because by 1965 his career had probably peaked. It's only lately that I have learnt about his individual style.

However I did spend some time with him and I looked to him for advice. I first looked for a business related to the transport industry and, by pure coincidence, I rented an Avis car and thought, there's got to be a better way to do this, or certainly a cheaper way. I realised that the industry was more or less dominated by Avis.

By another coincidence, the man who ran Avis heard that I was back and told me he was going to introduce a second-brand car rental company, in keeping with the two-brand strategy like the Myer and Target stores. He had registered a company called Budget, and after some fairly lengthy discussions he wondered whether I would like to run it for him. It wasn't getting me into a business that I could own, but it certainly was giving me the opportunity to start from scratch, so I accepted his offer. There were other reasons for accepting as well. The job would at least provide me with the opportunity of building a business and, secondly, I had very limited financial resources, so this was a perfect way to start off.

I proceeded to develop Budget as a national company and we were competing as aggressively against Avis as we were against anyone else.

In 1973, the man who hired me died very prematurely of cancer. I put together a consortium between AGC (Australian Guarantee Corporation) and me to purchase the Budget company. In December 1974, we started working towards breaking the monopoly that Avis had had for twenty years at Australian airports. We had a few hiccups along the way.

Ansett Transport Industries bought Avis in 1977 from the same estate that I did, and TAA bought Hertz. So we really had a polarisation between these two giant organisations fighting it out in the marketplace against Budget. By 1979 we had broken the Avis monopoly. Within seven months we knocked Avis off as market leader, and subsequently continued to increase our lead on them. Today we have 55 per cent of an industry which has grown in proportion to the growth of my company. We really have been responsible for making rental cars in this country a commodity, a service which is used in every strata of our community. The average wage-earner in Australia uses rental cars far more frequently for far more reasons than is the case in the United States. Although America is the world's most developed country with regard to rental cars, only an estimated 13.6 per cent of the population has ever rented a car. Because of the visibility and the competition we brought to the industry, that figure is about 20 per cent in Australia.

I knew from the very beginning that I was entering a highly competitive industry, one in which Avis dominated 85 per cent of a very small market, with a total turnover of $10 million a year. Less than three per cent of the population then had rented a car. Today the market is $150 million, we have 55 per cent of it and Avis has about 17 per cent. All that has happened in 19 years, because what I did made a lot of sense although it was considered unorthodox. The first thing I wanted to do was to create a team involvement, a very competitive one which recognised achievement, provided job satisfaction, looked for enthusiastic people and nurtured that enthusiasm; in other words, an environment that encouraged winning. I feel there is no sense in competing unless you propose to win, although you should top it off by making it as much fun as possible. Through the years we have stressed that message over and over again: win, but maintain the fun side.

Every day we try to ensure that something new and exciting happens, and we've sustained that as well over the 19 years. Because we were very limited in funds for marketing, we did no advertising until about 1969 although the business started in 1965. The only option available to me in those first years in order to build an awareness of Budget was to become a very visible manager. Later that led to presenting my company's service on radio and television, and adopting a fairly high personal profile. Subsequently I became president of the Melbourne Chamber of Commerce, chairman of the North Melbourne Football Club, and so forth. All this was part of the visible management concept that I had introduced. For the past four or five years I have been involved in making over 100 public speeches a year, all over Australia and overseas, because again, this sustains the principle of visible management and gives me an opportunity to move into the marketplaces and expand my philosophies on management and marketing. Also, we have about 200 offices around Australia, so it is a task to get around and see them all quite regularly.

These sorts of management techniques that others have called unorthodox were born out of necessity for me. It was the only thing that I could do to build an awareness into my company. I had to rely almost entirely on my own ability to do that, and later, as we took on the two airlines and the Department of Transport, and later again the Department of Aviation to break the monopoly, all the things we did were somewhat controversial, and certainly created a very public awareness of Budget. In fact in 1979 I was told by an independent research company that Budget had had more free publicity than any other company in Australia during the previous 12 months.

It started out by my being very confident of our ability to be successful almost from the outset. There is no doubt that the time I had in America was invaluable. I understood competition. When one thinks back to what Australia was in 1965, the business leaders tended to hide behind the mask of corporate anonymity. Other than my father and perhaps a few others, you did not have many well-known businessmen in Australia. Most of them were vague, shadowy-type people with thin ties and grey suits. There was a proper way of doing things, you didn't attack your competitors publicly, you behaved in a certain way.

Budget was a very colourful company from the start and we were doing much better than we had a right to do, because we were limited in funds and were very, very small. When I became the spokesman for the car rental industry, we had only about five per cent of the market and Avis still had about 70 per cent. However I was so confident that we were going to be successful that in 1977, the year when Ansett bought Avis and TAA bought Hertz, I coined a simple corporate statement: 'Number One In 1981'. All the Budget people wore badges stating just that. It meant we had to break the airport monopoly to reach our target, because 70 per cent of the car rental business was done at airports — and Avis had that business exclusively. It required lobbying almost weekly in Canberra, public petitions, interviews on all the current affairs shows, and the support of newspaper editors. Finally, the then-Prime Minister, Malcolm Fraser, intervened and ensured that the monopoly would be broken and there would be competition.

It took us a concerted effort from 1970 to 1979: nine years before we won the right to compete in the so-called free enterprise environment. After we won the struggle in July of 1979, we took $17 million worth of Avis business in the next seven months. This struggle focused attention on all the wrong things associated with monopolies and regulated markets, because when the public has the opportunity to express a freedom of choice, they will support a company that goes in and busts a cartel or a monopoly. We had the recognition of the underdog and the street fighter who backed it up with quality service and a quality product at very, very competitive prices. All those things had to be in place. So Avis, like anyone who is the beneficiary of a monopoly, just could not respond when exposed to competition.

I look at so many protected industries in Australia and I see the same situation illustrated over and over again. It's a pity, because the thing that brings out the best in all of us is competition. When the going is tough, then we draw deep, we draw on latent skills. Budget had one challenge after another, from the day we started in business. Those challenges enabled us not only to build our share of the market, to become a highly successful company, but also to build the industry that we operate in. The two are inextricably linked.

As I said earlier, an entrepreneur in Australia faces the difficulty of funding his idea, but another difficulty he faces later is that unless he has inherited wealth, as he gets more successful and the business grows, the harder it becomes to fund. The only way to do it is either to go public (which I really wasn't in a position to do, nor did I want to at the time) or to sell equity in your company. The more successful I became, the more equity AGC picked up. Because they are 78 per cent owned by Westpac, they got cold feet in 1983 when we looked like buying East-West Airlines. AGC saw that I would apply the same tactics to aviation that I did to rent-a-cars. The banks work in a pretty protected environment, and they thought that they would be terribly exposed to criticism if I came out and started to attack the two airlines. In fact, the two domestic airlines had already warned Westpac that I was getting too aggressive anyway. So AGC vetoed our plan and I said, 'In essence, this brings our partnership to a close. Somehow I'll find the funds to buy shares in the company.'

I do think that I must lead a charmed life, because the Australian recession came and business dropped. Our profits dropped, AGC went through a major management change, then I put an offer to them that they accepted. A year earlier they wouldn't have accepted the offer and I couldn't have afforded to make it anyway. When an AGC senior executive came in as a minority shareholder in Budget, we raised the funds and hocked ourselves for the next 100 years, and we now totally own Budget. AGC are out of it.

Budget has fought the regulations and won. A good example of that is the battle of the airports, both in Australia and other countries, which is now swinging our way. In New Zealand we're fighting the same battle. We know how to go about doing it now. We're also diversifying into areas such as Budget Air Services, in which we're bringing together charter operators around Australia under the umbrella of the Budget system and offering a national air service. We're into chauffeur-driven vehicles in a big way now, and we're constantly seeking compatible ways of expanding and diversifying our company. We will also be looking very seriously at moving into total leasing, which could even involve the leasing of aeroplanes. We won't expand just for the sake of expansion, though. Our policy is to 'stick to the knitting' — continue to do the things we know we do well.

On a personnel level, Budget encourages schemes which aid the welfare of employees. For instance, we try to discourage smokers by offering them incentives not to smoke, and we have had a fair bit of success. All this goes along with our fitness programs, the running and training and other schemes that are all part of Budget's culture.

Most of my goals are business-related, but there are personal ones. Two years ago I set myself a goal of running a marathon, which I achieved, and I have now decided that I'll do one every five years to test myself against the time of the previous one. That gives me incentive to sustain a certain level of fitness and mental attitude. Each year I want to have an adventure, such as going down the Amazon, because these adventures are part of a physical and intellectual experience that I want to continue. It's important for me to have a break from time to time. I'm getting a little wiser; I usually get out my diary at the start of the year and pick a couple of weeks that are spread apart. We have a townhouse in Surfers Paradise, and we get up there for a couple of weeks in the year. We also set aside time for an overseas trip.

Perhaps the more significant goals are the ones that I set on a regular basis for the continued development of my business. However there's a third dimension, and that's my involvement with the North Melbourne Football Club, which obviously requires setting a clearly-defined goal of what you want to achieve and how to take the steps that have to be taken to achieve those things. That's the third or maybe it's my second interest — the experience with a professional football team.

I think the time that I spent playing football taught me something about the nature of pressure. What people term 'the pressure of business' is something foreign to me. I become a little surprised at how many people find great difficulties in dealing with pressure, because it is really something that has never had any influence on me. When I was playing football, before the big games I was conscious that my colleagues would become very toey and excitable, behaving in a different way than I would. The pressure of the game didn't seem to have any effect on me, except maybe that the adrenaline pumped a little more than was usual. All my life, this has been the case.

I have seen, not only in my company but in other companies, the detrimental effect of pressure on other people. I suppose it's part of my genes. For example, no matter what challenges are faced in a day and what tasks and targets are set, at the end of the day that's the end of it, and I don't deal with it again until the next day. I completely close off. In fact I discourage people from ringing me after hours unless there is a real emergency, because I don't let anything lie heavily on me at night. I sleep well and I exercise well, as I believe a balanced life is important. I don't stay out late at night. I enjoy a drink but I don't drink heavily. I maintain a fairly moderate lifestyle and therefore I don't have the build-up of pressures on me at all.

After all, an entrepreneur has to bring great energy and enthusiasm to the development of a business, and must infuse the organisation with a similar energy. I think energy is the number one thing — the energy quota, rather than the intellectual quota, is paramount. The entrepreneur must be prepared to take risks, to back his judgement and to be consistent, to always be inquisitive and curious about how things could be done better. He must always set out challenges for himself and the people who work with him. That's the difference between an entrepreneur and a manager of a big enterprise which has become a bureaucracy. The latter job becomes an administrative function as opposed to a creative function. An entrepreneur is a creator. That's not to say you can't have an entrepreneur in a big organisation, but they're becoming increasingly rare because they're bogged down with administration and don't have the energy left at the end of the day to be creative.

When I look at achievers and particularly at those who have built enterprises or been successful in whatever their field of endeavour, the motivation is largely to create wealth for themselves and others. In all honesty, it never has been a factor with me. I never had a primary profit objective. I have always felt that if I do the things that are necessary to provide a service and run a successful business, profit will come. It's important that you have sufficient profit to be able to invest in the expansion of your business. Too often, businesses and individuals set the creation of personal wealth or the maximisation of profits as the primary objective. That's never been my style, and it won't be.

Until very recently I lived in a very small townhouse in Kew that was rented. Even now I don't own my home — the company owns it and I rent it from the company. I've never really had that sort of drive toward personal wealth and materialism. I'm not poor by any means, I live a very comfortable lifestyle and have a reasonable sense of financial security, which is fairly recent. Four or five years ago that wasn't the case, but now I feel reasonably secure and am fairly confident that if my kids need financial support of any kind, I can help them. I believe nobody begrudges me whatever success I may have achieved.

All my assets are in the company and probably always will remain that way, so I doubt that I will ever think of myself as a wealthy person because I'll never realise those assets. My standard of living is fairly simple. I don't possess a lot of material things other than my recent interest in good, contemporary Australian art, and I look upon that as being among my most prized individual possessions. I derive no great satisfaction from material ownership. Instead, I get a sense of achievement out of building a business that is dynamic, that encourages others in the company to develop their own creativity and to grow with the company.

I've found that as you move through a business career, if you're on some sort of a success path your horizons expand. I'm deeply involved in spreading the Budget network to the whole Asia-Pacific region. If you wish to succeed, you should have a single-minded confidence in yourself and your ability to deal with most situations, because no matter what you do in life, whether it's in a profession or in business or in school, it's never smooth sailing. You always have your ups and downs, and the key to me is to be able to deal with the down periods with confidence, enthusiasm and cheerfulness, and not reflect any noticeable despair. The moment that you do that it becomes infectious, and those around you acquire the same behavioural habits, which is very detrimental. Consistency of performance, confidence in yourself, an awareness that leadership is probably the single most important factor, are all essential. You have to behave as a leader and lead by example, rather than by instruction. But the charmed life I lead even shows up in little things. For instance, if I park in limited or no parking zones, very rarely will I get a parking ticket. When we go to the theatre and there are no parking places my wife always marvels, because she knows someone will pull out, and they always do. I chalk that up to thinking positively and just having confidence.

I'm such a heavy believer in myself that when I face what appears to be a very significant adversity, I don't worry about it, because I know it will all turn out favourably in the end. If I make a decision, I'll do what's necessary to make that decision have a successful outcome, although the idea could be ahead of its time. But if I devote my resources to marketing the idea, it will be in its time rather than ahead of its time. Other people may come up with a new idea, give it a shot, and when it fails they complain that it was just ahead of its time. Five years later someone will do it and make it work. Well, that's nonsense. The first people didn't make it work because they didn't put enough effort into marketing it.

The primary philosophy that I follow is: we are in business to create a customer, then service the needs of that customer. We must constantly ask the customer what it is they want, then find a way to provide it in an efficient and cost-effective way. Run your business to suit your customer and not yourself, and your business will succeed. Finally, fairness is fundamental. Fairness to the customer, fairness to your employees, and fairness to family.

I really enjoy testing myself. I enjoy challenges and fights, not merely for the sake of fighting, but if the cause is right I like to win. For example, I was recently in court over the claim made in a magazine by a competitor that they were the leader in luxury cars. Well, that was not true. Many businesses might accept such a claim, saying, what harm does it do? But it's wrong and therefore misleading, so we'll spend hours in court and probably $20,000, but we will win the case and again prove to our competitors that you don't make untrue statements.

From time to time there are setbacks, but I try to restrict the awareness of them to as few people as is possible, which in many instances is only to myself. In such situations, I have to find a solution to recover the lost ground, so I tend to occupy a lot of my private time in trying to determine how I can overcome that setback. For example, when we were the prime mover in causing the Trade Practices Commission to take an action against Ansett Transport Industries, (when they acquired Avis and we thought that it was in contravention of the Restrictive Trade Practices Act) it was a lengthy court case and a very expensive one. We were unsuccessful; one of the few times we have been unsuccessful in court. However we didn't run the case, the Trades Practices Commission did. Because it was such a public issue, when the case was lost by the Commission, I invited all the media down to our boardroom, which was in an old building across the street from where we are now. The media photographed us drinking champagne and saying, okay, we lost this particular battle but we sure as hell aren't going to lose the war, because what we're going to do now is capitalise on the fact that two competitors (by then TAA had bought Hertz) are now owned by the domestic airlines, which traditionally have avoided competition as if it were a plague. We announced that our competitors from that moment forward would be Ansett and TAA. All this appeared on television that night. From that moment onward, we attacked Ansett and TAA in every single thing we did. We were still able to project the underdog profile, because we weren't fighting rent-a-car companies, we were fighting the two protected airlines. That was turning adversity into a clear goal which we ulti-mately would achieve. So although there have been setbacks, I honestly can't think of any that were of great significance.

By the same token, I've never really sat down and evaluated what success means to me. Because life seems to move at such a fast pace and the challenges are always in front of me, I've never really had a chance to reflect on success, the meaning of it, or whether or not I and my company have achieved it. I like the thought that my company has moved in 12 months from being rated the 453rd largest company in Australia to 350th. We have jumped over 103 companies in a year and I see that as a successful year, but it's not the optimum and I won't be satisfied until we are number one. That always has to be the goal, we ought to be the biggest and the best company in Australia, because we are good enough to do that.

Success is a fleeting thing. You can say, okay, we have achieved success in getting where we are but we still have this huge challenge in front of us. We became the best in our industry, the biggest in Australia, but we are no longer satisfied with that. We are now developing ourselves in major marketplaces such as Japan, all of South-East Asia, China and Korea, and until we are leaders in those marketplaces we are not successful.

As long as the challenge is there in business, there are no other challenges that have a great attraction to me. I was once involved with politics in the United States, but I doubt that will happen in Australia. Still, I like to be able to express myself on issues that are of importance to Australia, and, increasingly, I seem to have the platform to do that. I believe that I can do more in a private sense rather than a political sense, where your views are so heavily polarised, as a Labor Party member or a Liberal or a Democrat. If I'm seen to be a member of the Liberal Party, then I'm seen to be biased in everything I say. If people do listen to what I have to say because they want a view from someone who isn't committed to the political parties, then I am in a good position to do just that.

One thing I do feel very strongly about is that Australian business must come to grips with the importance of venture capital. Deregulation of the financial system is a very positive step that will help this development to emerge. The next step is for major enterprises, such as the oil and manufacturing companies like BHP and Comalco, to provide annual funds for a general venture capital pool, because there will be distinct benefits and returns for them if they do that. This is what has happened in America. I think almost a third of the money

Above, getting ready to annihilate the competition. Bob Ansett and Budget's Queensland manager, John Stevens. Below, Josie and Bob Ansett, July 1979

that comes into the venture capital pool is from operating companies, because their management knows that ideas come from entrepreneurial companies. If they're clever and offer venture capital for these entrepreneurial companies, when the big idea is produced, they may be able to manufacture, distribute or market it — all the things that perhaps the entrepreneur can't do.

Government regulation, however, is still very excessive. It's all part of the self-perpetuation of the bureaucracy and is a total deterrent to the development of business. We have to be clever enough to scrap the enormous bureaucracy that we have built up in this country. It's obscene and obsessive in its task of perpetuating itself. It's not interested in anything other than self-perpetuation. This is very, very contrary to everything that a young country requires. It's going to take some dramatic changes, great energy and effort by a lot of people to change the situation, but it can happen.

If we were to go back to a zero-base budgeting, say, if we were to start this country again right now, we could start by eliminating many areas of government. Calvin Coolidge said in 1922, after his first year of Presidency, 'You could shut down the entire Federal Government of the United States and it would take six months before anyone knew the difference'. Well, things haven't changed.

In Australia, we still abide problems such as restricted trading hours and penalty rates for the tourist industry, yet we're trying to compete internationally in a major growth industry. The structures which are in place are no longer reasonable, the attitude of the trade union movement towards employment is, at best, ambiguous. It is primarily interested in protecting the jobs of members rather than in recognising the need to create new jobs and new industries, particularly for youth who are not being employed because they must be paid at an adult award rate. That's ridiculous, to have a 15-18 per cent unemployment factor in our youth because of the paranoia of unions that the young people may take jobs away from adults. There could be something like 200,000 new jobs created by the dropping of penalty rates, by offering services on weekends and in the evenings.

As an exporter, Australia must be careful not to rely too heavily on our mineral wealth, natural resources, and food stuffs, as we have done in the past. This does tend to lull you into a sense of false security and you become very dependant on other nations' needs. We have not looked at exporting some of the other things that we do well. One of the reasons the Department of Trade has been watching Budget's achievements in Japan with such interest is that we are the first company which has actually exported a service to Japan and sold to a massive population base those techniques and methods which we have developed in a very small marketplace. In fact, a film has been made of our performance in getting into Japan — the challenges that we faced and the achievements that we have enjoyed. It will be distributed through all the various Chambers of Commerce and manufacturers, and we hope to see it on commercial television.

Budget sold the Japanese on the fact that we do what we do better than anyone else in the world. They came out, looked at us, looked at other companies which offer similar services and were convinced that I was correct in what I had said to them. They also looked at their own industry; while it's five times larger than in Australia, it is not successful or profitable, because it's not being innovative in ways to expand its base. So they recognised they needed our help. One of the good things about the Japanese is that they aren't afraid to draw on the experiences of other countries in the manufacture of products, or for that matter anything else. Generally, they enhance the quality of services. We recently had a Japanese gentleman here, the managing director of Budget Japan. In his summation of his two weeks in Australia, he said, 'The Japanese worker works much harder than the Australian'. He's absolutely right, but he also said, 'Somehow, in Budget, you have a spirit that is greater than the spirit engendered in Japanese companies. I'm perplexed at that, because everyone thinks the spirit of people in Japanese companies is so high. But you've demonstrated to me that the Budget spirit is greater than any spirit we know in Japan.' He thinks this is because of our aggression towards our competitors and towards winning, and our ability to instil that in the psyches of all our employees.

We get this idea that it's wrong to say we can learn something from other countries, yet the reason for doing so is that we are a microcosm of the United Kingdom, the United States, and Japan, and we ought to be able to learn from their mistakes. Unfortunately, what we tend to do is to build this enormous bureaucracy that regulates against almost any sort of risk-taking, either from the producer's or from the purchaser's point of view. While such administration may be justified when you have the 220 million people of the United States or the 100 million-plus of Japan, it can't be done in Australia with only 15 million people.

Yet we are more cosmopolitan overall than, say, the Americans now. We have our own style of life, which is very different to that of the Americans, our own tastes, our own fashions, and a different way of running businesses. I think that American industry became very stereotyped in the conduct of business, because leadership of most major enterprises emanated from people who gained their diplomas in schools of business, thus creating an executive that was predictable. You knew precisely how they would behave in a certain circumstance, because they would look in the book and the book would tell them to behave that way. As a consequence I think America stagnated and permitted countries like West Germany and Japan to make huge gains in international trade.

We are more innovative than America and in many ways that country can learn from us. I don't think there are too many things that we want to learn from America. They have a visual pollution that will probably never be corrected. We have to be careful about extremes: on the one hand we must be concerned with pollution of this country, but the extremes of the conservationist ethic would have us produce nothing. We must tread a middle road and I think we are doing that pretty well. From time to time an extreme approach gets the upper hand, but we are developing a society that could ultimately be the envy of the world.

I think you have to look ahead, not 10 years but say 40 or 50 years. If we continue the way we are going and overcome some of the structural problems that I have already mentioned in respect to the growth of our bureaucracy — which is really intolerable in a community the size of Australia — we can go a long way toward ensuring our future. Unfortunately government growth has increased further, as real growth in employment over the past five years has largely been in the public sector. In constantly feeding the public sector we are eviscerating the nation.

If we can fix the bureaucracy and come to grips with the fact that our wages system and our industrial laws are antiquated, we can preserve the advantages we have over the rest of the world. Take, for example, a recent week. On Monday night I attended the premiere showing of an art exhibition called 'Turner Abroad' — some 65 works of art from J. W. Turner. A few nights later I attended the Sydney Dance Company's modern ballet called 'Other Rooms' and, again, this was of world standard. On the Saturday I was in one of the world's greatest sports arenas to watch North Melbourne beat Richmond in one of the unique sporting events on earth.

These are things that we tend to take for granted in Australia. We recently saw the London Philharmonic Orchestra perform in a vineyard on the Margaret River south of Perth, out in the open, with about 6,000 people listening to the orchestra. That's something which has never happened before, and the orchestra had to compete with the kookaburras. It was a unique experience. That's innovation. That's what is so great about Australia.

This country has something altogether different to offer. What we have shown, probably because of the size of our population and the enormous geographical dispersion of our major population centres, is that we have to be very creative people. When you look at what Australia has to offer, some of our artists and professional entertainers are world-renowned. Australian medical science has made profound breakthroughs in specialised areas. Our business entrepreneurs have shown themselves to be some of the world's greatest. As a nation we have produced skilled people who have made a name for themselves on the global map. This is because we have to be more innovative in Australia than Americans are in America, because we have a much more limited audience to promote or sell to. Aviation is an example. We were world leaders in the development of aviation for 30 years, and it really wasn't until the socialisation of the airline system in Australia that we ceased to be leaders. We thrust towards this egalitarian society and stress the benefits of socialism, but the very nature of socialism works against the creator. That's a risk which we truly face.

Australians are complacent. We have a good lifestyle and, 'She'll be right, Jack' is still a very profound statement of Australian attitudes. If you're doing well in your own marketplace and you're a big fish in a small pond, sometimes it's more attractive than being a small fish in a big pond. Advancement requires putting yourself to the test, shaking off the complacency, taking risks, and being prepared to learn. You find out quickly when you get into international markets that you're not as good as you think you are and you must be more creative and innovative than ever before, and you must take greater risks. The really dynamic businesses in Australia are going to have to go offshore and offer their wares in other countries.

I've had the opportunity of seeing a major change occur amongst Australians. A nationalistic spirit has evolved very quietly over the last 10 years. In 1965 we were knockers of ourselves and we had enormous inhibitions. Generally, we didn't think we were particularly good. I saw the change occur when low international airfares came in, and for the first time Australians at all levels of our society travelled overseas and saw the rest of the world. They came back with a new sense of confidence. So although historically we have not been a very nationalistic country in comparison to, say, the United States, this has quietly changed. That effect has flowed on from our win in the America's Cup challenge and the triumphs of our other sportsmen. We don't have quite the same attitude towards business, though, which is a pity, because we have some great international entrepreneurs, such as Rupert Murdoch. We can be very proud of some of our businessmen. That's very healthy, and I feel it's important that we build our own image and a feeling of pride in our country.

We're a very organised community, yet we like to think of ourselves as the great outdoorsmen who are laconic and have a great sense of humour. This is not altogether right. We are a very urbanised society, more so than America. We are a nation trying to find its identity. I don't think we have gotten there yet, but we are working at it. It will happen in the next 20 years and I think we could be a very interesting race of people, because we had the influx of various ethnic groups after World War II. We now have an Asian influence, and I think out of all this we are going to become a very interesting country.

Travelling enables me to see how Australia is viewed by the rest of the world. Australia has quite a glamorous overseas image. Wherever I go in the world, I find that people have a good feeling towards Australia. Their perception is that we have one of the greatest lifestyles in the world. We have a good climate, we have beaches, we don't seem to have to work that hard, and although we obviously do have shortcomings within our industrial system, we're a free country and we have people who are characters. The Australian character is unique in the world, and all that is very much appreciated and admired abroad. Many people see Australia as being a country with a great future. We're still under-populated, we're a wealthy country in terms of natural resources, and we have all the tools necessary to be an important country in the next 100 years. Certainly, having travelled to most parts of the world, I wouldn't live anywhere other than Australia, and I include America in that statement. I'm here for the duration, despite the problems entrepreneurs face.

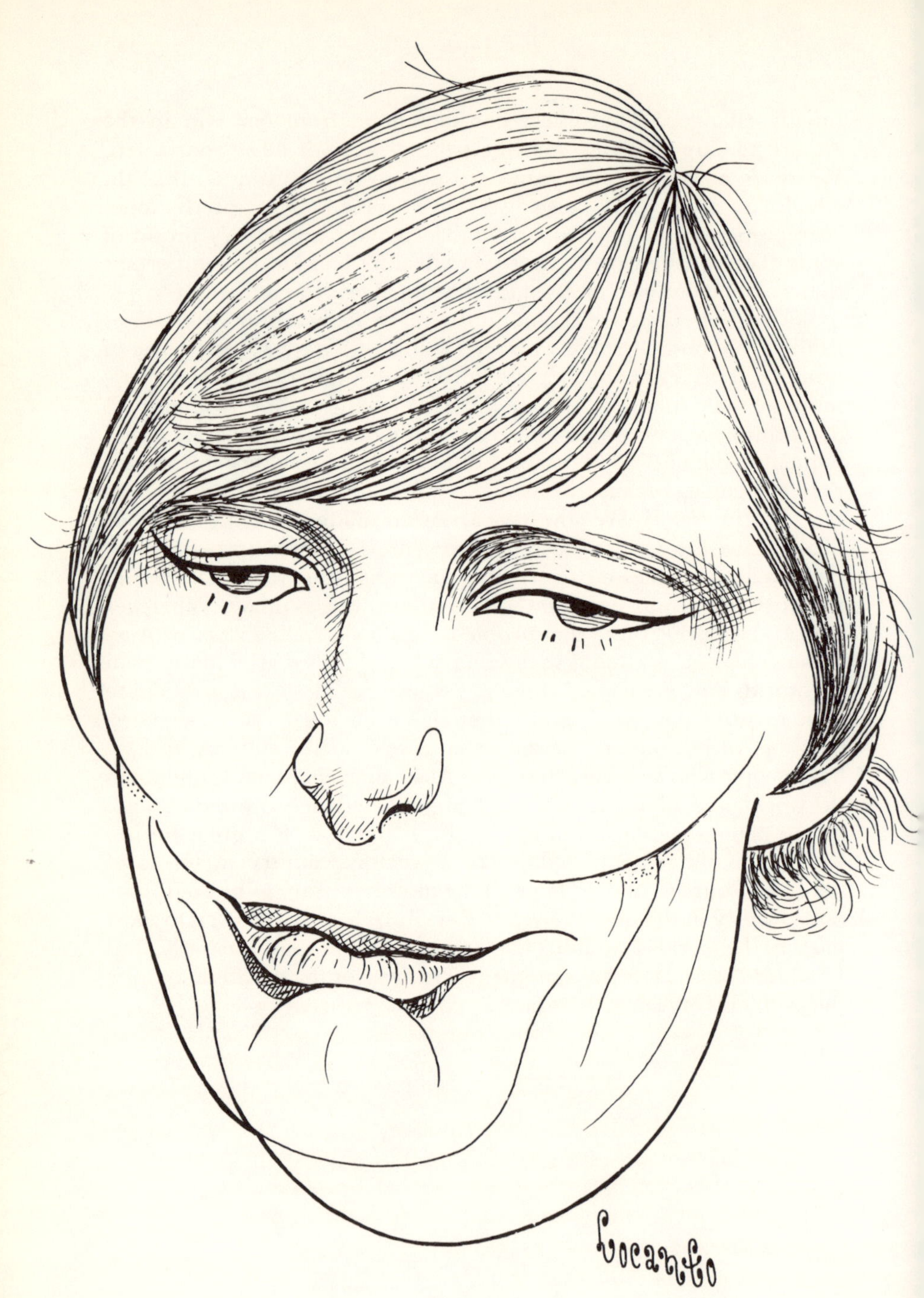

Fred Schepisi

In the late 1960s a handful of directors spearheaded the revival of Australian cinema as an art form of international stature, and Fred Schepisi stands equal first among them. Yet while his work has been critically acclaimed worldwide, the box office smash hit has thus far eluded him.

The reasons for this phenomenon are many, and have much to do with the tribulations of an Australian pacesetter operating in the often-devious world of Hollywood movie-making, as Schepisi graphically portrays in this interview. However, his words speak to much more than merely a hard-learned acceptance of disappointment. They reveal an eagerness to turn the lessons of frustration into formulas for future success. They demonstrate the mental strength of an artist to whom the retention of integrity is a triumph in itself, and perhaps most of all they show that to be an influential Australian abroad can reap continuing benefits, not only for the individual but for his country and the world at large.

Even more so than some of his Australian contemporaries, Schepisi developed an early, broad-ranging expertise in the film medium, which has stamped his best work in a way at once indigenous and international. He recognises an enormous personal debt to his days as a writer, director and producer of commercials, documentaries and features with Cinesound, a Melbourne film company which he and partners purchased when Schepisi was a mere 24. That company, now called Film House, still thrives, and Schepisi hopes to return soon to become an active part of it again, while still making films for the global audience.

'Plenty', his latest picture, which stars Meryl Streep,
looks at last to be the one that will not only wed quality
with mass appeal, but will be given the star treatment by
distributors as well.

Thrice married and the father of several broods,
Schepisi's personal life has been no less tumultuous than
his professional one, but in both the feelings are big and
bold. If Fred Schepisi does return home soon, Australia
can welcome back one of the finest film talents she ever
has nurtured.

What's the appeal to me in making a film? You get totally immersed in it and various aspects of you come out at each stage. When you're on the floor, the adrenaline pumps through to get you thinking fast, there's humour and tension and pressure. You work with the full spectrum of society, you're not closeted away with just the upper or lower class, you're working with labourers, electricians, writers, and big business: a full spectrum.

You go to exotic places, every day is different. The simplest days turn out to be the most difficult, the most difficult turn out to be the simplest. And Hughie the movie god has a surprise for you every five minutes. It will rain when it should be sunny, you'll transform deserts into lakes, and everything is in a state of flux all the time, like canoeing down a fast-flowing river, trying to stay between the banks and avoid the crosscurrents. I love it because it's a living organism, constantly growing and changing. The minute you commit the first thing to a film it says what everything else will do, it makes more things necessary or less things necessary. This is why you have to have a very specific approach to design and attitude, so you can know how to make the changes. It keeps growing and you grow with it, you learn from it and re-inject things into it. It's a fascinating process, discipline and improvisation in one.

People come into film-making for various reasons, but a lot of people who want to direct get a shock. They have no idea of what is involved. In the end, it's 90 per cent grind and it can be up to 16 hours a day in parts of the film. A lot of people think it's very glamorous and yes, there is that attraction. I know many people think of the involvement with actors and actresses but that certainly is not what attracted me. I wanted to enchant, tell stories and teach, as the novelist (Vladimir) Nabokov said.

When I was 12 I got the vocation to be a religious teaching brother, a Marist Brother. Instead of being horrified, rolling over and playing dead, my parents let that notion run its course, which I later thought was pretty sensible of them. Dad was the son of an Italian migrant who married an Irish lady. My dad followed my grandparents into the fruit business, then went into one of the first used car groups around. Then he went into used trucks and commercial vehicles, and then into real estate. My mum came from Brunswick, a working-class group of mostly Irish descent, and she helped my dad in all of his various enterprises. Their main goal in life was to make sure that their children had better opportunities than they had, make sure we were as educated as we could be, and they encouraged me in almost everything I did.

I had a form of tuberculosis when I was six, so I had to go up to the country and spend some time. Because I had to stay there to get over the TB, I went to boarding school at the age of eight for five years, and much to my 10-year-old brother's horror, he had to accompany me. I was there for 18 months, in the Marist Brothers' Juniorate, after which I went to a day school for six months to finish my leaving certificate. At 14 I wasn't much in love with schools. If I had done my matriculation I would have had to repeat, because I was too young to go to university at that stage.

My parents weren't very well off. They struggled hard and became well off, but not while we were going to boarding school. After my older brother Barry and I, there was a gap in the family because of the war, then a younger brother and sister came along. My elder brother is in computers, my younger brother is a doctor in Bendigo, and my sister is fast becoming a very popular leather fashion designer in Melbourne. She's very good, very creative, and designs all her own stuff.

I had no goals as a child, except when I wanted to become a Marist Brother and teach in religious orders. With goals I might have gone on to university, but I don't have any regrets about that at all. I didn't find that schools prepared you for anything you were going to do when you came out. They gave you thinking patterns but there was no practical education as to what opportunities were available to you. I thought I might be a motor mechanic, because dad had the used car business, but it was soon obvious that I wasn't any good at that, nor did I like it very much. My mother always said I was going to be a journalist or a novelist, because I was very good at English, then somebody said maybe I should consider advertising, because you get paid well for being good at English. That sounded okay, so I went along to a vocational guidance person who said, 'What are you interested in?' I said, 'I think advertising is all right, because you get paid for having good English'. He said, 'Let's find out. Would you like the short test or the long test?' I was 14. I said, 'I'll take the short test, thanks', and I'm not kidding, he held up three cards and asked me the colour of each. I got them all right and he said, 'Perfect. Advertising!' He picked up the phone, rang a mate and the mate got me a job.

When I turned 15 I went to work in the agency's despatch department. I used to drive the production people nuts until they gave me things to do. I delighted in doing the jobs so fast that I'd be back almost immediately, standing by their desk. They'd say, 'Did you do that already?' and I'd say, 'Ages ago!' I recommended to the firm that they needed a driver instead of having three despatch boys, so they closed down the despatch department and I went into press production for a while. In those days they didn't have copy writer/art director teams. The account executive seemed to do a fair amount of that stuff, so I wanted to be an account executive. At that point I was about 16½. Fortunately television came in, so I got into writing, production, and media planning for television and radio. At 17 I was the first person in the official TV department. My job really wasn't like being in charge of the television department, though, because there were so many people involved. I was an assistant to a lot of people and did an enormous amount of work.

The office was quite a hotbed of creative people. There were a couple of authors who were account executives, a couple of fantastic art directors, John Pinkney was there then, Phillip Adams, Jeff Underhill, and a lot of people who were wanting to be novelists and in the theatre all happened to be in this one place. Phillip Adams actually wasn't there at the beginning and didn't last long. Not that he wasn't any good, he just got a better offer. I was very enthusiastic and used to drive them mad asking them to give me opportunities. Phillip and I were much the same age, quite a bit younger than the others.

I got more and more responsibility, then Phillip went on to Paton Advertising Service and offered me a job from there, as the person in charge of television and radio production. I took that, because I had gotten married when I was 20 and already had children. When I got married I think I was earning 12 quid a week, but I did manage to buy my wife a small pot of Danish caviar every week. I was about 21 then.

At about age 15, I was doing a course at Melbourne Tech and started going to see Continental movies. Originally it was for the wrong reasons, but I became overawed at the brilliance of these pictures, and when Phillip Adams came along he introduced me to the world of film societies and festivals. Then I wanted to be in films. At the same time I was becoming disenchanted with advertising. I didn't like the morality of it — the whole system didn't appeal to my integrity. Having been fortunate to get into the television area of

Above, three-year-old Fred Schepisi with his father and brother. Right, 16-year-old Fred with his clarinet in a commercial for BP petrol

advertising at that time, I met a lot of people who were experimenting, so I had the opportunity to experiment with them. It was more like being with a film company than in advertising, and I met some extraordinary people who really were making something happen in the industry. I liked that world and I liked those people, and I knew that's where I wanted to be. Yes, I had set some goals by then. I was going to have my own business at 25, I was going to make my first feature film at 30, I was going to win the Cannes Film Festival at 35. I did have my own business at 25; I didn't quite make my first feature at 30 because that was more difficult in reality than I had realised, but I wasn't far off it. I was in a festival at Cannes in 1976 at age 36 and I was in the main competition at Cannes at 38, although I didn't win it.

After moving over to Paton with Phillip, I stayed there for a couple of years. During that time a guy named Jeff Pollack and I put in a submission to buy Cinesound of Melbourne. We didn't have any money but we had a one-page report which we presented to the owner. I don't know why he didn't laugh us out of his office. We tried to convince him that if he gave the business to us with no down payment, we'd take this heavy load off his shoulders. He listened to us for quite a while, actually. About two years later I put my age up by a couple of years and got the job of managing Cinesound Melbourne. The owner didn't know I was the same guy who had tried to buy the business, because it was a very small branch of a subsidiary of a larger company. A year-and-a-half after I got the job I bought the business, under much the same conditions that we had originally set out.

It was in 1964 that I went to Cinesound and in late 1965 that my offer to buy was accepted, because in the first seven months I was there Cinesound Melbourne made the first profit it had ever made. Then it started to make more than the main office, which apparently was an embarrassment. So in February 1966 it became Film House. We did commercials, a little television series for Kodak, and a lot of documentaries, and we were always trying to get other things going.

My partners, Alec Stitt and Bruce Weatherhead, had their own design and animation studio and also a toy factory. They were designers who got this brilliant idea to design, manufacture and sell toys. They took a little long to capitalise, which I think was unfortunate, because it was probably one of the most exciting ventures in Melbourne at that time. It deserved to succeed; they just needed a little more money and some better advice. They were constantly getting in and out of financial problems and that's why we separated.

You get into a business and sure, you do make money, but you're on this enormous treadmill which only keeps going as long as you keep running. You get off, it all falls over, and your money goes with it. I think we all got nasty shocks as to what was involved in business and what the problems were. We weren't shocked at the responsibility, it was just that we couldn't stop this darn thing. We had started Film House with the express idea of making very good commercials and we were a little arrogant in our approach to that. Perhaps we were just being idealistic; often, idealism expresses itself in the wrong way. We were breaking ground, not letting clients look through cameras and allowing only so many clients on the set, tearing up scripts and doing all kinds of strange things. In the first six months, we got almost no work at all, then things turned around and we did quite well. We were going to build a studio and get some really big things happening for the film industry.

But I was misguided in the use of money at one point and we over-extended ourselves. It was something I had been aware of but it was demonstrated to me that money wasn't a problem. Of course, it did turn out to be a problem and that set me back for two years. As you grow and expand, you take on other people and you have to listen to their advice, but you should listen to your instincts as well.

It took us a little while, then we were winning a hell of a lot of awards. Even when we were Cinesound, we went out to get the best people we could. Peter Purvis and Brian Cavanagh, then Volk Mol and Ian Baker came. We got graduates from the Swinburne Film School and people used to call us 'the university'. We wanted to create the best environment we could. I got a lot of the credit, but really many of the people who were there had an enormous amount of input. Alec Stitt, Bruce Weatherhead and I used to write a lot of our own stuff. Sometimes we'd get a live action job and decide it was better as animation, sometimes we'd get an animation job and decide live was better. After a while, you never really knew who did what. We were also able to use the best of the freelance talent that was available. It was at that time that I got involved with the composer Bruce Smeaton.

In the Cinesound days and partway into the Film House days, we did a lot of industrial documentaries. What we did in the documentaries we applied to the commercials, and vice versa. I think that had a lot to do with developing a particular style, how to bring design and graphics to the documentary field, how to work at random, capturing what you can, and working with amateurs and getting them to act like professionals. With the high graphic design style I was learning from

Alec and Bruce and the commercial side — because of the strange way you had to work with the agencies — I was learning a kind of patterning system, almost like a modular film-maker: pull something out of here, plug something in there and it still should work, because of the amount of design and the logic and discipline. Then you added that to the documentary and you came up with a better style. Likewise, in working with semi-amateurs, I developed an unusual style of working with professional actors as well. I found that the two approaches went hand-in-hand.

We had an exciting group of people working there, people who challenged everything: traditional casting concepts, production concepts, the quality of sets and designs, photography. Film stocks were getting better then, but we used to bring in still photographers and try entirely different lighting techniques even before the stocks had improved, just to get rid of the kickers and liners and trims and backlights and all that traditional lighting, to see if it was possible to come up with some really beautiful still photography effects. As stocks go better and faster, we were constantly experimenting both with the look of things and with the shape and structure of them.

We were all there to make feature films; it was just that the realities of business overtook us for a while. The reality of making films was that no-one was handing out money at that point and the cost was more than we could handle. Then things started happening in the film industry. The Experimental Film Fund was started up by the government, and I joined the Producers and Directors Guild, which in Melbourne was a terrific group of people in theatre, television and film who were all interested in getting something happening. We came up with the idea of having script competitions and producing them on stage, television and screen, using Swinburne students. We were biting off a bit more than we could chew because we were educating everybody at once, but some very interesting films were made by people like Tim Burstall, John Murray, Oscar Whitbread, Chris Muir, and David Baker. There was real energy.

We were trying to create a little world where we could work outside of commercial pressures, to develop and showcase our skills in an experimental way, and I think we were successful in that. We were led up the garden path a few times but what we learnt each time was great. We wanted our projects to span the different media, but of course we eventually headed off in our own directions. In 1969-70 I made a film called 'The Party', then we did 'The Priest'. One of those two got Experimental Film funding and one got a Developmental

Film Fund grant, but neither was for much money. We put a lot of our own dough into them. The projects were also produced on stage and were meant to be produced on TV as well, but that didn't work out. But at least we got the chance to work outside of commercial pressure. That group influenced one another in the very best spirit of co-operation. We all went to see one another's pictures, and we all read one another's scripts and pulled them to bits. It was really good.

We put 'The Priest' through as a Film House project and shot it in six days. We were doing commercials right up to the time of filming and right after. I don't think we found the blasted house for the set until the night before shooting. Trevor Ling, who's a terrific designer, was directing commercials through the Film House. He did up the whole location the night before filming. We cut it fine.

I was working very long hours. In the early days of Film House I ran it as well as directing and wrote a hell of a lot of the stuff, and we were getting an enormous amount of work. I always tried to involve my family in what I did. I've been married three times, so it's hard to say if I succeeded. I tried to give time and enjoy my family as much as I could. We all went out together. I had four children from that first marriage. I would go out a couple of nights a week and get drunk or play cards, but the weekends were for us, the family. We went somewhere or people came to us. I always considered that to be important.

My first wife helped to stabilise me — I was fairly wild and neurotic. I guess it had something to do with my boarding school upbringing and various things in my background. She certainly did her best to encourage my good points, to get me reading good books and using my brain. She was always incredibly supportive. I was married very young the first time and we had a lot of children quickly, but that didn't affect anything from my point of view. I suppose I grew away from that relationship a bit, although I know I am very much who I am because of that relationship. It was a great influence on my life and we were very, very close for a long time. Also, I was very strongly attracted to my second wife, which I guess had much to do with the breakup of my first marriage and a lot of guilt accompanied that.

My second wife worked in the company, doing production. She cast 'The Devil's Playground' and 'The Chant Of Jimmie Blacksmith'. For a time, she was very actively involved in the work, and again was always very supportive and encouraging. People you live with intimately can help. You are what you are because of your involvement with them. Fortunately, for the most part, they endeavoured to encourage the better instincts in me and I owe them a hell of a lot.

My second wife and I had two daughters together and we had some absolutely wonderful times, but we are both rather tempestuous. That caused us to clash strongly sometimes and it became a problem. I don't think anyone is to blame, it was just who we were at that time, but we loved one another very much. I don't know whether going to America broke down that relationship or whether it was just the similarity in our temperaments that caused the break. Those things are always hard to sort out. I had a lot to do with the break-up of my previous marriages. It's hard to put a value on the time that we spent together, but there was a great value and there is now.

I met the lady I'm married to now 14 years ago in New York. We were friends for 10 years and I don't mean anything naughtier than that. We used to see each other twice a year. Our paths didn't cross romantically until around the time that my second marriage was breaking up. It's been great, we have one child, and my wife's a supportive, quite calming, steadying influence in the family.

Anyway, back to the 1960s in Australia. There were a few streams, as it were, of film-making in Sydney and in Melbourne. I approached film entirely differently to other film-makers because of my involvement with animators, designers and advertising. The Film House group were going along in a specific direction, with our own individual outlooks and attitudes to what filming was about. We ran a very open company, people all had their own responsibilities, their own areas where they were as free as I was, so we were experimenting on every level. You would meet people in other groups and get involved in that as well, but there was a separateness at the same time. We really were quite different. It was very exciting, the camaraderie and the help which you got were great, but it was also bloody frustrating because it was so hard to get anything done.

The Experimental Film Fund really kicked things off. It seeded a lot of pictures. Guys used to take their $700, would you believe it, or $7,000 if they got the top grant, and multiply it magically. Tim Burstall could take $7,000, multiply it into quite a considerable amount of money, and produce something as brilliant as 'Stork'. It was the raw energy that guys like Burstall applied, with others like Phillip Adams working behind them, and men like Hector Crawford and John McCallum of Googie Withers fame that brought the film revival about. They gave the government the courage to put in extra dough. In the late 1960s and early 1970s the extra dough was attributed to the

Film Development Corporation, which in reality invested only about 10 per cent of the money that went into films at that time. But the FDC gave credibility to what had been considered a fly-by-night industry. With that credibility, Tim Burstall pictures were suddenly out and making money, the Bazza MacKenzie pictures made money, then Peter Weir came along and made money with 'Picnic at Hanging Rock'. Suddenly there was an economic viability and a proudness in Australian films, but we still found it very hard to get money.

When I made 'Devil's Playground' nobody believed in it, and it took me a long time to get any money or belief in it from the Australian Film Commission. Over half the money in it was mine and I raised a great deal in $500 lots. The day after I made it I was back shooting commercials. I was doing two shifts a day to keep the money coming in so I could finish the darn thing. Then I couldn't interest anybody in distributing it so I had to distribute it myself, and I had to get as much money again to do that as I had personally spent on making it. I had to work my butt off, and it is a very disheartening and demeaning thing to step off a feature film and have to do commercials two shifts a day. That energy would have been better expended in polishing the picture, for starters, and then getting other enterprises going.

Nobody thought that 'Devil's Playground' was a good script, so I got some advice from Phillip Adams, who led me to some people that he'd put Bazza MacKenzie through. They had some faith in it and they let me run. My mates in the advertising industry, Alec Stitt and Peter Clarke, invested in the film and helped design the advertising campaign, but apart from them nobody believed in the blasted thing. So it surprised everybody when it ran and ran and looked like a commercial success. We got our money back but it didn't break records.

Because of the success of 'Devil's Playground', I was able to get money for 'The Chant Of Jimmie Blacksmith' within three months. The Australian Film Commission had sorted itself out by then, the Victorian Film Corporation were looking for a star vehicle, as it were, and they were very generous and supportive. Nevertheless, I put more than a quarter of a million dollars of my own money into it, and I raised other funds in $1,000 and $5,000 lots. The financing came from businessmen, mates and relatives. Hoyts, who had just gotten a charter from Twentieth Century Fox to invest in Australian films, were going to invest $50,000 here and $50,000 there, but I convinced Terry Jackman, the general manager, that he should go for broke on 'The Chant Of Jimmie Blacksmith'. He was very supportive and I wish it had paid off better dividends for him. 'The Chant Of Jimmie

Blacksmith' didn't make any money. People have gotten about one-fifth of their money back, maybe a third. It was a great critical success around the world but if you read the reviews, they say, steel yourself, this is a film you must go and see but be ready, it is tough.

The film wasn't sold very well internationally. I went to a lot of trouble to select the right selling group, but nonetheless they rested on their laurels. They had taken on too many things to sell at Cannes. 'Jimmie Blacksmith' was the hot film at Cannes but it didn't screen until late. They could have made a lot of sales but they misjudged two things: the distributors' reaction to the picture, and the fact that it was on so late in the festival, meaning that the distributors had already spent all their dough. The film hardly sold anywhere; it was a crying bloody shame. It was sold in New York and they released the blasted thing at the same time the New York festival was on. 'Jimmie Black-smith' has a great reputation but as a friend of mine says, 'Give me three dollars instead of three cheers'.

Make no mistake, the film didn't get into Cannes just on its merits. Fred Schepisi and a number of other people did a lot of lobbying and flying to Paris to spread the word. At the Cannes Festival, it's not possible for one film to win for best picture, best director, best actress. It should be but isn't. They spread the awards around, and to be the first Australian film ever in the festival was our award. I knew exactly what I was getting into. The criticisms of the film in the French papers were 50-50, but at the reception that night it got a five-minute standing ovation.

On the whole, criticism doesn't worry me. It's just people's opinions. I'm never going to make pictures that will please everybody and I tend to make pictures that polarise people. You either love the films or you hate them. I know that, I don't get puffed up if there's a great review, and I don't get upset at a bad one. Fortunately, as far as reviews go, I've generally done well.

After 'Blacksmith' I had a chance to write, produce and direct a comedy from an idea of mine. It was called 'Bitter Sweet Love'. I was contracted to do it by Alan Ladd Jnr and Jay Kanter, who were the powers-that-be at Fox. I wrote a first draft and just as I was about to leave for Hollywood with the draft, I received the news that Ladd and Kanter had lost out in a management power play. In fact, they were escorted off the lot by armed guards. I wasn't sure what to do, so I took my agent's advice and waited until a new president was appointed. In fact, I took the first holiday I'd had in a long time. Eventually, a new president was appointed and he was somebody I knew, Sandy Lieber-son. I called Sandy and he said come over in a couple of months, which I did. But just as I arrived somebody was placed between him and the chairman, which meant that Lieberson's position had, in no small way, been usurped. He resigned and I found myself in these rather silent, painful corridors of Fox, with a script and nobody to sell it to. Anyway, I convinced the management to let me do a rewrite and collect my money, but that was rather sad because although the script had some great things in it, it had inadvertently become mid-Atlantic and I really needed help with it. Lieberson had helped me with the 'Jimmie Blacksmith' script and now I was looking for the same help, but of course he was gone.

Then I got co-opted onto two pictures. I was going to supervise, rewrite and direct a picture called 'Partners', which was a tap-dancing film, and supervise the rewrite of a thing called 'Raggedy Man', by Bill Whitliff. After I collected my rewrite money for 'Bitter Sweet Love' and came home for Christmas, I went back to America to work on the other pictures.

To direct 'Raggedy Man' I first had to be approved by Sally Fields, who was supposed to star in it. I met with her and it was obvious to me that she was never going to make this picture. It wasn't obvious to any-one else, although I tried to point it out. After two months I was finally appointed director and Sally Fields was told to make up her mind. She went away. Then there were negotiations with Sissy Spacek, whose designer husband had a contract with Universal to direct his first film, except the script they had for it wasn't very good. Then, Bill Whitliff had written another thing called 'Barbarosa' and via his producers, through my agent, and unconnected to Bill, I was asked to direct it, because they thought 'Jimmie Blacksmith' was a great Western! The Barbarosa script wasn't great at that time but Whitliff's intentions were terrific.

For the first time, the reality of Hollywood slammed me in the face. I had only just broken the back of 'Raggedy Man', I was very emotion-ally committed, and I had put four months work into it. My agent and lawyer, who were the best in town, both said, 'Look, they're mucking you around on "Raggedy Man". Do you like this picture "Barbarosa"? Do you want to do it?' I said, 'Yes, I do but — '. 'No buts. This picture is a pay or play deal, guaranteed to be made within the next two months. You must take it, because anything can happen on the other picture.'

'Pay or play' is supposed to mean that once a film has been signed and it doesn't get made, you get paid. In other words, if they don't play, they pay. Then they also have a guarantee of a film being made within a specific time but with no specific timing, which enhances the pay or play, because otherwise they may be able to hold you over for a number of months. But the truth of it is, they often cheat you and do a deal at the end, and they have more ways out of a contract than you can shake a stick at.

Against my emotional judgement I said, 'Okay, I'll take "Barbarosa" ', and within one day Sissy Spacek signed to the other picture, her husband signed to direct, and they were turning around and calling me a bastard because I had jumped ship. I hadn't — they wouldn't sign my piece of paper. As my dad always said, 'In God we trust, and you ain't God', and it was true. If I hadn't taken 'Barbarosa' I would have hung around for another three months and then I'd have gotten the elbow.

I've now learnt how to hold back until you know that something is definite. But there's a point where you switch over and all your obsessions go into a film, you immerse yourself in the project that you know you're going to do, you give yourself to it, mentally, emotionally and physically. Once you've made that commitment and it's all whirring around in your head, you solve what you see as problems and you get excited by all the possibilities. To then just turn that tap off is really difficult.

A strange thing about a lot of American producers and executives — not all of them by any means — is that they admire what you've done and the way you've done it, but they want to apply that in some way to what they do. They want to mould and control your work and apply it to their style, which is incorrect. The success of 'Witness' is clearly what Peter Weir has brought to it, and what Bruce Beresford brought to 'Tender Mercies' also worked. You don't want to come on strongly, but you get a bit of a surprise when you find out you know a hell of a lot more than most of the people you're dealing with. You stamp on that, because you think, hello, my ego's running rampant, sit down, shut up and listen. I didn't go in boots and all. I wanted to learn as much as give.

On 'Barbarosa' I had a production manager who was telling me, 'That's not how it's done here, we don't do that in America'. In listening to him, I was being prevented from making my picture. Things didn't ring true and the producer didn't seem to know that much. I got tired of, this is how we do it in America, son. You little jumped-up fart, who are you? I ended up saying to the producer, 'Look, I have a personality difference with this man. He may or may not be right but I have a personality difference.' The wonderful thing about Americans is that they understand that and they separate you. What you also say is, 'It's either him or me'. So he left and then I had a man who came on with, 'You want to do that? Wonderful. It's not a question of how we can't do it, we have to find a way to do it.' This was like lifting tonnes of weight off me.

You have to know what your strengths are and not be foxed out of them. You must be forthright and direct in holding out for those things, but not in a way that stops information from coming in. That's hard, and you tiptoe around much more than you should do, then in reaction you barge in a couple of times when maybe you shouldn't. I don't think I'm guilty of that, though. For example, I held out for a great designer, Leon Ericsson, on both 'Iceman' and 'Barbarosa'. He's a figure who frightens producers in America, because he's so unconventional and weird and seemingly out of it, but he's brilliant. It's a matter of knowing how to let him work at his best and giving him the support he needs. Some producers don't understand that quite so well, it's all frightening to them. They'll let you go with the guy but they'll hedge the bet on how they back him up and in the ways they stifle him, so you have to try a little harder. But they like the work, they're stunned. I'm sure it's the same case with Bruce (Beresford) and the other Australian directors. We have knowledge, we actually produce, we're not indulgent and we know how to get value for money. The producers are frightened when you say, I want this, I want that. They don't realise that you know how to schedule and manoeuvre within a budget to get what you want on the screen. They're surprised that you even care about it. So on one hand they're surprised, but on the other hand they're suspicious. But generally, my experience has been that they're amazed at Australian directors.

I've had a very diverse upbringing, not only in commercials but in documentaries and running a company from the age of 24. Have you ever been in an area where you don't know what you're doing and you have to do it in three hours? You end up with all your clothes off, sweating. Somebody left me an unedited documentary in the early days. I didn't even know what it was about — all I knew was that there were thousands of feet of film and within two days I had to produce a half-hour film. I had only done a very little physical cutting. There was a lot of sweating and learning.

One day we went out and shot a commercial for kids' socks or something, and when the rushes came in they were all black. The cameraman had forgotten to open the shutter. I didn't know about variable shutters then but I soon learnt. I rang and made some excuse about the film being held up at the lab and we went out the next day and re-shot it without telling anybody, then presented it the next night. The learning process was extraordinary. Being exposed to still photographers, graphic artists and animators, as well as all of the Cinesound documentary work, I got every kind of experience and I think that is all now part of what I do. This very unusual upbringing probably gives me a broader knowledge than what is normally expected of a director. Because there was little money available to Australian directors in general, I do think our experiences are broader than those of the Americans. Australian film-directors are definitely much more practical than American directors. I think one thing we have in common to a certain extent is that we get value for money on the screen. American producers tend to love us altogether and they also tend to think we're interchangeable, which is a joke. I think we make entirely different pictures, although there are common aspects.

I was one of the first directors of Australian films to make the move to America, yet when we were setting up Film House I was very strongly of the belief that I should stay in Australia to make movies. That way you get to make the films you want, the way you want, without interference. I used to stand up on tables and spout this philosophy whenever I got drunk. Okay, we all change, it's the same as those statements I made when I was 16. I didn't know the realities. I think now that it's important I went away and got exposed to different perspectives.

Although my intention in going to the United States was to learn and to try my skills, it was a marketing exercise as well. In Australia, I had lost a lot of money. In America I was getting paid reasonably well, so that had something to do with the move. I thought if I could make two or three films and earn a reputation for myself, I could learn about their marketing system. If I was lucky enough to make a reputation, it would then be easier for me to market my Australian films.

Also, I might learn something from their approach to making films that I could incorporate in what I do. I frequently experiment with a simple, strong narrative line with layers underneath it, that hopefully bubble up to the surface for those who are interested. If anything, I probably make the front force too strong, so that on first perception people are swept along by the main story. I know that often, if they go along and see it again, they're surprised at what they've missed. One New York reviewer even went back a second time to see a film of mine that he hadn't liked, and he gave it a good review the second time around. I'm still trying to work out a balance between when you have to fulfill emotional needs in a picture and when information has to stop coming, so you can take the picture through to its emotional conclusion. If something is intellectual, don't get so intellectually clever that you don't deliver the physical, emotional impact which is warranted by any specific scene. I guess I'll go on learning that forever. Where you get killed easiest is when you're only commercially-minded. In other words, if I went to Hollywood and said, 'I'm going to make a really commercial exploitation film', bang, I'm history, they'd kill me.

I would like to come up with a new film form. It could be something entirely different: I've only started to scratch the surface of what I can do. In commercials and sometimes in film-making, Film House invented techniques. Shooting in high contrast, printing in bleach-out black-and-white, acrylic painting over film and matching the two so that you have a hard-edged screen in a realistic or non-realistic frame — we did a lot of experiments. My natural tendency, which you can see in documentaries, is impressionistic. These are things I subjugate to the making of a more conventional narrative film. I can incorporate them here and there, but the narrative film demands its own discipline. I try to enchant and present things in a new and challenging way as much as the subject will allow me to do, but I have a pyrotechnical side, if you like, that I wish to display. This is why I want to do a musical: you can be pyrotechnical in a musical. Look at the dazzle of Bob Fosse, look at the change of expression which Richard Lester brought to movies. There are many avenues yet to be explored in film, and I think eventually the cable and home video outlets will change the narrative demands on film, which will lead to just such exploration. Yes, I would love to have you sit in the cinema one day and see something that will dazzle you, that you haven't seen before; not because I want to leave a mark, but just because I think I can do that.

The trouble is, when you do that sort of thing you sometimes seem to go beyond people's preconceptions. It's not that what you've done is unacceptable, it's just that the viewers aren't ready to make that leap. So you hold it all back, don't you? I believe that I'm stylistically different. In the way I present film, in the way we edit and shoot it, I'm very different. But all that is subjugated to telling the story, so if the

Fred Schepisi at home in Beverley Hills making pasta

audience is wrapped up in the story they're not necessarily aware of such differences. When I see a film, if the story is interesting I don't look at anything else, I'm gone.

Studios, however, can hurt a story and its style by reading the wrong things from an audience, then trying to cut the picture into something it isn't. They go against its rhythms. You can make acting look long and silly just by the way a film is toyed with afterwards. It's quite amazing. In the film I've just done there's a five-minute scene which we call the omelette scene. There are four major shifts and changes in the drama and humour in that scene. At one point, we thought there was something soft and a bit odd about it and I thought, oh God, we'll have to do a major restructuring. We changed two takes, one of an actor and one of an actress, cutting in at a slightly different points, giving each cut just a slightly harder edge, which fixed the scene. Nuances changed the scene from one that had to be entirely recut to one that was just perfect. The solution can be as tenuous as that and it isn't easy to find. Unqualified people who play around with the final cut don't understand that discipline. A scene can be structured and you know how it's going to work, but until you sit down and go through the ebb and flow within that structure, nobody can judge the scene. That's why you say, 'Please don't come and look at a rough cut. It means something to me, it doesn't mean anything to you.'

I did 'Barbarosa' as offbeat entertainment rather than as a heavy intellectual piece. It has some things to say but it's first and foremost entertainment, so it hurt a little when it wasn't a big success. Going into it, you're aware that this might reach a large audience. But I enjoyed 'Barbarosa'. We also had our first two drafts in on the tap-dancing film 'Partners'. It needed a bit more work but it was coming on well. We agreed that it needed $15 million as a musical and that wasn't a lavish estimate.

While I was away on 'Barbarosa', the producers of 'Partners' rang up and said, 'Can you do it for $8 million?' I said, 'You've got to be joking. How are we going to do that?' They said, 'We're going to fly down and talk to you about that', but I said, 'You can't. I'm in the middle of shooting and I can't give time to any other projects. Just tell me how you think you're going to do it.' They said, 'You can do without this number and this number, etc.', and I said, 'Hey, then you can do without the director. Forget it!' So it never got made, though I feel it will come back again one day.

I finished 'Barbarosa', but while I was doing it the distribution company AFD (commonly called Another Friggin' Disaster) fell apart and was shut down. Universal took over all of their products and the man who came to power in the distribution side had quite a different attitude from us as to how 'Barbarosa' should be distributed.

All you can do is point out what you believe is right as strongly as possible without becoming a maniac about it. They say to your opinion, 'There's no evidence of that', and you say, 'What if I go out and get you the evidence? If I produce the critical acclaim for "Barbarosa", will you take a chance on platform distribution?' He says, 'If the critics don't like it, you'll kill the picture forever'. I say, 'I'll take that chance', and he says, 'I'll consider the evidence'. I took the picture to New York and got the critical acclaim. I gave them the evidence but they didn't take it. That kills you, that really pisses you off, but you realise at a certain point, hey, I'm not going to win. Stop it, get on with something else, get on with your life. Just forget it, the film is history, you've done it.

If you enjoy writing, then that's an end in itself and you get satisfaction out of it. The next stage is to produce or direct — which is also an end in itself — and at that stage you look at the writing ruthlessly. I enjoy all the stages. If we are writing or rewriting, I enjoy being involved in that. I greatly enjoy the making of the film as a separate experience. Similarly, post-production work is an end in itself. Like anybody else I enjoy going to work and I'm proud of what I do. I know, too, what I do and do not achieve. My craft under pressure has improved immeasurably, as much by confirmation of what I believe as by new experiences, and that's very valuable. It's no good harbouring disappointments. Enjoy the process. If the product happens to be successful, fabulous, but that's timing. You can't control the timing of a film, although you can try to control distribution, and I will, more and more. Bugger them, they're not going to screw me up again.

I don't know what a setback means to me. You get disappointed, you get really low, but you just have to face up to the reality of it. What's the great line at the entrance to Wimbledon? 'Beware of those two great imposters, success and failure'. I believe that. Give it everything you've got, keep your objectivity, and that's it. I don't really care whether or not I make a lot of money, and if you are trying to say things, what's the point of saying them to a minority who already believe? So a setback is when you put everything into a picture, you know it has a lot going for it, you know people will like it when they see it, and then for idiotic reasons it doesn't happen. What you've got to do is slam a door, shut it all out and get on with the next thing. There are plenty of examples. My inspiration comes from all over the place, from great musicians, classical and jazz, from art, from experimental film-makers, from the Canadian National Film Board, from a million unrecognised and unappreciated talents. Look at Abel Gance, for God's sake. Before the middle of the 1920s the man had innovated just about every film technique that is still employed today. He experimented and made an extraordinary number of terrific pictures, including 'Napoleon', which wasn't appreciated until recently, and he's only an isolated example. There's the little-known Czech Karel Zeman, also a great innovator, and there are many, many others.

Some people aren't commercially touched. It's the luck of the draw, it's not something to worry about, it's not even a question of working out how to get around the problem. All you can do is learn what there is to learn from what you've just done and apply it to the next thing that you're excited about. It will work or it won't work and that's it. Enjoy turning it out, though. 'Barbarosa' met a similar fate to its American one around the world. I think pictures are either going to take or they're not. It's a cult film and big in video sales; actors come up to me and quote lines from the film, they love it that much, so I know it has value. That's all that matters, get on with the next one.

After 'Barbarosa', there were about seven or eight projects that I was prevented from doing — two or three were right up on the starting line. I'd drop everything I was doing and then they'd somehow disappear. So I went through a series of frustrations until I got 'Iceman', which is a good film. It suffered an extraordinary fate. It's probably going to get its money back but just barely. I agreed with how they released it and I agreed with the advertising campaign, but they were never able to dispel the impression that it was a cheap science fiction horror picture. Of the people who went to see it, maybe 50 per cent loved it, another 25 per cent liked it with reservations, and the other 25 per cent hated it. The newspaper reviews in New York were among the latter 25 per cent, but reviews in the magazines were great and in the rest of the country they were extraordinary.

The acclaim means nothing, it really comes down to confidence in the finished article. Certainly, within the industry in America, I have a high reputation, because people are aware that I'm taking chances, doing unusual projects that can't be pigeonholed and that are not easily marketable. I'm not doing commercial exploitation stuff and I don't say yes to projects very easily. I think people are also aware that whether a film catches on or not is the luck of the draw. In that regard 'Iceman' surprised everybody, because it wasn't as successful as it was expected to be.

'Iceman' was made as an independent production of Norman Jewison's and Patrick Palmer's, financed by Universal. The arrangement was what is known as a 'negative pick-up', so we had a lot of freedom. We tested the picture, packed the cinema, and the people enjoyed it so we thought, hey, let's go for it. What happened then was completely the opposite to what everybody expected. We were dumbfounded. As I said, it's in the lap of the gods. We went through three different managements on that picture.

I expected Hollywood to be a lot more entrepreneurial, full of characters who really use their intuition. I didn't expect to find corporate bodies, the equivalents of advertising account executives and marketing brand managers, people empowered only to say no. Very few could say yes and very many were protecting their jobs and records. I expected to find people with challenge and attack, who ranted and raved and made comments and gave help.

As I was finishing 'Iceman' I made a pay or play deal on a picture called 'Total Recall', which I believed was very commercial. It was set in the future and it played tricks on the mind. You never knew whether you were in reality, in the guy's dream, or in an intelligence organisation's implants into the guy's imagination. It was very exciting, a thriller, allowing you to explore the future. The production designer had been hired, we'd had a conference, and the film was in early pre-production. Suddenly, to my horror, I was dropped. I threatened legal action to make them pay, since they weren't playing. After six months I was offered the picture again, only to find out that they'd reduced the budget. That was a little ruse, a joke. Now somebody else is on the picture, yet many of my ideas are still in the script, which angers me, and of course the budget has gone back up to what it formerly was. One thing I have learnt is that even if you're writing the words and handing across the ideas, you have the protection and small consolation of knowing that the project won't necessarily be realised by others in the way you see it.

At about the time that 'Total Recall' fell through, I was living in the United States and doing a certain amount of work on the post-production of 'Iceman'. Between 'Barbarosa' and 'Iceman', I had written 'Meet Me At The Melba' and 'Misconceptions'. The latter was an original comedy, a writing deal only, for ABC Motion Pictures, and I handed in that script just before I went off to do 'Iceman'. It was a very ambitious first draft. I made the mistake of trying too hard, putting in too much. Now I read it two years later and think, how confusing. I'm just in the process of stripping it completely and I think it will be a lot better script. You simply try too hard at some things.

After 'Iceman', David Foster was doing a film with Roy Scheider about public defenders. It was a murder mystery, examining the morality of public defenders, and it was quite a good story. I was involved in writing discussions and pre-production work on that, but at the same time I'd been approached first by the writer, then by the producer, to direct the film of the stage play 'Plenty'. There was a bit of a race as to which film was going to come off first. Kate Nelligan had starred in the stage play of 'Plenty' and was very keen to do the film, but because of the nature of the subject, if we had done the film with her, it would have been on a much smaller scale than otherwise. Meryl Streep was interested in 'Plenty', then not interested, then she became very interested. It was a complicated situation, because both films were likely to happen at the same, depending on which film could raise the money first. I spent weeks waiting and worrying. As soon as Streep committed herself to 'Plenty' it seemed that the money was in place, so I got on a plane to England and began spending money in pre-production. To the producer's credit, he went enormous amounts of money out of pocket before the deals were finally signed. He had to make it work.

'Plenty' is an unlikely film. It's a tough subject, unusually wordy for these days, but with really good language and not limited because of that. The settings span seven different time periods, from the war through to 1961. The main couple who marry represent two ways not to live. His way is apathetic acceptance, because of his upper class and diplomatic upbringing. Her way is high idealism and moral outrage. Without an ability to really change anything or to compromise or find other ways of living, she destroys herself and everyone around her. Meryl Streep is fantastic. This was one of the best acting/directing experiences I've ever had. There was no star nonsense, everybody in the film gave generously and whole-heartedly. When you consider the list of luminaries, that's surprising: Meryl Streep; Charles Dance, who you'll know from 'The Jewel In The Crown'; Sir John Gielgud, who you'll know from everything; Tracy Ullmann, who trained in theatre here and is a pop star and extraordinarily popular; Sting, who you'll know from the pop group Police and from other films; Sam Neil; and Ian McKellen.

Meryl Streep is highly intelligent with fantastic instincts and not at all selfish. She was completely concerned with the overall film. She had a very difficult part, but I think she has done it extremely well and she's proud of it. David Hare is a stage writer of considerable reputation. I thought the play had a couple of flaws and so did he. We talked about that, he did an enormous amount of rewriting, particularly during rehearsals, involving the actors in going back through the play to see if there was any character substance that had been left behind. Hare wasn't defensive once; he knew we were interested only in writing the best possible screenplay we could get. We ended up with about seven drafts of various sizes, and in the end he stepped back, as it were, reconsidered the whole thing and made it his own again. It was a wonderful working relationship, quite a joy.

After the deal for 'Plenty' was finalised, within a day-and-a-half we had packed our belongings, were on a plane, and in the United Kingdom. We've been here one year now. We've just finished the editing and the music, a marvellous score by Bruce Smeaton, but we haven't finished the mixing yet because we're waiting for Meryl Streep to come back from Africa to do some revoicing in some of the scenes. The projected date for release is October (1985) in America and Christmas in England.

I was considering doing something in Australia next but I stopped it, because I'm at the point where I have to take stock. This is a big film, I don't know whether or not people will go in droves to see it, but there is a chance that it will get a fair audience. It's a quality film, a thinking person's film. I believe the group of actors who are in it should attract a lot of people. Who knows? I think 'Plenty' is fantastically good and I know a lot of people believe there will be Academy Awards for it, but that's all beyond me, I don't really care. I know people will like it and people will hate it, too. I did it because it was something worth putting your heart and soul into. It had depth and intelligence, and that's what I like. I feel I need to get back a lot of control, to take a more official producing role, and I'm trying to do that.

For 'Plenty', I can only be involved in distribution to a certain extent. I've been compiling sample ads, trailers, I have a designer friend coming up with ideas for campaigns and I think they'll be good. I'll certainly say if I think the campaign is heading in the wrong direction but I think it's a bit of a danger when the director gets totally involved in the advertising. I'm emotionally involved in the picture, and what means something to me may not mean a damn thing to anyone else. All I want to do is raise the consciousness of taste and the effectiveness of the campaign.

I think the trailers I've done are good and people have become excited about them, but the trailers can tell you as much about what

Above, Fred Schepisi in editing rooms in Hollywood.
Below, with David Hare on location in London, 1984, for 'Plenty'

not to do as what to do. For instance, I thought the ad in America for 'Iceman' was fantastic. It was emotive to me, but to the majority of the world it was just a horrible creature. That's where you have to be careful. When a film-maker sees separate elements of a film he sees a whole history, an entire emotional background, but other people merely ask, 'What the hell is that?'

I have a couple of projects on tap now, including one idea that I've wanted to make into a film for a long time. All of a sudden, many ideas have centered on this one film and I have to decide. I can write and direct it in Australia and I think I could do it well, or I could control it and have it written for America. It's a real problem for me, because it would be a cultural study of Australia, a very funny, entertaining film, but it is also such a great way to examine an extraordinary superpower like America that it deserves to be made there. I really am torn. Australia has attitudes, a point of view, an outlook on life that is worth exposing to the world and certainly worth exploring for ourselves. America is a country that affects every other country in the world. To be able to get inside America and see what makes it tick on a common-man level is a wonderful opportunity. I have a real desire to go back to Australia and make films — that's why I'm in this dilemma. Because this new project started as an Australian idea and is based on some of my experiences, I want to make it in Australia. Two of my families are in Australia, an older family and a younger one, and I want to be with them. It's a difficult choice. I'd like to be able to live between Australia and America. When I did 'Iceman', I was in Canada; for 'Barbarosa', I was in Texas; for 'Plenty', I'm in England. You go where the film is. I would like to do films internationally and I'd like to do more films in Australia, but I have to balance out the economics of it as well. You develop commitments.

Having been away, I now appreciate that Australia offers the world virility, in the real sense of the word. It's a feeling that there are no real rules, that if you believe there's a way of getting or achieving something you just go out and do it, not allowing yourself to be hindered by the way it should be done. I'm not talking about morals, but about cutting through the nonsense and going straight for what you want with an innocence that sometimes protects you. Australians don't back off when they run into walls or say, 'It's five o'clock, I've got to to go home'. Knowing what you want and finding a way of getting it is an attitude that Australia has which is dead in some other places.

England is improving from the last time I was here but there are rules, stratas, classes, attitudes to overcome, set paths to be taken and methods that don't allow for new ways of doing things. Of course, that's not true of all Englishmen, but when you're dealing with the English you do come up against this problem time and time again. Many accept their lot in life as unchangeable. They feel that they should have only so much time at work and so much time at home and these are values that they needn't even try to go beyond. Many of them adopt strange attitudes; for instance, they might not want to serve you in a shop, as if to say, 'I'm not a servant and you're not really a customer'. I know that some Australians have those attitudes, but for the better Australians there is no wall, they have an open vision, and when they come up against an obstacle they do a bit of lateral thinking to work out a way around it. They'll challenge, they'll come up with an entirely different idea or approach to get where they're going.

The bad thing, incidentally, about Australians is their tendency to knock others. The good thing about Americans is their wonderful encouragement of talent; the bad thing is they think they can mould this talent to their system in order to make money out of it. They give you a go but once they have you going, they may try to control you in corporate ways. That's where America seems to be losing it, while Australians somehow seem to have retained an entrepreneurial sense. We're not as bogged down by corporate research, systems and institutions — we think fresh every time.

Australians are embarrassed about success amongst themselves and do like to knock rather badly, yet I know deep down they really are proud of people who do well, so it's a pity. Six years ago, you wouldn't go into a shop and buy a shirt with a flag or a koala bear printed on it, you'd be laughed at. That's gone, we're proud to be Australians now, and I think as that feeling builds maybe we'll encourage those who are doing well.

Australia could learn optimism from America, that wonderful frontier quality which America has, allowing people to achieve things and be rewarded. Of course there's a reverse side, a balance. Just what is the good life? Isn't it sitting on a beach and cooking prawns as well as working? There really is a good life in Australia, which shouldn't be mucked up with absolute dedication to careers and materialism, to acquiring property, houses, cars, designer clothes and labels. I like Australia. There are characteristics about it that I don't like but I appreciate the sense of humour, the ability to laugh at the pompous, to be irreverent about the institutions and imposing elements of society. I like the egalitarianism. In Australia, you don't tell anybody what to do, you ask them. To a certain extent you do what you do because you were born with it and I like that, except when it's applied to pull people down or to take away incentives.

Film House in Melbourne has been doing extremely well. It's putting out really good quality commercials, with very few staff changes. We're involved in another company called Entertainment Media, which is doing television documentaries with a view to getting into mini-series. A couple of features have also been done with Film House involvement. Our aim is to keep the commercial side going and to branch out and get into more television, then into films. This is one of the reasons I'd like to get back in Australia, to do a certain amount of post-production work and get some other things going as well.

What do Australian films mean to the world? They have a great reputation for being original, open-hearted, square-shouldered, direct, unabashed. Because of all those characteristics and because they speak with an Australian voice, a different sense of humour and a different outlook, they're exciting. Americans love them because they remind them of their past, the way they aren't now. Australian films are about an exotic place and exotic people, which is strange to think of but true. They have a following because they're different and honest. I think honesty, passion, integrity and a lack of cynicism are what come through most in the good Australian pictures.

That's what I want to maintain. I can't work any other way. 'Devil's Playground' has flaws in it but the truth, the passion, the integrity, and the intent that push through that picture override everything. That's the important thing in film-making, and should never be lost. I'd bugger up a James Bond film. They're good mass entertainment, make no mistake about it, with those funny ladies in bikinis tittering about on their high heels, their jugs jiggling. I'd try to make them sexier and more tasteful, which is why I'd bugger up a Bond picture.

Looking at Australian films, you realise that in almost everything we revere we either lost out or somebody died. Most of our history is about events we lost or people who got killed, which doesn't make for happy endings, does it? But if the pictures had happy endings and wonderful resolutions, they wouldn't get a larger audience. I had a belief, as did some others — and we had strong opponents — that the way Australian films would make it in the world was by being truly indigenous, very Australian, although with themes that were international, and that has been borne out. On the whole, pictures that try to masquerade as pseudo-Hollywood or pseudo-international productions tend to be discarded.

As more Australian pictures get exposed to a wider audience, will they ever get beyond the quality film market, the $10 million possible take? Probably never, because Australian pictures are foreign pictures in America. Should we Americanise them to get a bigger audience? Not at all, because we wouldn't fool anyone, we would just lose the audience we have. Maybe one or two pictures will break away, maybe 'Mad Max' could have broken away if differently marketed, but I think there is a market ceiling. You have to make pictures for the people in the country where you're working. Then if it takes off, fine. The English pictures that have taken off have been very English. 'Chariots Of Fire' did quite well, and going back further, films like 'Lawrence Of Arabia' have taken a nice slice of the market. That's about all you can expect.

The Americans want to see things about themselves. That may change. With saturation in the types of films they are getting, it is very possible that a film which offers them something entirely different may succeed, but you're never going to do 'Star Wars' business in Australian films. As for the idea that an Australian film which panders to the American market will become a big box office hit there, forget it. The Canadians have been trying for years, yet their most successful films are those that are unabashedly Canadian.

If you want to make international films, then go and make them in those countries, as some of us are doing now. Yet I'm sure all of us have a goal to return to Australia with greater objectivity and a different perspective. I still want to do a film on the Australian artist and writer Norman Lindsay. I think it would be a very lusty, bawdy, irreverent movie, and it would be about how much you give to what you do and whether you were better off in a country other than your own. There is something about him that fascinates me. From what I've read, he chose paths that are not ones I'd choose, but he's interesting.

'Burke and Wills' is a story that everyone has wanted to do a film of for years and it has a good director. If they make it with the integrity and passion that the story deserves, which I'm sure the director will do, then there's a chance that it will fare well. The explorers die at the end of that story and Americans generally don't like films about people who die, but then Butch Cassidy and the Sundance Kid died at the end of that film.

In Australia you tend to say, 'Right, I'm going to make this film called "Devil's Playground" or "Jimmie Blacksmith" ', then everything goes into that. Somehow you make it come off, although you have your frustrations along the way. In America, you must have a number of projects going. On one hand you're working in the mainstream, but on the other hand the projects that interest you the most seem unlikely for the mainstream, so a lot of them get turned down. You must have seven or eight things going at once. At one point, I was writing 'Misconceptions', supervising a rewrite of a physical, comic Robin Hood that I was going to direct, somebody was about to pay a holding fee for me to direct 'Meet Me At The Melba', I was getting nowhere on having Judith Ross's 'The Other Man' produced, and I was involved with David Merrick, who was trying to sign me pay or play to direct a musical called 'Road Show' starring Liza Minelli and Tommy Tune. New music was to be written by the composer who wrote the original show, 'See Saw', on which the film was to be based.

Out of the blue, three lady producers from San Francisco came to see me. They had been to see me 18 months earlier about a project called 'The Consultant'. I hadn't liked the way it was written and I gave them some advice on it. To my surprise they had rewritten it that way. They said they had $10 million, plus Jackie Bissett and Roy Scheider. If I would do it the money was there, I should drop everything and start immediately. The script explored political media manipulation and took a good look at that world, so I thought, beaut, I'll go for it. Next thing I know, I'm subject to Jackie Bissett's approval. Then the budget became $7 million rather than $10 million. The whole deal ruined 'Meet Me At The Melba', it buggered up Robin Hood, which might have buggered up anyway because of finances, and suddenly I found myself with a difference of opinion with Jackie Bissett. We've sorted it out since, but this wasn't a position I was meant to be in.

These people had been begging me to make the picture. When I said yes, it was such a coup that they went out of the restaurant crying, they were so happy. So here I found myself in the ludicrous position of being wanted by everyone on the film except Jackie Bisset. I flew to New York and had major meetings with Jackie Bissett, Scheider and the producers in the one room for hours on end, for three days. The situation did not get any better so I rang the producers and said, 'Look, you raised the money on Jackie, not on me. Rather than mess me around for three weeks, why not ring me tomorrow and tell me I'm off the picture? I'm angry, very angry. I didn't want to be in this position but I'll tell you one thing, she's never going to make this picture, with me or without me. So you have to decide between us.' Of course the producers made the money decision, stayed with Jackie Bissett and I was gone the next day. 'The Consultant' didn't get made. In fairness to Jackie Bissett and to the producers, there was one particular character who was lying to everybody and that was the problem. In my opinion the director's control comes first of all, in that he can refuse to do the project. If I didn't think Meryl Streep was right for 'Plenty', I wouldn't have done the film. I had control over every other piece of casting. The balancing out of such factors is very important.

It's the luck of the draw, and that was when 'Iceman' came out of the blue. The editor of 'Barbarosa' rang and said, 'You ought to read this, I reckon you'll love it'. He sent me a copy of the script, I read it, rang my agent and said, 'Get me this picture'. I had to convince the producers, two or three times, that I was the right person to direct it.

You do meet resistance in Hollywood as the new boy in town. Studio executives say, 'Why aren't you using our best people?' It's interesting, *their* best people don't use many of their best people. The few really good American cameramen are generally tied up by commitments. Ian Baker, in my opinion, is one of the best photographers in the world, but it's not because he's an Australian or a mate of mine that he works with me, no bloody way whatsoever. I'm not stupid. The same goes for Bruce Smeaton, who's not only one of the best composers but who also orchestrates and conducts. I want people that I can communicate with, I like working with highly talented teams, and by that I mean people who push my barriers and theirs, every chance they get, people who take risks but can also deliver and can judge their contribution in economic terms. How much time do we have, what's the reality in any situation, how can I be practical and yet achieve the best? Those are the sort of questions we all have to ask in films.

The union trick is different in every country. Unions, generally, are there for good reasons, although sometimes they're applied in a misguided way. It's the same in Australia as in America. I like to work with a regular team because we already have an understanding, we've sorted out the basics, established our bona fides, and when I say I would like something I don't have to explain why or go through a history of what he likes and what I like. All that trading off is already done, so we start at a high level. In the American films I frequently used the same set decorator and production designer, and it worked out well. There's an advantage if you use the same actors, too. If I'm fortunate enough to work with Meryl Streep again, an enormous amount of feeling-out will be eliminated from the start. We would be even more direct than we were on 'Plenty', which was pretty direct. You become an ensemble. These aren't always the affable, easy relationships. There's friction sometimes because everybody is pushing, trying to stretch the barriers.

I now have an impetus going but I could have been equally unsuccessful as successful. How do I define success? It's doing something to the absolute maximum of your ability and being satisfied with that. There's a joy if it's critically acclaimed and perhaps there's joy if it's economically successful, but those facts are immaterial. So far I've been critically acclaimed but not really economically successful. I get paid quite well and the fee goes up with each picture, but my expenses are high because I travel a lot to and from Australia.

In America, newer directors get about $150,000 or $200,000. The minimum DGA (Directors' Guild of America) fee is $50,000. Guys like Norman Jewison get $1 million or $1½ million per picture, and the rest of us are anywhere in between the high and low marks. But you start out with a good fee, then a fifth or a quarter of it gets deferred, which means you never see it. About 25 per cent goes to business managers, agents, lawyers, DGA fees, all of which you lose off the top. A lot of figures are bandied about but this is a business with enormous costs, and the figure the director receives is surprisingly less than what he signs for. Not only does your fee cover all expenses but it has to be spread out over however long it is between jobs.

There's money in television. Why do I have a resistance to that medium, when it reaches more people in one night than most of my films will ever reach? Economic restrictions prevent you from putting certain qualities into television productions which go into films, and then there's censorship. Not only does the government have its decency codes but there is also the station's own censorship, the watering down and sterilising of material so as not to give offense to viewers. I don't want to get involved in that, although I think television is doing some terrific things nowadays. It seems to be pre-empting some subject possibilities for feature films, quite serious subjects about defective people or wife-bashers, for instance. Although such shows are a bit antiseptic, I think this new development is terrific. Still, I don't want to do television yet. It's too instant, done and gone. You can't put across the spectacle that I think is possible in films.

Sometimes one film script a day will be offered to me, then maybe one a week, then one a month, then the offers increase again. It's an interesting process to read so many scripts but also a dangerous one. I read very generously, because I know the effort that has gone into them. Therefore I read optimistically, which is a bit of a trap, because I'm trying to like it. You read so many bad ones that you may too quickly skim one that has good qualities. Conversely, you may read one that isn't very good but it might be seventh in a line of bad ones, so it seems fantastic. In the end, if you are grabbed by something you put it down, then come back to it after the initial flirtation has passed, and find the depth to it. If you do that two or three times, it's because the script excites you and fills you with possibilities. Then you want to do it.

There's a list of directors and the scripts do the rounds of them. People try to make out that you're the first director the script has been to, but you ring up your mates and say, 'Do you have this yet?' I've been offered a few films that my compatriots have not wanted to do and vice versa. That doesn't mean you're good or bad, it's just that the films aren't right for you. There's a list of directors who are booked up for years, then there's a list of good directors who are available.

The business point of view is, will the film appeal to the 14-22 year-olds? There's a magic age for actresses, they should look 28. There's a whole pattern of who will appeal to whom, and the 'money people' try to make everything conform to that, because then they don't even have to read the script. If the film fails they can say, 'It wasn't my fault. We had this actor and this actress and that director and this composer.' They have a package. I'm talking about corporate executives who are trying to keep their jobs, and the best way to keep your job is to say, 'I did everything humanly possible to make this work. Look, there's the evidence.' But did they read the script?

If an executive leaves a studio and somebody else comes in, he doesn't want to make a success of the product that the person who just left was making. I can't understand that. To me, you should make a big success of that product for the sake of the company and to prove that you're better at marketing it than your predecessor was. But studio executives think in an entirely different way.

This is a unique industry. For instance, on 'Plenty' I had to choose between all the great actors in this country and the great actors in this country who are known. I went for ones who are known, because the film was a difficult and unlikely project, but also because I didn't want it to be perceived as a Meryl Streep vehicle. I wanted it to be perceived as a film from a great play, with a fabulous ensemble of actors, one of whom is the great Meryl Streep. Another reason for 'casting up' was to give Streep formidable people to play against. When that woman is on the screen she's extraordinary, and you need real strength to equal her. Casting up clearly works commercially. EMI, who are distributing the picture, had all their managers in from around the world for the screening. 'Wow, Meryl Streep', they said, and the film was a success in their minds before they even went into the screening room to see the damn thing.

The truism is that in the end, film-making is a group enterprise. No doubt about it, if you get the right people together, the right chemistry, then something extra will grow. The director gets a lot of the kudos but people forget about the writers. A terrific script is the core of a terrific film. Hollywood tends to change writers like underpants, they don't know how to work with them. They talk about taking the curse off a script. Bugger it, why not have a good script to start with? I think writers are paramount to a good film and the director's job, if he has a good script, is to do justice to it and to everybody else who is contributing to the picture. Then, hopefully, he brings some personal insight and contribution to it as well. It's a group art.

A successful picture demands dedication and determination. Do only things that you believe in, have a passion for them, keep your integrity, and work hard. Working hard is probably the greatest requirement to success in anything. Also, learn how to subjugate your ego, have opinions but don't be opinionated. Have attitudes but accept that other people have attitudes and that there are tastes which are different to your own, and don't shut them out. Don't be egotistical to the exclusion of other people's contributions. Obviously, everybody has to have a belief in themselves, but I think that's different to being an egomaniac. Know how to listen, really listen, and how to evaluate the contributions that are made.

Do you like jazz? Have you ever seen Gil Evans? His is a philosophy on life that I like to sit and watch. His group has 17 individuals, all with extraordinary talent, any of who can stand up and do a very original, improvised solo that will blow you away. Yet within half a beat they'll sit down and be totally in union with the other 17 people, not one of whom is out a beat. All this is done under direction, and yet there is complete freedom and complete cohesion. I think that's how life should be and how art or films should be made. Everybody should have that freedom of expression and yet be able to meld and become a greater element in combination with others. You don't get that unless you are really dedicated.

Personally, I want to be the best at what I'm doing. If you ask me who is the best film-maker in the world, I can't tell you, because I think there are 20 of them and I want to be among those 20. I want to make fine films that I hope will surprise people constantly, that will push the barriers of film language and grammar and be worth having done. I want to look back and be proud of every effort.

Locanto

John Leard

Some would call him the most effective business manager in Australia. He turned a relatively small organisation into the fastest-growing, most profitable corporation in the Western world. Then, at the peak of his success and while a still-young 49, John Leard walked away from it all. The challenge was gone.

Because he had negotiated for himself a unique profit incentive payment scheme, Leard had become wealthy along with the organisation. In 17 years as managing director of Australian National Industries Ltd (ANI), he had transformed it from a steel and engineering business with modest sales of $19 million per year into a diversified multi-national with a turnover of more than $1 billion per annum.

During that time, Leard engineered the successful takeover of 32 other businesses, while ANI's profit growth averaged 31 per cent per annum compound — an achievement unparalleled by any Western company of its large size — according to the respected New York investment bankers Kidder, Peabody & Co. Twice nominated as Australian of the Year, Leard became an adviser to three successive federal governments and played a key role in the first-ever National Economic Summit in Canberra in 1983.

Despite all this, in 1984 Leard decided that, like the Olympic sprinter he had once aspired to be, he would go out on top. ANI was having its best year ever and he was ready for new horizons. World travel (with a backpack rather than a berth on the QE II), perhaps more booklets like the three he has already written after visits to the Soviet Union, China, and the 1984 Olympic Games, his

sporting interests and more time spent with wife Pam
and their five children are high on Leard's priority list
now.

A lifelong teetotaller who puts great emphasis on
physical conditioning ('The thing he dislikes most about
running is stopping', wrote a colleague), John Leard is
already assaulting the second half of his life with the
same supreme self-confidence, boundless energy and
a penchant for the unorthodox that characterised his
talented youth.

Maybe the difference between the successful man and the unsuccessful man is that the unsuccessful man had the opportunity right in front of him and he didn't see it or he didn't take it. Courage. It's often easier, particularly in the Australian context, to say, 'Let's play it low key'.

I guess I'm stubborn, pig-headed, and determined. When I decide to go after something or do something, I'm fairly hard to divert. For example, I never would have bonus issues in the company — I felt that they were the wrong approach. Some of my colleagues used to argue violently with me in an attempt to change my mind. You make the occasional mistake but the important thing is to bounce back after you have taken one on the nostril.

In my younger years, I ran into the problem of, 'You're too young to do this job, you're too young to get support for this'. Going along and trying to get money out of the bank or the financial institutions was tough. Some grey-headed bloke who looked as though he'd been thrashed by life was more likely to get a loan or get money for his company than some young bloke who looked as though he was still wet behind the ears. I suppose that was the greatest of things I've overcome.

There were prejudices against me, prejudices coming from my humble background and not going to a GPS school. Those things I never found any great problem. I walk over the top of that sort of crap.

Since I was six or seven years old I've been accepting responsibilities, which I think has had a significant influence on my life. During my father's absence in the war, I used to have to get the cows in and get them milked. In later years, when I was strong enough, I chopped the wood. We didn't have a modern country toilet so I used to bury the toilet every Sunday afternoon in the paddock, look after the chooks, and take my sisters to school. We had a major bush fire there when I was 10. It was a different lifestyle to the average kid.

Our ancestors came from County Tyrone in Ireland in the 1830s. My father was a sheep station overseer in the Hunter Valley near

Scone. My mother was a Sydney girl who had gone to the bush during the depression. She worked in a local hotel, met my father and they were married. I was born in Scone, 11th December, 1934.

My father was working on the land. They were living in Bunnan, which is a little village outside of Scone. It was a very simple lifestyle, a bush town: no electricity, no running water, involved with animals and with farm life. We moved onto a station property. I suppose the one big influence was that my mother always told me from an early age that I was going to get a good education. Perhaps because she was from the city, she could see that kids were leaving home at 13 or 14 and drifting into dead-end jobs in the bush, and she made sure that I went off to boarding school at age 12. My father's a highly intelligent man who never had the breaks. Mother's determination to get me an education had a lot to do with what I subsequently achieved.

I have two sisters and both are married. One's a housewife and the other one works in a business. They are both very bright girls. As a boy, I won scholarships and I used to work during the school holidays to earn my pocket money. I used to work on the local farms, picking potatoes and digging wells and all sorts of labouring work. While we came from humble beginnings, we never felt that we were poverty-stricken or even poor, but today you probably would. We used to come to Sydney for four weeks' holiday every year. I guess my parents were fairly careful with their money and had their priorities right.

My mother wanted to make sure I went to high school and I think that was about as far as they thought. She just had confidence in a good basic education. I didn't go on to university. When I left school there was a fair bit of pressure on me to become a lawyer or a school teacher, neither of which appealed to me. In the early days, my grand-mother gave me a cow, and instead of selling it I used it for breeding purposes. I made some money that way and I liked the business-dealing, although I hated the local produce bloke, who used to try to screw me after the calf was birthed. So I had a feeling that I wanted to get into business.

I got a good pass in the leaving certificate and I won a scholarship to study accountancy. There was one scholarship given each year to the son of an ex-serviceman and I came first in New South Wales in accountancy. I decided then that accountancy would be a good back-ground to business. So I went to night school rather than university.

I came to Sydney in 1952 and got a job with an accounting firm called Smith, Johnson and Company, which is now Peat Marwick Mitchell. My parents had owned land out at Chester Hill (a Sydney suburb) for God knows how many years, and they decided to build a house. I supervised the building of the house during 1952, in my spare time. The following year my parents moved to Chester Hill.

I was active in sport. I chased a few girls around but was fairly dedicated to getting my accounting qualifications. I always put my career ahead of sport. For example, the accountancy course, I think, was four or five years. I got through in two-and-a-half years; you could set your own pace in those days. You studied at the college and then sat for the Australian Society of Accountancy exams. I gained a lot of honours, including first place in Australia on a number of occasions.

Going for jobs, I always had the frustration of being too young. I was a qualified accountant at 20 and a qualified cost accountant at 21, and at that stage of life, of course, you know everything. I used to wish that my hair would go grey and that I would get a few more wrinkles, because I went for job after job and people would say, 'You're just too young to be in charge of these people'.

I knew I wanted to get into business. Right from the beginning, I knew I didn't want to work in an accounting office. I felt that accountancy was the background and I wanted to understand accounting, finance, and balance sheets. There were two sets of exams I could have done, the Institute of Chartered Accountants' exams or the Australian Society of Accountants' exams. I chose the Society because that was the commercial or business accountant's course, as opposed to the professional accountant's course. In October of 1954 I left Smith, Johnson and Company and joined a commercial firm called Halstead Press, which was the printing subsidiary of A..gus and Robertson, the book publishers. I worked with them as an accountant for three years.

I remember saying once, 'I'll make three thousand pounds a year', which was a very big income in those days, but I think my main aim at that time was to get a degree of experience. I suppose I developed a corporate entrepreneurial bent later. I saw in those days that I didn't want to get into a small business of my own and build it up. I had an aim to get into something that already was a reasonable size, then control and manage it, rather than own it.

I didn't have any capital, but I've never been frightened of responsibility. I felt from a fairly young age that there were three basic unchangeables in life. If you go back over history, these unchangeables are power, money, and love. I haven't altered that view a hell of a lot over 30 years. I didn't have any money in those days, so I thought that perhaps the best way to get money was through power, getting hold of an organisation.

I think that to anybody who hasn't had a lot of money, it does mean a great deal — it's a strong motivation. But it wasn't an obsession. I've always seen money as a means to an end, rather than an end in itself. I've been poor and happy and I've been rich and happy, and I'd rather be rich and happy. I've always seen money as a means of doing things rather than something that you accumulate and worship every morning.

By this time I had developed a philosophy or a feeling that for a while I would develop my career in approximately three-year stints, expanding, progressing on a three-year basis. I went to ANI in May, 1957. I had just gotten married then and I went to ANI on the basis that it offered an extremely good experience in cost accounting, which I wanted to get. I took a salary cut in accepting that job. So I really went there on the basis that I would stay for a year to get that sort of experience. However, after being there for less than 12 months, I found that the place was terribly badly-managed. I said to my wife, 'I think I'll hang around a while because somebody's going to have to do something about this management, and there will be some opportunities to progress'.

Every couple of years I moved up the ladder, and that was reasonably in line with my aim of achieving something better every three years. In fact, I was bettering that timetable. After I'd been there about six months, being a sort of brash young man, I think I did say to somebody one evening when we were having some prawns and drinks, 'Within 15 years, I will be running this place'. That became a bit of a joke which some people forgot about and some people remembered. But that's what happened, in fact. I progressed through the organisation fairly steadily.

There was a lot of resistance, the normal politics and competition for promotion and prospects. However, I kept my basic strength in the accounting and finance side. I'd seen people who had that strength get fully involved in production and marketing and get cut to bits. I felt that you had to keep your home base, or keep your arse protected. The politics of moving through an organisation that's run-down and not well-managed are interesting.

I think right from the time I was a kid I had confidence in my own ability, and had a native cunning to smell trouble when it was around and keep an eye on it. I also seemed to be able to control most situations in which I found myself. I suppose throughout my life I've tended to dominate situations that I get into, which lots of people don't like, of course. And I used to work out my strategies. Occasionally, you'd see jobs up ahead of you that you'd like to have, and while you didn't white-ant the people, you saw that their performance was not up to scratch, and it was always possible that people would see that you were capable of doing that job.

At home, Pam and I grew together. I don't think either of us was struck by a bolt of lightning the first day. We grew together, we were different. For example, she was more involved in the church than I, and wasn't as keen on sport as I was. We had some interests in common, but it was an attraction of opposites to some extent, and there was a growing together.

I've never been a great believer that you must parade your wife to enhance your own business career and interests. In fact, I've had a few hang-ups about that. It's probably my chauvinism. I felt that you should be capable of making it on your own, so I told her that I intended to succeed and I suppose that we divided the labour. I worked and made the money and she stayed home and spent it. But she ran the home, and our five children, of whom we are both proud, are more of a credit to her than to me. Still, she was involved in the business, she went to company social functions, she represented us when I had to go overseas and she's met princes, governors-general, prime ministers, presidents and premiers. She's a lady of great charm and she's done a great job for the company in many ways.

As I've often said, quite facetiously, we both had tremendous background and preparation for the sort of high-flying, affluent world we found ourselves in, but she had much greater advantages than I did. She went to Chester Hill Public School and I only went to Bunnan Public School. We moved to the Blue Mountains in New South Wales when we got married in 1957, and we went to live in a home in Blaxland. We didn't like suburbia. I didn't have an awful lot of money and we decided to get out a bit. It was very pleasant. Since then, suburbia has rolled up and caught us, but it's still nice. Pam worked for three years and we used to travel to town on the train. I think the job she had has disappeared in the technological age, but she was a bookkeeping machine operator. We've done lots of things together. Probably the most worthwhile activity was our involvement in the establishment of several new Baptist churches in the Blue Mountains.

Going back now to the period from about 1957 to 1966, ANI's business was not well-run and hadn't been well-run for many years. It got into trouble in the early 1950s through some crazy bonus issues, wrong capitalisation and poor business decisions and management. I

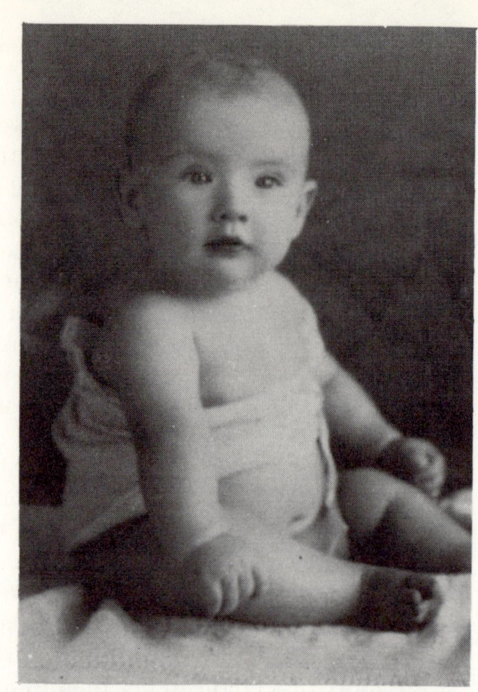

Right, John Leard, 1934.
Below, coming home after school,
1949

had two objectives. One was to develop a successful career, and I didn't want to do anything at ANI that could soil my career reputation for the future. So I was very careful that whatever I did at ANI was completely successful, because career at that stage was the most important thing to me. My second objective was to move through the ANI organisation with a view to getting the top job on my own terms.

I was probably the best finance man at ANI and I always felt that I had enough intelligence to understand what the business was about. I found no problem in dealing with production, engineering, and sales people. There were some casualties on my way through, there was lots of executive turnover, we lost some people we shouldn't have lost, but my job was done competently. In nine years, up to 1966, I received four or five promotions.

The big chance for me came in October 1966, when the senior financial position in the whole of ANI fell vacant and was offered to me. There was great feeling that I would jump at it, but I hesitated. I made the point of not being impressed with the company's performance. Suddenly, I was getting into a position where my reputation and my career, quite correctly, would be aligned with ANI's success or failure. I accepted the job on the basis that I would be listened to and that I would have some access to the Board.

I was 31. It really was from that point that I felt, okay, this is the opportunity I've been waiting for and if I can clean this place up on the financial side, I could be running the whole show. It was a reasonable-sized business, sales of $19-20 million, which back in those days was something worth getting hold of. I suppose this was the stage where I felt that in running the place one day, I could turn it into one of Australia's great companies. That motivation and that objective became primary in the whole exercise.

That was 1966-67 and the company was over-capitalised — it had a lot of inappropriate businesses in it. This was the period when a lot of takeovers were starting to happen. I said to the Board, 'We're a sitting target for a takeover, we have all kinds of good assets, we're worth 80c a share and our market price is only 30c a share'. I said, 'If we're smart, we'll do to ourselves what somebody who took us over would do. We should strip out the lazy assets, kick the arses of the poorly-running businesses, get rid of the managers who can't perform and genuinely shake the place up.' Of course, I thought this wasn't a bad idea, so what about doing it? I sold off some assets, returned some capital to the shareholders and got the capitalisation right.

We took three-quarters of a million pounds out of the overheads. Suddenly, ANI was starting to look good, and I suppose it was from 1968 onwards that I had a major say in everything that happened. The Board had been talking for many years about reconstructing the company. I remember the first time I put the proposal up to the Board, they said, 'It won't work', and I said, 'I think it will work'. It did.

Then we went on the takeover trail. I think we made our first takeover in 1969. Gradually, we spread the net. I'd noted that businesses of a single product or a single process had all sorts of problems, because the business cycles in Australia were fairly violent. In those days, they were more violent than today because we had periodical credit squeezes. I felt that there was strength in having your eggs in more than one basket, so I had a plan to get ANI into different market segments over a period of time. Some of the markets were in the consumer spending area, some of them in private capital, and some in government capital spending.

At the same time the rationalisation of industry was starting to take place and companies were dropping out. We were very small in the steel distribution business, but it was obvious that there was going to be a shake-out in that industry and there would be some good opportunities for those who got bigger and became survivors of the rationalisation. So that was the first area that we looked at. We made two or three takeovers in that industry.

Then we got into some heavy engineering operations, we got into some plant-hire operations, we moved across the whole spectrum. I suppose if you looked at where we were in the beginning and where we finished up, you'd say, 'Boy, oh boy, that's a massive change of emphasis in the business'. But it was gradual, and as we got more experience we branched out, until we finished up with what I think is probably the best-balanced business in Australia. It's a beautiful business to run because you're not subject to any one particular market segment. We tend to cross over the business cycles in Australia. If business is not spending, government is spending. So ANI tends to have tremendous resilience and strength.

I've always regarded myself as a corporate entrepreneur who just happened to study accountancy. I was a reasonably good accountant, but that was a long time ago and today I'm more a dealer in companies and businesses. You've got to have the capacity to look around and look ahead. If I had to put a quality on what I look for in a chief executive, it is the fellow who is able to anticipate changes. That's what we did very successfully at ANI. There are times when industries are running well and times when that particular technology falls away. Now, if you stick to the knitting, you'll have less and less wool to knit. Sticking to the knitting may be a philosophy which is reasonable for the operational man, but it's not for a corporate entrepreneur or business leader.

I'd always made it very clear to the Board that I worked for money and that I expected my income to increase at least in line with the company's prosperity, which meant that I became a very highly-paid man. In turn, the company benefited from my leadership and management contribution, so there was never any argument.

Money was always the reason I was working but I only wanted to get paid by results. So I don't think I ever worried whether I was going to be worth one million, two million, ten million, or whether I made $100,000, $200,000 or $500,000 a year. It was nice at the end of the year to say I'd made that much. Occasionally, you'd say, 'I'm now worth that much'. I think I was more concerned in those days with building ANI into a business that people could be proud of and which had a high standing in Australia.

I said to the fellows when I took over, 'In the past at ANI, prestige has been more important than profit, but as from today, profit is more important than prestige. If you want a fashionable office and surroundings, either go work somewhere else or have them at home, but here we will be fairly spartan. We're not interested in the bullshit and the trappings.' I always used to be happy when I saw some of our competitors take expensive offices in the city. You knew then that you'd knock the tripe out of them, because once they get in there they get lost. That's why ANI's head office is still in the back of the factory out at Lidcombe (a Sydney suburb). Nicely done, presentable, and it makes the people keep their feet on the ground. If somebody comes up with a harebrained idea, you can say, 'Walk down the factory and see what you think about that idea when you get out in the real world'.

I became growth-oriented and started to say, 'Each year has got to be better than the last'. I probably drove the managers mad and some of them into the grave. After we'd put up a five-year record in 1972, somebody did some analysis and said, 'This is the best growth record in Australia over the last five years. It's ANI.' Then I said, 'Look, we can get 10 years of continuous growth'. We did that through better management, expansion, and some takeovers. It was pretty clear at the end of 10 years that nobody in Australia had done anything like we'd done over that period.

I said to the fellows, 'Okay, we're going to do that for 15 years now'. Then the international people started to take more notice of us. A few of them, such as Kidder Peabody, said, 'We don't think anybody's done this over 15 years'. That offered a very strong motivation. I suppose it became a personal ambition of mine to run the company with the best growth record in the world. In many ways, in the period leading up to 1982, that was more important to me than all the money in the world. Even though I was making a lot of money, the achievement of the 15 years' world growth record was a critical thing.

After we achieved the 15 years' growth record in June, 1982, I started to feel bored and restless at ANI. I felt like the Olympic champion who had defended his title over and over again — what does he do for an encore? I felt that I had done it all in business, that the challenge wasn't there any more — perhaps I should have a change of direction.

The Comeng takeover was accomplished at the end of 1982 and I thought, maybe this will change everything. I'll give it another year and see how I feel. I worked like a slave that year to get the takeover bedded down. Probably the best year's work I did for ANI, in many respects, was in achieving the rationalisation of the Comeng organisation. It was a big takeover, five new businesses came into a group and there was a massive increase in business and capital employed.

The strike at Comeng's Granville plant that followed the takeover was a fight that had to be. It was not just a union problem, it was a management problem and an industrial problem. That particular plant was very poorly run. Management had never been properly backed up by the Board of Directors in the company. As a result, the management had become gutless and not very effective. The unions had become arrogant, and it was in many ways a last bastion of what the unions would call workers' rights. In Sydney's western suburbs area these people were labelled the untouchables, and it was thought that nobody would ever clean up the situation. So whichever way we could have played it, it would have been a difficult stoush. I took the responsibility to screw it right down and play rough as guts from the start — give them nothing on the basis that there would have to be a settlement at some point. Whatever we gave initially, we'd only give more later, so give them nothing to start with and you were then in your best position for negotiation.

In all industrial disputes, and we've had some, our relations with the unions were pretty good. There are two groups in the unions: the moderate element and the radical left-wing communists. Our objectives in the dispute were very much different to the unions, because we wanted to fix the place for the future and get the right working conditions and concessions on the bad work practices which existed. The issues, as far as the workers were concerned, were the conditions of redundancy and severance payments. In the end, we got all of the work practices that we wanted and they got their severance pay. It was a long dispute but it wasn't very costly to the company at all.

When I left, Comeng's Granville plant was five times as profitable as when we bought it in 1982, and that's what it's all about. I've always been a great believer in softly, softly. Talk about it and do it behind the scenes. However, you do get all sorts of situations in business where you can't do that. Sometimes you've got to stand up and be counted. Today, that business and its 500 employees have some sort of future and job security, whereas in 1982 they had no future at all.

The Board of Directors once said to me, 'What happens if you get hit by a tram?' I gave them a program, the way I thought the place would need to be run by a committee, but I said, 'This is the man (Neil Jones) who will ultimately come through and run it'. When I decided to retire, I gave Jones more training. I didn't tell him for a while that he was the man, but I gave him more responsibility so we could have a good look at how he performed. I'm not sure that you can always have your successor trained. I wouldn't agree that that is one of the most important things for a chief executive to have planned well in advance. Somebody sitting on his arse for 10 or 15 years waiting for the boss to pass on is not the bloke to give the job to.

At this point I was getting a bit disenchanted with the way things were happening in Australia. The election of the new Labor government didn't do much to excite me that it was going to give incentive to people. The sort of socialistic, bureaucratic approach to life that we have in this country ultimately gets people down.

Although people have accused me of being a workaholic and that ANI is the only thing in my life, it *wasn't* the only thing. I have a tremendous interest in many different activities, the church, my family, sport, writing, speaking, and even studying from time to time. Travelling is an obsession with me. It wasn't as though suddenly cutting ANI off would finish my interest or vitality.

At the end of 1983, I still felt the same as I did at the end of 1982. So in January, 1984, I went away for a couple of weeks on my own up to Surfers Paradise, and wandered along the beaches and just thought and thought. I just had to make up my mind whether it would be this year or next year. But I'd always wanted to go out in a year when there was plenty of growth left in the business so the new man wouldn't be inheriting something that was fragmented. I could see that 1984-85 would be a good year for the company. It's very hard in Australia today, with all of the government policies of both Labor and Liberal, to look two years ahead. I thought, 'I'm not sure how good 1985-86 will be. This is the year.' It's the best decision I've ever made. I have other things to do, and I feel very comfortable about it.

I think my parents were very proud of my success — they have stacks of press cuttings. It's been a great thrill for me to see them happy, because they both contributed a lot of hard work to get me educated and gave me some good advice along the way. So they've got great satisfaction out of it. They're both getting old now and I think it's nice that they've been able to see it happen.

I was never fortunate enough in business to work with people of great competence or people who I could look up to — it's just one of those things. I worked with some good men, but not people that you'd look up to and say, 'My hero, my idol'. I suppose Sir Charles Court would be an Australian that I have continually respected over the years. I'm not a great admirer of politicians. I guess the more you have to do with them, the more cynical you become about them.

I was offered Andrew Peacock's job a week after I resigned from ANI. I said, 'If I go into politics, I might become Prime Minister. The money isn't good enough and the family doesn't want to live in a smaller house.' I'm sure Bob (Hawke) would be highly impressed.

I started off by being no great respecter of persons and I don't take myself as seriously as other people take me. I was very impressed as a young man by W. J. Smith, who was the managing director of ACI (Australian Consolidated Industries). He was known as Gunboat Smith, one of the old business buccaneers. I happened to come in touch with him when I was an audit clerk with Smith, Johnson and Co. I used to do the audit of ACI and he took a shine to me when I was a 19-year-old boy. Arnold Glass, the founder of Capitol Motors (which we took over in 1977), would be by far the most outstanding businessman with whom I worked during my career. The headmaster of my school, a man called Russell Hodge, also had a great influence on my life.

I've enjoyed meeting some of the world leaders. I enjoyed establishing a business in the Philippines and having contact with (President Ferdinand) Marcos in the days when his regime was more successful than it is today. I think he is an example of somebody who has held on too long. I don't know, I'll keep thinking about that one.

I suppose I make friends sparingly. I never felt that it was all that wise to have the people you work with as your best friends. I think that it creates conflicts and potential problems. I like people but I don't need to have stacks of people around me to enjoy myself. I can enjoy my own company.

I was always regarded, and regarded myself, as somewhat of a loner. I suppose it developed. There was a time when people perhaps viewed me a bit differently. When my mother sent me off to get an education, the other kids in the community tended to say, 'He's different to us now'. I'd come home and ride in the gymkhana and they'd try to ride me off the track. At work I was one of the boys sometimes, but as I perceived leadership I realised one of the things you deny yourself is the right to be 'one of the boys'.

I think the entrepreneurial spirit is something that we should encourage and even when entrepreneurs stub their toes we shouldn't can them. I think they're to be encouraged at every level. Our big businesses have become too bureaucratised. Many top business people are really running bureaucracies rather than businesses.

I'm more of a corporate entrepreneur than a private entrepreneur. I saw a way of making money through earning high income out of a company and having a minor stake — it was still worth a lot of money but wasn't a 50 per cent stake, such as Alan Bond or Ron Brierley might have. Maybe if I had gone the route they've gone, I might have made more money than I've made, but I might not have had as much fun.

In the corporate structure, I think that I'm very different from the normal corporate executive. I'm individualistic, tend to be authoritarian, and tend to run the business as I would my own. I have found none of these conflict, provided that the shareholders and the company are benefiting. Lots of people would say that's the wrong attitude to have and somebody shouldn't be allowed to run a business like that, but I think it places more pressure on you. It doesn't mean that you don't listen to your subordinates. In fact, you listen more intently than other people do, because you know that your decisions are more vital and your mistakes are more damaging. So I think that my individualistic and unorthodox approach to management, my emphasis on profitability and growth, would be quite different to a lot of the people who get to the chief executive positions in large corporations.

It is lonely at the top but I've never lacked confidence, even though there are times when you wonder like hell whether your decisions are going to be right. You're standing up there holding your own hand and thinking about the decisions. But if you've got confidence that you'll do it successfully, the loneliness is not something that bears down on you. I don't think there is anything wrong with feeling lonely. For the fellows who have that problem at the top, it's not so much the loneliness which crushes them but rather that they're lacking confidence and ability.

I believe that performance is everything, whether it's in sport, in education, or in business. I'm a believer in competition. I like to be the best when I do something — I like to come first. I suppose that's the background to what makes you perform and achieve.

I've always had a saying that arse is better than class. I think having an inquiring mind is important. I used to drive people mad, I remember, when I worked on farms and earned pocket money during the school holidays. The farmers used to say, 'For God's sake, shut up, you're driving us mad'. I used to ask, 'Why this, why that? Why is something being done like this?' If the answer is, it's been done that way for the last 25 years, that's probably a good reason to change it.

Keeping your eyes open, being in the right place at the right time, and seeing the opportunity are critical. Alan Bond, for instance, has made lots of mistakes as he's gone along, but he's been in the right place, seen the opportunity and grabbed it. That's a part of success.

I've led a pretty successful, contented life. As I've gone along, even though it's been hectic at times and people around me probably thought that all hell was breaking loose, I felt completely calm and relaxed about it all. Even during the Comeng strike, the only thing that worried me was a threat at one stage to get at my kids, which I think was only the ravings of a lunatic. I didn't worry about it. I used to give $2 to the strike fund every morning as I drove the Cadillac past the strikers collecting money. It never worried me too much.

I've got a quick temper, though. I get annoyed and unhappy. As my wife said, if I blow up it's usually over something small, and if there's some major crisis or big problem, I'm ice cold.

Success has meant the personal satisfaction of achieving something, and on the business side it's meant money. It's been the opportunity to travel, to meet interesting people. You feel that you've contributed something to Australia's well-being. I suppose there's some ego-massaging, but I never thought that ego was a bad thing

John Leard with wife Pam and daughter Shelly

unless it's out of control. I suppose you enjoy the plaudits of people, to some extent.

I've never taken well to discipline, but was always very self-disciplined. I had lots of troubles at school, for example, because I wouldn't wear the school uniform for the whole five years. It sounds crazy when you look back now. I always wore something that wasn't quite regulation, whether it was the wrong socks or no tie or a different-coloured shirt. I've always been an unconventional dresser. When I was younger, I used to wear shorts to the office at ANI. I didn't wear a tie for years, although I always had a tie in the office to impress the right people, if they turned up to see me.

I've never been a conservative in the sense of being conventional. I suppose I'm non-conformist and unorthodox in my approach. I have always been regarded as a rebel. Actually, people perceive me a bit differently to how I perceive myself. The fact that I work hard, don't drink, like to keep myself fit, and tend to be a little bit of an exhibitionist are some of the reasons I'd be seen as a bit eccentric.

In this day and age, my devotion to the free enterprise system and the profit motive in Australia is not on, in some sectors. I like to drive nice cars: there's a bit of flamboyance in that. The company has a jet which we used to float around in. I like to travel well. I suppose that has become normal for me, although other people might see it as opulence, extravagance, or flamboyance.

I've never gone overboard. I'm a cautious investor and I like to see the odds in my favour. The high rolling set, because of the type of business they're in, sometimes have a need to impress people. I tend to say, 'Well, the record's there, you'll be impressed by that'. I get a great deal of satisfaction out of being the most successful or the best at something, but I like to have my opulence and my extravagance relatively privately. I like nothing better than to get on a Barbados beach for a couple of weeks and live it up.

I'm a great believer in self-discipline. I've been enormously self-disciplined and I think that's one of the reasons that I've been successful. I'm my own harshest critic. Everybody makes mistakes in business, and the business community and the press are very quick to criticise you, but it's never worried me because I've always been able to say, 'You're dead right, I spotted that mistake myself months ago'.

I tend to dominate things. I can look back on my life and see that it happened at primary school. If a game was to be run, I'd organise it. Even though I might have been seven or eight and some of the other kids were 13 or 14, I'd be running the game. For example, I came to

Sydney for a year when my sister was sick in 1944. I was 10 years old. I learnt how to play Rugby League, which had never been played back home, then I taught all the boys in Bunnan how to play Rugby League.

In 1968, the company sent me to the Melbourne University Summer School. I'd been working pretty hard at ANI by then for about 10 or 11 years, and I had probably gotten slightly more insular than I'd realised. There were 70 or 80 blokes at the summer school and it was supposed to be the cream of the up-and-coming Australian business executives. I remember coming back from that and saying, 'Oh, hell, they're all pushovers. If that's what the world's made of, we'll eat it all in one day.'

I've played 20 sports, and I've got a tremendous respect for my body. I take some satisfaction from the fact that I have almost the same body measurements I had at the age of 25. I exercise my body every day and enjoy the things that I can do with it — I'm a fairly physical person. I used to get into plenty of fights at school.

I'm a student of history. I wouldn't say I've taken a calculated approach to it, but I enjoy reading history. I've studied the disastrous effects of socialism and communism around the world and I regard myself as being reasonably well-versed in what the communists are about. I also enjoy the writing that I've done. I enjoy talking, I enjoy making the odd speech. People have been kind enough to say that I speak fairly well. I've been invited to go on the lecture circuit but that doesn't appeal to me at the moment.

I do get a tremendous amount of interest and satisfaction out of seeing our children achieve, progress and develop. I have no dynastic ambitions at all for them, which I think is a real blessing for them. No, I think I've resisted that temptation. When we could see that we were succeeding more than most people as a family, we tried to shield the children from the worst features of that sort of thing. We felt that we didn't want them to be little prigs and say, 'My father is John Leard and we're millionaires, so we're better than you'. They have had a well-balanced and down-to-earth unbringing. That, plus the Christian training they have received at home and from the Church, should stand them in great stead in their futures.

There was a period I went through where I wanted our children to succeed and I think that some of them got the feeling that I was pushing too hard. It comes out in little ways. One of our daughters is married, my son-in-law is a nice lad and he and I get on well together. Every now and again we'll be talking about one of the family and he'll say, 'He'd probably do a bit better if he didn't have father's successful image held up in front of him all the time'. I've encouraged them to work hard, to study hard, and to improve themselves, but I've also encouraged them not to neccessarily do all the conventional things. None of them are drop-outs or hippies; quite the opposite in fact.

If somebody makes a million in the United States, the attitude of the fellow next door is, 'Good on you, buddy, I'll try and do the same thing'. In Australia we say, 'You must be a crook'. We Australians say to our children today, 'Succeed, work hard, get a good education, join a profession or a company, spend long hours at work, and improve yourself'. Then at age 27 or 28, when they've done that, we tax them 60 cents on the dollar for the rest of their lives. We kill incentive, and it's little wonder that some of them say, 'This is not for us, let's get a few birds and go to the beach and have a good time'. This disincentive is a problem for lots of people in Australia.

In my own situation, I used to say jocularly, 'I'll work for myself until 3.30 on Tuesday afternoon, and the rest of the week I'll work for the government'. When you make out your tax return at the end of the year you sometimes ask yourself, 'What's it all about?', even if money is not your prime motivation all the time.

I want to become more knowledgeable about the world. The more I look at the world, the more parochial it is. I'd read in the press, 'Isn't Australia a dreadfully parochial country?', which it is. Then I went to England. I found sections of England dreadfully parochial, and of course America is parochial squared. They can't even run the Olympic Games without parochialism coming through. It impresses me that there aren't many people who have a view and a knowledge and a feel for the whole world. That's something I'd like to get, just for myself. I think I'd be a better person, and it would give me great satisfaction to understand the world much better. I can afford to do that but it will mean effort, both physical and mental. I think I'd like to understand something more of the political processes that are going on in the world. I see communism and socialism as disastrous developments in the last 50 years that somehow or other have to be turned back. Is this so-called New Conservatism the answer? I suppose I'd like to become a wise old man.

I'm a great admirer of America. Although there are things wrong with any society, I like their approach. I think their defence of individual freedom, the way they stand up for their personal liberty and their desire for freedom generally. is something that is to be admired. We tend to let the politicians and bureaucrats walk on top of our individual rights in this country.

I don't think that Australia can be neutral in the world's scheme of things. We are a country that is very rich in natural resources, we've got the capacity to grow enormous amounts of food, and we are very strategically located. We're a big country, the size of America, and in this sort of satellite world that we're becoming, large land masses are important. So I think that Australia has got to make a choice as to whether it is part of the liberal, democratic, Western alliance, or whether it's part of the totalitarian, communist, socialist axis. I think most Australians have already made that choice.

I believe that what America has to offer us is the umbrella of the Western alliance, the pursuit of freedom for the individual. Neutrality, in the world power play, is not a luxury that we enjoy. That doesn't mean we need to give up our independence, nor does it mean we don't need to influence some American thinking. But I think in freedom and democracy and liberalism the Americans have a lot to offer us.

The nuclear era is a fact of life, and while we'd all like to see the nuclear threat wound back, it can't be unilateral. Whether or not we can trust the Russians is the question for us. Their problem is probably whether or not they can trust us. I think it would take a very brave United States President to say that he is prepared to trust the Russians. Jimmy Carter half-tried it and he got buried.

ANI has a number of investments in America. It's the greatest market in the world, it's still relatively accessible, it may be parochial in some ways, but it's growing. I don't think any Australian company that looks overseas can go past America.

Generally, Americans tend to see us as one of the last frontiers. I think we've probably oversold that, because we are in fact one of the most urbanised societies in the world. But the American perception is that we're a bit like their Wild West of 150 years ago. I think the development of our resources has brought that about.

We have a fairly good rapport with the United States. Business people generally get on well together. While we speak the same language, we don't always mean the same things, which is a problem. To some extent, we're less attractive to American investors today than we were 20 years ago. I really don't foresee any tremendous investment for them here, other than perhaps in the financial services area with the new banks coming in. I don't see American industry being as keen to develop its roots in Australia as it was 20 years ago. We have become a less competitive society and other parts of the world offer the American manufacturing and industrial companies better areas for investment.

In many ways, Australia has taken some bad turns, both industrially and union-wise, in the last 20 years. We tried to push the import and placement side of our manufacturing industry well past the point where it was viable to do so, and we're suffering the effects of that. Since 1969 the trade unions have been above the law, and in many ways the unions run the country. Investors now say, 'Let's invest in some other country where the unions don't run the country'. Australia has some deep-seated problems which you would have to be a pretty big optimist to feel are going to be solved quickly.

The British don't see themselves as quite the bastion of freedom that the Americans do. The British are not as concerned or worried about Australia, and our ties are tending to be more with the Americans. As the increasing ethnic influence in Australia develops over the next 50 years, the original ties with Britain will weaken further.

The Japanese are our mortgagees. They're basically providing the funds which allow us to live beyond our means. We're borrowing from the rest of the world to support a standard of living we're not prepared to work for, and if anyone calls up the mortgage one day, it will be the Japanese. I think they see Australia very much as the long-term jewel in their crown, achieving by financial means what they didn't achieve in 1941 by military means. They're going to own this country one day, whether or not they ever fly the Japanese flag over it.

The Japanese are in an awfully strong bargaining position and they're very shrewd. In the coal fields of Queensland and New South Wales, they've encouraged every man and his dog to develop mines. They've done the same thing in Latin America, in the African countries, and now they're playing one off against the other. They've been shrewd in how they've manoeuvered Australia into developing its resources and then having to sell them at very competitive prices. Of course, if we don't sell them at the right price, I guess they just don't send their ships.

There's an enormous nationalism in Japan which I think is strengthening, if anything. People talk about some of the old customs fading away, but I think that the Japanese national spirit is just as strong today as it's ever been. Japanese people tend to work for Japan Incorporated, and their company structure is such that the old Zaibatsu (financial clique) strength of pre-war days has really come back. It might be called by a different name, but it's there neverthless.

In Australia, I think that we're going through a melting pot situation nationally. In many ways, there's less nationalism today than there was when I was a boy. Empire Day, which was celebrated on the 21st of May or something, nobody even hears of today. Anzac Day is pretty much a non-event; Australia Day a complete non-event. There's nothing like, say, the Trooping of the Colour in England, Bastille Day in France, or the Fourth of July in the United States.

In Australia, the conflict, at least of ideas if not physical conflict, between the original Irish immigrants and the British settlers still exists today. But that is complicated by the fact that at least 40 per cent of the population today is European post-war immigrants. I see that as one of the great strengths of the country, in the long-term. I think that there are attitudes of laziness and apathy which the Irish and the British have brought out here that we could well do without. I see one of the strengths of Australia as the maturing of the multicultural ethnic grouping which is now coming of age in the country. But I think you're talking about 40 or 50 years' development.

The rigidity of our wage structure has obviously worked against us, but the most prosperous times in Australia were the times when we had a rapidly-growing population. There were growing pains and problems with social issues, many of which tended to be solved by the families of the day, but since we've tried to institutionalise compassion in the last 20 years, we've got a field force of social workers who are self-perpetuating. If they solved all the social problems we have today, they'd have to create more problems tomorrow, or they would be out of work.

It's been fun to have Irish ancestors, but I've got no emotional feeling about Ireland. That's never been an issue with me. We've traced our family ancestry back, though, and it's interesting to know where we came from. I think there was a fellow called John Leard who felt that Ireland was stuffed, and he wanted to go somewhere else. I've told my children that they shouldn't necessarily feel that because John Leard made that decision in 1830, every succeeding generation of Leards should live in Australia for the rest of their lives. There may come a time when one generation says, 'Look, we'd best uproot and go somewhere else'. I hope that if there is anything we gained from our Irish ancestors, it will not be hang-ups about Ireland, but rather the courage that Leard had to see the writing on the wall and move to where he and his family would be better off.

I suppose I'm a patriot. I've probably tended to become a bit of an internationalist, too. I tend to see the whole world, and I suppose to that extent it belies my patriotism sometimes. I see Australia as a country with a lot of problems, none of which we are addressing very smartly, and I don't see the Hawke government being very much different from the Liberal government in the long term. We are a country where 55 per cent of the work force is unionised, as opposed to 18 per cent in the United States. So you must recognise that under the Labor government, you've got a coalition government. The ALP and the ACTU (the trade union movement) are really joint partners in running Australia. The fact that the ACTU is not elected by the people, but still runs the country, is offensive to me and to a lot of other people as well.

We have a bureaucracy that is self-serving. We have a political structure that is capable of running a country with 70 million people. We are the most over-governed country in the world, with one of the highest proportions of politicians per head of population. People love power. They love organising and influencing decisions. You're a dreamer if you think that suddenly the unions are going to let go of that power. On the other hand, you're not a dreamer if you think that their power is going to be counter-productive to the best interests of many Australians.

We are in competition with the world. Maybe we'll become competitive by debauching our currency, but weak currency ultimately does no good to any of us other than to keep us all at home. Maybe that's what some of the socialist elements would like in Australia, to stop the natives getting overseas and seeing what the real world is like. And debauching the currency is one of the ways of achieving that.

I fear for the future of Australia, particularly for the young people. If we're not careful we might well create a brain drain. Some of the smart young people might look at Australia in the way that the Leard who left Ireland in 1830 did, and say, 'Hell, there are plenty of places to live and work and bring up your family'. I'm a great elitist. I believe in leadership — it's the top 15 per cent of the people who make it happen. If you lose them — that's what happened in Russia, Stalin chopped their heads off — the country will suffer from it, as Russia still does.

If you can get the unions to keep the shit off our beaches, they're the nicest beaches in the world, with one of the best climates. Australia is less complicated than lots of other places to live. If you've made it, it's a nice place to live. The difficulty I see is for the young people who are coming up. There will be plenty of opportunities, but whether or not there will be enough opportunities, whether or not our unemployment goes from 10 to 15 per cent, is hard to say. We haven't been all that good at solving our problems in the short term. We're not as good at that as the Americans.

I think the 'lucky country' syndrome is still with us and we've got that British feeling, like Mr Micawber, that something will turn up. Don't worry too much, it will all be okay. Most times, something *has* turned up to pull us out. There still is the feeling amongst most people that the world owes us a living. In Australia, you've got a proportion who feel that socialism is an answer. In America, despite the political conflict, you've got a two-party system that supports free enterprise.

I'm a great supporter of freedom. That's freedom of the press, of assembly, of worship, of enterprise, freedom to vote. I'm constantly surprised by the people in the press and the churches and businesses who can't see that in bringing in a totalitarian system or supporting socialism, they're the very people who are going to be the first losers. You don't help people by doing for them what they should be doing for themselves. I think that's one of the hand-out mentalities that we've developed in the world.

I'm a bit of a Philistine on education. I think that people tend to get over-educated, particularly in the formal education system. Education, as I see it, is basically trying to put an old head on young shoulders, especially in the area of business. That's what I always felt the people who taught me accounting were trying to do.

I'm a great believer in keeping things simple. One of the things I don't believe is that the most intelligent people necessarily make the best business managers, which is something we could talk about for hours. Success in business is 90 per cent perspiration and 10 per cent inspiration. Ultimately, the market is the master of us all in business. The feel for the market is the critical thing in any business situation. That's how a businessman anticipates the changes and development which are going on around him. I think the ability to smell out where the market's heading is incredibly important. A sense of humour is also important, being able to laugh at yourself. Don't take yourself too seriously, don't believe your own bullshit.

They often say of me, he's a tough businessman. I've always thought that inner strength in your decisions and convictions, coupled with compassion, is better than all the toughness in the world.

Stefan Ackerie

If you're stodgy enough to dismiss hairdressing as a frivolous pursuit, chances are you don't live in Queensland. There, the name Stefan Ackerie commands a following which may be second only to that of Sir Joh himself.

Even while we spoke with Ackerie beside his swimming pool and tennis court at an exclusive spot on the Gold Coast's sparkling blue waterfront, the tour boats cruised by their guides pointing out his elegant home and detailing over loud speakers the story of his rise as Australia's hairstyling guru. Ever the gracious and unflappable host, Ackerie merely smiled and waved to his floating fans.

He's big on service with a smile. In fact, he has parleyed that skill, combined with exceptionally good taste and a casual yet convincing personal style, into a hair fashion empire that pervades Queensland and is now coming to the rest of Australia. It all began with his dad, a Lebanese hairdresser who brought his family here when Stefan was a teenager. Through him, Stefan learned early about the rewards of excellent service.

Yet that alone wouldn't have enabled him to achieve his boyhood dream of a chain of hairdressing salons. To do that he needed the capacity to work long hours, an unerring eye for profitable enterprise, financial daring, unusually good communication skills and, as he says himself, a high threshold of pain. He had all of those traits. As a result he now owns 60 salons, including million-dollar plans and projects in the Sydney market, he's branched into restaurants with six successful Jo Jo's outlets, he has a weekly hairstyling television program in Queensland and an annually televised Christmas Show extravaganza, he leads some 800 employees and has many thousands of young people vying yearly to work for him because of his reputation as a fair and generous employer. A multi-talented sportsman, a cautious and structured thinker who likes to express his ideas with the aid of almost constant doodling, Stefan Ackerie has the bottled energy of someone who is not only well in control of his booming business life, but is also a long, long way from peaking.

I wanted to go to Darwin and Mount Isa when I was in my early 20s, to see the Outback. So I took off in my little MGA and at Longreach I went into a pub to have a drink. Twenty years ago, when you arrived in such a town in a blue sports car that had wide wheels and a pack-rack and which made this beautiful noise, you wouldn't dare walk into a pub and tell them you were a ladies' hairdresser. A fellow said, 'Hey, where are you from? Brisbane? What do you do?' I said, 'I'm a ladies' hairdresser'. His face beamed and he said, 'You one of those poofta bastards, eh?' I said, 'Not a poofta bastard, just a ladies' hairdresser'. 'Smart bastard, too, eh?' I said, 'No, just a ladies' hairdresser'. Then it was on. We had to have a fight, because I was supposed to be a poofter.

I've always been able to take care of myself, always had something to do with fighting. In those days you couldn't kick anyone or fight dirty because the bar would all turn on you. I knew that, but if you could have a nice, clean fight and put on some entertainment, maybe you'd shake hands afterwards. The fellow was pretty drunk but he was tough. I just couldn't knock him down, couldn't knock him out without hurting him seriously. Then this other fellow rushes in. 'Are you the ladies' hairdresser bloke? Do you want a job?' I said, 'If you stop your mate, we'll have a chance to talk'.

So he stopped his mate, we shook hands, then the second bloke bought me a beer and said, 'I'll give you 17 pounds 50 a week'. I said, 'I can't accept that', and the other bloke said, 'See, I told you he's a smart bastard'. I said, 'One of us is a smart bastard and it isn't me'. The second bloke said, 'You can't go, you have to work in the shop. It's the only hairdressing shop in town except for another one which isn't much good, and it's closed. The people in this town need a hairdressing shop. It's my shop, it's empty, and it's in the arcade.'

I said, 'You've landed me with all your problems, without even considering mine. For me to live in this town I'd need 25 pounds a week. By the time I pay my car, food and hotel, I'd need that much to live. I can't live here to do you a favour and be out of pocket.' He said, 'The shop has never made 25 pounds in a week'. I said, 'How about I give you 25 pounds a week for the shop and I'll work at it, and when you get someone to replace me I'll move on?' He said, 'But it doesn't take 25 pounds'. I said, 'Don't you worry about that'.

I made about 100 pounds the first week and 150 the second. That's as much as you could make. To do that, I was working from about seven in the morning until about 10 at night.

My father is a hairdresser and I used to help in his shop after school. I always got the most tips. I realised very early that when I'd brush the hair off the customer's back with a bigger smile than the other kids, I got tips. So I was about eight when I became aware that if you serve people well and make them happy, you'll be rewarded. Also when I was about that age an American came to our little village of Batroun, in Lebanon. Somebody said the man had seven hairdressing shops. I knew then that I would have more, although my father had just the one shop.

My father came to Australia the year before I did, and I came a year before mum. He had to establish a house and see if this was the right place to live for the rest of our lives. It was lucky that we came here and not Peru. My father's father lived in Australia and my mother's father was in Peru, so there was a choice of where to go. We chose Australia, because my father used to fight with his in-laws.

It is no big deal for Lebanese to migrate, they're nomads. There are more Lebanese living outside Lebanon than in it, and that's before the trouble started there. It's a small country, it has a lot of ambitious people and they just have to get out.

My father set up a little shop in South Australia, doing hairdressing, so the whole family moved to Adelaide. There were my parents, myself, and five sisters. One sister worked with me when I first started hairdressing on my own, then she left and got married. Another sister has been with me for the last 10 years. She left for a while, went to Sydney, and then came back. We're good friends, we get on very well, we help one another, there's not an ounce of jealousy, and there is an absolute trust. That's very special. I have confided in my sister so much, it's a fantastic relationship. My dad is terrific, too. Once, when I was short a couple of thousand dollars, I wrote him a letter. In those days it was a lot of money, especially to someone who doesn't have a lot, but he sent it to keep my shop going. I don't think he would have thought my business would turn into this, but one thing I admire him for is when I needed it, he sent that $2,000.

When I came to Brisbane I knew the city would suit his health and lifestyle, so I suggested he come and maybe settle here. He came up, had a look, and liked it. My mum and dad had split so he moved here, got a nice shop, and he's happy. I see him a fair bit.

I was about 17 when I came to Australia. I had three years of boarding school at Marist Brothers just before we left, and although I never really wanted to go to school here my grandparents wanted me to be a doctor, because it was a status symbol to have a doctor in the family. They thought I might be the one. But I was educated in French and it would have meant wasting another two years to learn everything in English, so instead of going to university I went into hairdressing, which was very natural to me. As a kid I'd helped dad roll perms, clean up the rods and wash the hair, so hair was never foreign to me. I don't even remember learning hairdressing, to be honest, it was such a gentle transition.

My dad was happy to see me snipping at hair, so I did an apprenticeship with him in Adelaide. I began wondering how I could make some more money, so I thought, where else could you cut hair except in the shop? I was only an apprentice, earning maybe 12 pounds a week, so how else could I make money? I couldn't cut hair at home, because dad would hang me. He'd say the customers should come to the shop and have a haircut. The hospital seemed a very good idea. It was logical, there were a lot of people there, and they would want their hair done. I rang up to see if I could come and cut hair and they said yes. I got on well with them and used to earn about two bob a haircut, although I wasn't speaking English when I first came to Australia. Monday, Tuesday and Thursday nights I went to night school to learn English.

Wednesday afternoons I used to go to the hospital and cut hair, and I got so good that they asked if I would come Saturday afternoon as well. Sure. Then they said, 'Look, we want to have a meeting', and I thought, Jesus, they're going to sack me. Why would they want to sack me? I've never done anything silly. We had the meeting and they said, 'Look, you're making so many people happy, would you please come in and work Sunday as well?' I said, 'You don't have to beg me to come, I'd be delighted. You know, I'm in business', though I wasn't really in business then, I was still an apprentice. So I started cutting everybody's hair in the hospital Wednesday afternoon, Saturday afternoon, and all day Sunday. I did that for about three years.

To me the money was big, because it was equal to my wages and I could put it away. The way I used to see it, it was money I got for nothing. It was money I didn't need to spend, so I hung onto it for my future. That was when I finished working with my dad. We were

Right, Stefan Ackerie as a young
boy in Lebanon. Below, with his
youngest son, Mickey Ackerie

different, he wanted to do things certain ways and I wanted to do them other ways. I had no right to try to change my dad, so I left and started my own little shop in Adelaide. I was 20. The shop was very nice-looking, everybody liked it. It was all blonde wood with a pink and grey floor, which were Elvis Presley's colours. To have a pink floor then was unheard-of.

You know, it doesn't matter how good you are, if your place doesn't look right no-one will have anything to do with it. But then I said, 'Hey, this isn't me, I'm not going to hang around here all my life', so I said to my mother, 'I'm going to sell the shop'. She said, 'You'll do what?' and I said, 'I'm leaving'. She started crying, who's going to look after you, who's going to wash your clothes, who's going to do this and that. It was a nightmare trying to leave my mother. I said, 'I'm a big boy now, I've been that for a long time'. But no-one would buy my shop. They were scared that when I left it, people who came a long way to have their hair done by me wouldn't come anymore. Finally I almost gave it away, just to get away from it.

I had that shop for two years, then I went to Melbourne and worked for the biggest hairdressing chain in Australia at that time. I was there for about a year and then I went to Sydney. In those days, unless you'd worked in Sydney you were nothing. If you wanted to make the big-time, you had to say Stefan of Sydney. Stefan of Melbourne, Adelaide or Brisbane was nothing. Stefan of Sydney, wow, everybody looked. When I got to Sydney I couldn't believe my eyes. The hairdressing was nowhere near as good as Adelaide hairdressing. Adelaide is small, but there are a lot of Italians in hairdressing and it is very competitive, they are all good. Competition improves the breed, you know. But to please the people you had to come from Sydney or be trained there, so I spent time in Sydney.

Then the company I worked for in Melbourne said they needed someone in Brisbane badly and would I go. I always wanted to see Brisbane so I said okay, but I could only go up after two or three months. My ambition was to sell my shop in Adelaide, travel Australia, then go overseas, come back, and settle down somewhere. I had a very clear goal. I'd done Adelaide, Melbourne, Sydney, so now Brisbane was logical. I came to Brisbane, worked for about four or five months, and took the shop from $400 to $820 per week. It was a shop in the main street, same staff, but I doubled the taking.

It's so simple, but everyone wants to make it so complex. That's the amazing thing. It's just the same as when I brushed the hair off people's backs in the shop when I was a kid. I would predict then how much of a tip I was going to make. The more I smiled and the more I looked after the person, the better tip I got. Of course, you must have a team of people you can work with. We now have in excess of 800 staff and I venture to say they are all beautiful people. They understand our principle and our philosophy, although lately I feel a bit frustrated because I haven't had the chance to catch up with all of them. I have a conference starting next week, a two or three-day seminar, just to get to know one another again and refresh our thoughts and ideas about what makes things work.

Just plain treating people well is the basis of it, but you must be honest. You can't jump up and down and say, 'Hey, I think you're terrific', when they know damn well that whatever you are complimenting isn't terrific. It is so fake to tell someone it's nice when it isn't.

At the Brisbane shop, they promised me that for every 100 pounds I raised the weekly take, I'd get five pounds. I was getting a lousy salary but I had come to Brisbane just to see Brisbane. I put the shop in the high-profit league and the guy said, 'Oh, you're getting good money now, you're getting more than I am'. I said, 'That's not the point. The deal we made was for every 100 pounds, I'd get five.' Then he said, 'We'll pay you', but I had already lost respect for him. It was time to move, anyway.

That was when I went to Longreach and ran the shop there. When the word got out on the bush telegraph and the shop did well, I thought, maybe it's time to start my thing. I went to a bank manager in Brisbane and said, 'I want to start a chain of business shops. Where do you think is the best place to start?' He said, 'Maryborough. There's more money in Maryborough than anywhere else in Australia.'

So we started the shop in Maryborough. Leather chairs, beautiful shop. They'd stand in the door and say, 'How much for a haircut?' I'd say, 'Six and six', and they'd say, 'I can get it for five and six down the road'. I'd say, 'Then you'd better go down the road', and they did. They kept going down the road for about three months, so I said, hang on a minute, this is not business, it's not working. I'd better change my tune. I'd been thinking about that all weekend. Monday morning, when a lady came in and said, 'How much?' I said, 'Whatever you want to pay. Just come in.' I started doing her hair almost for free for three or four weeks. Then people started to see how good the work was and it got going.

At first I couldn't understand why they didn't like the leather chairs, the marble, and all this magnificent luxury, but it wasn't important to them. I learnt a big lesson there. I learnt that it is easy to go broke, and that not only do you have to be good but you have to fulfil the need, and the need varies a lot. And it is no different now than it was 10 years ago. The combination was more than a nice shop, a fancy sports car and good hairdressing. It needed one more dimension and I learnt that lesson in Maryborough. To this day we would be the best value hairdressers in Australia. Even though the shops look nice and the girls are nice and the products we use are of a very high standard, it still has to be competitive. I owe that to Maryborough.

After about three or four months the shop became busy. I had about seven staff and I thought, now I can leave it alone. So I went looking for another place. I went into Rocky (Rockhampton), didn't like what I saw there, so I went into Mackay. I'd never been there before, and as I was leaving this fellow said he knew where there was a beautiful shop. It was a restaurant upstairs but I could see that it could be a beautiful hairdressing shop. The fellow who had shown me the place said, 'You're mad, it's upstairs, it's out of the way'. I said, 'The worst is that everyone will tell everyone'.

The chain has just kept growing. I enjoyed Mackay so much I stayed there for nearly two years. It's got the harbour and the reef; I fell in love with Mackay, as it were. In Mackay I had the biggest shop I ever had in Queensland, bigger than anything in Brisbane, and yet it was a country town. The staff of 27 were dressed up nicely and they stood out. I was 25 years old at this stage.

But the bank manager had given me terrible advice, because if there's one place you don't start a business, it's Maryborough. Once I realised that everybody can't have a chain in the one place, Queensland made sense. I don't think I worked very hard or long hours, because when you enjoy what you are doing it's not like that. When you like it, it's not hard. It's only when you are not interested that the energy becomes hard to generate.

I've had a very good social life, which has never been hampered by work. I don't need toys to enjoy my social life, I'm happy to play golf or go water-skiing. My handicap in golf runs from, say, between 10 and 13. I'm also a kung fu black belt. The difference between kung fu and karate is that kung fu is Chinese and karate is Japanese. I hadn't studied kung fu in Malcolm Sue's school prior to the episode in Long-reach. I wish I'd known then what I know now; it would have been quick and painless. I play golf, a lot of people play golf, I race boats, a lot of people race boats, I fly aeroplanes, a lot of people fly aeroplanes. I see myself as very normal, very ordinary. It's just that I have these things together, and they work.

Back to business, I always knew I'd be setting up in Brisbane but I wasn't going to come until I was ready. Then a rep came and said, 'There's a shop in Brisbane which will go broke next week. If you want to buy it, there's a chance.' It was a big shop, in the main street. I said I could make that work. This was a Monday. I moved in Saturday and the staff were in chaos.

I said to them, 'Those who like what I plan to do are welcome to stay. Those who don't, let's split now and split nice and clean, instead of dirty.' The shop became an instant success and grew up to nearly 60 staff. It was an unbelievable jump. My goal was never money — it was always growth and the enjoyment of the work.

Everybody tells you about the stump you can't jump, but because you're ignorant you just think you can do it. Of course, you have lots of financial crises on the way because some things happen that are beyond your control, and your inexperience can get you into a lot of trouble. It's amazing how you can do dumb things, but as long as you don't do too many at one time it's all right.

For example, in 1970 the wig industry collapsed in front of my eyes. I had about one-quarter of a million dollars worth of wigs that I was committed to purchasing from the Bank of America. In 1970, that was a lot of money. I had to withstand that loss and I could very easily have fallen out with the bank, but that would have tarnished my name. One very special thing for me has always been my name. The bankers sang out, bankruptcy is so easy. No way; I paid them every single cent.

Then I started big-timing, playing the stock market. It was like the real estate boom on the Gold Coast, it didn't matter what you bought, you sold it for more the following day. I said, how long as this been going on? By then I guess I was starting to get sick of hairdressing. I thought I'd go big-time, so I said to the broker, 'I'm going overseas for a month or so. Things are very hot. Why don't I clean up everything and when I come back, I can start again?'

I had 500 Poseidon shares at $500 each, but when I rang up from Japan they had gone from $480 to $435 to $250. By the time I got back the following day they were at about $290 and everyone was in a state of shock. Some people were saying, don't worry about it, they'll go up to $800. We have proof they're worth such and such, the miners have such and such in the ground, so I thought, they'll be all right. At $90, hang on a minute, now you're starting to think of survival. I let half of them go at $90 and then the other half a week later, at $75. Quite often, I get into conversation with people who let their Poseidon shares go at $2. But I survived that and learnt not to play the stock market ever again. I never got caught in speculating on the property boom on the Gold Coast and I would have been susceptible to that. I could have signed anything but didn't; maybe I'd learned from the Poseidon boom/collapse.

I once asked a real estate investor, 'How the hell do you guys not get caught by such collapses? Are you so smart?' He said, 'It happens so slowly. You guys don't get in it until the last minute but we buy the land five years before. We submit plans two years ahead, we start the building for a year or two, and if it turns around the last year we can hardly be blamed.' It makes sense, doesn't it? So I learned not to get carried away too much, although it is my make-up to get carried away and it's very hard to fight my natural instinct.

Once the Brisbane shop took off, I could see the idea of a chain becoming a reality. I went to America in 1969 and could see shopping centres coming in around New York. I said hey, I'm going to get into one of those here. To do that you had to have a good name, you had to be known, you had to be clean. In those days the odd shopping centre went up in Australia and everyone wanted to be in it, but I got clever enough to make them want me. I did that by having the best shop in town, the best image for hairdressing, no drama, no complaints.

That's when I went from about one to seven shops, the first big turn-around in my career. The thought that came all the time was that I wanted to do well. I now have 60 salons, six restaurants, and as I said a total staff of about 800.

The biggest problem I had, and the biggest problem everybody has on the whole, is this: in a conversation, one person may be going this way, one may be going that way, and they wonder why they never meet. It's interesting for me to listen to people talking. I'll notice that one meant something, the other meant something else, and their minds never met. This started to become a problem when I got to about 90 staff. I couldn't handle it any more, it was so frustrating, but I used to think it wasn't me. I thought, now I know why people can't have lots of staff, because the staff are so much trouble. So I had to learn to overcome the problem and this is when the second major turn-around in my career happened.

I learnt how to master communication, though the word wasn't used then. I learnt that when I am saying something to someone, make sure we both know what it is that we're talking about. Say a girl comes in and says she wants to be a hairdresser. I tell her, 'To be a hairdresser you need to be efficient, you need to work, you need to be on time, you need to be a nice person, sincere, and please your clients'. She says, 'What's all this? I want to be glamorous and not do much work and tell everyone at the parties that I'm a ladies' hairdresser.' She doesn't really want to be a hairdresser, she should perhaps be a model. By such communication we eliminated the big turn-around, and now I have a very high rate of success with my staff. Among 350 apprentices I've had incidences with only three. I know some shops with staffs of 10 which can have that amount of troubles. It has to go back to basics. Everything is basic. Every time a situation becomes confusing, it's being turned into something which it isn't.

Then you have to teach the girls to manage. Today, management is very responsible for the bad things they do to their staff. Management must give their staff a clear direction. If the management is unfair, it's like throwing a kid into business or throwing the lamb to the wolves, the staff don't know what they are doing. They can't succeed and the minute they don't succeed they feel awful. When they feel awful they don't succeed, it's a Catch 22, so the management is responsible to guide their people.

I remember one girl we had who was a third-year apprentice. When the shop she was in closed she had to leave, because after three years she still couldn't do anything. I sat down and had a staff meeting with her, and within three months that girl was a senior hairdresser. Maybe it's a skill or a gift I have, an awareness of what is needed.

I went to my first management seminar when I was about 32, and by that time I already had 90 staff. When you have 1,000 people and they're all nice people it's easy, but if you have 10 people and they're rebellious it's hard. I guess I've always been aware of that. Another thing too: not everybody likes you. Some people don't want to work with you. I'm lucky, that trouble has now become minimised, because before we start, if they don't like what we stand for we part, and there are no hard feelings. Once I worked out these problems it was obvious that I had to have an office, a nerve centre. I always believed in good headquarters.

I have been looking for a man for a long time to be our administrator, and I think I've just found him. As soon as he starts I'll be free to go back to the salons. That's where I'm happiest. I needed to learn the administration side, I needed to learn a lot of things, but I've done that now. There's a fantastic conference room in the head office and that's where I'll operate from, training the kids every day, hands and heads. Other times I will be going into the salons. That's where I'm best, that's where I contribute the most.

I became conscious of the fact that for a company to be successful it needs a good nerve centre, a good heart, a good base, and then I realised that's the office. Again, nothing develops overnight. There is a fantastic administration centre there, which is now very congested and small. I've reached another peak but I don't want to expand yet, because sometimes by expanding you get fat, and I'm in the process of getting lean again. It's very easy to surround yourself with too many toys. I want to make the business more efficient.

I am very conscious now of developing. When people start out to be hairdressers, they think it's just haircuts. Today it's communications, serving people well, it is so complex, a lot more than just cutting hair. I want to put a lot of effort into that, it's my next gaol, to prepare the staff, really prepare them well.

Getting to this point was hard, I made a lot of mistakes. When you're desperate you'll tolerate someone who you wouldn't otherwise tolerate. I would rather lose 10 people than lead them on. When people don't fit they cause a mess. My staff must get on with one another. As soon as one doesn't, we let them go.

It reminds me of the story about this fellow who comes into a town in the old days, when towns used to have a wall around them. He knocks on the gate, says, 'I want to come in', and the gatekeeper asks, 'What are the people like in your town?' The fellow says, 'They're awful, terrible people, that's why I want to leave'. The gatekeeper says, 'Mate, you'd better keep going, because the people here are the same'. At the next town the fellow knocks on the door, and when the gatekeeper asks, 'What are the people like in your town?' he says, 'Beautiful people, everybody is nice'. The gatekeeper says, 'Come in, because the people here will be the same'. The guy at the gate is the equivalent of today's Immigration Department who question you about what the people were like in the place you just left.

You see a girl who's rebellious and you ask, 'What is the manageress like?' She says, 'She's terrible'. Every manageress isn't perfect, but then she's not likely to be terrible either. When a girl doesn't get on with a group of people, most times it's her problem.

The large number of applicants we get for a job is really an awful thing, but at the same time it's a compliment. It makes me feel sad, though. It's very common for us to get 4,000 to 5,000 applications. Now, there are fors and againsts. A lot of people are starting to see no sense in applying, because they believe they can't get a job here. That's not always good, so now we have to change this image. It's like a girl that 5,000 guys are trying to take home tonight. Would you attempt to take her out?

The thing that I hate to see happen to young people is that they are so unprepared about the position. 'What would you like to do?' I ask. 'Anything!' they say. 'There isn't an anything company. You want to be a hairdresser? Why?' 'My mum said it would be good'. Our interviewing processes are a lot better nowadays, more fair to them. Before we start we tell them that it's quite obvious we can't put them all on, and it's quite obvious some of them aren't ready. I try to get them to experience a good feeling in the conference, so that they are leaving in a positive and not a negative frame of mind. We make the deal before we start that no-one is going to get hurt out of this, it's quite obvious I can't put them all on. We see that they all accept that and we have a nice little chat, and they normally go to dinner at Jo Jo's, have a bottle of champagne, a free hairdo, and everyone is happy, so they leave without a kick. My grandfather said, 'Do good and throw it in the sea. You never know when you are going to drown and it will save you'. I find it is easier to leave people feeling good than otherwise. It requires more effort but it's still easier.

I learnt such things by trial and error and pain, lots and lots of pain. For someone to succeed, one of the things that is very necessary is that your threshold of pain must be high. But I've never really cared; if my business hadn't worked, I wouldn't have cared.

Part of the popularity of my salons comes from the fact that 20 years ago we started our television programs. At first, the station management said, 'This man wants to talk about hair on TV', and they wouldn't cop it. I took the risk of having pilot tapes privately done to show them what I could do and how I would do it. Then they said they'd be happy to talk to me, and next thing they accepted. Public response was almost unbelievable. After the program, the phone wouldn't stop ringing for about an hour-and-a-half. This went on until we did the Christmas Party program, which is put together by our staff.

My restaurants began next to a hairdressing shop we had upstairs in the heart of Brisbane, on the corner of Queen and Albert Streets. It was a bridal shop, 3,500 feet of space, but it wouldn't work. It was upstairs and people wouldn't go up. We used to have our monthly party there, then the area became too small because it could hold only about 200 people. There was a junk shop up there and when that company went bust I thought, hey, if I took this whole area over and

Above, Stefan and his first sportscar in Adelaide. Below, with sister Josie

had a coffee shop here, a nice coffee shop, we could have sandwiches here with our clients.

I'd always wanted to run a restaurant. The owners were convinced they were going to rent the space to some more junk shops, but I thought, that will be bad, like last time when they'd had signs everywhere, 'We have the right to search your bags'. Here are all these beautiful people coming up to have their hair done and walking through and seeing these ugly signs. I thought, I'll take the space.

Taking it was one thing, but what the hell was I going to do with it? I thought, everybody likes Lebanese food, everybody likes Chinese food, everybody likes cake and coffee, everybody likes good cappucino. If I put them all together and do them well, it must work. I really could see it as it is now. It took 18 months, because we had to get the decoration right, but it was an instant success.

The hairdressing shop was still there but people said, 'What are you doing with a hairdressing shop in the middle of the restaurant?' I said, 'I'll never close down the hairdressing shop', but then I said to the guys I worked with, 'Rip it out and if I come back here and say don't rip it out, tell me to get lost. Better still, come in tonight at one o'clock in the morning and rip it out.' They did, it was Thursday, and on Friday at 12.30 p.m. the restaurant was full.

For the next Jo Jo's, at Southport, we spent about $100,000 on a revamp. There is a lovely little bar and a lovely barbecue area for steak, fish and prawns. We call the place Jo Jo's after my sister Josie. We used to call her Jo, and when we got mad at her we'd call her Jo Jo. She's in charge of whatever she wants to be in charge of. At the moment she's happy with the restaurants, but believe it or not her brain is so good that she's wasted in the restaurants. As soon as the novelty wears off I'm hoping she will decide to go back to hairdressing.

The restaurants and hairdressing salons complement one another, in a way. They're not really different, it's just back to the same principle again, making people feel nice, serving people. I mean, everybody can't cook good food. If you are going to take short-cuts with the ingredients, it isn't very easy to make good food.

When I went into the Sydney hairdressing market and got involved with Jo Jo's, everybody said, 'You're mad, you've done two major things at one time'. Of the six Jo Jo's that I have I would like to relinquish three of them, and I think I've just sold one. The Jo Jo concept again has to be right. The Jo Jo's in town is right, the one downstairs and the one on the Coast are right. The ones in the suburbs will be fantastic businesses for somebody, but the hours for food in shopping centres are very short, from 10 to 12 and then 12 to two and it's gone. That doesn't suit the Jo Jo's system of food, which needs a lot of people. Unless the food turns over it doesn't stay fresh and the concept doesn't work. I think there should be a Jo Jo's in every city in Australia, in the heart of the town. The concept should be repeated six times in Australia. But the new buyers are also welcome to use the name Jo Jo's if they want to.

My Sydney hairdressing venture had to have a little rest. I always knew that to make it in Sydney you had to have the best shop, and our shop in Centrepoint is now accepted as the best, you can't dispute it. It's the biggest, the nicest, it's luxurious, a shop that cost our company in excess of $500,000. There aren't hairdressing shops in the world that cost anything like that. You've got to believe in something to put in that kind of commitment. This shop is now working very well, with a fantastic team of people. I now intend to live in Sydney two to three days a week and develop business, because the Jo Jo's operation is running fantastically. So it hasn't been too silly doing what I've done in Sydney, because it has now given me the team and the base. When you say Stefan's in Sydney, everybody knows what it stands for.

My plan is to spend $1 million in Sydney this year and buy 10 shops. You can see the media potential. Advertising is important and advertising in Sydney, I don't have to tell you, is very expensive. But that's my plan for Sydney this year and I look forward to doing it. I had lots of real estate but now I'm bored with it. I'll just get rid of that. Perhaps I'll put all my money back into hair.

When I went to Sydney everybody came to see Stefan, and I'll never forget a reporter saying to me, 'What is the latest for autumn, and what's the latest in Paris?' I said, 'Do you really think that the French are so clever that they could produce something for autumn, for spring, for summer, for winter? Don't you think it would be far more intelligent for you to think of the communication process, understanding your type of hair, learning to handle it? Wouldn't that be the most essential part of a successful hairstyle, instead of what happens to be the latest in Paris in autumn?' She said, 'No-one has ever had the cheek to tell me that. But it's true, isn't it?'

I used to go overseas a lot. As I was growing and becoming a name, people used to say, 'What's the latest, what's the latest?' I used to find it hard to tell them what the latest was, because there's no such thing in hair. Surely there is an evolution that takes place, but punk, for instance, didn't happen in one week. It took years. Nothing develops in one spring, autumn or winter, either.

One day, I was coming back from Paris and I could see that there was nothing new, but how dare I tell the public that? The only thing new was that the French woman wasn't sitting in the chair having her hair tizzed every week anymore. It was now going to be natural work, because people could no longer afford to sit in the chair for so long and so regularly. The cost of living had become so high they couldn't have their hair done as often now. So this was an opportunity to tell people what I really wanted to tell them: that things don't change over-night and that I've always liked natural work, I've never liked the tizzy work. Twenty years ago I was doing what they are doing today. So the newest thing from Paris was that you don't go to the hairdresser as often any more, because the French woman is now going to work, like the French man. Therefore we have natural hairstyles that you can do at home. It makes sense.

I've never been one to follow what London or New York or Paris says, I've been one to do what is best for you. How is the latest in Paris going to influence your life when you live in bloody Coogee? The latest in Paris for a trendy little blonde model is to go into the bar and get pissed every night, with her hair messed up all over her face. Here, a wife is going to look after two kids, waiting for her husband to come home. How is Paris relevant? For years I was forced into that mould, I resented it and was so happy when I could break out. I'll always remember that reporter in Sydney, she couldn't believe what I was saying, but it was true.

I think everything I do is real. If you are a high-fashion person, I will take care of you as well as anybody, and I'll be reliable and consis-tent. If you are a nice, lovely person who has five kids and you want something you can handle, I'll also take care of you, because I can do that very well. What I try to do is fit the square peg into the square hole, fit the game.

My formula for success it to be honest and fair, to yourself and to the people. You can't be fair to other people only, you must be fair to yourself. You must have good staff and you must always honour what you say you are going to do. If you say to a person that you are going to do something and that person doesn't like that, then you must do something fair about it.

On a plane once I sat next to this guy who had a pump in his hands. I said, 'What the hell is that thing?' and he said, 'It's a pump'. Really broad accent, beautiful accent. I said, 'I know it's a pump but what do you do with it?' and he said, 'I pump enthusiasm'. He started pumping and said, 'Imagine that I just put this in a 1,000-foot well and I'm pumping, pumping, pumping. Everybody quits before the water comes out, they think there's nothing there, but I keep pumping until it comes out.'

So many people quit just before it is going to work for them. It could be a 1,000-foot well or a 20-foot well, I don't know what their well is like. Yesterday I was in a boat race and this guy didn't want to go out in his 16-footer. He said, 'Why don't you go out in my 16-footer?' and I said, 'I don't want to, I want to go out in my 36-footer'. Everybody chooses their well. If you happen to choose one that's deep, then you have a lot of pumping to keep doing.

There's a story that is supposedly true about a guy who bought a gold mine. He dug and dug, found nothing, and finally sold the mine. The bloke who came in dug another two feet and found the greatest gold reef in the history of mining. Motivators are full of these stories. Whether they are true or not I don't know, but I do know a lot of people quit just before they make it. I'm lucky. Because I've got a very high threshold of pain, I don't quit.

Success makes me feel good about myself, it makes my mother happy. I am very fortunate to know what I'm doing. Just to be able to fill your day so well is fantastic. I'm never, ever bored. I also understand that a loss of privacy is the price that you pay when you become known. If I didn't want that then I shouldn't have done what I've done. I'm very fortunate that people accept me.

I respect success, I don't abuse it. It is not something that belongs to you forever. If you don't treat it with respect you could lose it just as quickly as you got it. Don't take any success for granted. You see so many politicians and great people who abuse that which made them successful. It doesn't take them long to lose success, does it?

If I felt I could be really, truly useful in politics, I'd think about it, but I'm not going to sit on the backbenches and argue and carry on like a lunatic for ten years. In and out of politics, I admire lots of people. I admire the good sense and quickness of Bobby Mathers, he's a shoe retailer. He's been a critic and a friend, a good, fair, positive critic. I admire Keith Williams's determination, I admire our Premier, I think Bob Hawke has been an inspiration, though they're hassling and distracting him too much now, which is a pity. I get a very positive feeling for athletes, because their threshold of pain is not the same as business pain. The pain in business is having lunch, whereas the pain in breaking half a dozen tiles with your hand is real pain. My biggest thrill was to break six tiles, and the day I did that I don't think I could have walked in the door, my head was so big. I've always had a lot of respect for athletes and for martial arts masters. Malcolm Sue, for example, is a small person in size but a big person in heart. He's like a leopard. There are a lot of martial artists who are masters and their threshold of pain is enormous.

Australia is the lucky country and I don't know what I've done to deserve living here, but whatever it is I will not abuse it. I think it's a fantastic place. However, I would like to see the government put more money into training people, instead of giving people money to waste and squander. A lot of young people don't really want to go off the track but they don't know how to get on the track. I think if you give somebody money and you don't teach them how to use it, it's very bad. I would much rather see these people earn their money, I would much rather see them being educated and trained to cope with society off their own bat, not with handouts. A quote we use at work is, 'Teach people how to fish and you feed them for life. Give them a fish and you feed them for one day.'

We have a lot of wasteland here, land that is not producing anything. We have to become competitive in marketing what we have and the things we have are natural resources. Perhaps one day we can become a major supplier of grain or sugar or meat and dairy products, but at the moment we are so inefficient in producing that we are not competitive. I would love to see everybody pulling together to become competitive, because everybody's standard of living would then improve. I'd like to see business leaders and leaders of all types communicating, because only by communicating better are they going to utilise what they have. It is unfair to see ships waiting outside Sydney for days on end. It is unfair to everybody, and I think that it happens because of bad communication, bad guidance. The Australian man is very decent, very gutsy, very ordinary, and by ordinary I mean there is no bullshit about him — what you see is what you get. People don't want to do the wrong thing and it's so much easier to do the right thing, but at the moment there seems to be confusion. I look forward to the day when this disappears.

I feel we have a lot to learn from Japanese workers. They believe in constant improvement and they're proud of their work, their companies, their country. So are we, but perhaps we can be a bit more proud of our workmanship and understand better what competition is. We can't live anymore without the world market, because we can't buy or use all our own products. Look around, everything we have on this table is imported.

Australia is very much Americanised. Some people take offence at that but I wouldn't. I think if you can play tennis as well as Jimmy Connors or John McEnroe, it's nothing to be embarrassed about. America is the greatest country on the face of this earth. If we can be going on a similar path or we can be compared to it, that's a compliment to Australia. Look at the boats, the lakes, the lovely homes, the cars. That's the American dream coming here now. We speak the same language, we have a similar heritage. What makes me laugh here is when they talk about New Australians. Everybody in this country is a New Australian. That really breaks me up. Americans are aware that the different cultures mixed together make one better culture but some people here don't understand that, and yet their heritage is all foreign. Americans and Australians come from all over the world, there is similarity in the size of the countries, both produce the raw materials of grain and other food, so the techniques that have worked in America must work here.

As to making my own techniques work, I would now like to make Stefan's succeed in Sydney, and after that I'll decide about the rest of Australia. I'm not going to go into every city in Australia just so I can say there's a Stefan's in every city. That ego thing has gone. It's more real now, more interesting. I have done a good job in Queensland, though it's not half-done, and I'm represented in every major shopping centre in the state. Now I'd like to achieve that kind of thing in Sydney.

Meanwhile, for every one of those people who gives you the tall poppy treatment, there are 99 who give you the positive treatment. The tall poppy is a syndrome that perhaps will disappear one day. I think it starts with people who are a little bit jealous. They haven't succeeded themselves; you never hear successful people gossiping. I have a little saying for that: 'The gossip people indulge in is a reflection of their inner selves'. I always feel sorry that they are wasting energy instead of seeing ways to succeed, because they are so convinced that they're not going to succeed. That's their problem — it's a pity.

The other day I heard the Premier making a speech at the opening of a new building. He said the developers deserve a gold medal, they've taken a derelict area and turned it into a magnificent complex, but tomorrow morning you won't see anything about it in the news. If someone were to run over someone else, then it would be all over the news. If a guy wins a race tomorrow, it will be all over the news, and yet this is a race but we don't hear about it. In this country, if someone succeeds he is supposed to have made his money by some devious means. If somebody does something exceptional, you don't hear about it. It is a pity but it's changing.

Actually I don't even know what kind of millions I have. Money hasn't ever really interested me and it probably never will. I get my high from seeing people happily doing business with me, to see my staff happy from achieving. Naturally if you do all that, then money comes also.

Unfortunately, my marriage is one thing that didn't work. I've been divorced for about 10 years, after eight years of marriage. I don't blame the failure on the business. I think if the marriage is working and is a happy thing, then the business contributes, it makes the marriage closer. If the marriage is not working, what could be worse than for some guy to be home at five o'clock, nagging his wife, when he could have been there at 10 o'clock, nagging her?

Having a full-time partner who you get on well with is the ultimate thing, but to have a partner you don't get on well with is the opposite to the ultimate. The support I get from my sister is wonderful, she's a friend, but that doesn't fulfil the role of someone you want to be married to or live with. But you can't force that either, and unless that happens right it is better not to happen. I guess you develop a freedom, and when you're travelling as much as I do you don't want to hurt anybody. You are more cautious, you don't want it to not work.

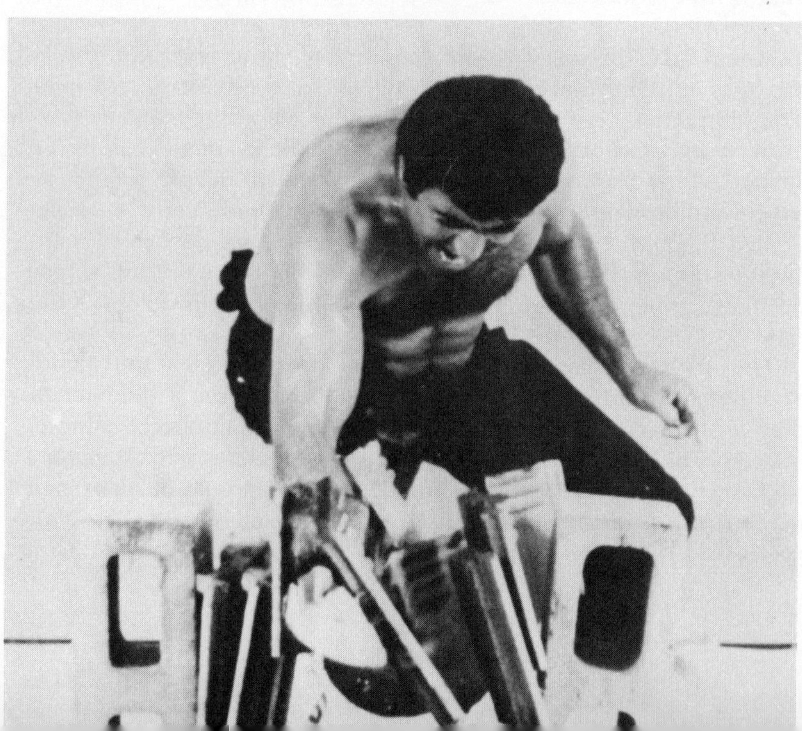

My goals now are more personal. I would like to do well in the off-shore speedboat racing championships. To finish up with the best boat in Australia is a personal goal. I'd also like to guide my children. The next three years are very important, that I don't let them take one road instead of another. The peer pressures on them petrify me. If you can protect your kids until about 16 or 17 then it won't be a problem, because they start to know right from wrong. So my goals have changed a lot, although, of course, one goal is to keep my business going as well as it is and spend more time with the staff.

I wanted to become a pilot and became one. That was a major goal for me, because flying a twin-engine aeroplane when you are a hairdresser is different. It's like giving some scissors to a Qantas pilot and saying, 'Here, go and cut hair'. That was a major goal, but my goals now are my work and my children. I don't like goals that aren't realistic. For the next two years, that's what I'd like to do. My motivation now is to see what I'm doing work.

Should some young kids read this, I'd like them to understand how special they are, understand the resources and energy they have. A typical example is, a girl goes home and her mother wants help. The girl says, 'Can't you see I've been working all day? I'm tired, I can't move.' Then the phone rings, the girl gets an offer to go out, and she's out until four o'clock in the morning. All of a sudden, she's not tired. We need to encourage kids to use that kind of energy for something that guides them into their own destiny, instead of wasting their energy or using it the wrong way.

And if they want to become a success, they must learn a skill. Then, don't give up on it, stick with it until you reach a level that's decent. And don't think you are doing people a favour when you do business with them. I'm not doing you a favour today, you're not doing me a favour. We both want to do business with one another, so let's do it nicely and be as friendly as possible to one another.

If girls who serve behind counters resent serving, if they behave as though they resent people, get out and don't serve. If you want to serve, feel lucky that you have someone to serve. That's the only way to become a success. A doctor serves people, a politician serves people, an aeroplane pilot serves people. Don't forget that without people, business can't function.

Locanto

Millie Phillips

She was a woman alone in the Australian male world of
the 1960s. She was poorly educated, almost penniless,
divorced, and a mother of three young children. Astonishingly, Millie Phillips not only defied these obstacles to
design her own house, write a book, and become a real
estate and mining magnate, but she now declares it was
quite easy to make a fortune. In fact, she can't understand
why everyone doesn't do it.

One reason must be that most people simply aren't
blessed with her qualities. At once shrewd and caring, a
person who has balanced extraordinary business acumen
with sensitivity and a God-given instinct, Millie Phillips
flourished in a time when a woman doing a man's work
was considered little more than comic relief.

When she walked out on a bad marriage in 1960 with her
children tugging at her skirts, Millie figured there were only
two choices: street-walking, or taking on boarders, and as
the first option was unpalatable that only left the second.
Not many years down the track she was worth her first million, mostly in the accommodation business. Later, as head
of the International Mining Corporation, she fared equally
well in the volatile field of mining exploration. At one point
in the early 1970s, a nickel find boosted IMC shares from 10
cents to almost $10. Yet she has never sold a share in the
company, which is now sitting on substantial oil shale
deposits in Western Australia and Queensland, drilling for
oil in South Australia and exploring gold mining prospects
in Western Australia.

Today, although her private empire employs about 500
people, Millie Phillips remains unchanged. A down-to-
earth achiever, she is a living textbook of how to be an
indomitable spirit.

In answer to your question, yes, I possibly am the richest self-made woman in Australia. I arrived in this country in 1938, when it should have been mandatory for all Jews to leave Poland. My parents were small business people and their background was one of extreme hard work. I entered the work force at 15 and was married at 17. By age 18 I had my first business, and I have been in business ever since. Work and I have had lots of time to become old friends.

Actually the working for myself came in two sections. Firstly, I was a full business partner with my former husband, and during those years my only rest was to take three weeks off to have three children. I became involved in business when my parents wanted to get out of their shop in Sydney. They had a great deal of ancient stock that had sold well in the war years, but the war was over. My husband and I had saved the hard way, by sharing cigarettes, eating lunch in the park, and not going anywhere. He was very good at saving. Whatever money we had we gave my parents, and in exchange I had a shop filled with unsaleable stock. I was all of 18.

The shop was in Paddington, 310 Oxford Street, opposite The Regent. I turned it into a children's workshop, painted over the unpleasant colours, brightened and cleaned it up, and then got rid of the old stock. Among that stock were some Melanese women's bloomers, extra over-sized, which I had to turn into cash to make something else work. My husband wouldn't do it — he was above that sort of thing — so with two suitcases in hand I got on a tram, rattled down to Paddy's Market, and called out, 'Two and six a pair', or whatever. I felt about *that* big. Every so often, a kind man would help me lift these horribly heavy suitcases. Really, I felt slimy and small, but it had to be done.

In those days, of course, everything was sold in quota. We didn't have a quota in the shop because we had gone from one commodity to another. The people my father dealt with knew me, but I couldn't do business with his country mates the way my father did. I remember a time when I bought things in Gowings store in Market Street, and between Gowings and Paddington I could run a mark-up and make a profit by selling the goods in Paddington. Honestly, though, I didn't feel terribly happy about that.

I know you're interested in personal matters but I find that my marriage years were a time that I don't want to talk much about. It was a hard time, very unhappy and unpleasant, and it's all past anyway. When I left my former husband in 1960, I walked out with the children and literally the clothes we stood in. At that point, my eldest child was six and my youngest was 18 months old. The story of those years is part of a book I've written, which I'm told is very readable but unfortunately suffers from the fact that it's highly defamatory. It will be published one day, because sooner or later one of us is going to die.

There are few things which a woman with three tiny children can do, and to compound that problem I had very little training. One of the traditional options in such a circumstance, of course, is to take in boarders. I did that on a massive scale. I found a property which the Baptist Church wanted to sell. The arrangement we made was probably unique — I have never come across a similar situation since then, but it seemed ideal for me. The church officials wanted a 12-month deferred settlement, because the property they were selling was a girls' hostel and they needed time to relocate the girls.

That plan turned out to be a breather which didn't work for me, because by the time I was ready to take possession of the property, the money that I had expected to have from the partnership with my former husband was not available. To make matters worse, the government legislated against new borrowings in 1960, so I found myself in possession of a property that I couldn't afford to purchase. I had borrowed 3,000 pounds from my father as a deposit on the property, anticipating that the balance would come from first mortgages and the settlement of my own company's finances. Those hopes collapsed overnight and I was forced to enter into a most unfair, horrific financial settlement with my former husband. Because he had the advantages, I was taken to the cleaners. I have remained single and partnerless ever since then.

There's little need to discuss the bruising. I think we all experience similar pains in broken marriages and I've never been one to fuss over what I didn't have. The mess in which the children and I found ourselves was a challenge that had to be overcome, and our acute money shortage could only be resolved by acquiring funds. The gall of losing a nice home, comfortable income, good motor cars, fine clothes, furniture and so forth, had to be pushed aside, and my energies directed

*Right, passport photograph of
Millie Phillips, 1938. Below,
16 years old in 1946*

instead into planning a future that at the time seemed so impossible to attain, so far beyond my grasp, that it was only a daydream. At that time, I challenged myself to give the children a future that would be better than whatever they could have had during my marriage years. It was up to me to ensure that this dream became a reality.

That probably means I'm an optimist, because instead of looking at the misery, I strengthened my resolve and set myself a target to earn 100,000 pounds in 10 years. It did seem to be a ridiculous goal at the time, because I had a myriad of debts. To complete my purchase of the Baptist Church property, I found that the shortfall in funding could be made up by borrowing 500 pounds here, 600 pounds there, and so on. Meanwhile, the children were very unhappy, missing the environment they were used to. In any event, ironically enough and long before the 10 years were up, I had made my first million. Mind you, it helped that we decimalised!

I acquired property and motels, nursing homes and hotels. In 1967-68 I had a hotel in Darling Point which was doing a roaring R & R (rest and recreation) trade. The hotel was for non-commissioned soldiers, all of whom seemed to be about 18 or 19, no older than my son. When they arrived from Vietnam, the soldiers would tell each other, 'You have to stay at Mum Phillips's, it's the only place in Sydney'. They became like an extended family.

I used to organise parties for them, and as a result of one of those parties I came in contact with a guest who was involved in mineral exploration. We had a conversation which convinced me that mineral exploration in Australia was the most fascinating thing in the world. A large part of the country hadn't been mapped, and it seemed to me that the continent was big enough for Millie's name to be written on it somewhere. I decided to go into tin mining.

In my first venture, the tin had supposedly been found already and only had to be dug out of the ground. My associate was the extraction arm of the project and I was the cash arm. It was unsuccessful, but I had fallen in love with mineral exploration. I had come to the realisation that everything around us comes out of the earth, and that we know very little about this country that I love so much. There had to be a mine that Millie could find.

I went to Alan Voisey, who was Professor of Earth Science at Armidale before he went to Macquarie University, and said, 'How do I get into mineral exploration?' He said, 'I know a number of top geologists who can help you to find acreage'. Some were experts in Tasmania, others in Western Australia, and one was a metallurgist who had just returned from America. Eventually, I decided that I wanted to buy into the Prudhoe Bay exploration in Alaska, because it looked as though oil would be found there. I had my bank manager in Oxford Street ring the bank manager in Alaska. I heard the two of them talking about the investment, seemingly forever. At the time, I was too naive to realise how many millions would be needed to produce the oil. That investment didn't pay off either, but I was right: Prudhoe Bay did have oil.

A geologist who had grown up in Western Australia told me he used to stub his toes on nickel there. I employed a spotter who was the geologist's relative. The spotter, who lived in Western Australia near the town of Southern Cross, was to watch for relinquishments of areas, because Western Mining Corporation had huge slabs of land there, and by law a process of dilution must occur from time to time. His job was to notify me whenever the mining company was relinquishing supply. The purpose of relinquishment is to prevent vast tracts of land from being tied up by people who are not exploring that land. For instance, my company recently reduced by half the area we have near Ravenswood in Queensland, and our holdings at Mt Coolon are down to a bare minimum, which the government realises. At Mt Coolon we've spent a lot of money on a deposit of shale oil, which of course is not a viable energy source at present.

The team I assembled came up with mining targets, but I realised that I didn't have the money to support such massive projects. In 1969 I turned to the public by floating International Mining Corporation. We found nickel in 1970 and the company's shares went crazy. I didn't sell because I thought the whole market was mad, and it was. To sell would have been wrong, like taking candy from a baby. The high price of nickel disappeared when a strike in Canada was settled, and the price of my company's shares receded again, which we knew would happen sooner or later.

I floated another mineral exploration company, called Mt Hope, which came on the market at an inopportune time, so I absorbed it into IMC. I've continued to look for minerals and we did find the oil shale deposit in 1979-80. It looked very promising until the price of oil suddenly dropped considerably. We're now searching for gold. I feel I'm positioned not far from the mining success I would like to have. I'm unashamedly in love with the company's prospects. It's a very undercapitalised company and always has been, but it has survived since 1969 without yet finding a viable ore body. I haven't mined the market because I don't believe in that, but I will mine the ground

The delights of oil shale from Mt Coolon in 1981, before the price of oil dropped

when I find a deposit — and I still refuse to sell my stock until I have a viable deposit.

You want to know about the difficulties of being a businesswoman in the early days? I'll give you an example. Although during my married years I had been the active business partner, and although I elected to stay with the same bankers when I went out on my own (incidentally, they were the very bankers which my parents used and I'm still with them) I nevertheless found that it was suddenly impossible for me to raise money from the bank. Obviously the fact that I was a woman on my own was a severe handicap. I was exposed to indignities, because, let's face it, I was different, I had changed roles. Perhaps others saw this as a threatening situation. Remember, we're talking of a time that preceded Australia's divorce law reforms. In fact, I was among the first contingent of women who, as a result of five-year separations from their spouses, could receive divorces. I recall I used to laugh at the fact that it was so easy to marry and so difficult to become unmarried, and I was determined to remain single until they evened the score. I guess that's why I'm still single.

Another thing you should know about those days, in case anyone is silly enough to want to relive them, is that I wore blinkers. I suppose in many ways most of us who are successful continue to wear blinkers. My life was the children and work, there was no time for socialising. The luxuries of a relaxed young woman were not for me. I was very serious and determined to achieve the goals I had set.

Those who have read my manuscript, *Clouds of Glory*, tell me that I've led a hard life. Frankly, I can't see that at all. Of course, it would have been wonderful to have had an understanding adult partner instead of a man whose delight it was to attempt to show the children on every second weekend and half the school holidays how bad their mother was. Needless to say the richer I became, the more he resented my success, and my hapless children were the victims of his jealousies. When I left, I wanted nothing but a severance of our ties. I didn't ask for maintenance or alimony, but the court insisted that I accept maintenance, otherwise there could be no divorce. We settled on four pounds per child per week.

By the time of my divorce I was already worth a lot of money, yet it was mandatory for my father to stand in the witness box and undertake to care for my needs. I could have bought and sold my father probably 500 times over, but because I had refused alimony it was impossible for the court to give me a divorce unless a man undertook for my personal care. It was most humiliating. At the time — and I'm not sure about now — a woman with any abilities was not even treated as a second-class citizen. At best, she was a precocious child.

My consistent view is that a woman has no right to be supported if she wants to leave the marriage. Marriage is not a meal ticket. It should be a relationship that two independent, caring people want to continue. It should be possible for two adults to say, 'The marriage isn't working. You go your way, let me go mine, and for heaven's sake let's do nothing that will injure the children.' I suppose that's a dream which may one day become a reality.

At any rate, I was now divorced and I owned a number of properties, accommodating more than 200 people in my boarding houses and a further 180 people in my chain of nursing homes. I remember when I saw my first nursing home, I had been enormously pregnant, which I suppose accounted for what happened. It was a terrible place, dark and gloomy. The people sat huddled against the cold and the walls were dark grey. I was brought up to respect age, and it seemed to me that people should be allowed to grow old in a better place and with much more grace than this. I determined then and there that I would build a nursing home which would be what a nursing home should be.

In fact at that point I had already found just the property for such a home. It had been standing empty for about five years, but it wasn't zoned for the development purpose that I needed. I told the Council that I had bought the building and would let it decompose until it became the greatest white elephant in a very expensive district unless they changed the zoning. I did create a nursing home out of that building. It was fun but hard work, and one did not know what one was getting into.

On the day we opened, doctors and others came and said they couldn't get over the ambience. The walls were light-coloured, the bedspreads were white, the curtains were pretty, pictures were hung, and it looked like a home. Everyone said, 'My goodness, this is exactly what a nursing home should be like'. Nursing homes were my first love. I lost that particular business when I walked out of my marriage, but I wanted to go back to that field of endeavour.

Following my divorce, the second business I acquired after the Baptist Church property was financially very successful. It was a property owned by a company then known as Alliance Finance, who specialised in mortgages of possession. I acquired the property via the expediency of borrowing 1,000 pounds from my accountant to pay the legal and stamp duties. I was in business again, in a bigger boarding house. This building had the distinction of having been a motel, although its location, in Walker Street, North Sydney, was wrong for that use. I bought it for 75,000 pounds.

Years later I negotiated the purchase of the property next door, because I knew that rezonement was just down the track. However, there was a 'Catch 22', because this was when high-rise buildings were going up in North Sydney. The Council wouldn't approve my proposed development, so I took them to a land court that the State had established to overcome the impasse of Council imposing their own ideas on everybody. The case dragged out for a number of years but I did subsequently sell the property for $2 million. Today I guess the same profit would be $6-$8 million.

I suppose I was born with an independent soul. Of course, I know that I'm a woman and that my limitations are that of a short person, but in another sense I don't recognise that at all. I don't know that there is a difference between me and the six-foot male company director. That's what I found so frustrating when I was younger. When I wanted to communicate mind-to-mind, the other party could only see me as a woman, and at that time this barrier seemed impossible to break through. In those days, not only was it a handicap to be a woman, but I used to think that for a woman to succeed she had to be ten times better than any man. In fact, it is harder for a woman to be a chief executive than a man, because we have to fight against our natural inclinations.

My personal inclination has been to put my children's needs first and foremost. Of course, this is not always possible when you're in a senior executive role. It's trite to say that nature has created woman differently from man, but it's also true. After all, woman was created in order to guarantee that there would be future generations, and in my own make-up there is a strong nesting need. This instinct is paramount in women and it's often at war with business achievement. For this reason, I believe that a lot of women opt out of the work force and lose themselves in mind-numbing, undemanding and mundane pursuits. They probably see no way out of the conflicting roles of self-determination and a career versus the demands of home and family.

You see, the very abilities necessary to be a successful businessman are the abilities most admired by women. A man's aggression is seen as a prized quality, a trait that makes him very attractive to the opposite sex. For women, the case is quite the reverse: aggressiveness is unacceptable. I recollect hesitating once before entering into a very large business deal, because I was uncertain of how it might affect a relationship that I valued at the time. I don't suppose there are many men who would even have given thought to such an absurd notion. Generally, I suppose that the richer a man is, the more desirable he becomes. He can then attract a very young wife, society awards him with all sorts of honours, he is invited to sit on boards and to display his intelligence, because after all, if he has the capacity to make so much money, that ability should be tapped for the good of everyone. That's not the way it has been for women in the past, but I believe things are changing — although it will take a while. Such changes inevitably must be preceded by a few individuals breaking ground.

Let me tell you a story. Many years ago, I used to attend certain company directors' luncheons that were always opened by Sir Creighton Brown with a 'Good afternoon, gentlemen', which I stoically suffered, although it would have been hard to imagine any-one looking up at Creighton Brown, who was less like a gentleman than well-padded Millie. On one occasion, Sir Creighton had a most embarrassing task. His guest speaker was the newly-elected leader of a decimated opposition party. I squirmed as, with much condescension, he smilingly introduced Margaret Thatcher. Very coyly, I thought, he said, 'Who knows, we may even one day have a lady Prime Minister'. He made it sound so very unlikely that I gnashed my teeth. Whether or not Mrs Thatcher is a good Prime Minister is academic. What I find amusing is the epithet 'the Iron Lady'. Had she been a man, she would be praised for having firmness of character and, let's face it, who in their right mind would want a weak Head of State?

The changes have been happening around us, though. I notice that approximately one-third of all law graduates are female. I see them practising in any number of firms, looking very feminine, and they seem able to express both career and domestic ambitions. Just last week the largest Council in Australia elected a woman as Lord Mayor. She's a mother of five children and has a husband who is a very successful doctor. Instead of sending her a letter of congratulation I sent it to him, because it is the proud husbands who will give the world the 50 per cent of the intelligence it is currently not tapping.

It isn't necessary for a woman to be bitchy to succeed, it's just a matter of firmness. My own management style is relaxed and prob-ably reflects my lifestyle. I play it low-key. If I wander into one of my businesses at a time when my chief manager is out and I'm not recog-nised, I consider that to be a sort of victory. It gives me an opportunity to see how things are really being run when the chief supervisor is away.

I impose my will if necessary, but I prefer to manage by consensus. My view is that people work best when their functions are fulfilled within a loosely-structured environment. In my experience, this brings out both the best and the worst in people. Successful men are always seen as tough and ruthless, and the respect that attaches to these qualities saves such men from a lot of the clean-up problems that I have. I dislike the naked use of power, it embarrasses me, yet after each clean-up I promise myself to conserve energy by showing my jack boots earlier next time. Nevertheless, my preferred method of management, discussions with staff to arrive at common objectives, remains.

This isn't a complex procedure. I hold meetings with line managers and we talk about pursuing common goals which, needless to say, are the ones that I believe would be most beneficial to the business. However, it's important to me that I have a consensus from the line managers that they feel entirely comfortable with our objectives. Then I expect them to manage their day-to-day matters within the framework we've hammered out together. The hardest thing a senior executive has to learn, I think, is to keep from meddling and getting too close to the day-to-day running of affairs. It is hard to give up the immediate pleasure of rolling up your sleeves, getting the job done, and feeling very impressed with the fact that you've achieved the impossible. It's especially difficult if you like being creative, because in return for keeping your distance, all you get is the more distant satisfaction of seeing your plans mature successfully. I see this happening around me with young management — and you must remember that my education is strictly on-the-job. I suppose that there is a certain amount of knowledge which one can bring to one's work which makes it easier to succeed quickly. However, sometimes acquired knowledge, especially if it is very academic, is a stumbling block that has to be overcome before one can relax into creativity.

To be an entrepreneur is largely a matter of driving by the seat of one's pants, I've always thought. I know that sounds hazardous, but in any situation one must look at the blackest, then the brightest, and settle for the middle of the road. I attribute my success to the fact that I have an ability to view each situation through several eyes, including a creative one. After all, the way an entrepreneur works is by re-arranging a product, whether that product is a mousetrap that can be improved or a property that is already serving a function and creating a reasonable return, but which can be transformed into a first-rate property that makes a fabulous return. This requires imagination, skill, and a knowledge of the market. I believe one must be as well-informed as it is possible to be. Information must be ingested constantly and it should come from as many diverse areas as are available. This means you must be a ferocious reader, and I am. It also means you must be disciplined about what you read or else you'll suffer from a chronic shortage of time.

Decision-making comes easily to me. I have one speed, and that's fast. I know quickly whether or not I'm interested in a deal. It's often not terribly hard to know what and how other people are thinking. Somehow my antenna seems to be ever at work, picking up information, even when I appear to be disinterested or not paying attention. To be successful in business you need the right mix of instinct, reason and advice. Also, as people who know me realise, tenacity is the key. I have had some spectacular disasters but they've always been containable. You must know what you can afford to gain and lose.

My business philosophy has been a basic one, in that I assure myself of a healthy cash flow to support long-term developments. I'm comforted to know that money is coming in while I'm developing long-range projects which necessitate borrowing. In that, once again, I'm slightly different than many men. Whether it's the natural caution of a woman or whether it's insecurity, I don't know, but I tend to dislike being over-extended. My gearing is not of the magnitude of many very successful companies which, it seems to me, take gambles that I would not be prepared to endure. I dislike having to lose sleep because of creditors, which is why I run my affairs in such a manner that at any time I can pay out and still come away intact, unscathed.

On the other side of that coin is the potential that big gambles have for returning many millions of dollars. For example, I have friends who develop large properties. They'll attempt to make 20 per cent profit on a $20 million development, which can be organised by borrowing 80 per cent of the financing. I don't have that kind of courage. I prefer to do much smaller developments with lower gearing, which of course allows correspondingly smaller margins of profit.

In a way, learning to take profits was traumatic for me, and being the boss was embarrassing because, after all, I cut my teeth on dialectical materialism. I was never a member of the Communist Party, but during the war and in the post-war years it was natural to want to believe that communism was a way of life which did not equate need with ability. The concept of power is still somewhat unacceptable to me, and at first it was very hard to be the boss, to accept the knowledge that I had the total power to hire or fire people. It still does seem somehow wrong to me that people have such power. Likewise, I found it awkward and unpleasant to know that people depended entirely upon my goodwill. I do what I can to avoid hurting, I do what I have to do, but I make certain that no blood is spilt. No-one should have the right to take away another person's pride and dignity, but of course I realise that this sometimes does occur. Every redundant person must hate the one who has given them the sack, and that's easy to understand. You see, I couldn't fit into a large organisational structure where it's dog-eat-dog and people climb over the bodies.

I don't think there's anything unpleasant about my work, whether I roll up my sleeves and get into the muck or sit at a desk organising large fund transfers. It's all one thing, a matter of getting the job done. I think the work ethic is somehow slipping through our fingers. Australia is constricted in its production by the small population and by the fact that its people want to enjoy one of the world's highest standards of living without necessarily working as hard as other nations which have earned high standards of living. I don't have to tell you that this country is fortunate to be able to live this way, because of the wealth in the ground and above it.

We're not taken seriously in Europe, we're not important. There are so few of us we really are a backwater as far as the rest of the world is concerned. Among those who might identify with us are Californians, because of similarities in the countryside and climate, and Australia has been an escape for a number of Californians who came here as migrants. Yet most of them would consider us to be unsophisticated, and they're probably right.

If you were a true Continental you wouldn't feel comfortable in this country. All the things that I love about it would perhaps terrify the Continental, who's used to living closely packed, who wants the cafe society, the security of numbers, who would die of horror to be in some of the places that I go to. When I'm the only person standing in a section of the Outback, with nothing around me, I think it's heaven and wouldn't replace it for anything. Continentals, however, wither and die here. People are shaped by their environment, they carry the needs of that environment around with them, and I'm no different.

I need the openness of space, while Continentals need to be closed in. I feel insecure in crowds, they are insecure in vastness. When I travel, my eyes always hunger for vistas. Out west the horizon seems a million miles in every direction from where you're standing, with nothing in between but green trees, a few birds, and a blue, blue sky, yet it doesn't feel as though you'll be crushed under the weight of all those clouds. I love Australia, it's my country. I'm Australia's great ambassador. The farther I go from home, the more flag-waving you'll get from Millie. If I could snatch half the world and bring it to Australia when I travel, I'd probably do so. Yes, there are things about this country's attitude toward work which are irritating, but people are as they are and one must accept them. Australians simply are not geared to productivity, they're not go-go Americans, for example, or saluting Japanese, or machine-like Germans. However I do think they're wonderful people.

It's strange that Americans worship money in a way that we don't. In 1972 I went to a Harvard summer school in Honolulu. For six weeks I did nothing but talk business with 59 men. It was a wholesome exercise, pursued enthusiastically by some of the highest-paid, most intelligent people I have ever come across. The Harvard professors' business was to teach people how to make money. I thought to myself, 'All this time, Millie has had an awful secret to hide, that she could do this wonderful thing, and now they're telling me it's a unique experience'. A seat actually was established at Harvard to study entrepreneurship. It was a brand new world for me, starting in 1972.

In Australia, of course, the ability to make money is not a desirable trait. In my married life this skill was valued but played down. Since my divorce, the children were encouraged by their father to hate that trait, which created all sorts of conflicts and problems. To a large extent this acted as a brake on my achievements. Behind most successful men there is a very ambitious, pushing woman. Nobody has ever been pushing me. There's nobody in my corner saying, 'Go on, rah rah, Millie's getting there'. Mine was a creative exercise that grew out of itself, without any nurturing from outside. Perhaps that's pure entrepreneurship.

I suggest that in Australia, the pendulum has swung too far. We began with a non-caring industrial system and have ended up with a government-run system of over-care. Also, as the computer takes over from the worker, we need to fight to keep the work ethic alive. To me this is a most important area of study, and one for which our scholarly system is not geared.

A paper I gave some years ago to a group of startled business course students advocated a reassessment of the way we manage our unemployment benefits. My proposition was that we ought to tithe money received from the public to use for the public good. There's nothing wrong in expecting some return for the money we pay out to support the unemployed. I can think of hundreds of organisations that could gladly use the extra help, Meals on Wheels being one example. It doesn't take much imagination to see how useful society would find this additional help. There is a crying need for cost-free workers to assist in all sorts of programs for the needy, such as domiciliary care of the elderly. Why can't we organise teams to cook, clean, paint, or come to a gloomy house and say to an old person, 'Hi, how are you going today?', then settle down to listen for an hour or two. We have thousands of charities and government-funded institutions that always need extra help, that all have work beyond their budget crying to be done. I see nothing degrading in a former high-level executive rolling up his sleeves to bring brightness into someone's life. It's an equation in which everyone wins.

For me, there would be nothing more demoralising than finding myself on the redundant heap, becoming a recipient rather than a giver. In that case, self-pride would have to be rediscovered by assisting others who are less well-off than I am. I believe that both here and overseas we have diluted the work incentive. Of course, there are many unemployed people who sincerely want to work, but seriously, we're beginning to find it more and more difficult to attract a junior who's old-fashioned enough to make teas, do some filing, run errands, or take a turn at the switchboard. I suppose my generation was too hungry for the 25 shillings a week to turn down that kind of job. It isn't that I want to turn the clock back, I would be the last one to want that, for in an economy where the work-earning expectations and living standards are low, entrepreneurs like Millie can't thrive. In such an economy, the system remains locked into two stratas: the very wealthy, and all the others, who are poor.

I suppose some of these concerns I'm expressing arise from the experience of my early teens, when I leaned strongly toward communism. I lived in a slum neighbourhood and my closest friend became a prostitute at age 15. I was surprised at the time, because she seemed to me to have had a much more sheltered environment than mine was. Her family lived in a house and her father went to work, while we lived at the back of a shop and both my parents worked, so I didn't receive the mothering that she had. Yet, I dare say, she had a need for things that had no priority with me. My head rang with the wonders of Tolstoy, Wells, and Shaw, so I fell for dialectical materialism and the need for a socialist state.

As I said, during the war and the post-war years, many of us were like that. Don't forget a lot of us had gone through the ugliness of the depression, and whilst I never suffered from hunger, I certainly was exposed to every other kind of need. While I was still too young to join the Party, lo and behold, I found something that really delighted me. Zionism contained the same belief, and as a bonus it wanted to bolster my self-image by teaching me that Judaism was not what the Nazis wanted us to believe it was. Instead, it was something special, something that deserved to have its own homeland.

My love affair with Zionism started then, and truly it has never ended. In fact, I married my former husband because his ideals matched mine. We had planned on his demobilisation — he was in the British Navy — that we would quickly make our way to Palestine to help build the homeland, using our young muscles to care for the remainder of the holocaust's survivors. It all sounds terribly melodramatic now, but I can assure you it wasn't then. That was simply the way it was, because in those times everyone lived on war emotions.

As it eventuated these plans did not mature. My former husband fell to, if you like, the fleshpots of the easy life. By the time I left him, it was too late for me also. I was by then an entrenched Australian, and all my energies were directed to financial security for myself and my three children. Even so, I'm still unashamedly in love with both countries. Australia draws me to the extent that I feel physically involved with the land, and that's probably why I became involved in mining. Israel draws me because — well, can you wonder? — I came from Poland, where anti-Semitism is learned at the mother's breast.

My formal education was very limited but I have never stopped learning. I'm an avid reader, though I often half-jokingly curse the fact that I'm not illiterate. I drive myself mercilessly to achieve, in the sense that no day ever holds enough hours. If I find I have any time, I plan and fill it up with far more than I could possibly fit into it.

I have no social ambitions in the way of people who join clubs and become accepted by groups. I'm socially inept in the sense that I have no small talk, and let's face it, as a partnerless woman I'm no hostess's prize. I relate easily to men, perhaps because my nearest sibling was my brother, and I find that I can talk factual matters far more readily with men than with women, although that's changing. When I was a young mother, I experienced all the guilts of being a working mother. In conversation, other mothers tended to look down on what they saw as my neglect of the children. In succeeding years the tables turned, until now, when I ask women what they do, they quite often apologise that they're only housewives. I don't really mind not being socially lionised. I like my silence — it's always peopled with thought — and to tell the truth I like Millie as a person, I enjoy her company. Still, I recognise that I must be self-opinionated, because I prefer talking to listening, although when it's advantageous to listen, I do. However, I don't often indulge in idle talk. Time is too precious to waste in chatter, and I find such talk not only tedious but tremendously wearying.

I think I ought to elaborate on my communism versus capitalism beliefs, because obviously I have ambled comfortably across to the side of capitalism, where I am now entrenched. There was a time when the workers — and you know one must sloganise to say these things — were downtrodden, deprived, and exploited. The pendulum has swung in this country as elsewhere, and it's the unions who have become the tyrants. On the other hand, I have to tell you that I'm glad communism exists and functions, because it has forced capitalism to change its social conscience. As a result, we no longer need to rely on good will or paternal (in my case, it would be maternal) attitudes to provide the higher standards to which workers have become accustomed, or to provide an environment in which all people can compete on a more or less equal level. Education also is readily available for virtually all of our people.

Yet I remain apolitical. Some years ago, friends asked me to stand for the Australia Party and I laughed at the notion. Being a true activist, I would find it impossible to achieve within the frustrating confines of politics. That doesn't mean I don't appreciate the fact that many people in politics could be successful in the marketplace but have forsaken the opportunities of the marketplace in order to work toward what they idealistically believe will be a better government. To these people, I'm grateful. They obviously have an ability to contain their frustrations to a greater degree than I have.

I believe that I work harder than most of my staff. I enjoy housekeeping, cooking, and shopping — I find these things relaxing at times, although at other times they just become chores. Now, however, my children are old enough for me not to have to worry about those chores, and for the first time in my life I can concentrate on what Millie wants to do and to be. That's not as easy as it sounds though, because whilst one is in business income is produced, which in turn requires investment, which procreates more profits, necessitating further investment. It's a monster, a who's-riding-the-tiger sort of thing. Mineral exploration in particular is a teasing exercise, because areas are usually acquired with very little background knowledge. As a rule, the exploration is a grass-roots operation. After the funds are expended and the exploration is carried out, there comes a time of

Above, on site looking for copper at Cobar, NSW, 1970.
Below, with controversial former NSW Premier Jack Lang
at the opening of a nursing home, 1972

decision: do we relinquish the area or hold it? Then new areas have to be found and we're back on the hurdy-gurdy again.

Obviously, I like to be kept busy. The profit angle of what I do is probably not as important as the achievement itself, although in the game I play profit is the score. I like to think that there will come a time when we will all view our wealth differently, when instead of accumulating more wealth in order to buy more valuable paintings or silver or properties or whatever we invest in, our consciences will suffer from the cries of the needy. It sounds rather at cross-purposes to live in a house as luxurious as mine and talk about the needy, but I do contribute. I don't want to paint myself in the colours of a saint. I don't give the Biblical proportion on an annual basis, but I do my best to get as close as possible to that benchmark and I do allow my conscience free expression in the form of giving to those who haven't. I hesitate to call this charity, because to need is not to be in need of charity, it is to be in need of help. I think that giving to those who need help should be a natural outcome of maturity. It's a privilege and an opportunity which should never be passed up. I think we ought to embrace this philosophy in every part of our life, and, as I say, it is happening through social systems all over the world, yet I think it needs to gain more meaning.

For example, last year I celebrated my son and daughter-in-law's marriage. It was all very beautifully catered for and very expensive, and it bothered me that in a world where so many are hungry, such a vast amount can be spent on flowers for a one-day occasion. To soothe my conscience, I gave a sum equal to the cost of this very beautiful wedding to both Israel and the Children's Fund. Israel got a forest, and the Children's Fund were told to feed 100 children for every guest who attended the wedding. That may seem like a huge amount of money but it was embarrassingly small. I hope the time is not far off when we're ready to accept the responsibilities of living in a world which is so disproportionately catered for. Otherwise, we're going to have a lot more problems.

I'd like to talk about women in management and women who are trying to break into chief executive roles. Women have succeeded in the arts and fashion and cosmetics and so on because it seemed, I suppose, a natural outlet for us. This has yet to come in commerce or in politics. Again, I am optimistic, I think it's happening. I must have been born an optimist or I wouldn't be mining, I suppose.

It's harder for women to create good management teams than it is for men. I think most people still prefer to work for a man, because it's easier to follow the tried and tested than the new and unknown. I keep saying things are changing but changes takes a long time to happen. I don't think that the business world is ready yet for a female Robert Holmes à Court, because not only does that require great know-how and nerves of steel, it also requires the kind of organisation where chauvinism, sexual competition, and personality conflicts can be kept to a minimum. So much energy and effort are required to get the job done that anything unrelated to the success of the achievement is not only a handicap but becomes a danger. When you're juggling large sums of money, you can see the need to minimise those dangers.

Many years ago I looked at a situation that was begging for a takeover, but I decided not to do so. I think I would still make the same decision about not proceeding today, probably because of the dearth of women in senior management. The team I would need to run such an organisation would have to be diverse, it would have to be tried and tested, and it would have to be capable of taking over whatever positions within the organisation were suddenly vacated by the departing executives. Every takeover must contain an element of fear among the organisation's staff. There would be fear that my leadership might not be acceptable to men. When I was much younger, most of the people would have been senior in age to me and probably senior in experience, and they would have felt so. Whereas if a man came in as chief executive, he would be assessed not so much by his age or experience as from the points of view of power and his ability to manage money.

When I decided against that takeover, I could almost feel the thoughts and interactions of the people who would find themselves subordinate to a four-foot, 11½ inch ex-Polish lady whose knowledge of the business was not as great as theirs. It would, forgive me, screw up matters, and that is not what business is all about. It's hard enough to get the machinery rolling smoothly. To iron out personality interactions, and the potential abrasiveness and catalyst to danger that my presence might have been, posed such enormous problems that I decided the ultimate result would have been a loss in profits. Nevertheless, I like the challenge of having a crack at cleaning up a mess that others have left behind and putting a run-down business back into the black. Of course, I would then immediately put myself into a position of more travel, more work, and more supervision.

The time must come when women play this role. The time must come when women are seen as being 50 per cent of humanity, with a great deal to contribute, which must be used for the potential good of all. Sooner or later, we're going to have a brave woman who will jump in the water and test it for all of us. Perhaps the place where this could happen easiest is America. The Equal Opportunity Act certainly has smoothed the way for women to rise to the top there. I think that if Australia is to treat its women equally, we must produce similar opportunities, if for no other reason than to remove the disincentive of the old boys' network. The disincentive, of course, is that the boys have managed it for a long time, they think they know how each other feels, they have a common language, common interests, and these interests exclude non-members of the network. I think that North American men are much more ready and able to accept capable women and yet still see them as females. They don't seem to feel as threatened as our men are. They seem to enjoy the company of intelligent females, and indeed, seek them out as full partners in intellect, in achievement, and in maturity. In this, Australia is behind.

Wealth hasn't affected me greatly, although I do live in a very nice house, surrounded by nice things, I have a country home, and I drive a fast English car. It's good to know that one can buy the things one likes, within limits. It's always a matter of degree; I'm not a billionaire. To buy a Rembrandt, for instance, would be quite out of the question. While my needs admittedly are those of the very wealthy, I don't live high off the hog's back and could not possibly be described as a silver-tailed person. I see myself as a worker, which is my own excuse for being a capitalist, because I don't sit back and collect money that others are slaving to earn for me. I'm not a capitalist in that sense, because I work as hard as my people. I certainly make a lot more money than they do, but then I carry more responsibility and plan more. In fact, I never stop planning. True capitalism is the acceptance of wealth. It has nothing to do with an ethic of building for the good of all. Let's face it, we live in a symbiotic society. I can add to the public good by creating income and generating jobs. Yes, I live well, but it's nice to know that through my efforts, not only have my children been fed, but many others have benefited as well. Giving should be an accepted part of having.

To me, capitalism is inheriting money and then not working it, because money is like a farmer's land: you have to keep it, cultivate it, do all the right things to make it produce, and in its production it will create more work for more people, improve standards of living, and feed children. The most important ingredients in achieving success in any discipline are to set high goals which at the same time are realistic, to have a flexible mind and the ability to work quickly. Last, and I suppose most important, is to love your work in a way that makes it not just work but a hobby, an entertainment, and an all-fulfilling experience.

Richard Holden

The Australian who leaves home in search of a fulfilment that apparently only the outside world can offer
is one of this country's oldest stories and greatest
banes. Richard Holden's story, however, has a double
twist. First, he capped a young life of sailing the South
Pacific and demonstrating against the Vietnam War in
the political hotbed of San Francisco, circa 1964, by
exchanging his Australian 'frontier' heritage for the
even more remote frontier of Alaska. Second, he
wants very much to live again in Australia after more
than two decades abroad, but not until he has completed a project that he hopes will place Australian
wine among the world's most popular vintages. He's
already well on the way to accomplishing the latter
goal, via a very expensive two-year-old marketing
plan that he expects will increase Australia's wine
exports to America by at least 50 per cent within four
years.

Raised and trained in Melbourne as an architect,
Holden has many years of experience in Alaskan
government under his belt, and in recent years has
made a fortune in the private sector with his construction consulting firm. A big, imposing, confron-
tationist-style man who drives possibly the only 911
Porsche Targa in Alaska, the 46-year-old Holden is
nevertheless private, and even modest, under that
thick hide. Though he doesn't mention it, his generous contributions to charities for orphans, the
handicapped, and for sports teams, are well-known
in the land of the midnight sun.

Our talk took place, in part, on the site of a hotel
he's building on a magnificent waterfront setting in

Juneau, Alaska's capital. The Alaskan community
has, in fact, done much to fund Holden's daring and
exotic venture with the Australian wine industry,
under the Chloe label. But among other talents,
Richard Holden is a hell of a raconteur; what say we
let him tell the tale himself?

Grandma Holden told me that my great-great-grandfather stole a side of ham from a parish priest in Ireland, who turned him in. They gave him death or transportation to Australia. He chose transportation. He wrote a letter to his wife in Ireland in the 1830s and said, after seven years, he wished he'd chosen death. He was so upset about being transported that he changed his name from O'Brien to Brien; he hated priests thereafter so he dropped the 'O'.

My mum and dad met in the early 1920s in Brighton, Melbourne, and married there. My father was a mining engineer by trade: he had a foundry and he was a gay blade. I was born on 12 April 1939. My father's foundry was making good money but his accountant ran away with the dough, so my dad got into the bottle and became an alcoholic. He got himself out of that in 1953, then went up to the Snowy Mountains and worked on the Snowy Project for the rest of his life. He stopped drinking and became a hell of a good man.

My brother has built his own Optical Science research group at the University of New South Wales. He practically invented the soft contact lens and is the first optical scientist ever to win a Fulbright Scholarship. He lectures half the year abroad. Smart little bugger, he's the academic of the crowd. My sister went to Star of the Sea College in Melbourne and now we're putting her two daughters through the same school. We were pretty poor, that is to say from the time that I was about seven, dad wasn't of much help. The poor bugger just fell to bits so mum had to go to work, which in 1949 was a bit of a disgrace. She worked as a secretary at a wool mill up in North Brighton, but if she'd had the opportunities that young women have now, she'd have starred in whatever she wanted to do. In those days, of course, she was lucky to get her high school education. She got a succession of jobs and finished up as de facto general manager of a mill in Melbourne before she retired. She's 77 now, fit as a fiddle, and has gone to every Collingwood game for the last million years.

Australia is a great country for growing up at any income level and not feeling inferior. I think that's one of the reasons why when

Australians go abroad, they tend to make it fairly easily, because they're not constrained by the social world. There aren't many countries on earth where a person can grow up in modest circumstances and still have a good life. Australia might be the only one. There are only 22 functioning democracies in the world that give you enough room to move around without having to have an internal passport or other constraints.

I'm an Australian. I'll die an Australian. I'll never quite fit in here. I'm controversial here and that's because I don't like people telling me one thing when I know they really think something else. One of the things being Australian teaches you is to understand where you stand. Around the world, an Australian is identifiable as a certain kind of person. That is to say, Australians are not capable of being anything but where they came from and what they. are, which is egalitarian, kind to neighbours. They don't look for trouble but they stand still if they have to have some. Not that this is good or bad, they just have these attributes. They say, 'Okay, if trouble has to happen, it has to happen. It wasn't my idea but you are going to suffer the consequences.' That's the defensive side of Australians, the side that appears to be aggressive but really is saying, 'Look, mate, I have a good idea here, I think it'll work. Why don't we try it out?'

What I revolted against when I was growing up was, 'She'll be right mate, no worries'. I said, 'Wait a minute, I'm 23 years old, I have a mind and I have to have somewhere to put my ideas'. You can do that in Australia now, you can use your ideas, but when I left Australia there was practically no room for people like me. I was one of a generation of people who left Australia in droves in the early 1960s, many of whom are still abroad.

I won a scholarship to St Mary's Christian Brothers' College at St Kilda, where I matriculated, then I went to the Royal Melbourne Institute of Technology to do, for some reason, radio engineering. I ended up doing three years of architecture, then I did a bit of night school to get the diploma and I was working as a draughtsman for architects in Melbourne. I was on my way to becoming a nice, happy young architect. I was sailing, skiing, surfing, doing everything I wanted to do — part of the great middle-class Australian life.

A bloke I did a bit of sailing with reminded me one day that he was going around the world on his 47-foot ketch. He said one of the other blokes had to drop out and asked if I wanted to go. I said, 'How long do I have to make up my mind?' He said, 'Thirty minutes'. I sat at my draughting board and thought of calling my fiancée, but I knew what she'd say. I thought, for the rest of my life I'll have a nice house at Balwyn, I'll go skiing at Mt Bullen, we'll have a summer cabin and we'll go to Fiji and to architects' conventions around the world, and I'll probably become an insufferable son-of-a-bitch, because I'm a loud-mouth by nature. I thought all of that out in about 30 seconds instead of 30 minutes, called him up and said, 'You're on'. The family were in an uproar, my mum threatened suicide, and I lost my fiancée who didn't want to take the chance.

In Bass Strait we got into the worst summer storm they'd had in 35 years. We had a good 40-foot sea, about a 70-knot wind, and we nearly lost the boat. Seven days out in Bass Strait I started learning a lot I didn't know about myself, including that I was capable of becoming absolutely shit-scared. I had a marvellous friend on board, Jack Ward, who later became dean of the Australian University librarians before he retired. He'd knocked around the world himself, he was a radio operator on the first two Australian Antarctic expeditions, among other things, and he taught me a lot about what to do when you're frightened.

Although we had intended to go to Auckland, we had to backtrack to Sydney via Bateman's Bay, so I thought I'd go down to Melbourne and see if my fiancée had changed her mind, because there was now space on the boat. I said, 'Phil will marry us at sea', but she said, 'I don't know', so the space was filled by someone else. We sailed to the Cook Islands, then up to Tahiti. I'd been bothered by sinus infections all the way across, and when we got to Tahiti I came down with amoebic dysentery. The boat had to sail without me and I was stuck in Tahiti on my own, with a fever of about 105 degrees. I got chucked out of the hospital because I ran out of money, and I was sitting on the beach with my fever, thinking, what the hell am I going to do now? The nearest British Consul was in Fiji and there was no Australian Consul at all.

There was an American pharmacist on the island that I begged some penicillin from. I told him that I needed somewhere to sleep and he said, 'What can you do?' I said, 'I'm a trained architect', and he said, 'I have a concrete block shed out the back here. You can sleep in there, and when you're fit enough you can draw additions to it, how's that?' I said, 'It's a deal'.

It took about three weeks to get the fever down, then I drew his building. I had another four months on my visa and didn't want to leave there; it was paradise in those days. The pharmacist said, 'I'll tell you what, there's only one architect here, Christian Regault. I'll talk to him.' Regault needed a designer, so I got the job. I had high school French and nobody in the office spoke English, so I thought, I have to do something about this. I bought a copy of Camus' *L'Etranger* in French and English and read it to myself in English and out loud in French. In about a month I taught myself how to get along, and for the next four months I lived the life of Riley. I was the only Frenchman in Tahiti who wore a beret, I had a Vespa motor scooter, and I lived in a little encampment of a dozen grass buildings, three miles from the road to town. We'd go to work at 7.30 p.m., and at 11.30 we'd knock off for lunch until about two, then work until about 7 p.m. I had the time of my life, the ladies were friendly, everything was great.

Monsieur Gigi was the police inspector in charge of tourists. Once a week, he would see me sitting in a cafe having my aperitif. My visa was going to expire and I tried to make as discreet an enquiry as I could to see if I could get it extended. Regault was trying to do the same for me, because I was in the middle of the design for the Territorial Assembly Building. Everybody knew that Regault had an alien with no work permit doing his work for him, and every Thursday the building committee from the Legislature would come up to look at the progress, so I'd have to hide in the broom closet. From there I'd explain everything I was doing so Regault could explain to the committee. They all knew I was in there but I wouldn't come out until they went away. Then we would go back to work.

One afternoon Inspector Gigi said, 'Richard, are you enjoying your stay with us?' I said, 'Inspector, I couldn't be happier'. He said, 'It is a beautiful island, isn't it? It's a pity more of our foreign friends can't partake of it for a longer period. I understand you are a student of architecture, Richard. I also understand the Legislature is having a new Territorial Assembly Building built for itself.' I said, 'Is that right, Inspector?' 'Yes,' he said, 'and I understand that the design will be completed in about another month.' I said, 'Yes, it should take a good month, maybe two', but the inspector said, 'Oh no, Richard. Monsieur Regault absolutely guarantees to me that it won't take more than a month. I understand your visa is up next week, by the way.' I said, 'Yes, Inspector', and he said, 'Well, a month from now, Richard'. It took another six or seven weeks, not because of the architecture but because the Assembly had a hang-up about some decision-making. I never said a word to anybody about this and Regault never talked to me about it, but around the third week before the month was up I had a similar conversation with the good inspector, who gave me one more month. Two weeks after that, he said, 'Richard, I understand there is an American boat in port which is going to leave here soon on its way to Honolulu and they need a crew member. I recommended you with the highest of honour.' So I got on the God damned thing and had the worst trip in history.

The mizzen mast broke four days out and I got a hairline fracture of the elbow. The master was a chap of about 65 who had done very little blue water cruising and didn't demonstrate any knowledge of it. The radio was shot, the motor seized on the way down, and the sextant was out by a good 10 seconds, which meant that you could quite easily miss an island by 2,000 miles. The woman the master had brought along with him for a bit of companionship decided she didn't like him, she liked me, and I couldn't stand the sight of her. Here I was with a fractured elbow, the water went bad in the tank 10 days out of Honolulu, and we made the longest, slowest passage imaginable from Tahiti to Honolulu — 28 days.

At one point, we were going down the Molokai Channel with no mizzen, we had the boom slashed forward, and we had the jib out on a spinnaker boom, so we were wing-on-wing and surfing with no steerage whatsoever. On the the south-west corner of Molokai Island there was a military reservation. We came down in the middle of a war game. You could see the marines landing on the beach and the fighter bombers were dropping napalm all over the place. It was like being in the middle of a Cinemascope movie, and right in the middle of the Molokai Channel sat the USS *Enterprise*, firing off jet planes as fast as she could go. A helicopter took off about 200 yards from us and we were just flopping down the channel, doing eight knots, no steerage whatsoever, just trying to keep her from broaching. The pilot got out his Aldis lamp and signalled us to change course, so we got out the flags and signalled, 'Sorry, can't change course, ship in distress, no mizzen'. The bastard came over about 200 feet from us, turned sideways and blew us flat, which was a bit of a risk in that boat because if he had come up forward of the jib the jenny would have gone under, and we would have gone down by the bow. I ran up a signal that said, 'Fuck you', and we could see this fellow sitting up there in his helicopter with his orange helmet, looking up the signals in his book. He looked and looked, then flew away. The *Enterprise* had to stop work, all the jets started circling, she got up steam and got out of our way, and we spent about three minutes coming down beside them. There must have been 2,000 blokes standing on the deck looking down at us. We got to Honolulu and the Naval Military Police were there. 'We want your ship's papers. You have an alien on board?' They were going to confiscate the ship and the radio. They were going to put me in the slammer until they could find out who I was, but Sparkie, one of our crewman and an American, talked his way out of all that. So that was my introduction to the United States.

I only stayed in Honolulu for about a month, then got a job on a boat which had won the Bermuda Race in 1936. We made a two-man passage from Honolulu to Newport Beach, California, in 15 days, including three days of more than 200 miles each. I got to Newport Beach in October, 1964, and ran into the police. I had a big, red beard, I'd been almost a year in the Pacific, and I was going to stay at the Salvation Army in Los Angeles until I could scout another boat to keep going on. While I was waiting for the bus down at the Newport Beach station, I went for a stroll along the street. There were a lot of boats tied up and I was looking for anybody I knew. A police cruiser came down the other side of the divided road, got about 100 feet past me, then turned on his siren and lights. I thought, this is exciting, this is America just like on TV. Lo and behold, the car jumped the median strip, roared up, and stopped opposite me. The cop got out of his car, pulled out his gun and said, 'Assume the position'. I said, 'I beg your pardon?' and he said, 'Come on buddy, put your hands against the wall'. He said, 'Let me see your ID', but.I didn't know what an ID was. He said, 'What are you, a wise guy?' I said, 'Look officer, you're point-ing a gun at me, which makes me nervous and frightened. I don't know what the bloody hell you are doing, but the first person I'm going to phone is the Australian Consul and I suppose he'll call the Chief of Police and have something done to you. You can't be doing this in the street.' Little did I know. It turned out they were looking for a guy with a red beard.

I got to Los Angeles and took a job working for a big architect, but I couldn't breathe because I'd just spent a year in the cleanest air on earth, so I went up to San Francisco. In November I was living in Berkeley, and the fiancée of this fellow I'd met said, 'Do you want to go watch the demonstration?' I thought that would be interesting, so I went along and was standing on the corner when the Oakland police began going about the business of hauling these students out of the administration building. They were obviously enjoying the work. The students were being passive resisters and were getting dragged across the ground with their heads bumping on the sidewalk, getting bloody, while the cops were pushing and shoving. The next thing I knew, I was in the back of an Army truck with a sore head. I spent the night at a prison farm, where the others told me, 'We're the free speech movement. They won't let us put out literature on the campus against the Vietnam War.' I thought the students had a bloody good idea, because it was a dumb thing that the Americans were doing in Vietnam. The students agreed, particularly because they knew who was going to be doing the fighting.

Having had my fill of the West Coast police and their various manifestations, I said, 'I'll give you a hand'. I had been in the Labor Party in Melbourne, and when I was vice president of the student representative council at RMIT we started the campus bookstore, which is now the second biggest book shop in Melbourne. I still hold share number one in that store. So I'd had a bit of political organising experience and could help set up mailers and that sort of thing. Then I met my first wife. Josie and I got along like a house on fire. We moved in together, then I applied for a green card, which wasn't too difficult to get in those days, and got a job working for an architect in San Francisco.

That lasted about a week, because they wanted me to wear a tie in the office. After looking for five months I finally got a good job, and the third day I was there the office manager said, 'You've organised the job very well, Richard. We really think things look good. Office policy is that we wear a tie to work.' I had a tie on the next day but I let it down. The manager said, 'You must have it done up', and I said, 'Mate, I don't think we're going to make it'. He said, 'Didn't you tell me you had looked for a job for five months before you found this one?' I said, 'I don't need this one that badly'. The next day, I walked around the corner and found another job, designing fly-by-night hotels. It was the best architectural production experience I've ever had, learning how to churn work out for money, because you're not taught that at school.

In the meantime I got married, so it was only a matter of time until I got the Green Card. I went down for my first formal interview with an immigration inspector named Perryman. Question number 17 was, 'Have you ever known any communists?' Americans are very religious about that sort of thing, which I knew, but I thought, bugger them, I'm not going to start life in a new country by lying to them and subscribing to what I feel is hypocrisy, so I said, 'Yes'. The inspector looked at me and said, 'Richard, I'm going to start this interview again. Why don't you think about your answer?' He went through all the questions again and when he got to that one, I said, 'Inspector, the answer to the question is yes'. He said, 'Oh, Richard. Now we have to go to Supplementary Form 2A and start recording this interview. How many communists did you know?' I said, 'Buggered if I know, probably 35 to 40'. You see, I used to argue with them on the bank of the Yarra River every Sunday afternoon. I thought a lot of them were nice blokes, but they were silly buggers — they were always getting things wrong — so we used to go down and debate them. The Liberal guys were there, the Labor guys, and the communists.

That was the last I heard of Inspector Perryman for about four months. In the meantime, I was piddling around with what came to be called the Vietnam Day Committee, headed by Jerry Rubin, Abbie Hoffman and those guys, and I was getting pretty good at organising. For the first Vietnam Day rally there were about 8,000 of us. We got a permit and marched down through Berkeley to the Oakland frontier, where the Oakland cops were in this phalanx at eight o'clock at night, with baseball bats, dark glasses, and white helmets, just dying to have a go at us. The group were very smart. Instead of trying to confront the police, we just skipped down the open line and the cops followed. We all marched back to the Berkeley City Park but the cops wouldn't let us in. By the next day, the Bay Area newspapers had picked up the story and there were 25,000 people at the park. That day the Oakland cops let the Hell's Angels in through their police line to bash up the protesters and marchers. The Hell's Angels really enjoyed that sort of work, but they made the mistake of breaking the leg of a Berkeley policeman, so the cops drove off the Angels.

Then the Harvard Medical Faculty chartered a jet to come out, Bertrand Russell sent a telegram, and the next week we were going to have the rally that we'd had in mind all along. Norman Mailer and all these famous people were going to be there, and they were going to have me up on the platform giving the Australian perspective. Not that I was important at all but I was a bit of local colour.

On the preceding Wednesday, I was having dinner with an architect who, more importantly, was the Californian chapter president of the ACLU (American Civil Liberties Union). I told him what I was going to be doing the following Saturday, and he asked, 'Do you have your Green Card yet?' I said, 'No, I haven't'. He said, 'I'll tell you what's going to happen to you. You'll sit on that platform, you'll make your few remarks, and then you'll be very quietly surrounded by four guys in grey flannel suits. When you get off the podium, they'll put you in a limousine, drive you to McCord Air Force Base and you'll be deported. You're working without a Green Card and they don't like your politics.'

Left, 14-year-old Richard Holden heading off for Melbourne Christian Brothers College in 1953. Below, with wife Judy on their way to the governor's inaugural ball, Alaska, 1983

I called up Dick Miller, who was organising the event, and said, 'Dick, I'm going to chicken out'. I told him why and he said, 'Boy, you'd better, yeah, we don't need you taking that sort of risk. But we have your name on 400 posters all over the Bay Area.' I spent Thursday night and Friday going around with two other people, fading my name off the posters. Friday night, I drove down to Monterrey with my wife and we spent the weekend with some very respectable lawyers and doctors. The following Tuesday, I got a phone call from Inspector Perryman. I went down to his office and he handed me an envelope with an invitation for an interview two weeks hence.

'Inspector, you could have put a stamp on that thing and mailed it to me', I said. 'Richard, I want to have a little chat with you', he said. 'You want to be a good citizen and all that?' I said, 'Yeah, all that, but I want to exercise my constitutional rights, too'. He said, 'What were you doing last Saturday? Why would you want to hang around with that bunch of scabs?' I said, 'Inspector, I don't know what you're talking about. I spent last weekend down at Monterrey.' He looked at me and I looked at him. 'You're sure you have an alibi?' 'What do you mean, an alibi?' I asked. 'Did I do something wrong?' He said, 'Your name is on posters all over San Francisco, to be speaking at that rally in Berkeley with all the scum over there'. I said, 'How many Richard Holdens are there in the San Francisco Bay Area?' He said, 'Four, and you're the only one it could be. Let me give you some advice. If you run with skunks, the smell will rub off.' I said, 'Thanks for the advice, Inspector'. No Green Card.

In December, I saw an advertisement for a job in Fairbanks, Alaska, for a fabulous salary in 1965 of $12,600 a year. I'd never been to Alaska but I wrote to the employers and got the job. I wanted to take our little Volkswagen up there, pack our goods and cat, and drive up the Alcan (Highway), but to do that I needed a Green Card to get back into America. I called up Inspector Perryman, explained my dilemma to him and he said, 'How do I know you have a job up there?' I gave him my letter of engagement, he called up and talked to the partner who hired me, then said, 'Richard, if you go to Alaska, will you promise me you'll never come back?' I said, 'Inspector, I'll swear on 1,000 oaths of communist non-conformity that I'll never come back'. I got the Green Card the next day and off we went to Alaska.

My wife didn't like it at all. We spent five tumultuous years in Fairbanks. I thrived on it but she hated it. I designed the Alaskan 1967 Centennial Celebration Exposition up there, went to several schools and did some university work. At the end of 1967, I went to work as a draughtsman at the university. The financial device that Americans usually use to fund capital improvements is a general obligation bond issue. The first big bond issue the university ever had, I think, was $20 million. They didn't have any construction department, so in January when they decided they needed one, I said I could set one up. I gave myself a raise and started managing the projects. In 1968 I set up a planning operation and that worked too. The next year I got involved in lobbying for the university capital improvement program and started figuring out how the political process worked.

The nuances of the American political system are altogether different from parliamentary politics. In the first place, you have two Houses of the Legislature, and in Alaska you have 20 Senators and 40 House members. The Senators have four-year terms and the House members have two-year terms, so you have only 10 Senators running every two years. Since they have such longevity, the Senators tend to stick together regardless of party affiliations, so you really only have to worry about five guys out of 20 if you're in trouble at any time. In the State House it's madness, because 40 guys are running every two years. Then you have an elected Governor who runs the Executive and pits the Senate against the House to get what he wants. Half the time he's opposed by his own bureaucracy, which doesn't want to do what he wants, so what you have is a great big mess. With respect to a normally functioning government, it doesn't work nearly as well as a parliamentary system does. You have crisis after crisis all the time in a bureaucracy because of conflicting policies, and most often what you get is no policy. It's a very anti-planning political system and it causes itself a lot of trouble. Anyway, I spent a long time at the university developing my understanding and practice of the political system.

By 1975 I'd been exposed to it enough to get invited, by a new Commissioner of Public Works for the State, to come to Juneau as his Deputy Commissioner. I accepted that position, and it was my job to abolish the State Departments of Public Works and Highways, which were very powerful in this country. Public Works ran the Marine Highway and State Ferry System, which is the biggest passenger ship fleet under the United States flag. My job was to abolish those two proud agencies and create a Department of Transportation and Public Facilities. Over a five-year period I did that, and I also had the DOT building built, though it wasn't to my design. It was much bigger than what I'd intended.

Because I was frustrated by several experiences with the press, I figured that the government couldn't talk to the people easily enough, so we started mucking around with telecommunications, having the Governor talk to the folks on Monday night. The folks then voted on capital improvement programs, using the TV screen and electronic voting techniques. We ran the program from Anchorage to seven Alaskan towns.

Of course when you do that you bypass the media, so we attracted a lot of attention. Because it was a pilot program, I had given a consulting contract to some media people who were familiar with the techniques. I was accused of being a crook, giving away a contract without competitive advertising (which was not required, because it was a consulting contract not a construction contract). Nevertheless, that became front-page news for about a month, during which there were probably 10 headlines about me. You start to realise you're not as tough as you thought you were when the newspapers want to do it to you.

That was in 1979. The year before, Alaska's Governor had been re-elected by a very narrow margin. My wife Judy said to me, 'You promised you'd quit the government a year after Hammond got re-elected. Keep your word, because if you don't, I'll quit my wife duty forever.' So I quit, but I thought, what am I going to do now? I hadn't lined anything up, I had $27,000 in the bank which was my contribution to retirement, and that was it.

I was sitting in my office the day after I resigned when a bloke came in who was a board member for a rural school district in Alaska. A large part of Alaska is not incorporated in any political sub-division. In 1975 the Legislature set up 21 autonomous school districts, which were 100 per cent State-funded. At the same time the State government agreed that it would build a high school wherever there were eight students or more, which in the last 10 years has been an expenditure of about $350 million. That was one of the programs I was in charge of.

So a bloke from one of these districts walked into my office and said, 'We need you. We have a school building program that won't grip, so why don't you come and work for us?' I said, 'You're joking, did somebody put you up to this? Yesterday I quit, and today you're offering me a job. I'll tell you what, I'll go to work there as a consultant.' In three months I had six school districts as clients and was running a construction consulting firm.

I was doing much more work than I could handle, so I got Keith Gerken in as a partner. Then the State started funding schools in the urban areas and along came the big oil money. Juneau had a building construction program for $40 million which we picked up, then Fairbanks had one for another $50 million which we also picked up. In the space of a year I had a thriving consulting firm and started thinking, maybe it isn't so hard to make money in the private sector. I'd had some tough fights in the government, doing good work, but it wears you out. I thought, what do I want to do now? I'll wait and see for a year.

While I was waiting and seeing, I bumped into an old friend of mine who had made a very good living in the last 10 years building leased office buildings for State workers. He said, 'I wish they'd bid that Labor Building in Juneau', and I said, 'I can get them to do that'. 'No you can't,' he said. 'The Indian Corporation that represents the tribes of Juneau has that locked up with the State government'. I said, 'I'm not going to put the fix in for you but I'll make sure they advertise it'. He said, 'If they advertise it, we'll win it and I'll give you 25 per cent of the thing'. I said, 'You will? I want 40 per cent.' 'No,' he said, '10 per cent.' I said, '40', he said, '25', and I said, 'Done'. We bid it, won it, built it for $5.5 million, and it was then appraised at $11.6 million. All of a sudden, I was a millionaire. I thought, that was pretty easy.

In the meantime, all the consulting firm work provided me with a salary so I had time to think. At about that time I was trying to work out what I wanted to be when I grew up. It's not difficult to make money, knowing what I know about how the machine works, but why do I want to do all that? I was 41 years old and I'd only been to Australia once in the last 14 years, when my father died. If I went home, I would bring my big, tall Sioux Indian wife with me. I could just see her walking into a public bar and a bloke saying, 'Ladies' lounge'. She'd reach over and clock him. This is my third wife, Judy. I had a second wife up in Fairbanks but that only lasted a couple of years. It was a mistake, we agreed it had been a silly thing to do. Judy and I are competitors. I keep getting together with women who are competitive. What I want in a relationship is a complex question to me, because I've been divorced twice. Nobody has ever looked after me, and I keep meeting women who turn out to be competitors rather than partners. That's probably something to do with my character.

Judy and I went over to Australia right after I quit the government. Lo and behold, the place had changed 100,000 per cent. I couldn't believe it. There are BYO restaurants with the finest food for money in the world, all over the place. Everybody is all mixed up together. America is called the melting pot, but if you go to Chicago, there's Polish Chicago, Jewish Chicago, Swiss Chicago, German Chicago. You go to Melbourne and it's Melbourne, all those people are mixed up together. The pubs are open late, *The Age* is still one of the finest newspapers to read in the world, *The Sydney Morning Herald* is tolerable, my mate Morris Lurie, who I went to architectural school with, is now a famous novelist, my mate Peter Sheehan is in the think tank for the Federal government and is a chief economic brain for Australia. I thought, what the bloody hell has happened here? It's all changed.

The thing that impressed me most was that the rural towns had been cleaned up. All the pubs, which were run down when I left and had great holes in the tin, had been painted. The beautiful wrought iron was restored, not just in Carlton, but all over Melbourne and up in the bush. I went up to Bendigo and couldn't believe it. But all of a sudden I thought, I can't live here because I've made my living over there. I'm used to dealing with Governors, State and United States Senators, I know my entire Federal Senatorial delegation. If I had to see the President, I could do that. I can put $20 million deals together and go to a banker who buys my lunch, but I can't take those contacts to Australia. When I go home, I'm the kid who left.

One day Judy and I went into Young & Jackson for lunch. As usual in a place like that there were piles of bottles on the floor, so Judy grabbed a bottle of Wynn's Coonawarra. She took a drink of it, got this great, big smile on her face and said, 'This is damn good wine'. I said, 'Yeah, that's Coonawarra, it's good claret', and she said, 'It's Australian'. Then it occurred to me Americans don't know anything about Australian wine. They haven't got a clue that Australia is the third great winery of the world.

There was a thought to be had there and I started wondering about developing a little deal to get wine from there to here. I didn't want to be a farmer, nor did I want ties that required supervision of a manufacturer. I don't know anything about wine either, except what my stomach and nose tell me, and I probably only have an average palate.

When I came home we got busy building a firm, getting enough money in the bank so that I didn't have to worry. In about the middle of 1981, I began asking people how to go about doing such a thing. I got talking to Eric Eckholm, a young media guy and good thinker who had run a very good monthly documentary called *Alaska Review* on public television. He was a bright guy who knew about worlds I didn't know about, like marketing, film-making, media, and publicity. He was running the Alaska Seafood Marketing Institute at the time, which is a big, heady trip here, and he said, 'I'm going to quit in 1983'. I said, 'Why don't you let me know when you quit? I have an idea.'

By that time I had figured enough of the economics of it to know that, technically, it was feasible for Australia to make wine cheaply enough so that even if you added the freight and other basic costs, it ought to be fairly competitive here. I said, 'Eric, how about if we import Australian wine? How would you go about doing that?' He said, 'We'd need a good hawker'. He came to work for me on July 1. We got a letter on July 5 from a man named David O'Connor from San Francisco, who was the senior vice president and West Coast executive in charge of a large national firm, Cunningham and Walsh. His letter said he wanted a few good clients. Eric said, 'Do you know who this guy is? He had the Qantas account for 18 years.'

We met with him and he said, 'Have you guys got any dough?' I said, 'I have $100,000 right now and we'll put another $100,000 in, but that's it for this year'. He said, 'We can do it for that'. He set up a market research team which, if it were a firm, would have the best qualifications in San Francisco to do the job I needed done.

I said, 'I have an instinct. I don't know if it's any good or not but we're going to try it out. Americans eat a lot of sugar and they like flavour, but they're brow-beaten about wine. I don't like to drink a lot of the Californian wines because they don't have much flavour, and they're making it that way because that's the way French wine is. The French can't make wine with flavour because they don't have any good soil except in the Rhône Valley. They have to really struggle to make a full-bodied wine, so the French style is elegant, understated, very complex, but with little flavour. The Californians have started to emulate the French because to be Francophile is to be in. In addition, the way the Californian wine industry advertises itself is almost like going to church to drink. I think Australians make good, solid wine which is fun to drink, and that's what I want to test. I also have a notion that we must find out what adjectives people would ascribe to Australians, because if they're the same as they ascribe to Australian wine, we have an automatic marketing bridge.'

We did these research tests and that's exactly what we found out. Americans think Australians are wonderful. They think they're bold and generous, full-bodied and hardy; all the things that go into making traditional Australian wine. I said, 'See?' but O'Connor said,

'You can't do that, because it won't fit in with the Californian varietals'. I said, 'David, you're the marketing man, you're thinking about getting the wine on the shelf. I don't care about that, that's your opportunity. My opportunity is that I think Americans are right about Australians. Now we're going to find out whether or not they'll drink Australian wine if it has the same characteristics they ascribe to Australians.' We did that and, lo and behold, Americans loved the stuff.

We did very sophisticated research. For instance, we set up an eight-foot cubicle in a very fashionable shopping mall outside a wine shop. You spot a guy who has just bought a bottle of wine and you have him come into the booth. 'Excuse me,' sir, we'd like you to fill out this three-page, multiple choice questionnaire. If you would do that for us, we'd be happy to have you select any wine of your choice from the rack provided over here.' Americans love to fill out forms, in my opinion. So you get your free wine and you leave, and then as soon as you're gone, we chuck the form you've filled out. Then we check the video parked behind a screen which is mounted behind the wine rack. It photographed you selecting your wine, because we want to see why you picked that label. That's the real test. We tested 200 labels and 100 names before the research pinpointed 'Chloe'.

We had another test where they wire a joint of your finger, like a lie detector. We flash labels at you, in random order, then sort them into random order again, then flash them again, to see the reaction. To find out what it is you're reacting to, we do that for half-an-hour, then put the results on a card index and test the ones that got any reaction, to see which are best. We did that for a year, from July 1983 to July 1984. It cost us a quarter of a million dollars. The whole project has cost nearly $750,000, of which about $200,000 was my own money. The rest came out of the firm and through sales of shares.

In the meantime, we started to look at varietals. We had John Gay, a premiere wine-taster, on board and we went around San Francisco buying all the wines we could. There's a lot of it there, although much of the Australian wine on the West Coast is sitting on shelves so dusty you could write your initials on them. In Australia, the domestic wine consumption went from a gallon a head in the 1960s to seven gallons a head in the 1980s. Because the domestic market boomed, planting boomed two years later. Planting is still booming but the domestic market's rate of growth is slight, and now you have no body of expertise in the trade in Australia concerning the export of wine. The advertising industry doesn't know how to do it, the legal profession doesn't know how, so what you get are wine farmers flying over to

CHLÖE
CHLÖE
CHLÖE
CHLÖE

America with a case of their best. Every Australian vintner we talked to had a story about how they were had by the Yanks.

What they don't know is, Americans do business after they get a contract. If you don't have a contract, forget it, because Americans are good, tough businessmen, they're ruthless and they're going to make bucks. America makes bucks better than anybody else; these jokers are working 16 hours a day, they don't take time off — that's why they die at 55 — but they're rolling.

Australia sold 62,000 cases of wine to the United States in 1982, which is less than Israel did. Every country on earth that makes a grape sold more wine in America than Australia did. We made our business plans. We targeted 5,000 cases the first year, 10,000 the second, 20,000 the third, and 40,000 cases the fourth year. On its own, that four-year plan will increase Australia's wine export of varietals to the United States by 50 per cent. I thought to myself, that's it, that's how I go home. If I can put together a little marketing operation that increases Australia's wine export to the United States by 50 per cent, then I can go home. Everybody in Australia drinks wine and Australia is terribly export-conscious, as it should be, because it lives or dies by its exports. We can help to develop a whole market, not just for our products, but for any Australian wine, and we have a lot of plans on how we can regulate people who start to bring inferior wine in. Because we are creating a market now, I can go home and take a reputation with me that has already been made in Australia.

Our goal is to spend six months of the year in Australia — the summer there and then the summer in Alaska. I can't imagine a better thing to do. When I go home, I want my accomplished friends to say, 'Well, Holden, that was a good thing you did with Australian wines'. Why is it important to me what they say? Perhaps because I was poor when I grew up. Actually, it isn't as important what people think about me as that I want to be able to play there in the playpen I've built here. The games I play here are games of power and structure, and they use all my talent. If I went back there, I couldn't play those games. But I want to go home and play around in Sydney and Melbourne like I can play around in San Francisco.

Before our marketing effort, I saw two promotions of Australian wine as an export to England. One was a red called Chateau Kangarouge, the other a white called Wallaby White. The wine didn't sell and the marketers thought there was something wrong with it. I was talking to the Deputy Director of Trade in Victoria, who said, 'They've started another promotion that you won't believe, but they're trying it out in England': Revogel (word spelled back to front). I thought, my God, they're making a mockery out of a magnificent industry. Some of the best wine in the world and they're doing that to it. The Deputy Director said, 'They've decided that they're not doing too well, so they're just going to advertise in the *Wine Spectator*', (a national weekly for wine in America). I said, 'How much do they have to advertise with?' and he said, 'Half a million'. I said, 'You could drop half a million in New York and you wouldn't even hear it hit the pavement. If you're going to advertise in the *Wine Spectator*, that's a $5 million dollar operation. Look, the best thing they can do is nothing. They'd help the product better if they just let that stuff gradually go off the shelves rather than make fools of themselves.'

We're not doing any advertising, that takes millions, but we will in about three years. In April 1984 John Gay, Eric and I started going to the wineries. John tasted 500 wines in 10 days and we got good stuff, Chardonnay, Semillon, Shiraz, Cabernet, Riesling and Muscat. In San Francisco we have a test lab, and every time we get a shipment we test it against the original bottle we bought, to make sure we have the quality.

We ran 'focus group' tests in San Francisco, and the Australian wines that we bought consistently won against the best of the American wines, although people couldn't figure what the shiraz was because they're not used to that beautiful, burnt-toast, smoky kind of grape. We finished our testing at the beginning of July and said, 'Okay, now we have to go fly a product'.

I went back to Australia in August and ordered 200 cases of each wine, with a 1,000-case reserve. They didn't want contracts because they didn't know who we were, and we didn't want contracts because we didn't know if we were right. We had budgeted to make five mistakes, five lots of 1,000 cases. Nieman-Marcus in San Francisco was the wine shop we went into for our first food conference convention, then we did a series of events at I. Magnin (department store). The night the Australian Trade Commission, magnificently supported by Trade Commissioner Graeme Rice, launched the second Hogan ad, we brought the wine.

We had a big launch at the Trade Commissioner's house, with 40 of the wine press there. We flew celebrated Australian gourmet writer Elise Pascoe over to do our cooking, and she did a magnificent job of classical dishes. Then we gave some interviews and tastings for the food press, because the Americans' whole thing is wine with food. We had stuff in the shops six weeks after the launch. San Francisco is the toughest wine market in America, perhaps in the world. We know if we can do it there, we can do it anywhere. We don't even have to prove that we can do it anywhere else, because San Francisco has the biggest wine snobs in America, in a market where nobody needs another wine label.

Then I began to wonder if I could get Alaskans to have a go at funding a similar project. I needed half a million, so we put up a prospectus. I didn't know anything about stocks and bonds, so we hired a guy who put together a prospectus for a corporation with $20,000 share lots, for $10,000 a year over two years at $10 a share. In order to start selling them around Juneau, we bought about 20 cases of good Australian wine, which we found in San Francisco, and we had a big party. Bugger me if six people didn't buy shares the next week. I thought, cripes, that's another thing that isn't so difficult to do.

We started going around the State. There are a lot of people around here who can throw $10,000 together. It isn't true at home, but in Alaska, for instance, there are a lot of government workers who, as married couples, are senior enough to pull down $130,000 a year between them. Plus it's great fun for them, an adventure. We told them the plan might just fall in their face and they would be out $20,000, but in the meantime they'd get good wine and the idea that they owned a wine company. I just sold the last share yesterday.

We're going to seven cities next month: Denver, Phoenix, Seattle, Portland, Salem, Eugene and Spokane. In September we'll go to Houston and Dallas, with enough promotional support to make the retailers want to buy the wine, because they'll be able to see what we've done in San Francisco. I think we'll leave Los Angeles alone until next year, because it's a big, powerful, piranhical market. If you get caught in Los Angeles you can do your whole lolly. I think next year we'll do 20,000 cases, so we're rolling.

Most of the big boys in Australia have tried to export to the United States. There have been some notable failures, even with hiring firms in the United States to do their marketing. We have to be sure that what we are doing is sound, on behalf of our shareholders, who are all Alaskans, plus the Australians we have with our Australian company, Australaska Pty Ltd, in Melbourne, and our suppliers.

What you have going on in Australia right now is the same thing the wine industry has had going on in California for years. That is, there are bulk wine manufacturers and boutique wineries. All but one of the big Australian wineries are owned by American or British companies, whose purpose it is to make money. These foreign companies that dominate the Australian mass producers of wine are not interested in expanding the market itself. All they care about is expanding their share of the domestic market, which is becoming more and more competitive. It serves them no purpose to try to export to their own markets, because they have other companies there that don't need those markets. Their purpose is to drive the medium and small wine producers out of business, if they can.

In Australia right now there are about 6,000 grape producers and about 600 vintners, of which five or six have around 50 per cent of both markets. The Labor government tends to look after the grape producers, who sell more votes to the big guys, because the big guys on their own would just let them go broke, buy them out, and then have their own means of production. Then what you'd get in the Australian wine industry would be a 'vertical tier' operation, like you have in American agriculture. In America, you don't have protection of the small businessman like you do in Australia. That is to say, the commodities markets are manipulated by the giant companies, who can then drive small businessmen out of business, buy up their holdings at a fraction of their cost, and dominate the industry, in which case they can choose whatever varietals they want to buy for table wine purposes.

Any wine industry is carried by its leaders. French wine made it, not because of vin ordinaire, but because of the high quality of good value table wine. Unless the Australian government is prepared to spend a lot of money either on promoting table wine or on protecting grape producers, who are the planters to boot, then the big guys will gobble up everyone else and high-quality Australian wine will disappear before anyone else in the world ever really knew about it. If that happens, then the world will have lost a wonderful opportunity to savour a product which is unique. I don't think we have to suffer that. I think that even in America you can get a market going which will demand Australian fine wine to a point where medium and small producers have an argument to make it on their own.

Americans haven't adopted cask wine because it is not respectable. They tend to drink wine for status as well as pleasure. In America, you buy a $5 bottle of wine when you're going to have dinner with the wife. If you have the boss coming for dinner, you buy a $15 bottle of wine and you leave the price tag on the bottle. We're going into cask wine soon, because another reason why Americans don't drink cask wine is that it's made from very inferior grapes in the United States. That gives us another leg up.

This sort of snobbery reminds me that where I grew up, we didn't like tall poppies. There weren't enough people where I grew up who were used to making money. The middle class didn't have access to the banking system, you couldn't go to the bank and say, 'That's a good idea, isn't it?' and have them say, 'Yes'. It's the most profitable banking system on earth and it's accustomed to milking middle-class people. I think one of the great things the Hawke government has done is to open up the banking system, which frightens most of the domestic banks.

It always pisses me off when you see the biggest trading economies in the world having economic summits in Europe, and Australia isn't there. The reason is because it's isolated from the world community and it hasn't made the necessary impact on the community that surrounds it, which is Asia. It's only recently that they started to do deals with the people they have to live with for the next millenium. That will make Australia the bridge between Asia and the rest of the world and that's a wonderful opportunity. It has to be done.

I'm making money but I'm now saying to myself, 'Heavens to Betsy, other people think I'm a success, now what do I really want to achieve?' The answer is peace and quiet and tranquility. I'm going to get there, but I'm now starting to try to figure out what the devil do I mean by peace and quiet and tranquility, when everybody around me says I'll never want those things. At the moment, though, what I want is to keep doing what I'm doing.

I'm hunting now for some land on the north Queensland coast, just south of Cape Tribulation, if I can get it, because the rain forest is there. If the rain forests die, the race will die. What I'd like to do is find out about the rain forests. In a few years I'd like to channel my energy into a microcosm and see what I can contribute, because if you don't do that you die. If I keep doing what I'm doing for another 10 years, I'll also die of old age at 55.

In the past I've had no goals at all. I was just wandering around doing what came naturally until this year. My body is changing, I can feel it. Oh, sexually it isn't changing, in fact I'm as active as I ever was, but like most people I want to live to an old age. I don't want to vegetate and be bored, so what I'd like to do is contribute to the places that have contributed to me. We all must share. If we want to be predators forever, then we'll destroy ourselves and the insects will take over.

Until I realise my Queensland plan, I'll spend my spare time reading *The Observer* and paying bills. I also make furniture. You see, I live in a cold country that I don't enjoy physically. I did downhill skiing but it's a bit of a pain in the arse now. I used to act in plays twice a year but I suppose now I don't take the time to indulge in hobbies. What I do is get away from the world in my shop, where I make things. When the phone rings I tend to want to smash it, and in the workshop I have all the tools to do that. I also like the company of my eight or 10 comfortable acquaintances around here, and I dive into them like a swimming pool. Also, I still do occasional sailing in the summertime and I'm going to get myself a 43-foot centre-cockpit sloop in the next couple of years.

Do you have a good idea? Then I'd say, trust yourself. But have you figured out the forces that are going to be triggered for and against or neutral to your proposal? Because you're not going to do anything on your own. Whenever you try to do something, you're going to invoke a reaction. Have you figured all that out? If you haven't, then you are going to get a brutal and basic education. If you think you have figured out the reactions in advance, then you're going to test your perceptions. You have to understand the world you live in before you try to execute an idea. Otherwise you'll learn later rather than sooner. The people who don't plan that way, who plan with ego instead of intelligence, will spend a lot of money and then wish that they'd spent more time and fewer dollars earlier.

You also have to work hard. Hard work isn't necessarily digging ditches and it isn't necessarily the Protestant work ethic. If you're going to plan ahead, it's not because you spend 12 hours a day at a desk. In my opinion, sitting 12 hours a day at a desk, thinking you are creative, is often a substitute for creativity, it's often a drug. Hard work as we are taught it is often a means of avoiding decision-making. The first thing that's going to make you successful is to know how to make decisions. Know when you should decide and when you should ask for more information, because decision-making at the right time, given the right level and quality of data, is what makes you successful. Sitting at a desk is not in itself a factor at all.

Determination is everything. You have to know you are going to do it, until it is clearly not do-able. Self-confidence is a prerequisite to making decent decisions. If you're not confident in yourself, you'll make excuses to cover your lack of self-confidence. You cannot give what you don't have a surplus of. Nothing sets me apart from my peers, except that I'm not afraid of failure.

A setback is the emotional consequence to you of an uncalculated or unforeseen stoppage. You were going hard to do something, you fell right on your face, it hurts, and you think, why didn't I figure that out? Am I not the person I thought I was? That has happened to me lots in my life, I've been slammed and I didn't think I deserved it, but you start to figure out after a while that nothing's fair and you have to work out how to get back on your feet. What you are and are not going to do again are the questions to ask.

For instance, we're now doing a $500,000 analysis for a $25 million hotel project which will be put up in downtown Juneau. It's not a *pro forma* thing to do in this town. A couple of hotels won't be full this summer because they're at the mercy of the large tour companies. In the last couple of years, the tour companies have decided not to over-night their tourists in Juneau. This year, the hotels which used to be full will be half or three-quarters full.

The way you reverse that is to make Juneau a tourist destination, which it already is in its own way. It has many natural attractions, but the problem is that the people in Juneau are inured to dealing only with the State government. They're not used to thinking, if I put $10 out of my pocket into that pot, then I'll get $500 back. Also, half the people in Juneau are civil servants, and they don't care whether there is tourism or not. In fact, tourism is a pain in the arse to them because it ruins their summers.

We're going to put up a six-storey hotel with two floors of condominiums. One level will be apartments for legislators who come from other places to be here during the Legislative session, which by Constitutional mandate runs from the second Monday in January for 120 days. That means we know when the legislators are going home. We can then move their furniture out and install the hotel furniture in June, which means we have a gift, for all practical purposes, of 32 hotel rooms out of 22 condominiums. It's a good deal for the legislators too, because they get security while they're gone, and they don't have to have somebody stay in the place for nothing, just to make sure it doesn't get burgled. They also have room service and whatever the hell else they want while they're staying there, and they can walk to work. They also provide a residential component to the downtown area, which all downtowns beg for.

Alaska is a third world state in the world's most powerful nation. Some of the world's poorest people live in Alaska. Eskimos still die of old age at 58, in a country where white people die of old age at 72. We haven't done much to look after the heritage they gave us, which is very similar to what the Australians have done. It's only recently that the Aborigines were given enough ground to live a fruitful life. Did you know that the Labor government has given the Aborigines 13 per cent of the continent? Potentially, it's very valuable land. If you don't look after where you grew up, you betray yourself. If you grew up on the east coast of Australia, where I grew up, the country is so extraordinarily beautiful, compared with almost any other land on earth, that you'd feel criminal if you desecrated it. I think many Australians and Alaskans have that in common: they respect the land. Both places also have a common sense of isolation. When Alaskans find out that I'm an Australian, they say, 'If I hadn't come to Alaska, I would have gone to Australia'. Many of the people who live here say that to me.

Australia offers the world a kind of social integrity. That is to say, the Australian political, social and economic systems work to a balance, so that everybody has a shot at something. It's probably the most economically and socially egalitarian society on earth. That used to be bought at the price of excellence, but no more. An American woman such as my wife would say Australia is maybe 15 years behind the United States socially, but I think she's looking at something that started off 100 years behind and is growing fast. Australia has the capacity to absorb races. It allows people to get along by being themselves, that's what it really has to offer. No other country can say that except Alaska.

America is a great market, and if Australians organise themselves they can penetrate it. There is a vast market here for goods and services, to anybody who's innovative and understands how the Americans think and what they'll buy.

Ralph Sarich

Australian inventors have enormous difficulties in marketing their products, which in itself speaks volumes about some of this country's most entrenched problems concerning innovation and competition in the world marketplace. When an inventor breaks through such barriers, it's often because he or she has combined the development of something useful and original with skill in selling it to sceptical investors and manufacturers. The classic example, one of the wealthiest and most creative of living Australians, is a beguilingly modest man named Ralph Sarich.

For most of his 46 years, this Perth-born genius of high technology has doggedly pursued a dream, sacrificing home and job security, with the blessing of wife Pat, to create an engine with the capacity to revolutionise the world's transportation industries. Australian corporate giant BHP has been convinced since 1972 that the Sarich orbital engine project will lead to a smaller, lighter, cheaper, more fuel-efficient and durable replacement for conventional engines. In December of 1983, General Motors became involved by setting up a division for quick access to the new technology and to transfer the know-how to American staff. Mercury Marine and Outboard Marine, the world's biggest corporations in marine engines, also jumped on the bandwagon after noting that amongst other advantages, the orbital combustion process (OCP) engine reduces hydrocarbon pollution by up to 80 per cent, compared to conventional marine outboard engines.

With the orbital combustion process engine taking up only 40 per cent of the space required by conventional automobile engines, the implications for car design are staggering. Sarich and his wife already rank among the wealthiest of Australian families, and if the value of the stocks continues to soar as expected, they could end up as the most elite of all the country's 25,000 millionaires.

To Ralph Sarich, all this means very little. He and Pat live with their two children in the healthy and unassuming way of many Perthites, and they also hold a devotion to Western Australia which is peculiar in its passion to the citizens of that faraway place. On the subject of devotion, Sarich is something of a lay expert. Not only has he devoted every job taken, every experience gathered, to the eventual goal of becoming an independent inventor, but having achieved such a grand design he has now developed the best high technology of its kind in the world. He has introduced management techniques so stirring that they have captured even the stodgy imaginations of some of America's greatest corporations. The staff loyalty at his Perth headquarters is a local legend.

An electric talent with an unswerving vision of the brain power that, like Australia's mineral wealth, remains yet untapped, Ralph Sarich and his Orbital Engine Company shine like beacons into an Australian future that only poets and thinkers dare to foresee.

A special earth-moving scoop was my first significant invention. Along the line there have been a lot of little inventions, an hydraulic pump, a transmission later on — I guess there are about 20 or 30 inventions you could tally but not all are patented, because in a lot of instances it isn't worth the cost. Internationally, patent costs are sometimes far too high to be worth the risk. Even so, our company spends at least $100,000 per year on patents.

As a young man, I couldn't see myself marketing the technology that I developed unless I had business experience, so it was my objective to get that experience. I also felt that sales were going to be important, so I spent a year selling heavy earth-moving equipment, industrial equipment, General Motors' engines, that sort of thing. That job was a mixture of engineering and sales, and it was very interesting because the machines were interesting. Something else I wanted was practical experience, so I worked for Theiss Brothers as a plant engineer on heavy earth-moving equipment. It was there that I learned a lot about scrapers, bulldozers and other similar types of machinery.

I followed a planned course because I felt that practical experience was essential to be an inventor, marketing was important and business was extremely important. I believe it is essential to have some formal education, and the units I did in engineering proved to be invaluable later. I really should have done more but I guess everything has fallen into place anyway. In fact, the whole business is bigger than I thought it would be. I am the negotiator for OEC in business deals with various companies, control all the engineering operations of the company, and the finance. However, I'm not formally qualified in any of these areas. It has been a matter of self-education, good fortune and experience, I suppose.

I was born and educated in Perth. My father left Yugoslavia because fortunately, he didn't consider it a good place to raise children. He contemplated America, then decided to migrate to Australia. He came unassisted, unlike it is today, paying his way by working at chopping trees in Pinjarra. He was here when the depression hit. He had to live in a tent in Pinjarra, under water-logged conditions. All he could afford at first was a mattress and bare existence. He kept my mother in Yugoslavia, sent her money, and was finally able to pay for hers and my elder brother's passage to Australia. They settled in the Swan Valley and saved enough money to buy a property. I was born on 12 December 1938 in the Perth country suburb of Herne Hill.

My father not only had a job, but also ran a vineyard and an orchard and raised sheep. The wine from the property was so terrible that it was only in later years I was able to drink wine again. Because we lived on a property, I was interested in farm machinery and electrical equipment, which of course then was far less sophisticated than it is today. I was interested in anything technological or scientific, and engineering dominated later.

Although my father thought I should take on farming he must have felt I had potential, because he insisted that I go to engineering classes and do correspondence. I wasn't a star at school, my reports said that I had potential but that I wasn't realising it. I found concentration at school difficult. I always wanted to be inventive and creative and had my sights set on that before I even started school. I used to tinker as a kid and couldn't see the relationship between subjects such as history and geography and what I was aiming to do.

My elder brother was educated in Perth, too, and I have another brother, Eric, who was a star League footballer in Victoria. He currently works on ABC television in Perth. He has represented Victoria in State football. I also have a sister who's a year younger than I am, who was probably the best of us all at school. She became a clerk/bookkeeper. My other brother is a farmer.

I didn't finish my secondary education until I was about 16, after which I did night school, technical college, and day school. Up to the age of about 22 I was studying engineering units, but I didn't complete the full course. As with my primary and secondary education, I had the vision of trying to be creative, doing things somewhat differently, trying to use foresight, and I didn't feel I was being taught that. In fact, I found if I was inquisitive of teachers on certain subjects, I was told to do as I'm told. In the end I concluded that if I devoted the school hours to business, I could in turn employ mathematicians, if I wanted to, and be creative in ways that weren't taught at school. You could say that what I'm doing now is what I aimed at during my school years.

At the age of 19 or 20 I had started a part-time engineering business, which I expanded after quitting tech. I was designing and building agricultural and industrial equipment, then I took a job with Tutt Bryant in sales engineering. The job was partly marketing, partly engineering. Later I became the northwest general manager for them, covering the area from Carnarvon to the Northern Territory. Then I came back and was placed in charge of Pacific sales in Perth. I also invested in real estate and other businesses during this period. The Tutt Bryant job was to earn a living and my business activities on the side were designed to generate extra income, because I wanted to be able to do what I'm doing today.

I had a pretty severe car accident at the age of 22. In fact, I was on the danger list for a little while. I had internal injuries, multiple fractures, and for one period alone I spent two months in hospital. Several other times, I had to go back for facial operations. After that I decided to get married. I thought I was walking a tightrope, so to speak. My brother Eric and I were pretty wild in those days; we used to love having a great time. I had known Pat since she was about 16, and when we got married we were fairly broke. We were on the wrong side of the financial ledger, because the accident had cost me a great deal through loss of work and very heavy medical bills. When we got married, we bought a house on no deposit. Pat operated an orchard and held a job as a bookkeeper, whilst I operated my engineering business and worked for Theiss. Financial survival was a case of working seven days a week, every week. I often didn't get more than two to three hours of sleep a day, but Pat and I combined very well and we built ourselves up.

Another reason my schedule was full was because I played sport as much as I could until I was about 30. When I gave away tech, I then put those hours into business, learnt to invest in real estate and other business activities, started my own business and operated that, sold it, went into a job, and continued to invest in real estate. At the right time I decided to get into the area of technology, which had been an ambition all my life. I quit the job and went full-time into the automobile area.

When I reached the economic point to be able to do that I thought, okay, I'll cut down on expenditure and start. I discussed the idea with my wife, then we sold the home we'd built and had for only about a year. It was on a five-acre block of land 12 kilometres from Perth. We put the proceeds from that sale into the project, so we risked everything to achieve the ends that I was aiming for. My wife and I felt that

*Above, Ralph Sarich, winner of 'The Inventors' Grand Final, 1972, being
congratulated by the Acting Chairman of the ABC, Mr A. G. Lowndes, and by
panellists Diana Fisher and Leo Port.
Below, with wife Pat and children Jenny and Peter*

if I did fail, she could always go back to work as a bookkeeper and we could do what everyone else does: put a deposit on a home and pay it off again. Fortunately, it didn't work out that way.

Our two kids were only little when we built and sold the house, which was a dream home for my wife, a very nice place. We went to live in an old asbestos house in Morley. That was a rugged home compared to what we'd been used to. We took it on because it had a workshop and bush all around. Although it was in a residential block, it was an area that hadn't been developed. So I threw security out the door and my wife supported me.

Without Pat, none of this would have been possible. It all goes back to when she was prepared to commit her house and security to my ambitions. She's not at all interested in engineering, she just wanted to let me fulfil my ambition in life. She's like that, the only thing she won't let me do is learn to fly. She reckons I'll kill myself. I book flying lessons, she cancels them, and that's been going on for a few years now. But it is essential to have somebody like her. I think she's been critically important for me, because I like a close family and we are very close to our two kids, Peter and Jenny, who are 21 and 19 respectively.

Any time I've wanted to do something, Pat has backed me all the way. She's always there to put questions to, which is very important. Otherwise, I believe there is no way that I could be doing what I'm doing today. We're very compatible, though we look completely different. She's blonde, fair and slim, whereas I'm rather the opposite. She's been a tremendous mother and has raised the kids excellently. They're well-mannered and not spoilt in any way, despite the fact that they know they're well off. Peter has been out with the roughest kids in the neighbourhood, as well as with rich silver spoons. We rarely try to influence him as to whom he picks for friends. As far as we're concerned, we like our kids' friends. We're completely against drugs. Our kids have led quite an ordinary, typical Australian life. They are, I believe, well-mannered, honest kids, and Pat deserves all the credit.

To be quite honest, for a long time I didn't really have very good contact with the kids. I used to be up before they got up and home after they had gone to bed. Pat used to insist sometimes that I take a Sunday off and we'd go on picnics or some other outing. We now have very good memories of those times with the kids, and again, she's responsible for that. We still go to various places with them, for example, we all went to Hawaii. We're hardly like parents to them nowadays, because they talk with us a lot about the things they do. Even if they do wrong things, they're not afraid to tell us.

Peter and Jenny were little when I started on my very ambitious project, but I had supreme confidence in what I was about to do. However, I very quickly began to question that confidence, because I hadn't realised how conservative the engine industry really was. This jolted me, to discover that the task would be a hell of a lot harder than I had thought. What I had to do was just work that much harder and be a lot smarter. I had to sharpen up all around.

I used to do the designing, draughting, in fact everything, by myself. Then I employed a fitter who, by the way, still works here. Bruce Fairclough was my first employee and he had some draughting experience so I used him as a fitter cum draughtsman. Subsequently, we employed another two people — both of whom also are still with us — Ken Johnsen and Colin Pumphrey, who were both kids then. Ken was 16 years of age when he joined us and is now the company's commercial manager. We currently have about 120 people.

When I started out on my own, I didn't have any clear idea of what I wanted to create. I had a drawing board and a drawing machine, I looked at a blank sheet of paper and thought, where do I go from here? I guess a few thoughts were going through my mind without reference to an exact concept, but I certainly had thoughts that there was a place in the world for a more advanced engine. I thought the size and weight of car engines at that time weren't in keeping with the modern world. My vision was to build a very compact engine with good fuel economy and hopefully lower cost, which would also comply with emission standards. Of course, those standards weren't as stringent then as they have become since. All of a sudden, both fuel economy and emission standards became critical concerns, and the motor companies began to pour in far more money than they'd ever put into such projects, so we were fighting against a fast-moving target. According to a published report, Ford invested $200 million to improve fuel economy by 1/10th of a mile per gallon. That's what we were competing with, but we were only spending tens of thousands or hundreds of thousands of dollars to try to catch up with such targets.

We took on minor partners eventually. Sir Charles Court heard about my company and sent some officers from the Western Australian Government to have a look at what we were trying to do. One of the people he asked to have a look at the project was an engineer named Tony Constantine, of Wundowie Steel Industry. As soon as he saw what I was trying to achieve, he was insistent about making a personal investment, so he acquired a 10 per cent share holding. A friend named Roy Young also wanted to buy 10 per cent, and between us we funded the whole project. From there onwards it was a partnership. Then on 23 November 1972 we signed up with BHP. We'd had a lot of approaches from other people but we elected to go with BHP mainly because Tony Constantine had quite a good relationship with some of the BHP executives through Wundowie, and he thought that BHP had some very good people. They've never let us down and have turned out to be very good partners.

Initially, I studied all sorts of different geometries for an engine concept. The over-riding criteria was always that we would look for a compact and lightweight engine which, as I said before, had to have fuel efficiency and low emissions. We came up with the orbital concept. One of the things that attracted us to it was that it had compactness, but I considered one of its most vital attributes to be a unique gas motion characteristic. Experts did not agree with us at that time. They didn't believe the engine would create good combustion, but they weren't in possession of information that I had concerning two-fluid injection. So we started with the orbital engine and developed the combustion process on it, but to make the engine work properly we had to develop a new fuel system. That was something we hadn't banked on at the beginning, simply because I thought, science being what it is, somebody out there will have a thesis we can use. Then we discovered there wasn't such a thesis, so that provided another challenge and, I suppose, an opportunity.

There were a lot of people who had put their confidence in us, including Sir Charles Court, and the feeling was that we couldn't let them down. It was just a matter of designing the fuel system, which we did, and which is now the very best in the world. It produced the right type of fuel atomisation and patterns. We then achieved such impressive success with the orbital engine that we were able to obtain a commitment from one of the major United States manufacturers. But we could see that even if a prototype was delivered to them of a high performing standard, they would still have to design production equipment for it. This meant they would have to go through the prototype procedure again to manufacture the engine. After that, they'd have to modify the engine to suit the production equipment. We could see that to produce a viable engine was still a tremendous way down the line, so we decided to look at the possibility of converting the combustion technology of the orbital engine to the conventional engine. We found that we couldn't make much headway on existing automobile engines, but our engineers came up with the idea of fitting our combustion process to a standard marine engine. To the engine block itself we applied our technology on combustion, fuel systems, aero-dynamics and thermodynamics, with the result that we've produced an engine which can now be manufactured on existing tooling. The engine incorporates all the original key objectives of the company, so it has now achieved everything in one package.

The orbital combustion process engine has aircraft, marine, indus-trial, motorcycle, and snow plough applications, as well as auto-mobiles, so it's useful in all areas. At the moment we're working on non-exclusive marketing arrangements. However, we have been approached for exclusive licensing worldwide. Which way we go depends on the magnitude of the payments. Looking at the engine's potential the payments would have to be very big, because just in the automobile area, by 1986-87 there will be about 35 million cars produced worldwide. If we penetrate even two-thirds of the market, that's 20 million cars. The royalty rates should be about $35 per automobile on average, but if we look at even a $25 average, that's something like $US 5 billion over a 10-year period.

I am still responsible for all of OEC's negotiations. I try to be fair at all times. I look at what's reasonable and fair for our company and for the companies we negotiate with, and I feel that anything we present is balanced. If we think a business proposal is equitable, then we will stand very hard, but we do look at the situation carefully from all aspects, including from the point of view of the potential client.

The Australian market is just not big enough to justify the sort of investment you have to make to do the research, development, prov-ing, and then setting up and establishing the manufacturing facilities. We deliberately targeted to get General Motors and Outboard Marine Corporation involved. Both are the biggest companies in their respective fields. It was also quite deliberate to go to the Americans, because we felt that they had been upset by the Japanese manufac-turers getting inside them with better technology. My belief is that once somebody has pushed them a little bit, the Americans are very determined people. They were down, and I felt that they'd be looking for a step-change in technology to help them take on their previous position of superiority again. The other thing, of course, is that they are the biggest. In spite of the fact that people always look to the Japanese as being big, General Motors and Outboard Marine are a lot bigger than any Japanese manufacturers in those respective fields, so we thought our marketing plan made sense from the strategic viewpoint of the market itself and the determination of our targeted clients.

I've never really had trouble getting investors. There's a lot of public misunderstanding about when I used to have a dash at the government concerning lack of support. That wasn't because we couldn't get private funding, we could get it, but governments in all other countries were supporting high technology projects to a far greater extent than we were being supported. On a relative basis, we weren't asking for anything outlandish. What I was really completely against was that the government wasn't trying to support technology ventures at that time, which could create a lot of employment for the country and introduce a much more sophisticated standard of high technology to this country. I felt, why should private individuals such as myself be trying to do it on their own, when a lot of such work is actually very much in the public interest? If we had only been interested in the money from investors, then we would have been better off in the United States. Yet I'd personally committed myself far more than anybody else in the private sector and had gambled, relatively, on the orbital engine, which is valuable to Australian high technology.

People in business usually can't understand technology well enough to weigh its potential and viability. Therefore, it's natural that they are very guarded, very sceptical. It's up to the technologist to put across the argument properly, to convince them that a project is worthwhile. The manner in which you approach that task is the key. People must first of all trust you and trust your motives. In fact, no-one is a comprehensive expert, but people have to get a feeling that you know what you're doing and that you're a reasonable person to deal with. Negotiation is a matter of working out each individual situation, as the case may be, but I have found that first of all you have to work out what the other party's problems are. You should anticipate, if you can, what their objections will be, and then work out the answers very carefully before they've asked the questions. That's a policy I always use.

There's no doubt in my mind that success comes from fierce determination. You must also at all times be logical in your thinking, constructive, critical; you must try to operate without being biased and without doing things that you'd like to see done rather than what is constructively a reality. By that I mean that often people will head off in a certain direction because they would like something in particular to happen, but they don't face reality and they go in the wrong direction because of that. Be constructive and try to think freely. I also believe that you must not only have confidence in yourself but also look at your weaknesses, which a lot of people fail to do. Listen to people's criticisms of you, encourage them to do so, so that you can see how you look in other people's eyes. A lot of people are blind to that, but it's important.

One other outstanding thing is the importance of being able to read other human beings. The only way you develop that skill is by contact. Your intuition tells you roughly what you think the other person is thinking and you work on that. With regard to influencing BHP, my prime objective was to work out who I was dealing with, to see how they think. At BHP, just like most large corporations, there may be in true reality half a dozen people who make decisions. One person might think one way, another might think another way. I try to work out how the key decision-makers think, what they like to see, then I work on that.

In respect to confidence in my ability against others, I guess I felt that I could do better, but whether that's right or not is another thing. Still, you don't do anything unless you have confidence in yourself, and generally I was very confident that I could do better than what I had seen other people do and I was prepared to gamble on my ability to do just that.

People often think that our company's ability to keep its staff is due to the fact that this is an exciting area, but of course there are other research programs around that don't attract the same loyalty. Right from the outset, I looked at my own career working for other people and I could see the faults of companies that I worked with. I tried to eradicate those faults in our management here. Above all, if we employ somebody we respect their intelligence, and therefore encourage their contribution to how the company should be run.

We try to get the employees to participate in how the company should operate and we do small things that help the working environment and atmosphere. My attitude is that, for example, employees can be put off working somewhere if the place of employment looks shabby and neglected as they drive up to it. So they can be against it before they even start, and if it's untidy inside as well that further aggravates the adverse attitude.

We try to keep our place from being a typical industrial-type facility or laboratory. We try to make the gardens nice and tidy, and we have plants inside the building. In other words, we try to create a pleasant environment first. Then, as I said, we encourage people to have an input on how the company operates. We can have a full meeting and

With an early prototype of the orbital engine

the floor sweeper can stand up and say, 'I think this is being run the wrong way by management'. As long as it's done in a respectful way, we listen. Anyone is entitled to put forth their view on what is wrong with management or what we can do to improve the operation of the company, from the standpoint of how the employees feel as well as their concerns about efficiency, because we are forever striving for greater efficiency.

In job interviews it's important to select the right people. When we interview, it's not good enough for us to merely select, for example, a brilliant engineer — he must have a personality that is compatible with others. So when we interview engineers, we select staff engineers at random to interview the job-seekers jointly with the management. The applicant doesn't know this at the time but he finds out later if he is successful. The policies of the company and what we are looking for in a person are stated when the applicants come in. John Hinton, the general manager, engineering, selects the interviewers and they are varied regularly.

All up, I guess it's a completely different approach to typical Australian industry. In fact, some very big American companies who have been here have been very intrigued by the Orbital Engine Company's methods, and they have told us that they were going to try similar techniques in their own operations. There are no hard and fast formulas — you can't say this is what you should do — it's a matter of getting a feel for what the employees want. It's impossible to know every employee, but you have to get to know enough of them to get a feel of what the general impression is of the company they work for. We try to make them feel that it's their company and try to break down the employer-employee barriers. In fact when the company floated, all the employees were allowed to get equity at the issued value. At that time we had 90-odd employees, and they invested nearly $400,000. That's multiplied by seven times now. Additionally, they are likely to be given a bonus which, based on our present value, is worth approximately $10 million. Payment of this is dependant on full commercial success.

To trigger full commercial success the company needs strong, irreversible commitments. If we get those, the value of the stock, which is about $7.30 per unit now, will probably double or treble. When the employees are doing a tough task like this they're apt to feel that if they succeed, in the end all the 'fat cat' directors and equity holders, the rich people, will make the money instead of the workers, who have put in all the sweat. So my family trust has allocated about four per cent as an incentive to employees, currently valued at $10 million.

The girls here work like heck, and they do so willingly and with self-motivation. Generally, the tradesmen are not as easy to motivate as the engineers. Obviously this is because some tasks are not as interesting as others, but we do try to counter this by providing an opportunity for elevation. We encourage the tradesmen to become technicians and engineering officers, we urge them to go to school and keep increasing their academic skills. In fact, we have a young lady here who started as a tracer and now has an engineering certificate. The company does everything it can to further the interests of its employees in making them feel that they are part of the company, so they have an interest in its welfare.

The best advice in this vein that I ever received was from a management course funded by one of my former employers. We spent a week training in management techniques, and in the end the instructor said, 'Look, I've only shown you the standard methods. If you're going to be exceptional, you can't follow those.' I guess he was being perfectly honest. He went on to say, 'If you want to be a success, you have to work out your own new and novel methods. I've given you what the copybook says, but educational institutions are churning people out continuously, all from the same mould. If you're going to do something exceptional, you must have an exceptional and different approach.' That confirmed what I had learned myself.

If I was going to be exceptional in design, I wasn't going to be taught that at tech, or university, or anywhere else. I believe it is essential to get an education — I'm an advocate of formal education — but once this has been completed a person should start looking for different horizons, be creative in what they do, and listen to other people. I've spent a lot of time listening and talking to people, particularly in my earlier years, to learn their views. You don't necessarily have to adopt those views, but sometimes what they say triggers a thought in one's own mind in some other direction.

Every person who works for OEC has been trained by the company. Considering the numbers of people trained during the development period, together with setting up the laboratories, this must be deemed an accomplishment in its own right. For some machines it is 12 months from the date of order to the date of receipt. So you can see that it hasn't been just a matter of developing the orbital technology. Over half the effort has gone into establishing the facilities and training the employees. The design engineers here are Australian.

The whole orbital engine project has been 15 years in the making, but it must be remembered that there is much more to the picture than that. For instance, General Motors reportedly spent almost $US 1 billion on the rotary engine and never made it a success. There has been the gas turbine, a sterling, and many other concepts. Ford was quoted in the *Wall Street Journal* as having spent $200 million per 1/10 mile per gallon on fuel economy improvement.

When one considers these facts together with the $US 10 billion we have spent, two-thirds of which went into establishing facilities, the Orbital Engine Company has performed very creditably, particularly because to do this in Perth is an enormous task in its own right. To develop engines, sophisticated laboratories are essential, otherwise it isn't possible to communicate properly with General Motors and other such corporations. The laboratory standards must be at least as good as theirs, including the standards of computer facilities, electronics and the reliability of test data.

Everything we buy comes in from overseas countries, such as Germany, Japan and particularly the United States. There are very few equipment distributors and no dealers in Australia who know what they're talking about when it comes to some of the equipment we need to purchase, so we have to chase around overseas to get information. Our own engineers spend considerable time studying equipment for the purposes of development and analysis. We spend a lot of money to help the engineers educate themselves in order to ensure that correct decisions are made on equipment purchases. They've been very accurate with selections.

Certainly there were many times when I felt like giving it all up. I think pride stopped me from doing that. I had committed myself to a task, and I think the fact that other people committed themselves and backed me so hard made me determined not to let them down. I didn't care how wealthy BHP or the investors were, I just do not like letting people down who have put their faith in me. It was an obsession to get the job done. The bad thing about obsessions is that a person can get rattled. Your health can suffer, which doesn't help anyone. I had to learn to ride the pressures, despite how heavy they were, without being stressed or depressed. I don't get depressed now but that's something I have had to learn along the way, because it is virtually impossible to bring off something like this without becoming very hardened. We certainly have had some severe reversals, things that at times looked as though they were going to devastate the company. I spent a lot of time working out my own psychology, and I'm quite a different person in a business sense today than the person I was when I started.

However, socially I haven't changed friends to any significant degree, and I hope I'm still the same person underneath as I was when I started, except for my handling of business and technical matters and troubles. In doing things that were very hard and sometimes distasteful, I've tried to get over my weaknesses. By nature, I'm inclined to be a soft person rather than a hard one. I like to be generous, but sometimes in business that's suicide. It has been a great experience trying to figure out the way people think.

I think a lot of people lose sight of what they're doing. A lot of people set out to make money to be comfortable, to be happy, then they start realising the power and status that money can bring. They become power hungry and off they go on a course of developing more and more power. On current market value, the Sarich Technologies Trust is worth over $250 million, which places it among the first 75 companies in Australia. In its own right, the Orbital Engine Company would have to be among the first 40 firms in our country. However, I think it's unfortunate that our society judges status by the amount of money a person has. I don't look at it that way.

To me, some of the engineers we have working here are on a far higher pedestal than some of the wealthy people we have in our country. From my viewpoint, those engineers are far greater contributors to society than some of the wheelers and dealers around town. I don't look at the amount of money as the measurement of success. What I will be satisfied with in terms of measuring our success will be the penetration and acceptance of our technology in a commercial sense by manufacturers around the world.

In the meantime, of course, I am likely to benefit financially, but my aim isn't to become a social climber. We do not have a desire for the high society scene. My aim is to use the money for development of other scientific projects and for similarly unique endeavours, but not solely to make more money. I will personally be investing quite a lot in projects that I know will never make money, such as in the areas of spinal research, biomechanics and selected biological regions. I know that a number of these projects will be total financial write-offs before I start, but I will derive satisfaction out of contributing to society, and additionally it will be interesting to me.

Perhaps these feelings have something to do with the fact that both my parents taught me strong principles. Although the old man was not religious, my mother was very religious. I'm biased and sympathetic towards religion but I don't go to church. The only religious group I generally donate to is the Salvation Army, because of the benefits I believe they provide for society.

My biggest obsession today is to make the Orbital Engine Company a highly successful international company in technology. I hope to see the OEC one day emulate United Technologies of the United States. To me, it's far more meaningful to see a big new Australian company born out of the use of brain power rather than out of being lucky enough to find oil or minerals or whatever. In that, you really are only exploiting what Nature has given you.

So far Australia has offered the world very little technologically, except in isolated instances. In general, I think we could do much more by using brain power rather than just by relying on the good fortune of Nature, and I think that's what Australia must wake up to. There is no doubt that Australians have the intelligence to be successful, but what's needed is to exhibit a much greater extent of desperation to succeed. The reason for this seems to be that our living standard, on a relative basis, is far too good for the amount of work we do, and I think that's not healthy. The Japanese, who do not have natural resources to speak of, not only work harder than we do, they are also far more dedicated. And yet their living standards are well below ours. It's inequitable really.

I wouldn't mind living in the United States. I like the American people, I like the country, it reminds me somewhat of Australia, so I guess it would be my second choice. But I love Australia and that's why we're still here. I particularly like Perth. I think the people are good and the rugged type of country here suits me. Certainly it's not as picturesque in some people's eyes as, say, the Swiss Alps, but I like the frontier feeling of Australia, the roughness of it. I think the Outback in the north seems almost as if it were on another planet.

I do not like saying what I really think of myself, except I find I'm pretty determined about things. Although I never used to have patience, I have developed it and now I guess it's instinctive to me. It probably comes from my mother. I spend quite a lot of time thinking things through and trying to work people out, which helps me a great deal in business dealings. Before I make a significant decision, it is usually the subject of a lot of prior consideration. People often think that I make spur-of-the moment decisions but I rarely do. Because I try to anticipate what will happen, I usually have many options thought out for each commitment made. I probably have an unusual way of approaching the study of a subject, but when I reach a decision

I am prepared to gamble significantly. Someone probably thought of the same things as I did, but if they did they obviously didn't act upon them. When I hear people say, 'Oh, I thought of that too', it's almost an indictment of themselves, in that if they had, then they should have done something about it.

I don't believe that superior intelligence is indispensable when it comes to accomplishing things. I suppose it's true, though, that some people are lucky to be born with the ability to be versatile thinkers. In my position, I have had to learn to reasonably understand finance, engineering, administration and marketing. A lot of people are fairly narrow in what they can do. If I was included in a cross-section of the population judged on intelligence, I would be lucky to be in the top 30 per cent. What helps me is that I think things through thoroughly, and am prepared to act on my judgment.

Vera Randall

Hearing Vera Randall describe herself, one might conclude that she showed few early signs of becoming the inspiration and prototype of success in business for a half-million female followers across Australia. Genuine though her modesty is, a closer examination of her words reveals a preoccupation with such attributes as strength, sharing, purpose, and vision. It is just those attributes, instilled in her from youth, which have enabled this gracious and amiable woman to found a franchising empire that has now begun to spread throughout the world.

It all began in 1970 when Randall went on holiday to Canada, and there discovered a quick-and-easy method of sewing knitted fabrics. The thrill of creativity hit home, sweet as religion, and she immediately set about adapting the United States-based idea to Australian conditions. With an untutored yet innate business sense, plus a $4,000 loan and boundless enthusiasm for spreading the word, within a decade Randall engineered the opening of 50 Knitwit sewing school/fabric stores. With the help of husband Mike, a marketing man, she has now expanded the business to New Zealand, South Africa, and the United Kingdom, and still has the ultimate goal in sight of bringing the improved idea back to its American birthplace.

Yet behind such grandiose accomplishments and plans, the shy and spiritual New South Wales country girl remains unchanged. When she tells you the motivation behind it all is simply to share the thrill of creativity with women who might not otherwise know it, you believe her. And when she reflects on the domestic joys of life with Mike, son Tim, and step-daughter Michaela, the complete Vera Randall emerges as a rare role model indeed.

Every Knitwit teacher must be nervous when they start a lesson. You are meeting a whole group of new people and you've got to establish empathy as quickly as you can, in order to share the excitement of the method. You've got to get to know people well and build up their confidence in you as teacher. Somehow I knew all of this, so I was meticulous in setting up my first classroom, the way it looked and the presentation of the lesson. A lot of preparation went into it. I just didn't go into a classroom and say, 'Look, I've discovered this method and I'm going to tell you about it'. I programmed what was to happen in each of the lessons and how long it would take, but I was very nervous.

Although most of my early customers were people that I knew, I don't think that made it any easier. I can remember the end of the first lesson more clearly than the beginning, because I walked out of that classroom three feet above the ground. I knew that everyone in the classroom was as excited as I was about the method of sewing. We all went down into the store and the ladies were all buying fabric to go home and make up garments, and I knew that the magic was there.

All of the things that I dreamed would happen were happening that night, and it was an exhilaration that I feel every time I teach or sit in a class or see a Knitwit fashion parade — the excitement of our customers and women sharing the success that comes from making something. We talk to each other about it, I meet women in airports, in the street, in the shops, and we can go up to each other and talk about Knitwit, and know without saying too much what it is that we are sharing, the feeling of being successful, of making something and being admired. It's become like a a big family.

It's a combination of the product, the method of sewing, the people involved in Knitwit, whether at the head office or in our warehouse, the store owners and their staff, all believing in the feeling of confidence that can be built up through success in completing a garment.

I knew what it did for me, and I was very interested to see how it affected other women, because I knew the feeling of having been successful with the very first pair of slacks I made almost as if I could have gone on and done anything. Women that come to our classes tell me this over and over again. They do a Knitwit class and often, for the first time in their lives, some women who never enjoyed the opportunity to be outstanding, or do something special, have this feeling of achievement and creativity that spreads over into other areas of their lives, so that they'll often go on to learn something else. Or they'll be more confident about, say, re-entering the workforce or leaving the workforce or making an important decision. It's not only the method and the success that comes from sewing, it's the sharing of it with other women around Australia, because we really have built up a network which we call our Knitwit family.

There are now almost 500,000 certified Knitwits around Australia. We give a certificate at the end of the eighth lesson to say the student has completed an eight-lesson course in the sewing of knitted fabrics and is now a fully-certified Knitwit. Women are so proud of that certificate.

When you come down to everyday things, failure can be devastating; things like trying to make a dress, and giving up halfway through because you don't know how to put in the zipper. You feel such a dill, fancy not being able to put a zipper or a facing in. But I handled that neatly with Knitwit, because we don't have any zippers. So anything I come across in sewing that I can't handle quickly and easily myself doesn't go in the method.

A lot of the time, doing things correctly was pure instinct. Background helped me a lot and training helped a lot, but I know that there is something instinctive and I know there is a drive. I think the most important thing for me was the ability to relate to other people. If I hadn't been able to communicate to other people how exciting the method of sewing was, how it took place, and how to go into the business, if I hadn't been able to communicate the dream, it wouldn't have happened. So I think it's a mixture of instinct and communication.

My drive comes from inside. I think it comes not only from my belief that there is a plan and path that I am following in life, but also from growing up in a small country town, because we had time to go tramping through the bush, dreaming and fantasising. I can remember walking for whole days in old creek beds just exploring, but all the time my mind was daydreaming about things that could happen. Once you have a dream, it's something to chase. People who don't have a dream and who don't fantasise may never have anything out of the ordinary happen to them.

I was raised at Schofields, a small country town out towards the Hawkesbury area between Blacktown and Windsor (New South Wales). My father owned the general store there. He was the local postmaster, general storekeeper, Justice of the Peace, counsellor, confidant, the lot. Early in my teens he sold his store and bought a poultry farm in the same town, but concurrent with that he owned a British Motors Corporation franchise, which later became a Leyland franchise, in the adjoining town. As I was the oldest of seven children, I guess he needed those two important projects just to bring up the family in the way that he wanted, and set the sort of standards that were important to him. As well, he has a strong work ethic that I also see in myself, in my son Tim, and in the whole family.

My father's family originally settled here from England. My mother's father came out from Norway. So on one side of the family I have the Norwegian line, and on the other British. I guess my love of the water stems from the Norwegian side.

My mother did very well at high school. She did a course at technical college and is a qualified dressmaker. She set up her own dressmaking business for a few years but then raised a family of seven. So I had these two role models at the same time: my father in business, with a very strong drive to work and make new commitments and do new things, and my mother, soft and gentle, with a flair for design, who made me aware of beautiful things. So it was a lovely balance between those two people.

At Schofields, when I started school at four-and-a-half, there was just one room to the school. It grew to be a three or four-room school before I left. Looking back, it was fairly unique to have all the different grades in the one classroom and to be literally learning the alphabet while the big boys and girls were doing much harder work.

From there I went to Parramatta High School, which at that time was a select school. I was quite thrilled to be the only person from that area to be chosen to go to that school that year. I wasn't on a scholarship, but they did call it a select school. Selected people who showed promise of academic achievement were brought together in one school. It's a system which has since changed. My mother also went to the same school under the same system. She could have gone on to be a high achiever, I think. She had all the ingredients but things were quite different then, and I think she was also very happy with the role that she undertook.

It was co-ed at Parramatta. Coming from that tiny school at Schofields to this very big high school, I'll never forget walking into

Above left, Vera Randall, age four, with sister Gwen, age two, 1945.
Above right, Vera Randall's mother, role model, mother of seven, and homemaker.
Bottom, with son Tim, age six, 1974

the quadrangle and seeing 700 boys and girls all assembled at once. I just about fainted with shock. Later that same day, we were measured back-to-back by the children themselves, to see who was the shortest in the school. It was me.

That first year I made a lot of friends. I was part of a group of about 10 who were very close. In my first year there I was elected class captain and was thrilled about that, coming from a small school. I wasn't outstanding academically. I think at school I was even a bit lazy, because I couldn't see any real purpose in the education system apart from the disciplines of learning. I was very anxious by the time I was 15 to get on with things.

I didn't complete the leaving certificate. At the end of the fourth year, I weighed up all the options concerning whether I was to be a teacher, or go on to university, or follow some sort of commercial path. I determined that it would be a commercial path, and within days of coming to that decision I left school and started at business college. I would've been 15½, which was quite young in those days to be leaving school. But having started at four-and-a-half, I was always a year younger than everyone else in my class.

My parents were a bit disappointed by my decision, but I think they also saw the value in it. They saw that I wanted to get out and work and get on with things, and didn't argue beyond a few days about it. They saw I was serious, I wasn't just quitting school to be lazy, I was leaving for a reason: to get out and start working.

All those years I had thought about being a school teacher, because in those days a female became a nurse or a teacher or did office work. I vaguely thought about office work, but deep down I knew it was going to be more. But I did the commercial course and enjoyed that, short-hand and typing and bookkeeping, and went off and did secretarial work for eight or ten years and loved it.

The third job that I took, within two years of leaving business college, was at Upjohn, which is an international pharmaceutical company. From the day I started there I loved the excitement of that place It was an American company and I loved the way they approached business. Before going to Upjohn, I knew that work should be more exhilarating than what I was feeling. I didn't want to just go somewhere from nine o'clock to five o'clock and spend time. I was looking for the buzz of work.

At Upjohn I worked for the same man all the way through. When I started working for him he was the accountant and office manager. As he was promoted to managing director and then Far East area manager, I was promoted along with him. So I went beyond the normal secretarial duties, and I was always thrilled when he gave me projects to look after that I could complete in my own right but under his name. Taking minutes of all the meetings, whether they were production, quality control, advertising, or general management, was wonderful grounding for all the things I've done since.

I met my first husband when I was working at Upjohn. I was 18, which seems terribly young to me now, and I was married by 20, which was fairly common in the 1960s. Looking back, I really didn't know what I was doing. I was too young and it was quite devastating to have our dreams tumble down later. I left Upjohn when I was expecting Tim, and enjoyed two wonderful years at home when he was a baby before I went on to discover Knitwit.

When Tim was 18 months old I went off on a holiday trip to Canada. I took him along with me. I kept my long-service leave from when I was working at Upjohn and used that money for this exotic, overseas holiday to visit friends. I was supposed to go for 28 days on an excursion ticket, but I ended up staying for three months.

It was on the very first night there that my friend, who's a very busy medical doctor, invited me to go to a sewing class. I couldn't believe my ears. Having travelled all the way from Australia to be invited along to a sewing class! In the past I had tried very hard to sew, of course, with my mother being a professional dressmaker and others in the family being able to sew. I was the one who kept failing in what I believe is a very important part of the Australian home-making tradition. I believe that women are the centre of the home. As much as we might share all of the responsibilities of cooking, cleaning, sewing, organising, and even doing the flowers, there has got to be someone who's in charge of that traditionally female area.

To me that traditional role is very important. I love it, I thrive on it. The fact that I can have both is, to me, what the women's movement has been all about, the fact that I can run this whole Knitwit thing, travel the world, and still come back and enjoy being a wife and a mother and the focal point of a home. Because to me the home is the most important part of our society.

I went along to the sewing class quite reluctantly, because having travelled so far it just didn't make sense. I'd literally given up on learning to sew. I'd tried very hard, I'd done sewing classes at night school and failed. There's nothing quite like failure to put you off something, and I really was off the idea of ever being able to sew. But I went along to that class to be polite. The lesson was by demonstration, and I saw the teacher make up a beautiful pair of double-knit slacks. She and the whole class enjoyed it.

I was first into the store after the lesson to buy the fabric, the pattern, the thread, the scissors — all of the things I needed to make the garment. By one o'clock the next morning at my friend's house in Vancouver, I'd completed the slacks — I had sewed them up and they fitted beautifully. I knew then that I had come across something that I wanted to share with every other woman in Australia, not only the method of sewing, but what went along with it: the feeling I had of being successful at this very important part of our home-making tradition. I stayed awake all night, realising that I had come across something important.

To create something is an instinct that's locked up inside every one of us. This creative urge is a part of us that needs fulfilling and I had not felt a lot of fulfillment in that area, because I'm not naturally creative. I've got a good sense of colour and harmony, but I'd never actually made something successfully. Sewing was the thing that I was looking for to fulfil a creative need.

All of the fabrics used in the method are knitted, and it's just the method of sewing the garments which manufacturers had been using for 10 or 15 years. It's very quick and eliminates all the tedious, time-consuming steps of home sewing that have been carried on from generation to generation, without change. So this whole new method made sense to me, it was logical, you literally traced off a pattern, cut it out, sewed it, and it was easy! You did all of the different steps for a reason and you could see how this whole thing was going together.

It was part of a very big business which was started in 1968 by a lady called Anne Person from Eugene, Oregon. She'd had access to off-cuts from a factory — they were knitted fabrics and ribbings and things like that — and she didn't know how to sew them. So she made it her business to go along to that factory. I don't know whether she got employment or how she did it, but she learned the secrets of the garment manufacturers and put them together in a sewing book, published some patterns, and started teaching other women her method. At the time I came across it in Canada in 1970, she had about 360 outlets throughout America and Canada.

I went down to the store the next morning, the same store that I'd been to the lesson for, and asked how it all worked. The lady there was very helpful. She explained that it was the method of sewing which Anne Person had pioneered and she had since franchised, and she explained how franchising worked. Independent women had set up stores similar to hers in their own communities and were in business, teaching the method and selling all the products needed to sew the garment. Having established that I stayed on in Canada for three months, and went to five different companies like Anne Person's company to do classes.

I learned the five different methods, and of course being a secretary helped. I recorded everything. I finally came back to Australia with 28 shorthand notebooks filled with ideas, a goal already established, and an objective written down. Within six months I'd written a business plan and gone along to my bank manager for an overdraft to start the business.

The research was important to me, because I couldn't sew and I had to learn everything about the manufacturers' method of sewing. But I learned very quickly because the method is so logical and sensible. So in a way, the mechanical side of it was fairly easy. How the business worked, how franchising worked, again was fairly mechanical — it was finding the way to share the excitement that challenged me the most.

The Americans and Canadians were incredibly helpful. Everywhere I went people were happy to give me information and to help me formulate my ideas. I don't think any of them saw me as a threat to what they were doing, because I wasn't going to compete against the principals of any of these operations. But I think to people on that side of the world at that time, Australia was almost another planet, we're just so far away. They couldn't see any threat and we were a tiny market. There was nothing patronising about their help, though. They were excited about the idea of me pioneering the thing in Australia.

At first, my mother was quite anxious about the fact that I was going out to teach sewing, having seen my earlier efforts. My parents were both anxious about the effect it would have on my marriage and on my role as a woman, which is understandable. But they were very supportive all the way through, there was never a day that they suggested I should stop. As parents, they were always worried about when I would arrive for dinner, say, on a Friday night or Sunday lunch, and then I would drop off to sleep a few hours later because I was at home and I could relax. They probably saw me at the times when I was looking the most vulnerable. But they're terribly, terribly proud of me. Even though it's hard for them to convey all those feelings, I know that they tell other people about them.

My first husband was supportive to start with, but I don't think he had the vision that I had as to how big this thing was going to get. I knew how big it was in the United States, and I also knew that the population in the States and Canada was quite disproportionate to Australia. But my enthusiasm was based on a need that I felt to share the method of sewing with other women, because it had done so much for me to be successful in something that I had previously failed at. It was quick, easy, and fun, and I got a feeling of success every time I made something. I mean, other people would admire what I made and actually challenge that I'd made it myself. So it did something to me every time I completed a garment. Then there was the aspect of being able to make garments that were individual. You didn't see things like them in the stores and you didn't see other people wearing the same styles of clothes. To me, franchising was the obvious way to share the method and the excitment of starting a business.

We've never gone out and actively sold a franchise. Whether it's in Australia or overseas, people have come to Knitwit wanting to own a Knitwit store. I sold the franchise for New Zealand to Janette and Mani Wild who, at the time, owned a franchise in Adelaide. In the United Kingdom it was Coats and Patons who heard about it through their Melbourne operation. They invited Mike and I and Elaine, my accountant, to fly to London to talk about it. As it turned out, within two years we'd bought the franchise back from that big company, because they didn't have the flexibility or the type of skills that are needed for opening small businesses. They had all the capital in the world but didn't have the ingredients necessary for success in Knitwit, which are a feeling for people, an empathy with the market, and an understanding of human needs. It's a people thing.

It was a mutal decision that this big multinational's approach to the market wasn't the thing for Knitwit. On the other hand, Coats/Patons own the franchise in South Africa and it's very successful there. It's a completely different market, more vibrant and in a country that's still in the pioneering stage. In the last two weeks I've had discussions with a guy from Manchester in England. He and his wife are now buying the franchise for the United Kingdom. I've had five Australians working over there for the last 18 months, but soon we'll see it being run entirely by people living in the United Kingdom.

I travelled around Australia with them over the last two weeks and across to New Zealand, sat up night after night sharing the excitement of the whole thing, and saw them off at the airport just a few hours ago, knowing that I'd come across the right couple. It's not a question of sale of a franchise really, or the money involved. To me, it's finding a couple that have a feeling for the business. They'll go out and want to share it with other people, just as Janette and Mani have done in New Zealand.

We are all part of the same Knitwit family. The people who buy franchises, a single store in Australia, or a franchise for a whole country, are still linked to us. We're the franchisor and we have a very strong relationship, in that the success of each of us lies in our interdependence. The success of an individual store is dependant on my success, and my success is dependant on the success of the store.

I see the European markets opening up, say, within the next five years. Within 10 years, I see us being in 10 countries. Ultimately, for an Australian to take the concept back to America and show them how to really do it is the goal. I love the United States market. It's exciting, it's fast, and I think in this particular area I've seen an idea, developed it, and made it work better than the original idea. I'd say we'll be in America within the next 10 years but I don't want to go too quickly. When the time is right, it will happen. When I find the right people to work with in that country, it will happen.

Germaine Greer published *The Female Eunuch* in the same year that I started Knitwit. I read that book with some interest, but at that time I couldn't relate very much to the goals and aspirations of the whole movement. But another part of me could see a way to involve other women in setting up their own businesses, and I couldn't see any reason why we couldn't do it. I couldn't understand the limitations that the feminist movement felt were being placed on us, so I quite quickly put aside thoughts of any involvement in the movement.

A lot of the publicity tended to be around the things that women couldn't do, the limitations in employment and the wages differential. Looking back now I can see that it all did exist, that it was all true. In the past it was very hard for women within the hierarchical system of business or government to achieve at the higher levels, but I think individual women in the professions were enjoying a degree of success. The thing that is new for a lot of men is that more and more women are becoming achievers. But men can share the achievement, so that it adds a new dimension to a relationship instead of being something that's going to take away from it.

I think the situation for women working in hierarchical-type systems has improved, although it's still got a long way to go. But I guess my background was quite different, growing up in a family where my father was always in business, and there was no reason why he couldn't go out and start a new business. I couldn't see any reason why women couldn't start and have no limitations, and there were very few. There were limitations like needing a male guarantor if you went along for an overdraft, but I wasn't going to wait around for 10 years for things to change and I accepted my $4,000 loan — with a male guarantor. It's interesting for me now to look back on what happened during those years and realise that while I couldn't feel involved in what was happening with the feminist movement, I still had a strong urge to get on with working with other women and to start Knitwit.

When I started the business I wanted to write in one sentence what I was going to do. I had my mind full of shops, sewing methods, designing patterns and fabrics, and when I got back to Australia it all felt quite overwhelming. But I still knew I wanted very much to do it, so I sat down and wrote down what it was. I've since discovered what I did was to define an objective. At the time I didn't know all these things, but I wanted to write down what I wanted to do. I wrote that I wanted to teach Australian women a fun, easy method of home sewing. So having written that, the next step was much, much easier. I sat down with a map of Australia and marked 50 locations where I thought a Knitwit business would be successful. Then I put a time limit on opening those 50 stores — 1980. The 50th store was in fact opened on the 18th of January, 1980. I set a goal and put a date on it.

I think the clever thing was actually publishing that goal. Quite by chance I did an interview with a newspaper in about 1974, and the journalist asked me how many stores I saw being around Australia ultimately. I said that I intended to open 50 stores by 1980 and she printed that. In every interview I ever did after that, the journalist would ask me how it was going!

At the beginning, I worked out the minimum amount that I would need to start the business. Having defined the objective and set a goal, I wrote a business plan. There were pages and pages of typing, all the details on what the corporate image would be, how the classroom would be set up, how many people would be in a class, and what would be taught in the classes, right through to how much money I would need to borrow to start the first store. I determined that if I could borrow $4,000 and lease fixtures and fittings and do my printing on a 60-day account, that amount would be enough for the first store. It was also as much as I dared to go along to the bank manager and ask for!

So I went along to the bank manager in the town adjoining Schofields, where my father had his business. I did it during an afternoon with a pile of samples of garments that I had made using the Knitwit method, the business plan, the objective, the goal, and a document for him including a cash plan for the first 12 months of the business, showing him how I would repay the $4,000. I was in the bank less than 10 minutes and he suggested that I come back the next afternoon and we'd talk about it again. I'd gone in expecting to be there for hours, but I went out the door of the bank thinking, there are other banks. Yet when I went back the next day he was a different man. He was very excited about the whole project. I now think that he probably went home that night and asked his wife what it was all about.

I knew from working at Upjohn that trademarks were important and that product identification was important. It took me months to put the name together. I knew that a trademark had to be an invented word and I knew the rules for registering, so I finally used a combination of the words 'knit' from knitted fabric and 'wit' being the fun of sewing it up, so it was a combination of words to make Knitwit. Then I realised the play on the word 'nitwit', which has worked well for us.

The first thing I did after getting the bank loan was to lease a store. I found a shop at Carlingford in New South Wales at a very good rent. A tiny store, it was only 700 or 800 square feet and had a classroom on an upper level, but it was clean and in a courtyard building. I contacted a shop fitter to fit it out in the corporate colours that I'd determined with graphic artists Colin Xavier and Norm Nelson. So the physical things were underway. What I didn't have was customers.

I had this wonderful method of sewing, I'd written the instruction manual, designed 16 sewing patterns and had them printed, but the $4,000 overdraft was all used up. Then I did something that I realise now was a direct mail campaign. Again, at the time I didn't know that. I sat down and wrote a letter to all of my friends and relatives and friends of friends of relatives, telling them what I was doing and how exciting it was. I told them about the classes, what they could learn in them, how much they cost and when they were starting, and booked the first series of classes from those letters. From memory, I sent out 60 letters and I had bookings for about 28 people.

The other thing that I did was letter-box drops. Being a secretary, I was able to design a very nice leaflet. I owned an electric typewriter, a Gesterfax machine and a duplicator, and I copied off leaflets on coloured papers to make them look interesting. I used to walk around on Saturday afternoons after I'd closed the store and put these papers in letter boxes. If people were out in the garden, I'd stop and talk to them and almost take the booking on the spot.

I did fail at different things along the way. It set me back temporarily but my whole purpose was so overwhelming, this need to teach other women this exciting method of sewing, that I very quickly picked myself up and said, 'That was pretty dumb'. And I got on with doing it right the next time. I've made mistakes but I don't dwell on them. I don't catalogue them or even think back on them, but I can remember after things went wrong that I said, 'Well, you won't do that one again'. My setbacks have been normal things in business, such as when it was difficult to find materials or importing laws changed, but I don't think I ever saw any of them as real setbacks. I saw them more as things that I had to find a way around. I think it was Robert Townsend who said, 'Problems are opportunities to choose between solutions'. I love that.

Being a small business at first, I knew there was no leeway for big mistakes. It wasn't as if I was a big company with a multi-million dollar backing somewhere. It was the bank's money to start with, the $4,000. There was just no room for doing things other than the right way.

For the first 10 years, I was teaching. I felt that it was very important that I stay in that classroom, in contact with our customers and with the whole basis of the business. As well, I was training all of the teachers for the first 10 years. I've since been able to employ a teacher/trainer, a fabulous lady, to do that, but I still go into most of the training sessions for part of the time. I can't teach now and I'm really disappointed about this, for the simple reason that I'm rarely in Sydney for eight weeks in a row. It's not fair to the class to start teaching for three or four lessons and then change teachers. It's important for the students to build up a rapport with one person.

The thing grew so quickly I found that before long I was teaching classes almost every day and every evening of the week. Tim was in a pre-school kindergarten and I was dropping him off in the morning at 8.30 and picking him up in the evening at 5.30, going home, cooking dinner, and going back to the store to teach another class and tidy up and prepare for the next day. So they were long, long days. As well, I was working on the franchising plan, to begin selling it to other women. But that wasn't terribly different because in the years before that, when I was at home or working at Upjohn, I was doing voluntary work for World Vision. I was literally going from one job to the other

Above left, introducing Mike to the world of Knitwit, 1980.
Above right, with Premier Neville Wran after receiving the Bulletin-Veuve
Cliquot Australian Businesswoman of the Year Award, 1979.
Below, with Mike, step-daughter Michaela, and Tim, 1985

at that time, so there was nothing unusual for me in working day and night, because I wanted to.

I just can't see a difference between work and play. I enjoy everything, whether it's working, cooking, going scuba diving, going out on the harbour, or being with Mike, Tim and Michaela. To me, it's all there to be enjoyed and it's all precious. Whether it's a walk down the street in Balmain or a trip out on the ferry, there is so much to enjoy. Those early years, while I was working up to 20 hours a day, I can even remember working all day and all night and going on the next day. There was an exhilaration involved that kept it from being a chore, and that exhilaration still hasn't stopped.

I kept up the direct mail marketing approach all the way through. Twice a year, we still mail to all of our customers. It is an important basis on which the business has been developed, because it provided a very personal communication. It is a *real* letter to our customers, addressed personally and delivered through the letter box, sharing our latest news about fabrics, new classes, and new patterns, and sharing the success of the growth of the business. So everyone that is part of the business, whether as a store owner or a customer, is kept in touch. And I say to this day that I share the success of Knitwit with every one of those women, because we really did share the dream.

My first franchisee was a lady living in Windsor. She wasn't originally a customer, she was a friend of one of my first students. At the time that I met her she owned a haberdashery store. Her friends had told her to have a look at what I was doing and she bought the franchise to open a store at Windsor within months of looking at the idea. She could see how exciting it was, and that store opened within a few years of my opening the first one at Carlingford. It was from there that the chain grew. Most of our subsequent franchisees were former Knitwit students.

The stores opened rapidly in the next five years, 10 in one year, 15 the next. After I had opened the fifth store, it was obvious that my first husband didn't share my dream and that our relationship wasn't strong enough to cope with the changes within our marriage. It's enormous, the sheer emotional trauma in the break-up of a marriage. At the time I was determined to make the business work and I knew I had to keep going and bring Tim up. Even though I knew the marriage wasn't sound almost from the beginning, the business probably escalated the timing of the break-up. On the other hand, I knew that it was the right thing for both of us. When the decision had to be made it was crystal clear that the time was right, but it was a question then of setting up my life independently with Tim and then seven or eight years of being a single mother running a business. It was hard but a lot of people were doing it at that time.

I was so busy opening more stores and keeping everything together that the excitment of the achievement didn't come until much later. I was aware that it was happening, and I celebrated the opening of the 50th store with the store owners in South Australia and it was published around Knitwit, but we were so busy with the day-to-day running of the company that it wasn't the high point one might imagine it could be. The high points have been meeting customers in stores and airports and other places, and hearing of how another woman's life has been changed through a sewing course. Our conferences — whether they're in Hawaii, Singapore or Australia — when all off us get together and share the success, are also high points for me.

One highlight, I guess, was winning the inaugural Bulletin-Veuve Cliquot Australian Businesswoman of the Year award. I was surprised at that. It was in 1979: someone had nominated me for the award while I was overseas. Then the people running the award came and interviewed me once or twice. I didn't think very much at all about the possibility of winning. When they phoned and told me I'd won, I was absolutely thrilled. It was like a dream to have that sort of recognition. I think we all need recognition and that's why I think awards are important.

My sister, Thelma, re-entered the workforce, having not worked for about 10 years, and I'm really enjoying having her work in the company as my secretary, just as in these last few years I've enjoyed working with Mike. If the people are right, it's magical to be so close. We have a wonderful team at the Knitwit head office.

I met Mike on the fourth of July four years ago. I'd had almost no social life in the years in between, running a business and bringing up a child. If I wasn't working, my place was at home with Tim. Through meeting me in business, Mike invited me to the opening of a restaurant here in Balmain.

He was a marketing consultant. That night at the restaurant he stayed fairly close and kept introducing me to people. I almost didn't go because I'd had so little social contact and I'm terribly shy by nature, so to go into a room full of strangers was a big ordeal. I got to the door and was about to not even go in but he came to the door and beckoned me in, looked after me all night and took me home, and I think within days we both knew that we'd get married soon, even if we didn't say it. He proposed within three weeks and we were married within four months.

Tim was thrilled for me. He met Mike within a week of Mike inviting me to the opening of the restaurant. The three of us had dinner together. Tim must have known that he was an important part of this new relationship. At the time, he was into making model planes and cars. He brought along a collection of them and displayed them on the restaurant table, obviously to make some sort of statement. I'm not sure what it was but he wanted to show Mike something. Mike's been wonderful to Tim and they've got a fabulous relationship. When I go away travelling, they are like two bachelors at home. They have a ball!

When Mike and I married, gosh, we thought we were being terribly sensible and sophisticated, saying, 'You do your thing and I'll do mine and we'll be supportive of each other'. This whole modern approach to husband and wife having independent careers didn't work for us, because we waited 40 years to find each other and wanted to be together as much as possible. I was interested in what he was doing, Knitwit was an overwhelming thing and he was fascinated with it, being a marketing man. One night, we just looked at each other and said, 'This is foolishness. We want to be together all the time, we love each other so much we want to share that love as much as we can, whether it's working or playing or being at home.' Seeing I had to travel quite a lot it seemed stupid to have this enforced separation during working time. So he came into the business and he loves being part of a team made up mostly of women!

There's no pressure working together because he's a little bit like I am — he doesn't see this dividing line between work and play. He enjoys everything he does, and even when we go on holiday or when we're travelling or entertaining, Knitwit is a fairly predominant thing. We live it most of our lives, and happily. There is no resentment about that. When you're meeting people with a common interest all over the world, it's very easy to work together and enjoy it.

I think it's sometimes hard for Mike, living with the whole Vera Randall thing. It's got benefits too, though, and he is aware of that. The hardest part was coming into the business without the 10 years' background that I had. He had to go through a learning process. Often it was a question of me saying, 'We tried that five years ago and it didn't work'. He's an ideas man and I think it must have been very hard for him to constantly have me say, 'Well, that won't work', and give the reasons why. But he's such a gracious person, it was never a big problem. He has made a big contribution to taking it from being an Australasian operation to being an international operation. I'd already taken the business across to New Zealand and it had been franchised there, but since I've met Mike we've opened businesses in South Africa and the United Kingdom.

But along with the work there are chances to take super holidays, even though they are only for one or two weeks. I can't imagine a three month around-the-world jaunt. But next August we may go on a diving holiday to Sri Lanka. We've got all the brochures on that. If it wasn't for work we wouldn't enjoy the lifestyle and the chance to have all those holidays. I could do without those things but we certainly enjoy them.

I have found a supportive man who is pretty unique. In the years that I was a single mother and in business, I really had given up on the idea of marrying again. But I knew that there was a dimension to my life that was missing. I had accepted that and when I did meet Michael, I couldn't believe that it was happening. Having been by myself for all of those years has made our relationship more precious. I really treasure having someone to share my life with. I wake up in the morning sometimes and think, 'Is this really happening to me?' Still, after four-and-a-half years.

A lot of the people that I have read about have motivated me. I avidly read biographies and autobiographies, the life stories of sports people, people in business, people that have worked with relief organisations. People that were models along the way were the founder of World Vision, Bob Pierce, who I met a number of times and worked quite closely with, and the people I saw doing relief work in, say, Vietnam or Korea or Hong Kong. These people, working with dedication, were an inspiration to me. You walk into a room and they have a presence that you can almost reach out and touch.

I admire a lot of Australians. I admire Maggie Tabberer — I think she's a fabulous lady. There's a lot of Australians in big business that I'm reading about these days that I admire, people with corporate skills. I admire Tammie Fraser as a woman, and Dame Pattie Menzies was a wonderful role model when I was growing up. It's almost a daily thing for me to pick up a magazine and read about someone that I admire. There are so many success stories in this country.

It's only been in the last little while that I've been able to go to motivational-type conferences and congresses. Recently I went to a sales congress and heard a guy called Zig Zigler speak. He wrote a book called *See You At The Top*. I'm waiting for his tapes right now. I love his philosophy on life: physical, mental and spiritual.

I went to that sales congress because Tim wanted to go. He saw a poster advertising it, and although he's still at school he felt it would be a good idea to go, because he does have a part-time job selling in a hardware shop. There were 4,000 people there, talking about life-planning and achievement. It was packed with motivation, making us all realise that we can do almost anything. The theme was 'The sky is not the limit'. To sit there with Tim and to hear people saying all the things that I would dearly love to have said to him over the years, but often as a parent couldn't express, was something special.

Learning to scuba dive was special in that way also. Tim learned when he was 12 and then persuaded me to learn. We switched roles, child/parent, parent/child, and he stood on the shore saying to me, 'Come on, you can do it', when I was exhausted. Our relationship has been terribly close, and I'm now also enjoying having a step-daughter and feeling we are a real family of four.

All the way through, the thing that I was scared of was what my work might be doing to Tim. I think the very fact that I was scared helped though, because it made me make sure that he always understood what I was doing and why. He was sharing in it as much as possible, visiting stores in Australia and travelling with me in the school holidays. I'd plan my overseas trips so he could come with me and see what I was doing. So he understood, all the way along.

He's been going to a good school all the way through. St Andrew's Cathedral School has been the one constant thing throughout my moving from one home to the other and travelling. I don't think school training can ever replace the home training, but the stability of that school and the teaching there reinforced my value system for him, which was very important.

I can't have ambitions for Tim; that's one thing that I have come to grips with. I want him to find something in life as exciting as Knitwit. If it happens that he comes into the business at some stage, of course I will be delighted, but I don't think that's important. The important thing is for him to find something that will give him the same excitement that I've got for Knitwit. Let's hope he finds it.

As for me, if it wasn't Knitwit I'm sure it would have been something similar. The background that I enjoyed was building up toward it. My commercial course and working as a secretary were building toward it. But there is a bigger thing. I do believe that we are all here for a purpose. I don't think we all just happen to be here on this Earth to muddle along, I believe that God's got this plan, even call it a blueprint, for every one of us. When we find what it is, there's a meaning to what we're doing. If you mix that with personality traits, success must surely be God-given. We were created to be successful! Now that I can look back, I see that there was a definite plan. I've found it, and having found it I feel completely fulfilled.

I think that true Christianity is reaching out to people and being a clear witness to what we believe in. But I think that in order to witness and tell people about our beliefs, we've got to do something to earn their respect and confidence. I don't think we can go through life expecting other people to believe. We do it by example. To me, sharing my success with others and the feeling of confidence that sewing has built up in me adds an important dimension to Christianity.

I feel the same about relief work. I'm still involved a little bit with World Vision, having worked with them for three or four years part-time while I was at Upjohn. The purpose of Christian organisations might be to preach the Gospel, but in order to earn the right to speak I believe these organisations should first administer to the physical needs of the people: the hunger, the cold, the need for housing and clean water, clothing, and medical care. Then, hopefully, the people will say, 'Why do you do this for me, what motivates you to do it?' And then we've got the right to speak about the love of God.

I'd say as a Christian person today, I've only got the right to speak about my beliefs to other people after I earn their respect and start meeting some other needs. I don't think that I was terribly aware of this, though, while it was happening. It's just part of the Christian ethic that I was brought up with. I saw examples of it in my own town, in my own family. It happened, but now I think it's fabulous to be able to look back and say, 'Hey, that's why'. The World Vision thing fits with this whole Knitwit thing but I didn't realise it when I started Knitwit. Through World Vision, I was learning how to reach out to people. I'd earned the right to talk to them and be an example to them. You've got to *do* something. Sitting at home, behaving piously, or even going to church is not what Christianity is about.

There's a correct way to go about everything. The concept of Christianity or the New Testament is one that we've based our whole law system on and I think that flows on. If you take into your business life Christian beliefs of caring for other people and how to respect other people's rights, you can't have a better program to work to.

Knitwit's now a household word. The Knitwit method of sewing is considered to be a generic term, it's a way of sewing knitted fabrics and it's a trademark. But I must say, almost every day I'm surprised at the acknowledgement of it, the fact that no matter who I meet or where I am, people seem to know about it.

Success is a hard thing to describe. I think it's the feeling of knowing that you've achieved what you set out to do. That's what I'm still sharing to this day with other women. It doesn't change the fact that I am as painfully shy today as I was when I first went to that high school at Parramatta. I am still that same person, it doesn't change any of those things, but it does give a feeling of self-esteem and confidence. Being a mother is a good leveller in all of this. A teenager can bring you right back to reality and I know Tim's helped me, through our shared activities, to see the beautiful things out there, the largeness of everything else.

Some people don't know exactly what they want to be successful at. They want to be successful but they can't say at what. Whether it's in the area of sport or home-making or business or a career, first of all, set some sort of goal. It might take years, as it did with me, to determine what it is. Then, determine whether it's realistic, whether you really want it or whether it's some sort of impossible fantasy. If you really want it, are you prepared for all the hard work that's involved? Defining an objective, setting a goal, writing a plan and then working very hard, I've since discovered, is a classic business strategy — and it works.

In about 1978 someone who was writing publicity started to wonder out loud whether Vera Randall might be Australia's first self-made millionairess. I said that was absolutely impossible and just forget about that line of thinking. It horrified me to be putting this monetary measure on the whole thing, but this person pursued that line, worked with my accountant, and figured out that Vera Randall, at least on paper, was a millionairess. To own something that was worth more than $1 million received some publicity.

The profits that I was earning were the means by which to expand the business and I could only ever see it that way. There never was any motivation to earn a millon or 10 million or even a thousand. It didn't happen that way. Profit was very important, though, because I could see clearly that without that profitability, the whole thing would crumble. On a more basic level, all I could see was all the women that I would be letting down if I didn't run a profitable business and keep it growing. There'd be women all over Australia that I wouldn't be getting to in order to teach them the method of sewing. So even profitability was motivated by a need to share something exciting with other women. It's only been in the last few years, when I've looked at expansion overseas, that I've seen the need for profitability. So for the first time I'm entering into this new phase, which involves financial planning other than for survival.

If I could choose I would be out at store level, working with customers and with store owners even more than I do. But I know that, being a franchisor, I have a responsibility to the people I have sold franchises to, to make sure they are successful. That involves administrative work, and while I don't get the same buzz from all that I know it's important, and every morning I wake up and want to get going.

My routine is getting up early and thinking first, when I'm in Sydney, about the organising of the home, seeing that everyone's off to do whatever they have to do that day. I then think about the evening meal and all the practical things. Then I'll go off to the office and work with the staff, doing paperwork or working on the telephone, and go home in the evening to cook. I just love getting into the kitchen at night. Sometimes it's six o' clock, sometimes it's nine o' clock. The family's learnt to have dinner when it's ready. I also love entertaining at home.

Or my routine could be getting up at 5.30 in the morning to catch a seven o' clock flight to any part of Australia and back in the same day. It could be flying down to Melbourne for a meeting of the Commission of Australia Post, because I am one of the commissioners. It's like being on the board of directors. It has outside commissioners as well as management people inside the enterprise.

I was invited to be a commissioner by the then-Minister for Communications, Neil Brown. Because it's a big operation, I thought there might be something I could contribute as someone who was close to small business in Australia. I have a strong awareness of my need to contribute to the free-enterprise system, especially in the small business area. I do a lot of work speaking to groups about that, but I *am* shy when I stand up in front of 200 or 2000 people to talk about being in business.

The postal system again is a part of our tradition. When Australia was first founded, letters going between England and the settlements were the main communication. Originally they went by ship and by coach, and now we're sending them all around the world by air. But it's still the same — very much a people thing. People communicating is an important part of Australian life.

Australia is the most wonderful country in the world. The opportunities for people like me to go into business still exist, and opportunities in the arts or music are still there. Our lifestyle, our weather, the beauty of the place, I sometimes find overwhelming. The free-enterprise system that we still enjoy in Australia is something I fight fiercely to protect and that's why I go out at night, speaking to groups of business people at conventions and conferences.

The fact that we are still willing to get in and have a go is one of our strongest traits. You show an Australian an opportunity, whether it's starting a little business cutting lawns or opening a retail store or giving up a job and pursuing a career as a painter, and Australians will have a go. I think some of the European countries have lost that urge. It's a very important trait.

Australians who are achievers become even more determined when things get tough. They get in and have a go and then they find a way to do things, even when it's tough. These are Australian traits. If we put them to work, even the small business communities can do almost anything. There's no limit to what we could produce and export or what we could achieve as a nation.

America's a big country and I sometimes wonder whether or not it's running out of control. It's so big and fast-moving that it could happen to that country. But Australians can still slow down a bit and enjoy what they are doing. I think what we can take to America, in particular, is not only our philosophy of having a go and finding a way to do things, but enjoying what we're doing. I think we're well-balanced. We want to use all of our senses.

The United Kingdom is a different market again, very traditional. I'm studying the market right now to find out what it is that's going to open that market up for Knitwit. We've got to find which button to press, because again, they've got millions and millions of people. Even if we capture a market of 10 per cent of the women who own sewing machines, we can do big things there too. We could have hundreds of stores in the United Kingdom.

For Australians to take a product into Europe and America is a traditional measure of success, whether it's in the field of entertainment, art, music, or business. I'm sure for me it's got a lot to do with pride in being Australian and wanting to show the world, because when you travel around people often don't quite know where we are or what we're all about. People think we're not nearly as highly developed a nation as we are. A lot of people, unless they've visited, haven't got any concept of the skills available here or the type of people we are.

I don't think a lot about Japan, apart from the textile industry. I know that the Japanese industry is very advanced. Though, of course, I look at it more from the point of view of whether Knitwit would be of interest to Japanese women. I believe it could be and I believe the marketing approach has to be quite different. But I'm not prepared to put it on record at this stage. I've got a strong notion on how it should be done there.

As an Australian, especially, to be heading up an operation in 10 countries in the world would be fantastic. I just can't imagine sitting at home for a day and not doing something. If anything, I'm a bit frightened of being an old lady who really should step down and refuses to do it, although I think I'm alert to the fact that one day I'll have to stop and hand it over to someone else.

My personal ambitions are to build my relationship with Mike and to stay as close as I can to Tim and Michaela. I realise that soon, as a mother, I've got to let go. I think I've started to do that already and I can see no further than that. I just want to enjoy everything to the fullest and share it with my family. For me, to start wishing about more things that I could have would almost be greedy.

Steven Rich

Steven Rich was born in Germany, but with the advent of the Nazi regime his family migrated via Holland to England and thence to America. Once ensconced in the United States, young Rich rose quickly in the ranks of Hunter Douglas, an American multinational founded by his family in the post-World War I years. He seized an opportunity to open the company's Australian operations in the 1950s, and with his responsibilities expanding over the next few years he flew millions of miles as the corporation's international chief. It was on one of these flights that he met wife-to-be Gay. Rich took up Australian citizenship about two decades ago.

At the peak of his career with Hunter Douglas, he gave it all away to spearhead Australia's first government-endorsed Development Corporation, in the then-Territory of Papua New Guinea. Sponsored by Australia's leading institutions and industrial companies, Australia New Guinea Corporation, with Steven Rich as chairman, made extensive investments in TPNG, with heavy emphasis on the primary industry sector. Traveland was founded in 1968, and under Rich's guidance grew to become this country's most successful fully-integrated travel operation.

Meanwhile, son Jodee has rocketed up the entrepreneurial ladder as founder and head of Imagineering, Australia and New Zealand's largest micro-computer software distributor. From an initial turnover of $30,000 in 1981, the 25-year-old Jodee Rich's business hovered around the $20 million mark in 1985. The younger Rich's renown as a gentleman also proves he has gathered more than mere business acumen from his father.

Steven Rich's own self-deprecating humour and disapproval of self-importance are keys to a formula for success that starts and ends with the human element. In keeping with the emphasis on family in Rich's life, his son still lives in a separate part of the house, and his daughter Nici, an architecture student, designed the swimming pool outside his mansion in Sydney's prestigious Bellevue Hill. Rich still travels, but for him and his the pilgrimage is over, and Australia is the 'richer' for it.

I was born in Frankfurt, Germany, on 4 July 1926. My father was a colourful man. He was a cigar manufacturer and later became one of the outstanding wine experts in Germany. I remember many years later in New York, during World War II, I took my then-best girl to a place called the Starlight Room. Although it was wartime, they were still serving German wines. The waiter brought a bottle of wine that I'd ordered, and he had uncorked it without showing me the bottle. I tasted it and said, 'No, this isn't a 1937', and he looked down his nose at me as if to say, who the hell does this callow youth think he is? He said, 'There's only one man in New York who could do that. Hugo Rich-heimer.' I said, 'Well, that's my dad'.

My family left Germany in stages. As you know, the rumblings of the Nazis started seriously during the depression, in 1931. I was five and I really don't remember anything about that. But in 1933, when Hitler came to power, we all left Germany and went to Holland. There were about 30 or 40 of us there, because we felt when Hitler came to power there would be an instant reaction, although this wasn't to be so.

The men mostly stayed outside of Germany, my father went on to London, and the women and children went back to Germany after some weeks. Then my father established his business in London and we moved there a couple of years later. Most of my secondary education was there. I don't know how I ever survived that, because what they seem to excel at there is the breeding of snobs.

I had to learn English, but it can be done very quickly when you're a child. I think that's the reason I'm fortunate enough to be able to speak a few languages, because most of these came to me when I was young.

As soon as we really settled down in England, the war clouds came and then there was the Blitz. I can remember even in the first part of 1939 collecting what we used to call 'fag cards'. Then about 12 months later you were giving up the fag cards, because cigarettes were hard to get and you were collecting pieces of shrapnel and pieces of bombs.

That was the sort of commodity trading that went on amongst kids. Of course, there were tremendous grounds for fear amongst Jews, and about a dozen members in my family didn't survive the holocaust. They had settled in Holland, where they were subsequently transported to Auschwitz. We had our share of casualties.

We left England in 1941, at the height of the Blitz. All Germans, whether they were refugees or not, were interned. They picked up my father, and it was only because he was so well-known in certain places that he was released. They then went after my brother, who was 16. So we felt that this was a hostile environment. It wasn't that we hated the place — we'd fallen in love with Britain — but this was a big disappointment to us.

My parents thought we would be better off in America, so we went by boat. Actually it was quite nice, a ship called the *Andalusiah Star*, a semi-cargo, semi-passenger vessel that went to South America first. She was too fast to be a convoy ship, she zig-zagged on her own, and I guess we were pretty lucky to have made it in those days, when 180,000 tons of shipping were being lost each week to Hitler's submarines!

We arrived in New York nearly eight weeks after leaving Britain. My brother Harry was the first one to go in the service. Our family name was Richheimer but under the war situation, when you became part of the American forces, if you kept your German name and the Germans captured you they'd just shoot you. You had no chance as a prisoner of war. Harry changed his name to Rich and I followed suit.

I finished my secondary education at New York University and was going to become a psychologist but changed my mind, took a year of medicine, then went back and finished with psychology and economics. I had already come to the conclusion that psychology wasn't for me.

I was a fantastic college basketball player! I played so well for New York University, which was, I guess, the top-ranking team in America, that after about half a season with them the coach told me I'd be a better cheerleader. So I took him at his word. In those days college basketball was already a big thing in America. Of course, there was no television, but we'd get 25,000 people into Madison Square Garden. I decided that if they had college cheerleaders at football games, it would be good to have them at basketball games. We got an incredibly agile and good cheerleading squad together, which sometimes got more publicity than the team, especially if they lost a game. I was very slim in those days, and the sports writers said I looked like

Frank Sinatra! I always had a lot of energy. I'm almost 59 today and I still have an above-average level of energy.

In 1945 the war ended, and in 1946 I started at Hunter Douglas, which was a family business, and stayed there until 1961. Some of the family had moved to America before us and they gave us a very warm welcome. My father, who had set up a business in America in the 1930s, took that on again, so it was an interesting time. My father was reasonably successful in America. He was almost artistic in his approach to business, because a good bottle of wine to him was a work of art, which indeed it is. So he was more concerned about the quality of his product than the material rewards that came with it.

Anyway, my brother went to General Electric and I was asked to join Hunter Douglas. In retrospect it was fantastic, because in the post-war period we were growing very rapidly. We were in the aluminium business and there was a factory on the West Coast in Riverside, California. They had decided to build a factory on the East Coast and I was charged with the responsibility of obtaining some very hard-to-get materials. The first thing I had to get was a telephone. An Irish gentleman who had heard of me because of my cheerleading career at college, of all things, took pity on me and said, 'I can't get you a private telephone but I can get you a public one'. I said, 'I can't get a phone booth in the room', and he said, 'No, you don't have to. You can put it on the wall.' So I had this machine on the wall, and of course you had to put nickles and dimes and quarters into it. I remember talking to someone in Virginia who had some second-hand roofing beams and I said, 'Of course we're a very big aluminium producer and you'll get a lot of business from us', and a voice came in, 'That'll be $1.50 for the next three minutes, please'. But we got the factory built, and I moved into my first district office in 1949.

The company was into Venetian blinds and I earned my stripes by developing a way to keep them clean. We built this big wooden box that re-circulated water and we put the blind inside it. The thing was an abomination, it was a real albatross, but it worked. By letting the water flow down the blind, it showed how durable the blind was, because it wouldn't rust, the tapes wouldn't shrink, and so on. It had only one problem. These boxes were meant for department store floors, but because of the water fall and the tinkling the old biddies in the department stores had to go running to the toilet all the time. So here were these great big ugly boxes with the Venetian blinds in them, which were supposed to be having streams of water running in them, all turned off because they acted as some kind of diuretic. I think it was then that they decided to send me out into the field.

I was sent to Oakland, California in 1950, and from there I moved to Dallas, Texas in 1951. I was in the southwest for a couple of years, and then one day I received a phone call from my chairman. I was told that the man they'd sent to Australia to open up operations there had contracted leukemia. Would I like to go to Australia? I said sure, but he told me to think about it over the weekend. So I went down to the Dallas public library to read about Australia. There were two books, both from the 1930s, and I remember clearly that one said, 'When going to the interior of Australia, it is advisable to wear a sidearm'. So that's the sort of picture I had of Australia.

I arrived here on 14 December, 1953. It was a stinking hot day, one of those Black Fridays, and I had come from Holland where we had our overseas headquarters. I was met by our agent and was taken to the hotel. Because it was Christmas-time, all the cockies were in town and you couldn't get a hotel room for love or money. The agent took me up to my room and it had a tiny little sink over in the corner. I said, 'Where's the bathroom?' and he said, 'You're looking at it'. I couldn't believe it. I said, 'Is there any air-conditioning in Australia?' He said, 'Well, we have one shop that has air-conditioning'.

We had a great time but I had a replay of my early days in New York, because although it was going on 1954 now, things were just as scarce here as they were in America in 1946. It was taking Australia ever so much longer to catch up. We had the devil of a time getting materials to build this factory. The most remarkable thing that happened was that although we were lucky enough to get two or three telephone lines from the Postmaster General, there was no switchboard. So the installation crew sat on the porch of this factory for two weeks, waiting for the switchboard. The only breaks they would take would be for tea, lunch, and afternoon tea. That was the PMG in 1954.

Because it was mid-December when I arrived, everyone had already stopped working and they didn't start again until February. So it was one long party really, or supposed to be. Since I was fairly intent on getting things done, it was like knocking your head against the wall. Nobody was home, no factory was open, and nobody wanted to do anything.

It has changed considerably. But I was lucky, I met some nice people here straight away. I had someone to show me around and it was a tremendously hospitable place, with people who had *joie de vivre* of incredible proportions. But this place was still suffering from the

Korean War and there was a lot of regulation. And there was a short-age of everything. If I went to America on a trip, I carried a kit bag to bring back things like spoons and doorknobs that you couldn't get here. The customs staff out at Mascot was so small that the guys there got to know me, and they even got to know my kit bag.

We had a remarkable group on the first aircraft that I took to Australia. I was horrified at the length of time it was taking, so I enter-tained myself with a game called Scrabble, which none of my fellow passengers had ever seen. We all became fast friends, and still are. One fellow is now a Supreme Court judge, another has retired as head of one of our largest companies, and another was head of a govern-ment department — they were all on that flight. One of my fondest memories of those early days was my membership in the Manufac-turing Industry Advisory Council. Such people as Sir James Vernon, Sir Ronald Irish, and Sir James Kirby were the chairmen, and it was an incredible group. I was on the Council for 13 years.

In 1955 I had a call from our people at Hunter Douglas, who said they would like me to come back to New York to look after the then-overseas division, which after the domestic company was sold included all the interests outside of the United States. In 1956 I was appointed executive vice-president in charge of the worldwide opera-tions of the company, and I did that for a number of years. I had gotten married in 1956 and Gay and I literally spent our life on an air-craft, because I never believed in sitting in a particular place and administrating. I always wanted to see what was going on and I still believe in that very strongly, although these days it's much easier to get around than it used to be and you can make much shorter trips. You have to keep in mind that my first trip to Australia took 72 hours, which included a night's stop in Singapore. Today you can get to the West Coast in 13 hours. In those days it was 40 hours, so you had a huge investment, not so much in money but in time. If you went around the world it would take you four weeks. I do that in five days now, sometimes.

Gay was a hostess with TAA. I originally met her in 1954 at the Queen's Ball in Adelaide, the first time the Queen came out, but we met again on an aircraft. We started going out, fell in love, and it wasn't easy to have a love affair over 25,000 miles because I was always going around and around. We got married in New York. Gay had a little red briefcase and the idea was that she would look after customs forms once we were married. She still has the briefcase, but instead of me being relieved of that responsibility, I soon found myself filling out two customs forms wherever we went. The story of my life.

Jodee, my son, was conceived in Ireland, in July 1959, the result of Guinness Stout and Irish smoked salmon. We were only there for three nights but Gay informed me on the aircraft going back to London that she was pregnant, and she was right. Nici, our daughter, was 'Made in Holland' and born in Australia. The kids became great travellers. I was always very mobile and Gay still continued to travel with me, but to a lesser extent after the children were born. Then as they grew a bit they came with us and finally, when the crunch came and they needed us, Gay stayed home, because we didn't believe in children being reared with nannies.

In 1961 I came back here to be in charge of this part of the world. We had set up operations in New Zealand and had expanded operations in Australia. But in the end, I decided that we had good management on the ground here and if I didn't strike out and do things on my own, I'd never know whether my success was due to family connections or not. One needs to confirm one's abilities, so I decided that I would give up the active executive role at Hunter Douglas.

We had lived in Holland for about a year, during the time of Indonesia's sabre-rattling with Dutch New Guinea, and we had gotten to know the Dutch Foreign Minister. One of the very first Australians I'd ever met in the 1950s was that great Australian Sir John Crawford, who in those days was the Secretary for the Department of Trade. Through him I got to know his boss, Sir John McEwan, and even today I have an affinity for the National Party. I can remember going to Jack McEwan's 60th birthday party, which Sir Walter Scott hosted in 1960. They had a table for the 'seniors' and one for the younger set. The 'youngsters' at that table were Peter Nixon, Doug Anthony, Mac Holten, Ian Sinclair, and myself.

In 1964 I was visiting Canberra and said to Sir John that I felt a bit uneasy about Papua New Guinea because of (Indonesian President) Sukarno. I told him about certain observations I had made in Holland and he said, 'Why don't you go and tell the Prime Minister that?' I said, 'Come on, he wouldn't listen to me', but I did get to have a word in Menzies' ear and he said, 'Why don't you talk to Paul Hasluck?', who was then the Minister for Territories and later became the Governor-General. Hasluck was very sympathetic and said why don't I form a study group for New Guinea. I said to the Minister that what I'd rather do was get a group of friends and acquaintances together and we would go and have a look up there. I talked to Sir John Marks,

Steven Rich at work in his office at his 17th century English settling table

Sir Ian Potter, Sir James Kirby, Sir Cecil Looker, the Hon. F. M. Hewitt (who had first interested me in investing in New Guinea), Sir Frederic Deer, Merlin Hansen, and Sir Roger Darvall. We decided to have a look for ourselves and all of us, except John Marks and Ian Potter, went up there.

We were appalled at the lack of attention and concern for New Guinea that existed in Australia. We came back, reported to Paul Hasluck, and were going to form a development corporation together with the government, but I think Menzies got advice from Foreign Affairs, who temporised things. Weeks went by and we thought, well, if it isn't going to happen, we should go ahead on our own. So we formed the Australia New Guinea Corporation, which was a first in those days.

This was a company which was made up of almost all the banks and leading insurance companies and our top 10 industrial companies, such as BHP, CRA, and ICI. They asked me to become chairman of the company. That wasn't what I felt I should be doing but I did it, and spent six or seven years of heavy concentration and time up in New Guinea. We had coffee plantations, and we also took a swamp of 1,000 acres and made it into the most beautiful tea plantation in the western highlands. We took expertise wherever we could find it. This happened to be mainly Scottish expertise, because the best planters in India were Scots. We got into timber and built the first high-rise building in Papua New Guinea, called ANG House. We built the township for the Bougainville Mines. We were very, very active up there, especially from 1965 to 1970.

When we got to New Guinea there were three major Australian companies. One was Burns Philp, another was Carpenters (Investment Trading Co.), and the third one was Steamships Trading. Everything was in their hands. We were the fourth denominator, which had the Australian business community behind it. That was the difference. All the high pioneering work, all the things that books are written about, had already happened when we arrived there. We risked our lives in a different way. I must have been nearly killed half a dozen times in light aircraft mishaps, but the true pioneers who had gone before were giants. We were catalysts of progress I guess you could say. Hell, we had the first elevator lifts in New Guinea. Hundreds of people watched their relatives disappear into this black box and then, miracle of miracles, they would come back in the other box, reincarnated. The New Guineans couldn't understand how people could go up in that box and then come out in another box. It was unbelievable!

Everybody thought we were mad to have a high-rise building in Port Moresby. There wasn't anything higher than six storeys north of Brisbane. Ours was only 12 storeys, but it was difficult to get Australian institutions to underwrite the building, so we went off to New York. I guess because of the tragedy of David Rockefeller's nephew being killed in New Guinea, Rockefeller had more than a passing interest in the Territory. His people underwrote 15 per cent of the financing of the building, then when the Chase (Manhattan Bank) came, others followed. It wasn't a hell of a lot of money but it was the principle of the thing. The building was an outstanding success before we even dug a hole. We had wonderful support from companies like TAA and the ANZ Bank, who took two floors each. Major companies operating in New Guinea underwrote each floor and it became almost a business community commitment. We finished the building and as I say, there wasn't any unoccupied space in it at all.

The average Aussie was not very conscious of New Guinea in those days, except for the war-time experience. The attitude was, 'It's a place that I've been to and thank you very much, I never want to see it again', but there was no consciousness about our colonial responsibility. Making sure that there was community support for the government policy was really our purpose. I dare say that there could have been some major problems with Papua New Guinea if a public awareness hadn't arisen. I can remember in the early Hunter Douglas days one of the young boys in the warehouse got a girl with child, as it were, and guess where he disappeared to? New Guinea. That's where you went to hide. It wasn't the most salubrious of places, and yet there were tremendous Australians up there, men of high calibre who had dedicated their lives to New Guinea. It was an interesting part of my life. I can tell you many a time we would say, 'Hey, this is what your mother sent you to college for'.

I once had a riot on my hands. Six hundred blacks were rioting because the pay hadn't arrived from Port Moresby. I had been told if there's a riot, you never get in amongst it, because that's when it really becomes dangerous. I chose not to take that advice and found out who the ringleader was. That was pretty obvious, because he was the leader of the charge. I just put my hand on him and spoke to him, and the frenzy subsided. You see, we were at a place called Cape Rodney, which only had access by air or by sea. The payroll would come in every Tuesday for distribution on Wednesday, but the airstrip had been closed for a week because of floods. So we had no cash and those gentlemen didn't like that.

The longest time we ever spent in Papua New Guinea as a family was when we had six weeks there once. We had a wonderful time, lots of experiences, and the kids still talk about it today. There were about 30 Europeans and 6,000 locals, so we were completely cut off.

Cape Rodney was where our timber operations were, and my first impression of it turned out to be the correct one. We never should have done that timber project. We later paid $3 million to have it carted away by a very large and experienced Australian timber operation, and six years ago they paid dearly to have it carted away yet again. In 1964 we landed on this little airstrip, and it was extraordinarily hot. We were in a light aircraft, looking for somebody to pick us up, and there was no-one. We had chartered the aircraft, so the pilot took off. There was just Gay and I. This truck then appeared and made straight for us and it somehow didn't manage to stop. The driver overshot us by, say, 100 metres, and then backed up and overshot by 30 metres. He leaned out of his cab, showing a lovely alcoholic face, and said, 'I'm sorry, we don't have any brakes on the truck, because the spare parts haven't come through'.

So Gay got in the cab and I got into the back on the flat-deck next to this great, big, mangy dog. He was hot and he was wagging a bushy tail back and forth in my face. I thought, this isn't something we want to be involved in. Next thing we saw was the sawmill. This was a little public company called Pacific Island Timbers. I thought, my God, this is unbelievable. There was a bunch of shacks, a bit of machinery, and that was it. In later years I asked myself, what made you do it? I guess it was the challenge. I think the seduction of challenge is both a human frailty and our greatest strength.

In New Guinea in those days we had absolutely no worries about security. We never locked the doors. Once, Gay woke up in the middle of the night and said that she thought there was somebody at the window. I said, come on, there's nobody at the window, so we went back to sleep. At first light I woke up, and sure enough, there was somebody at the window. That person had been waiting there patiently for hours, because he didn't dare make a noise to wake us up. His wife had delivered one-half of twins and the other one was stuck. He wanted to tell Gay about it, to see if she could help. And she did. The other baby was delivered, we whistled up an aircraft, and they took the woman into Moresby Hospital. There are many stories like that, it's an interesting place, Papua. We had black snakes and alligators and all the other goodies of that part of the world, but it's a time of my life that I wouldn't swap for anything.

For me New Guinea was never meant to be full-time, but it almost turned out that way. You see, I remained on the board of Hunter Douglas until 1982, when we had a difference of opinion regarding an investment in a smelter in the Hunter Valley that I felt the local company shouldn't get into. The cut-off of my involvement in New Guinea came when we had established other management there. Because I'd never intended to be as close to that scene as I was, it took probably two years longer than it otherwise would have taken to step back from it. In the end, however, we had very good management. Then, a bit like one's favourite prodigy, the involvement in Traveland was looming. That was accidental.

Fairfax, David Jones and I got together and decided to form a travel company in 1968. We thought it was something a store like David Jones should be in. The idea was that Fairfax would look after the media exposure, David Jones would provide the floor space in the department stores, and I was supposed to look after the management side. About two years later we had three branches. Fairfax had provided the media exposure, David Jones had provided the space on the floor, and we had selected the management. It didn't really work out and after two years my partners looked at me and said, 'We've done our bit, what are you going to do?' So I rolled up my sleeves and got involved in the show. I guess Traveland grew from there.

The travel industry in those days was in a very protected environment, so you had great difficulty breaking in. There were people then who actually considered themselves to be the travel 'establishment'. It took several years for them to take us seriously.

By the time I got involved in Traveland, I'd travelled three or four million miles as a passenger. I'd always been interested in that side of things. The real challenge — there's that word again — for Traveland, I think, was to start giving some service to the public. If we're anything at Traveland today, and there are about 600 of us, it's because of the people who, with the training we gave them and their own innate qualities, are able to give the public what they want. Hence our motto, 'Do as you say'.

The real key is being of service to the public. An experience I had once in the middle of the night in Chicago is a good example of that. We had boarded a 747 ex-Los Angeles. Something happened over Iowa and the pilot decided to go into Chicago. There was not another 747 on the ground so they had to change gauge, as they call it. We were put into a DC10, and because it was the middle of the night nobody was expecting us. We had to file up to have our seats reassigned. There was a little fellow in front of me who wasn't very happy, jumping up and down. When he finally got to the counter, he could barely see over it and he said to the girl, 'Young lady, do you know who I am?' She just looked at him and said, 'Sir, as far as I'm concerned, you are just a pain in the arse'. And she meant it. What that story tells me is that the pressure threshold, which is a big part of our training, is something that eludes us very often. There she was in the middle of the night wrestling with 250 people, and someone comes along and wants to be assertive. How do you train people for that? I'll tell you what, the crowd was with her.

The consumer today is totally travel-oriented. We still have a horrifically regulated environment in this country. There are those who would argue that regulation is good for us but I am not at all of that view. I think that although there have been casualties in America and, indeed, fanning out from America, because of the deregulation environment, it's the best thing that has ever happened. There are still those in this country who would like to see things go back to the so-called good old days, and the public be damned. In terms of what the public is paying, seat cost per passenger per kilometre is still way in excess of what they should be paying and what people are paying in other countries. It is just fatuous to say that our small population is the reason. That's just not right. Take, for example, the cost base of Qantas. It has a magnificent cost base, because it probably has the longest haul sectors in the world. It's a magnificent airline but we can still lower our costs here. I think one day we'll get into a different sort of environment with charters and so on, and there'll be further cost reductions.

Government and industry regulations are inextricably linked in this country. To start with, we have the two-airline policy domestically. East-West are strong, don't forget where they came from. In their first year of ownership I think they've done extremely well. They are considerably restrained with equipment, because they have small aircraft with low endurance. It's not a wide-bodied aircraft and it has a high operating cost, yet they're managing to make a buck with it. If you were to put a 767 or an Airbus in the hands of East-West, wow, the picture would change overnight in this country. The picture is going to change but not in the short-term. The Americans, coming across the Pacific, have given us some good lessons here. We have an extremely capable and aggressive carrier, called Air New Zealand, that I would put up with the other two pioneers in the international field, KLM and Singapore Airlines, in terms of aggression. It's no accident that all three of those airlines come from a small population base at home. They've had to earn their money with a 'fifth freedom-type' of carriage, which means, in effect, lifting people out from where you stop, en route to a place other than your own country.

In the United States it has been the survival of the fittest. The largest carrier in the world is still the largest carrier in the world, and that's United Airlines. It has survived that environment. It had a good look at itself, shook itself, and is going at it extremely well. Sure, they lost a bucket of money during the changeover and while the deregulation was grabbing hold, but they've done well. Other carriers haven't done so well, because they would not face the facts. Sure, Laker (Airlines of Great Britain) went to the wall, but that was a combination of things. Restraint of trade was one aspect but he had dollar exposure, the pound plummeted, and it was Murphy's Law.

This country has absolutely no excuse for its high costs, even internally, because the airways are free. You don't have to build roads or rails; all you need is navigation equipment and to fill that aircraft. They can't say that because we are a small country we can't do this or that. I've been very involved in my life with airline policy, and when Peter Nixon was Minister for Transport we had a very close relationship throughout some interesting times in Australian airline policy-making. There was a new fare regime five or six years ago, which for the first time was supposed to mean low fares to Britain. The Inter-departmental Committee for Air Policy (ICAP), had an excellent plan to close off the corridor between London and Australia to the two bilateral carriers, and increase the load factors to a point where they could lower fares (only to raise them later, of course, but they didn't tell you that) but they forgot one thing: the world is round and you fly over other people's air space. There was a tremendous international outcry against this plan, especially through the Asian countries. Singapore led the push to let people know that if that's the way you want to play it, you can kiss your landing rights good-bye. There was tremendous turmoil behind the scenes — I could write a book about those days.

Traveland continued to grow and amalgamate in the various areas of tourism. Traveland had 100 per cent of Viva Holidays, and the Westpac Banking Corporation had a company called Discovery Holidays. In 1983 we decided to put the two together. This means that we

*Above, in Garoka, in the Eastern Highlands of New Guinea, 1972
Below left, Palm Springs, 1949. Below right, with wife Gay, daughter Nici,
and son Jodee on board the 'Monterrey', 1969*

own 50 per cent of Viva and Westpac owns 50 per cent, but we manage it on behalf of the joint venture.

Traveland has a higher proportion of women employees than most companies. We're very strong on promotion from within and we have some very, very capable men and women at the top. I find our women are incredibly motivated and determined to prove that they are equally as skilled as their male counterparts. I also find that in many ways they're easier to work with because, strangely enough, they're not as thin-skinned as men. Yet women show their feelings more easily. I've often said that if men cried more often, they wouldn't get as many heart attacks. If a woman is in business and she's upset, tears will come, but that's fine, that's the outlet. At least you know where they are.

As for in-bound tourism, which is destined to become our top foreign currency earner, I think the future of Australia and New Zealand are closely linked, because most people come to Australia to see New Zealand as well. We mustn't forget that. This market has good expansion possibilities but I think there are other parts of the world that are probably just as interesting. Traveland has offered in-bound services to Australia only in the last year.

We're looking at a few other opportunities now. One of the obvious ones is resort development, which is about the only ambition we haven't realised from when we laid down our development plans some years ago. It's an elusive thing, resort development. It's a bit like the travel industry itself, because the returns from resort development are hazardous. You have to know what you're doing, you have to pick the right area, you have to know your market. Most of all, you have to have good distribution. It's the distribution part of it that we can bring to such a project.

I just spent last weekend up in the Whitsundays, where there's a whole smorgasbord of development going on. The biggest single thing that has happened there is Hamilton Island, and I saw you have Keith Williams on your interview list. He has literally taken an island that was just a plain old thing and done fabulous things with it. He's built an airstrip and literally moved a mountain. Someone said to me about Keith Williams that some people say, 'We're gonna', and Keith Williams does it. I wrote him a letter and said, 'You know, one of the human frailties is that we're envious when we see the monumental achievement of others', and I said, 'In this case, all I feel is pride'. I really meant that.

Personally, my first priority has always been to be happy. For me I suppose it's a challenge met. The material part of it has always tended to be more of a measure to me than anything else. In other words, possessions per se do not mean anything to me, really. I would hate to be without them but I have no need or feeling for materialistic expression. As a matter of fact, it's an abhorrence as far as I'm concerned. For instance, this watch was given to me 45 years ago. Once a year I change the band. I drive a good car but it's eight years old. When it says it wants to go, it'll go.

So success is also the satisfaction of seeing other people grow, and it has to do with the spirit. I think a lot of people are unaware of their innermost spiritual needs and tend to subjugate them. Without being overly introspective, you can pretty soon find out what turns you on and what fulfills you. If you can set that direction, then you can be one of the few in the world who doesn't have to follow. You can get yourself into a leadership position. Community work can be an expression of that attitude, and if I have any spare time I do a bit of community work. I've been involved with the Salvation Army now for 15 years, as deputy chairman of the Advisory Board and Red Shield Appeal, and that really has been rewarding. I enjoy my role there, and although it takes up a bit of time it gives you a feeling of contribution. I think you get back a great deal more than you put in, in terms of the rewards.

I've always had a need to talk to people. I like to talk things out, but at a certain point you draw the line. If you have to make a hard decision, you make that decision and you stick by it, unless there are overwhelming reasons why you have to double back. I think also you have to back your judgement and instinct, both with regard to people and situations — and not take things so terribly seriously all the time.

I saw a man at the airport yesterday whom I hadn't seen in maybe seven years. He's a bit older than I am, he'd been knighted since I last saw him, and he stood there so seriously and so full of self-importance, until we just started smiling at each other. He had cast his mind back to those days when things weren't as heavy as they are today. I think that's important.

I don't think I'm singular. I think most people who have been blessed with success are their own persons. I think you have to make sure that you can live with yourself, otherwise you do find yourself in isolation and loneliness. Most people will rationalise a decision, no matter how hard it is. I think if one is careful in the implementation of some of those decisions — in other words, it doesn't matter what you do so much as how you do it — then you can live with yourself a lot more easily and never feel your self-importance and self-satisfaction. I think that must be a terrible cross to bear, self-importance. I'm not saying humility is the thing, that would almost be hypocrisy. But a lot of people walking around today act so bloody self-important, and they really haven't achieved that much. Even the most sizeable achievers are only tiny grains in the sand of time.

Speaking of the sand of time, I'm conscious of my age, going on 59. When I turned 50 my mother said to me, 'The best pears have been eaten'. Somehow I don't believe that, and yet, although you might feel 28 physically, it is a fact that you're 59. So I'm thinking about a change of lifestyle, to find something that keeps me physically active. I have absolutely no particular time-frame that I'm working to. I do know that I have a responsibility to others to make sure that there is a succession, and I think I'm fairly successful there but no, I don't want to go on forever.

I've always got to be doing something, though. I was talking to Gay the other day about that. I might take up ballooning again. I used to be a very happy flyer, I enjoyed that very much. If I see a commercial opportunity with ballooning, I might do something with it. I can well understand what our friend from (Australian) National Industries, (John) Leard, is all about, because he did something at 50 that says, 'Hey, I want to switch gear'. It will be interesting to see where he turns up next.

As to where Australia as a country is going, there are two tiers of perception in America about us which are fairly interesting. One is the corporate perception and the other other is the public perception. The public perception has its roots in the World War II, when there were a lot of American guys out here who had fun, played a lot of games, went back, and have always longed to return to Australia, because the lifestyle was so totally different to what they had at home. So, we've had a niche in the American public posture, if you will, of being a wonderful, open country, a last frontier, which was considerably enhanced with the America's Cup win.

But I think the corporate image of Australia is the more important one, and the realistic one. Those companies from America that have invested here have usually done extremely well. I don't know of many major American corporate investors that have bombed out. There may have been some casualties, but by and large they have all done extremely well. But we have the classic problem of our labour industrial enviroment, which I think is very negatively perceived overseas. We do have a productivity problem; we have in this country a climate that was not created by the labour unions as much as by management itself. When I came here in the 1950s, the relationship between the factory floor and the so-called management was not good. There was an emulation of the British system, where the blue collar workers are one thing and the others up there have been ordained. That got very much out of hand, and the crisis we're seeing and experiencing today is the pendulum swinging out against us. It is a small population, and there will never be a leavening of that as there is in America, with its low-cost labour. In fact what keeps America going is its constant supply of low-cost labour.

America is a high population country with only 25 per cent of the work force in unions. I have no problem with unions per se but I think the biggest problem in America's perception of us is the feeling that productivity is not here and that maybe some other proprietary rights are being undermined to a disproportionate extent. It's not going to get fixed by union bashing, nor is it going to be fixed by union militancy. I don't know the answer to it. We had a tremendous climate in Canberra during the post-conference (Economic Summit) consultations, but unfortunately to just feel the climate was one thing and the reality was another.

Do you know what the 'dog-poop syndrome' is? Well, you're in a religious situation and you have the most inspiring ceremony. You walk out of your house of worship, inspired and eight feet tall. Then you get on the footpath outside and you step on some dog-poop. Suddenly, you get back to reality.

Nevertheless, this country is going to experience an absolute explosion of tourism. We're still a very long way from other countries, but people are getting used to longer flights and they're getting out to Hong Kong and China a lot more than they did. I think that Australia and New Zealand are going to see a lot more people, but when it gets down to the bottom line our biggest problem is going to be our small population.

I think Japan is going to continue to be our most important trading partner. I hope that we as Australians can go up there and learn from them. I was there a couple of weeks ago and the industry of the people is just unbelievable. We have an office there and we were concerned that they didn't answer the phone until 9.30 a.m., but guess what time they get home at night? Ten o'clock. This is sometimes seven days a week.

Now let's look at the other side of the coin. Who's right and who's wrong? In a realistic world, if we could get away with working 30 hours and picking the grapes off the tree, then let's do it. But that's heaven somewhere, some valley we haven't found. One day you might have 15 million people charging into this valley and saying, 'Hey, look what we found. We found the answer to the lot, we don't have to work and we can maintain a standard of living better than anywhere in the world'. But that's not the real world.

I became an Australian citizen when I first became involved in the New Guinea exercise. Menzies said to me, 'Mr Rich, when you say "we", we don't really know who you mean'. I said, 'I mean Australia', and he said, 'Well, are you an Australian?' I said 'No, I'm an American', and he said, 'We can fix that immediately'. I didn't know that the sly gentleman already knew I had an Australian wife and I could have fixed it without his help. So I've been an Australian citizen for 20 years.

I was a great fan of Menzies. I admire Bob Hawke, who I've known for a long time. I admire some of my friends who have achieved things, the people I associate with. I think there are some tremendous human beings there. But as public figures, I guess Hawke and Menzies, even though they came from different political schools, are high up on my list. The most successful people I know, whether they are artists, people in the business world or whatever, have all worked hard, known their subjects, and followed their instincts. And, most of all, they know what the customer wants. This is true of the creative person, it is true of the artist, and it has got to be true of the business-man. I think the single most important quality of success has to be to know what people want or to make them think they want it, which has a lot to do with marketing.

I don't think I've ever been afraid to make decisions. Also, it's important that you're comfortable in yourself, so that your psycho-physical resources are directed to the right area. Some of the zealots around the world are so uncomfortable, they have this incredible energy, but it's often so misdirected — energy looking for a place to go, rather than the person setting an objective and then asserting energy for it. The final word, I guess, is don't live in the past but learn from it, and always move forward.

John Laws

Talking with John Laws, it isn't hard to understand why radio and television audiences either love him or hate him. Every cliché in the book — i.e. a mind like a steel trap, doesn't suffer fools gladly, has opinions on opinions — seems to apply to this man, who nevertheless appears to have some internal radar which steers him away from the banal or the cliché-ridden statement.

A study in contrasts if ever there was one, Laws has the forthright honesty of a country soul, and a deceptively plain logic to fuel his extraordinary success as a conversationalist. A pioneer of the 'talk-back' or open-line radio program in Australia, his opinions have infuriated and delighted thousands for more than three decades, yet he claims never to be deliberately provocative.

Born on 8 August 1935 and thrice married, he now lives with his family in the Sydney suburb of Woollahra, has a palatial country home, and drives around the city in a Rolls Royce. He casts one of the most unapproving eyes in Australia on the 'tall poppy' syndrome, doesn't like the word 'mateship', and thinks he might have worked on the land if he hadn't become a broadcaster.

It was years before he even thought of radio as a permanent job, but if his current contract with Sydney's 2GB, reputed to be worth about $1 million a year, is accurate, John Laws may be the world's highest-paid radio announcer. Yet he says money had nothing to do with his decision, in 1985, to join the then lowly-rating station. He did it because if you're number one on the number one station, there's nowhere left to go. A few months after Laws joined 2GB — bringing an estimated 75,000 listeners with him — the station rocketed up the ratings.

Laws hated school, is largely self-educated and inarguably strong-minded, yet he claims that stupidity may be his greatest weakness. His only career ambition apparently is just to get better. He's an issues man, not given to deep philosophy, but often overpoweringly direct in expressing his thoughts.

If this sounds like someone who sees the forest by looking at the trees, maybe that's part of Laws's unsettling magnetism. Somehow, his ideas seem to lead by example rather than by tenet, and perhaps that's what this interview has most to offer.

My mother's father was Scottish. I don't know what my grandmother was — Scottish too, I guess. I've never been one to investigate what went on behind, because I can't do much about it. My father was English, my mother was born in Australia. His parents were English but I can't go much further back than that.

My father had two or three trade stores in New Guinea, which he ran quite successfully. We seemed to have a comfortable sort of life, but it wasn't flash. We left New Guinea in 1941 when the Japanese invaded, and we lost everything. My father came to Australia, and after the war he set up business. I suppose we had a middle-class lifestyle.

When we first came down to Australia we lived in Parramatta, where my father bought a small corner store which my mother loathed. After a while he got into the importing and exporting business. We moved to Cremorne, where my father died. I was 15. We bought a house at Lindfield after he died.

Had I not become a broadcaster, I think I probably would have remained in the country. I may have done something associated with motor cars, because of my love of them, but I remember applying for a job with a motor car firm on the North Shore after I left school. Of course, I couldn't get the job as a car salesman because my mathematics were so bad. So God knows what I would have done if I hadn't gone into radio. I really hate to think, because with my ability to excel at laziness at school, I certainly didn't have any qualifications to be anything.

There was enough money to get by so I could finish my education, for what it was worth, at Knox Grammar School. I loathed it as much as it loathed me, I think. I particularly excelled at recess. But I had to do a year or so at school after my father died.

When I finished school I was a nuisance to my mother, as most 16- or 17-year-olds are, and she came upon a brainwave to send me to the country, which suited me. I went jackarooing at Wellington in the south-west of New South Wales. I stayed for a bit over 18 months, then got into radio in Bendigo, Victoria. The man who owned the property that I was a jackaroo on was a Legacy man. He had a friend in Legacy who was involved in the radio industry and the friend said if I ever wanted to talk about going into radio, not necessarily to be on the air, then I could contact him. I left Wellington to hitchhike around Australia and found myself in Bendigo. No money, it was pretty cool in the night-time, so I saw the man from AWA Network and got a job there until I could seek proper employment. I was a Legacy child, they helped to look after me while my father was in New Guinea and when he died. There was a Legacy ball in Wellington which I helped to organise. I also did some compering for them and that was enough to get a job at the radio station.

I was a sort of general knockabout for a week or so, then I managed to talk them into letting me go on the air. I've always subscribed to the theory that there isn't much point in being in something if you don't enjoy it. In the same way, when we acquired a circus later, I figured there was not much point in having a circus if you didn't play with it. At Bendigo I wanted to go on the air and they allowed me to do that. Afterwards, I did everything. I used to work nights, mornings, and weekends. They wanted some help in the breakfast program, and I think somebody had just left or somebody was overworked so they let me do it.

I didn't prepare, I just did it, the same as I do now. I just go and do it. If you're a radio announcer, you just go and announce on the radio. I had gotten a bit out of my depth with a number of ladies in Bendigo, which is why I went to the far reaches of Townsville. The station wanted to keep me so they sent me to Townsville, but I only stayed about six months then went to Newcastle, then to Orange, and I got to Sydney in about 1957.

I suppose I could say this was a definite plan to get into Sydney radio, but it wasn't. It was lack of enchantment with the environment generally. I really liked country radio, I was very happy doing it, but I still didn't see radio as a permanent occupation. Even when I came to Sydney, I didn't see it as permanent. I thought I'd better get on and find a proper job. I was keen to get involved in advertising, but I didn't really know, because I didn't ever do any work at school and therefore wasn't well-educated. I think I was very late to mature, and because of that I had no great drive or ambition or desire. I didn't want to have a lot of money and I didn't want to have a little money. I just wanted the world to keep going on. It stayed much that way for me until I got married and became a father. Then I altered, but not very much.

By that time I had been in Sydney and had gone back to Newcastle because of a complication here with a man called Bob Rogers. I was at 2UE, and when he came to the station he saw me as some sort of threat. Then 2SM offered me a job for what at that time was considered to be a lot of money. It was 100 pounds a week or something, which in 1958 was apparently more than the Prime Minister got. As soon as I went to 2SM, the story is that Rogers allegedly had a clause inserted in his contract saying that so long as he worked at 2UE, I couldn't work there. So the management cleverly banished me to Newcastle, which was part of the 2UE Network, where I recorded programs that they then put on 2UE Sydney. It wasn't a breach of any arrangement they might have had with Rogers, because I wasn't working at 2UE, I was working in Newcastle. They had just brought me in the back door. I must have been in Newcastle for a couple of years. My first son was born, I had a little farm; that was a good time, actually.

You see, I love the country and I was able to have my acreage and a lovely 130-year-old stone house outside of Maitland, which was beautiful. Rogers really did me a favour. That was a very happy period of my life. He had also done me an even bigger favour because by causing this to happen, he triggered an emotion in me that hadn't been cocked prior to that. I became very determined that I was going to be better than him and I knew that I would be better, because he already had indicated that he thought I was. This gave me a reason to be more determined and to get on and do the job. You'd better not tell him that he did me a favour, though, because he's likely to suicide with the news.

I worked very hard and was generally enjoying life, but by 1961 I still didn't consider myself to be any great shakes and was quite prepared to look for proper employment and stop having a good time because I didn't think it was right to get all this money and have such fun. In 1962 I came back to Sydney, to 2GB. Then I got polio and that knocked me over, because all the fun stopped. I suddenly realised that life was a fairly serious operation and I'd better get on with it. When I came out of hospital, somewhat the worse for wear, I decided that I might as well stay in what I was doing.

I'd had polio before, when I was 12, but it wasn't too bad then. I had already had one or two of the three Salk vaccinations, so I was fortunate, because there were people in iron lungs around me. By comparison, I got off pretty lightly with seven months in hospital. I did a lot of thinking and drinking in that time, which was when my first marriage started to decline. I saw very little of my wife during those seven months. Then I realised that I'd better get on with something.

Even though I was little heard-of at the time that I got polio, it was front-page news. That started the publicity treadmill, and because of the publicity I had an appeal to people which I otherwise would not have had. Channel Seven offered me a television show called 'Startime', which I did after I came out of hospital. I did it for nine or 10 months and it was an underwhelming success. I didn't like it much but it put my name before the public eye more firmly than ever before. It got publicity that I needed then to recover from my time away, and it boosted my radio activity. I was at 2GB then. It must have been 1964 when I went back to 2UE, where I stayed until I joined 2UW in 1969. I finally left 2UW to return to 2UE a decade later in 1979, where I worked until late last year. Then I came here to 2GB in mid-April of this year after I had taken seven months off.

AP (after polio), I then went to 2GB and did the television show, which reeked of mediocrity, then I got out of radio for three months because 2GB didn't take up my contract. I wasn't fired but I couldn't get a job in radio, so I was unemployed for three or four months — didn't ever get unemployment benefits, didn't know they existed thank Christ — so I spent a considerable amount of time listening to records and drinking. Then 2UE employed me but for less money than I'd been getting at 2GB, because I was at a disadvantage being unemployed. When we did the first open-line program at 2UE, it annihilated every other program in Sydney.

With a few exceptions, personalities weren't terribly dominant in Australian radio until the late 1950s or early 1960s. In about 1964, I became aware of ratings. That was when I started the open-line programs. Up until that time there was nothing to win. You just did the job, got paid for it, and that was all there was to do. I suppose subconsciously I may have changed when ratings became important. I mean, I've yet to meet a man with a modicum of success who doesn't like to appear to be good. I need to be good, and I need to be told I'm good. If the survey tells me I'm good, then that's all right.

The station thought an open-line program would work, and it seemed like a good idea to me to be able to include the listeners. Of course in those days it was a fantastic novelty, people ringing and saying, 'You get stuffed'. It was extraordinary but it worked, and I dealt with it the only way I knew how: I dealt with the people the same way I'd deal with them if I were talking to them in the street. If they were troublesome, I told them to piss off. Not quite in those words, but my attitude to the people who wanted to talk to me was the attitude I've had toward fellows in the bush, or anywhere I've been. Maybe that's why it worked.

I'm not deliberately provocative. Contrived controversy doesn't work. I've seen a lot of people try it, even on this very radio station. I just say what I think. Perhaps I think in a provocative manner but it is not deliberate. I don't come in here in the morning and think, what contentious thing can I say today? But if I pick up a paper and see where some girl has been given $35,000 by the Equal Opportunities Board because she was discriminated against, according to her, or harassed by her fellow workers and she wants equality, I think that obviously doesn't mean equality. It means unequal equality — she gets $35,000, and a woman whose daughter was murdered by her husband gets $20,000, which is the maximum she could get. It infuriates me to think that there are those sorts of 'equalities', so I have grist for the mill in the morning but it's not deliberate.

That particular story about the girl getting $35,000 came in over one weekend, and I sat on it, waiting for a phone call from somebody so I could say, 'It's a disgrace'. Nobody rang so I said it anyway and people rang up to say, 'Gosh, you're right, how ridiculous that is'. Even the Premier was interested in what I had to say, so I'm not being contentious but simply obvious. I like to look at both sides of the obvious.

I can't remember, but I certainly hope there are times when I've changed my opinion in the past. You'd be some sort of blockhead if you weren't flexible enough to change. The world's full of those people. Generally, for any subject about which I'm asked to express an opinion, there's so much information available that I simply consume it from all sources and then I form my own opinion.

For anybody who writes a newspaper editorial or who expresses an opinion of any sort at any time, obviously, you base that opinion on the information which is available to you. I don't think that you should have to preface every statement by saying, 'From what I have learnt, this is the case'. Often I say, 'it would appear' that this or that has happened. Another thing that I do more often than not is express more than one opinion. I'll express one opinion firmly and then say, earlier this morning I said so and so, but if you were to look at that from the other point of view, you could see so and so — which I think is honest. That's what I endeavour to do with the radio programs, to give a point of view other than the fashionable one. Certainly I'll analyse the fashionable point of view, but then I'll give another viewpoint. That's what attracts a lot of people. Many people ring up and say, 'Really, I never thought of it that way'. If you can do that, you've achieved something. But my program, primarily, must be entertaining. If information is an offshoot of that entertainment, then that's fine.

I like to keep the conversations going as long as I can. Particularly, I have more fun with the people who want to abuse me than the people who want to be nice to me. I'd rather deal with the abusive ones, it's more entertaining for the listeners anyway, but I have a responsibility to those other listeners. If somebody is just going on and on and on, then I have a responsibility to terminate the conversation. There is only one way to do it, and that's by pushing a button.

Being my usual observant self, I noticed that as our success at 2UE increased, my salary didn't. I had an overwhelming desire to improve my lifestyle, so I thought I'd better find somebody who would give me more money. I talked to the Albert family, who own 2UW, and they were very generous so I went there. I suppose that was about the time when I got it by the throat, that was when I decided I would make radio work for me. Up until 1968, I'd been dominated by radio.

I saw that it was possible to get more out of work than I was getting, to make more money, to wield more power. Everybody likes power. Not too many people like to admit it, but I think it's a great driving force behind the designs of many men. I like power, so I headed in that direction. That was 15 years ago, and it was 10 years of fantastic fun. It all went so damn quickly, like everything. Then I went back to 2UE, at a monumental figure, because at that time they wanted me. It took something like two years to settle those negotiations. As soon as I got back there, with the exception of one or two people who were on-side at the executive level, I knew I'd made a tremendous error. I thought 2UE might have changed in the 10-year period I'd been away, but it hadn't changed at all. I'd had remarkable freedom at 2UW in every way. The Albert family were marvellous — they gave me a total freedom which allowed me to burst into the corridors of power, because I could do outrageous things. I'd ring the Prime Minister and do all those sorts of things which radio announcers just didn't do.

The first time I rang the Prime Minister from 2UW, his aides wanted me to ring back and make an appointment but I said, 'Look, we don't have time to do that'. I was doing a radio program, which seemed to come as a surprise to them. And I got the Prime Minister. I did that with a number of them, with McMahon, with Whitlam, and I rang Margaret Whitlam the morning after the election, when she became the First Lady. I spoke to her while she was in bed and

Margaret described the night dress she was wearing. I think that's the sort of thing people want to hear.

I suppose power really means the ultimate indulgence. Any sort of power: the power to be able to get where other people can't get, the power to be able to talk to other people who others can't talk to, knowing that you can pick up a phone and ring whoever it might be, the sort of person who generally isn't available, being included in areas where you can learn and diversify and be among the bigger and better minds of the world — like Kissinger's, for example. When Kissinger was here, I was able to sit down and spend time with him. That's the ultimate indulgence for somebody like me, who is interested in what other people have to say.

I think this is very good, it speaks highly for our system, that you can ring the Prime Minister or the Premier or whoever and say, 'Listen, that's a bit hot. What you've done there is a bit unfair.' He says, 'You know, I've never thought of it like that. You're right, we should look at that. We'll get back to you.' And they do. I was the one who set the ball rolling with the rural problems in the pensioner assets test. That was when I was at 2UE. I talked to Hawke about it and he told me that he agreed that it appeared to be an injustice, and he would certainly look at it and pursue it, which he did. There have been many other instances where I can go to bat on behalf of the general public, who under normal circumstances would never get close to those people. If the ministers of the government think that I gave them a bad time about their railways, Barry Unsworth will send me a ticket on his XPT, or whatever it might be. Everybody is pretty human, they're all pretty good. I don't think anybody takes my comments any more seriously than I mean them.

I see all this as being a very important part of my function in the community. I think it makes my function generally much more worthwhile. That's satisfying, to think that you can be helping other people.

But after I left 2UW, five years of discontent followed at 2UE. I did my programs, sometimes not as well as I'd done them before, sometimes better, and then I had a throat problem. I left the station with an arrangement that after six months I could go back to 2UE if I wanted to, but two months after I stopped 2GB came and talked to me. I saw this as an opportunity to get better at my job, so I took their offer. I think since I've been here I've probably made the best radio programs I've ever done. I hope I can sustain that.

I don't mean to be cruel but with the exception of John Conde 2UE, in my view, just didn't have any style. They didn't know how to treat people. You were even flat out finding somewhere to park your car. If you drove it into the chairman's garage, the sky would fall. Well, I can't deal with people like that. You have to have a bit of style, you have to send Rolls Royces out to get people and have a bit of glamour. I couldn't even get a proper office, so I was renting my own office space in Woollahra. I found their penny-pinching, petty attitude abhorrent. I think if you are in an entertainment industry, you have to be a bit grand, have a bit of pizzazz, a bit of sparkle. You can't be saying, 'Don't park your car where the chairman parks'.

At 2GB, I feel that I'm diversifying even more, becoming a bit more analytical, trying to become a bit more understanding. There are other areas, too, that aren't immediately noticeable. Presentation, putting the program together, making it go more quickly so that the three hours are gone and the listeners say, 'Where did that go?' That side, the production side, is important.

But I don't do a lot of work putting a program together. The girls do a lot of work before the event. We have a writer who discusses with me what I want to get onto that day, which line I want to take, and he gives me a series of points. Towards the end of my time at 2UW, when we were rating number one by a huge margin, I used to get to the station when the nine o'clock news was on. I never did a lot of work beforehand. I come in earlier here. Normally I come in at a quarter to eight, read the papers and have a yarn with the television on, just to make myself aware. That's the first thing I do.

One quality in Australia that I am aware of and sympathetic to, because I fell into the same trap, is an unbelievable immaturity. I was immature, and in many ways I may still be immature, but Australia is terribly immature about this tall poppy syndrome. For instance, I think that people who complain about the amount of money we pay our politicians really are imbeciles, because I would have thought the more you pay them, the higher the calibre of politician you get, and I still believe that to be true. I think the Australian government is probably about as good as any in the world, but the tall poppy syndrome is vicious here, almost to the point of fanaticism. I think that holds us back, it doesn't do the country any good. If we were more open, we would realise that the Prime Minister should be treated like a Prime Minister. When Malcolm Fraser replaced the dinner service at the Lodge, there were people screaming all over Australia because he spent $20,000 on it. They're just crazy. As the Prime Minister of a country, he's going to be entertaining dignitaries from all over the world. Surely we should have a decent dinner service, it's our country,

it's our dinner service. But they can't come to terms with that — very narrow thinkers.

Australia should learn to become broader in its attitude to things and people. We must get rid of this jealousy, this bitterness, this inferiority complex. We are the only country in the world which has a superior inferiority complex. I think Winston Churchill once said, 'I never met a man with an inferiority complex who didn't deserve it'. We deserve an inferiority complex, because in many areas we *are* inferior, and the sooner we realise it the better.

In the work area, for instance, you'll read that about 50 per cent of all upheavals on waterfronts happen in Australia. Isn't that a shock? I talk to a lot of overseas people who simply will not consider trading with Australia, because they can't rely on us. We just can't say that we *will* deliver our coal or whatever it might be. We're importing beef from New Zealand — that's a joke — because their presentation and formulation of selling is better than ours. This amounts to only one per cent of the beef consumption in New South Wales, but one per cent of something is better than 100 per cent of nothing. They're getting something out of it. So I think this trade unionism must be brought under control because it's throttling the country. We should have a fantastic tourist industry, there's no country in the world like Australia. Our Outback country is unique. I've seen all that country up around Katherine and through the Kimberleys, I've been around it more than once, but we can't take people there and show them because who can afford it with the penalty rates and all the other stupidities? There's John Brown, working his backside off trying to sell Australia overseas, and people can't afford to move internally. It's a generally backward attitude.

The way I see it, Japan, in particular, is probably becoming fed up with our inability to perform. Japan may be disenchanted with us. Obviously they've set up their own manufacturing business because they couldn't rely on Australians to get the job done, but I don't think anything necessarily sinister is happening between Japan and Australia.

I suppose our isolation is Australia's main disadvantage, though many see that as an advantage. There are many advantages for Australia: its vastness, its mineral wealth, its achievement in an amazing number of areas. There are hardly more people here than in New York City, and I don't believe that New York City has produced the calibre of people we have. We lead the world in microsurgery, we have Joan Sutherland, the best lady singer in the world, Robert Helpmann, and many other people of quality who have come from Australia over a period of time. I bet you couldn't find all those people coming out of New York City or London.

We're a nation of extremes. If you stop and think about the things that have been invented and perfected in Australia, and think of a little country like Australia taking away the America's Cup — that took a lot of doing — but then we turn around and let ourselves down in so many other areas. I think that's why I feel sorry for Bob Hawke. I mean, he tried to unite the nation when we won the America's Cup. When he was elected lots of things happened which gave him that opportunity, but the spirit existed and survived for about seven days, then fizzed again.

Australians are insular, we're inward-thinking people. A lot of people can't see past Australia. So until we rid ourselves of the inferiority complex that we may in some areas deserve, until we're prepared to think that we're worthwhile and able to compete with the rest of the world, I don't suppose we'll change. Also, we have to develop a system by which we can become a reliable and respected nation. Australians are known and loved all over the world and I think Australia is considered to be a great country, but in a rather novel sort of way. I don't think that we're looked upon as being particularly smart or reliable or capable, I think we're looked upon as being a lot of nice people who really try hard and often pull off the America's Cup and things like it, but that isn't good enough.

We're trying to change the wrong things in Australia. For instance, take the Discrimination Board's desperate, pathetic plea that we shouldn't discriminate. I mean, discrimination is a necessary part of life. I don't know how long the Anti-Discrimination Board has been in existence — five years maybe. In five years, they've tried to change humanity in Sydney, Australia. It has always been normal and natural, not pleasant or desirable, but normal and natural for people to discriminate against other people.

All of a sudden this bunch of do-gooders appears out of the blue and says, we're not going to discriminate against people. You can't say somebody's fat, you can't say that they're thin, you can't say they're homosexual or heterosexual. Now, you can't change humanity, you can't alter human nature, but if we had groups — like the greenies and the Anti-Discrimination Board and the Equal Opportunities Board and the women's liberation movement — if we had those people working as hard at developing pride and a work ethic in Australia as they are on those other projects, we'd all succeed. But they're all working on the wrong things. I mean, how can you change human nature, in Sydney, Australia? How can you change a human nature that has existed for thousands of years? If you see a fat person, you look at them. Yet some do-gooders want a race of perfect people who don't discriminate. It's an impossibility, it can't happen, we're going in the wrong direction.

Of course, there are different degrees of discrimination. As an example of the worst type of discrimination to which I'm exposed to on the program, here's a recent letter from a listener: 'I'm sick to death of people in Parliament telling the Australian people they're going to bring in these so-called badly-off Asians. The only reason they left Vietnam in the first place was because they were exploiting their own people. They left afraid of communism, because under that form of government exploitation is not tolerated to any degree, as it should not be tolerated here. I live in Cabramatta, amongst these people; it's a working-class area. Thousands of Australian men and women have lost their jobs because so-called employers put these people on. They do it because for one, the Asians don't join unions; two, they start work long before they're supposed to, for not one cent extra; three, they very rarely take a lunch break; four, they work for much less than the award wages; five, they wouldn't strike for one hour, even if their lives depended on it; six, naturally, the bosses will take them over Australians and laugh all the way to the bank. Talk about destroying the standard of living. There'll be none at all in another five years. What benefit are they to Australia? Name one thing. They won't assimilate at all, they marry Asians, they buy from Asians, Asians employ only Asians. If there was a war tomorrow, they wouldn't fight for Australia. They come here for one reason and one reason only: to make money. How dare Bob Hawke and Andrew Peacock tell the Australian people this is the way it's going to be? Ask the people. The politicians' motives for bringing the Asians here are just to import votes.'

All that sort of thinking aside, I must say that, personally, I've never even considered the fact that I might one day think, 'Forget work, I don't want to know about it'. I believe there's a distinct possibility that past-times could well become boring. In that period when I stopped radio work because of my throat condition I worked harder than ever, because I wasn't restricted to times that I thought I could work. I was in the country, so I drove trucks all through the night, ferried cattle around the country, and did all sorts of things. Everybody has to have a reason to live. That's why when they retire, some people do die, because they no longer have a reason to live. To wake up in the morning and think that I've no reason to get out of bed would be soul-destroying for me. Through work I can talk to different people every day, every day is different. I play music I like to listen to, music I'd play if I were sitting around the house. The only difference between my job and sitting around the house is that the station pays my phone bill. I do what I like to do: I love to talk about products, I love to read books and talk about what I've read, I love to tell people what I've seen in the world and hear what they've seen.

I would be prepared to admit that I'm unique in my work, but that doesn't necessarily mean that I'm the best. I mean, Jack the Ripper was unique, but I don't know that that's an accolade. Because there are so many facets to what I do in a three-hour program, from humour to pathos to out-and-out slinging to playing music to singing to reading poetry, I'm diversified, but I would not like to think that I'm the best.

You see, even if I was number one on a station, the station wasn't always number one. It was number two sometimes, or sometimes number four. If you're number one on a station which is number one, there's no reason to get better, is there? Everybody needs a little bit of discipline and I'm not absolutely fantastic at self-discipline. But I'm alert enough to know when you have your back to the wall. By coming back to 2GB in April of 1985, I deliberately put my back to the wall.

I had been at the top or near it since 1964. I'd been number one when the station was number four and number one when the station was number two. I thought that I could get better here, not because the station was number seven, but because I like the management and the environment. I certainly enjoyed the thought of trying to claw my way back up to the top, if being at the top is that important. It's important to the station managers. I certainly feel a responsibility, but don't confuse the facts. The desire with me is not to be number one, but to be better. If by doing things better you become number one, that's fine.

In fact, I've never had a driving, overwhelming desire to be number one. If I have an office, I want to have a nice office; if I have a farm, I want it to be the best farm; if I have cars, I want them to be good, clean, tidy, and properly cared-for. I love and collect books, a desire that has stood me in good stead. I like stylish things, but in order to have them you have to have money which means you have to work, so the treadmill became attractive to me.

I had a little fellow in here at half-past seven this morning, doing a school project. I spent half-an-hour with him and he asked me why I worked. I said, 'It's simply because I can't think of anything better to do. You get out of bed in the morning, you have to do something because you can't sit around the house all day, so you might as well work.' He seemed to think that was a pretty good idea, and that's really just the way I live my life.

A lot of people who are in this industry would like to feel that they are hounded to death. They're not. I don't think I suffer greatly from lack of privacy. Sometimes I'm hounded, in restaurants and such, but what does it matter? I have learnt to live with that. People stop me and talk to me in the street, or wave and say good-day, generally in a friendly way. I very rarely get abuse these days. In the early days, before people became accustomed to me, I got abuse. I went to a restaurant the other night for a quiet dinner with my wife, and a man and woman organised themselves at the table next to us. They might as well have been sitting at our table, because we spent all night talking to them. I was disadvantaged because I couldn't be openly rude to them. I didn't want to humiliate them, their intentions were good, but they were a pain in the arse. That was a nuisance. It meant that we left the restaurant early, when I had really been looking forward to a quiet dinner because we had family things to discuss. Those kind of things happen occasionally, but I don't run out in the street and get mobbed. As I say, there are plenty of people in this business who would like to think that that's the way it works. It doesn't. I'm more likely to suffer invasions of privacy at the airport in Hong Kong or Singapore or Los Angeles, where there's a group of Australian travellers who see you and really do mob you then, because you're out of your element. But you could walk up and down Rodeo Drive in Beverley Hills and see Robert Redford having coffee. Nobody takes any notice of him, so all that's a bit of a myth.

However, I can go to parts of Australia where people don't even know me, yet on a telephone switch-girls will recognise my voice. That's peculiar, it's rather nice, but it's peculiar. I remember going into a motel in Lightning Ridge. I had my children with me and was talking to them, and a woman on the other side of the petition called out, 'I know who that is. That's John Laws's voice.' Quite extraordinary. So I imagine my voice is distinctive and because it is, perhaps it's been a help to my career. It certainly hasn't been a hindrance.

The thing about criticism concerning people like me is it's so public, and I feel sorry for anybody who's humiliated publicly. I was sorry for Nixon when he was publicly humiliated. I don't think that's the sort of thing that people should have to experience, but that's one of the prices you pay for success. I'll listen to criticism, depending on from whence it comes. If somebody I respect criticises me, if Phillip Adams was critical of me, I'd be more likely to listen to it than if somebody I didn't respect was critical of me. There's a great ulterior motive in criticism and that's envy. In those cases I tend to dismiss the criticism. If you are a public person, you have to have an ego. If you have an ego, you're sensitive to yourself, that's what an ego is. So how can you be egotistical — and you have to be, to be public — and not be affected by criticism?

I don't analyse myself, I don't assess and consider myself day by day, what I am or where I stand, because it varies day by day. I don't describe myself, and in fact it's very rarely that a man does describe himself. You don't pick up the telephone and say, 'Good morning, I'm John Laws, I'm six-foot-three and I have green eyes'. However, I like to think that, professionally, my strength would be honesty. And stupidity is my weakness. Obviously on some occasions my main weakness is not being able to differentiate between the two.

To me, success simply means that you can have fewer worries in one area, but by having fewer worries in that area you have more worries in another. The more you have, the less you worry about not having it. The more you have, the more you get, and then you have to worry about what you've got: farms, employees, motor cars, shares, and nice, static things. I'm not sure that one offsets the other, but that's what success represents to me. I'm prepared to put up with that.

Honesty, awareness, and hard work lead to success. I have absolutely no doubt that these qualities work. Just be aware. I have a sister who used to say to me, 'You are so lucky'. And I thought, Jesus, am I lucky? Why am I lucky? I don't think I'm lucky. I was in the right place at the right time, but so were a lot of other people. I wasn't the only one at 3BO in Bendigo when the opportunity came along, I wasn't the only boy of my age in Bendigo at the time. But it seems that, when opportunity knocks, a lot of people are putting the garbage out or are in the bath. As for a setback, it's really just a nuisance. Sometimes I see it as a form of enforced rest, but it really just represents a nuisance. I don't ever think of it as more than that.

Concerning other well-known Australians, I admire an awful lot of them, such as Edmond Capon, Director of the NSW Art Gallery, or Lady Cliento, but 'admire' is a very loose word. Admiration and respect don't necessarily go hand-in-hand. You have to admire a man like Joh Bjelke-Petersen, but you don't have to respect his motives. I can't say that I admire people with immense power simply because they have immense power. I admire Neville Wran, but by openly saying that you admire people, you immediately link yourself with them by inference, and that's not healthy, because you can admire people for all sorts of different reasons. Although I admire Neville Wran, I may not necessarily admire his politics. I admire Bob Hawke but it doesn't necessarily mean that I admire his politics. I admire Paul Keating. You are more likely to develop some sort of admiration for people who are thrust in front of you, because you see them work. So in my position, I probably admire my wife more than anybody else.

I think it would be presumptuous of me to suggest that I had admiration for overseas personalities, because in order to have any real admiration for them I'd have to be familiar with what they do. I admire anybody who can create an environment which is a step closer to world peace. There seems to be a great shortage of those people in the world, because they are all telling us that we need world peace while they're pointing a nuclear warhead at us. I find it very difficult to admire that. I admire great artists; by that I mean painters, musicians, composers — people who are dedicated. If you were to look at a list of dedicated, successful people, then they're the people I'd admire. I don't think you necessarily have to name them.

There is, however, somebody that I'm frightened of. People tell me it's God, maybe it is. I don't know what His name is, but there is somebody who makes me stop when I might have done something wrong, or there's somebody who makes me think, 'That would be a nice thing to do'. It's not me who makes me think it, so I believe in Somebody.

Belief of that sort and admiration for friends or colleagues are of course different things, but on the latter subject I think mateship is a peculiar word. To start with, its origins: you know, a 'mate' originally was a sailor-boy on a ship who was put there for one good reason, so in its original form I don't subscribe to it at all. I think friendship is probably one of the most important things, but mateship, in the connotation which it has today, is a pretentious word really. I don't like the word. I think it denigrates friendship.

On the domestic front, support from wife and family hasn't been related to my career. I'm happily married. Lack of support from a wife that led to divorce has probably affected my career, or lack of support by me for a wife, whatever the case may have been, but there's been absolutely no association between work and home. While a marriage is at peace with itself, there's no association. The only desire I have for my children — and again, it's a very trite answer — is that they can love a lot, give a lot, and be very happy. I think directing a child into a specific area is a very dangerous thing to do, both for the child and for the parent. Generally, you end up steering the child in the wrong direction and you are very disappointed. I don't think you can live somebody else's life.

In terms of my own career path, the television part of it pays me handsomely, and I would like to see if it were possible to do something worthwhile in it. I've really just experimented with it. I like doing it, I just don't like the end result much. As in reading commercials or writing poetry, television is just part of the day-to-day things I do. I believe that a number of people have tampered with their own integrity in attempted dealings with me, but as far as my integrity is concerned, in doing things to the best of my ability I have never lowered my own standards. My goal, as I've said, is just to get better.

Prue Acton

Like creativity, the definition of talent can be elusive. Many of the people in this book have had to struggle hard to bring those two qualities to the fore in their lives, but Prue Acton is one who seemed born to achieve. A true artist, she demonstrated creative talent beyond the norm from the age of three. With the help of intelligent and even aggressive guidance from her parents, she set about a career that saw her well-established as a fashion designer by age l9. Today, with a daunting list of national and international awards to her credit, she is poised to become one of the world's premier names in women's fashion.

An incredibly prolific designer, Acton can turn out 35 designs in a single day, with a personal record thus far of 57 creations in one 24-hour period. Elected to the fashion industry's Hall of Fame in 1976, thrice-winner of Olympic Games design awards, named in 1982 as an Officer of the Most Excellent Order of the British Empire (OBE), Acton currently produces no less than 20 collections annually, of l50 to 200 pieces each — and still believes that the peak of her creativity is yet to come.

Gifted with an exemplary eye for detail and the artist's affinity for texture and colour, she feels blessed to have been born in a country famed for the quality of its light. Other nations have been equally impressed with the Acton style. Aside from sales in Australia, her own company also sells to the United States, Canada, Hong Kong, New Zealand, and Japan.

In 1969 she branched into cosmetics, and a complete line still bears the distinctive Acton logo. No less than $12 million worth of clothing and accessories are now marketed under her name.

Well-travelled and widely-read, athletic and strikingly attractive, the mother of two and the leader of 50 loyal Australian staffers, Prue Acton nonetheless seems almost unaware of the immense natural resource she embodies for this country. However, she's far from blind to her own potential, and has definite plans about how to achieve it. For the rest of us, this Australian artist's future progress should be a joy and an inspiration to witness.

If I walked down the street now, I could tell you within about 15 minutes what the best-selling clothes on the market are. I've always been able to pick a winner. Yet you can't research the future, you can only check out the past, and it mainly tells you what not to do. I work fairly instinctively, although if you wanted to pay me for a day's work, I could easily pull out a very precise recommendation on the 'why'. That's one reason I like working in my own company. When I've worked in major companies throughout the world, I've always had to back up my statements. What a bore! An idea that may have taken 12 months to create pops out and here it is, this is it. Then someone asks you to rationalise that product. Well, I can take you through all those steps and give you a rational answer, which sounds awfully good, but what a waste of my time. I could be onto the next idea.

I call it non-instinct, I call it my computer. I believe if I put enough information into my computer, then it's only a matter of assessing that information, which I usually do in a brainstorming session or a creative moment. For example, yesterday morning in the car, I came up with a new structure for a company. I've been thinking about it for about eight months and I was able to put every step down in one session, and then go and talk to someone about it. I could tell you, if I bothered to, where all those ideas came from that I've been filtering for eight months. On the 1st of July I have to have my winter colours and fabrics put down. They go on the market on the 1st of February next year, but already I've been working on that winter collection for probably six months, a little bit here, a little bit there, making notes, until one day, probably on the absolute deadline, I will sit down and do it. People think I've done it at the last minute, but I haven't. The computer has been getting as much input as I can give it. I think that's what creative people might be all about and why we work best under pressure, because you just keep on feeding in information, throwing ideas around, sleeping on it, and then on the final day, when you know, you go. I used to stay awake Sunday nights, and by Monday morning at 9.30 I had virtually done the week's work. Then I realised

I could sleep and when I woke up the same thing would happen. Perhaps it happened while I was asleep.

I have an open and broad mind, so I can take in a lot of influence and a lot of information at once. I try to never make a decision until I'm happy with the idea, which drives people insane. They think I'm not concise or decisive, whereas in fact, until I'm absolutely happy that that's the right decision, I won't make one. Some people consider this a disadvantage, and it can be. We call it procrastination at its best. It's making a decision and sticking to it. Also, if something is not working, I'm then able to say okay, slide around here. I have a backup in my mind on an idea and I'm quite good at futurising, I think. When I was thinking of this new company the other day, I imagined all sorts of ideas. I futurise, so when someone says so and so, I'm able to say yes. In this way, opportunity walks in at my gate. I recognise it, because I've already done the pre-plans for a number of eventualities. I can say no, I'm not interested, because I've done my pre-thinking.

I'm very affected by light, which I know is a sort of genius of artists. Light affects my brain in some particular way, and I think I can see the differences and nuances in light and colours. I can detect very subtle differences, such as a 16th of a centimetre at 100 paces. I can say that hem's crooked, and it is. That's something you're born with. Obviously you develop as well, and I was brought up in a family which had a good sense of design, so my critical resources were developed by that family. My mother dressed beautifully. In her 30s she was the most elegant of women, the house had beautiful flowers, and she was always decorating the house and garden, so I was surrounded by beauty.

There were a lot of other very creative women in our family who never were successful. They could sing and paint but they were obviously frustrated as artists. Actually there were many creative people on both sides of the family, but nobody else really made the most of themselves in terms of creative expression.

My mother's parents were born up in Gippsland. They were farmers, and my grandfather started off with nothing. He left home at 12 and became a fence poler, because he was the youngest, so there was no money for Baw Baws.

I was born in Benalla (Victoria), and as a child I spent a lot of my holidays in Gippsland. That was very important to me, because I witnessed my grandmother being an equal partner with my grandfather. She ran the property, drove the car, looked after 30 shearers, four kids and four more orphaned cousins, and so on. My father's parents, on the other hand, were public servants and shopkeepers — quite a difference.

My father was very young at the end of the war when he left the Air Force. He had a wife, I was a baby, and they had 600 pounds which my mother's father had lent them. My parents bought a grocery shop in Toorak Road and I was brought up living on top of that grocery shop. I was about 10 when we moved into the suburbs. By that stage my father and mother had gone into self-service, and in fact had one of the first such stores. Then they had one of the first supermarkets in Beaumaris, and my mother also ran a baby giftware shop at one stage.

I was a very shy child, although there were really two sides to me. On the other side I was a ringleader. My mother said that when I was three, in kindergarten at Christchurch, my teacher said to her, 'Do you realise this child has done such and such artistically, which no other child of that age does? This child has real talent.' The teacher had noticed little things like the paintings I did, where the sky was completely blue right to the horizon, instead of how most kids draw only a little line of blue. I never did draw like other people. Then I began doing a lot of portraits, which was what I liked doing, and teachers would come in the room and say, 'Oh, who did this?' That was when I knew I was good at different creative things. I was top of my class when I was interested in certain subjects, but often I couldn't be bothered with them. I have a very good memory, so I didn't have any trouble at school because I could learn everything off by heart. Also, I had an ability to rearrange the facts so that they came out concisely and simply. That helped when you were studying on the night before an exam, so I never had to work hard.

By the time we moved into the suburbs my parents had a number of shops where I worked during my holidays and after school, filling up the shelves, ringing the cash register, and doing all the things kids do when their parents are in business. So from a very early age I listened to business, heard all the discussions, and was always treated as part of the team. My parents used to say, 'Whatever you do, we'll back you, we're behind you', so from an early age I imagined myself running a supermarket. I just knew that I could run anything I needed to run. One night when I was 12, I decided that I wanted an allowance for clothes, so I designed a wardrobe. I worked out how much money I'd need, and that was the first collection I ever designed.

I didn't sell that collection, but I can still see today what those garments looked like. Before that I was making doll's clothes, heaps of them. Then I wanted to be an architect, so I designed houses and painted. I was also good at maths but I left school at Firbank when I was 15. I left because I was bored out of my brain, and because at school I wasn't allowed to do art and maths.

I was good at history and English as well, but I was scared that I'd end up a secretary if I dropped art, so I dropped school instead. My mother talked the RMIT (Royal Melbourne Institute of Technology) into taking me as one of the last two students who were accepted at age 15. After that, you had to be 16 and then later, of course, you had to have your matric. It's a lot harder to get in today, all of which I think is stupid. Anyway, I did advertising art for two years at RMIT and textile design for four years. By this stage I was making my own clothes and had to take off one morning a week to learn to sew and drape a pattern. I still can't do a paper pattern, I can only do a draped pattern. One morning a week for about a year I would cut something out, my mother would sew the hem up, and I'd have a new dress every Saturday night. I tried working at Myers in the Christmas holidays once and hated it. After that I started sewing for friends and for family, in the Christmas holidays, making bikinis. My bikinis became very well-known — not that I ever delivered on time! Then I started working for a Mrs Opie down at Beaumaris, sewing for 10 shillings every Friday afternoon. She just had a few machinists, a small business, but it was very interesting watching her because she was so quick and so good.

Both during and after my schooling my parents, as I said, were always absolutely encouraging in whatever I wanted to do. All their friends would say, 'You can't possibly back a daughter in business, what do you mean backing a daughter?' That didn't worry them, because my mother was always the entrepreneur in the family. My father was the money, she was the ideas, and they're both hard workers, so that was how it was in our family. My mother is not only creative, she's also a land developer with my father. She found out that my father has beautiful colour sense. I always thought a natural eye for design and style came through to me from my mother's side, but I think it came from my father's side, too. I learnt maths from my father, and from my mother I learnt the entrepreneurial skills — how to get out there and make it happen — which you have to do if you're a farmer.

At art school I did try to change over to dress design, saying I thought I could do both courses at the same time. However, the administration didn't agree with me. They thought I should repeat a couple of years, but I said no thank you and finished school. But I had begun to realise that I was interested in both disciplines, dress designing and textile designing.

When I left art school, I was offered a job as a junior designer. I quite precociously asked for 19 pounds a week (which was a secretary's wage at the time) when the going rate was about nine pounds. However the company closed down by the time I got back from my holidays, so there I was with no job. I had applied for a couple of jobs as a textile designer, but they didn't want me and I didn't want them, so it was mutual. As I said, I'd been making my own clothes and I had some beautiful clothes. I can't remember quite what happened then, but probably my mother said, so and so has a factory, why don't you go and talk to them? So I went to see this friend of my parents and I'm still with that factory, funnily enough. I designed five dresses there, and then my mother and I walked around Melbourne with them over our arms. I modelled them and we took our first orders. That was in February and we started shipping them just after Easter, which of course you're not supposed to do. You're supposed to show before Christmas for the winter season. We didn't know any of that then. We got a very good reaction and the clothes sold fast. After that, I didn't know that you had to do a summer collection in April. We learnt such things fairly fast. My parents lent me 300 pounds and we got a small place in Flinders Lane. It was only 500 square feet on the third floor, but I made it look quite pretty. I worked about 18 hours a day, because during the day I would be selling and showing and taking fabrics to the factories. When the lifts didn't work, I'd lug 60 metres of fabric up and down flights of stairs and then carry the fabric up to our factory on the corner. At night I'd sit down and do all the adding up of the fabrics. I had to devise and set up my own system, my father and brother did the bookkeeping and my mother helped with whatever had to be done. I was 19 at the time. When I was 21 and my brother was 18, he died in a surfing accident. I also have a sister who left home at 17 to live in London, then in America. She's a dancer and a teacher, amongst other things.

My father still had the supermarket business when we started up at Flinders Lane, but he retired when he was about 42 and then ran my company for a few years. We got pretty big very fast, although I never thought much about it. I never knew what was happening; I must have been too busy doing all the production and designing and selling. Then I got agents in Sydney and in Adelaide so I could go away and show the collection.

The Gown Of The Year was quite a prestigious award then; I suppose it was the only prestigious design award in Australia. I made a dress and came runner-up in that competition in 1965 and was thrilled. I was about 20 years old. To be runner-up was pretty amazing, because the people who were in the competition had been around for 20 years. I was up against all the top names in Melbourne, people who were famous in all the couturier houses and some of whom are still around.

Then, I guess, my name started to be whispered around Melbourne, and the clothes began flying out of the shops. A couple of years later we moved into Collins Street and I got a production manager. My parents employed Betty Harrison, who was the number one marketing salesperson in Australia. She came in as general manager. My father had retired by then, so my parents went off to the United States, Japan and England, where they signed contracts for my clothes to be produced throughout the world.

This was so unusual at the time that there was no provision in Australian taxation for such exports. As a result, we were being taxed 90 per cent on every dollar we made. Because no one had ever thought of exporting an idea out of Australia, we were being taxed both in the United States and on the original dollar by the Australian government. It took us three years and cost a lot of money to fight that arrangement. However, the clothes were a fabulous success. The first collection went into Lord and Taylor in New York, which also had Mary Quant's designs. Lord and Taylor had a department called the Young New Yorker, which was a terribly stunning place to be. I only had about five styles there but the store promoted me well, putting an ad in *Time* magazine.

I was just about to get married, so this was the mid-1960s. With our designer I went off to New York, where we were a bit of a rage, because we were wearing our mini-skirts. New Yorkers had never seen a mini-skirt in their lives, but we'd gone really well with them in Australia because Jean Shrimpton had come out with them. So we were having the biggest ball back here where the skirts were going up, and although the Catholic Mothers' Association wouldn't have bikinis, they nevertheless were getting smaller and smaller. The old pattern that I had made when I was a kid at RMIT turned out to be the biggest-selling bikini on the market. All the big swimwear companies were knocking off the pattern, and I'm right in saying 'knocking off' because it wasn't very nice, although later, when I began to appear on television, I had to learn not to say things like 'knocking off'. Anyway, my first collection was shown in New York and was a runaway success. The store ran a big ad that said, come and meet the designer, Prue Acton. Well, three people turned up to meet me and all three were Australian. One was a reporter, one was a relative, and one was a stranger. Yet the store sold 3,000 dresses. For Mary Quant, Lord and Taylor had done a promotion a couple of months earlier for which 3,000 people turned up but only three dresses were sold, so it was a bit of a difference. We were an amazing commerical success from the beginning. Lord and Taylor had taken me on before the Quant disaster, because such promotions take about nine months lead time or a minimum of six months.

My parents set that up by meeting with the number one fashion guru of New York. The only time she had available was to sit with them in the back of her limo, but they talked and she said, go to such and such a company. That company had lost a designer, and the head of the company, who was old, was looking for some marvellous miracle, I think, something to leave his company and his sons with. He took me on and then tied up with Lord and Taylor as the exclusive outlet, because that's what he had done with his previous designer. He had a lot of prestige in the market, he believed in the clothes, and they sold. Meanwhile, that one Australian reporter who attended the New York opening sent back a story to *The Sydney Morning Herald*, so I was front page news here because this had never been done before by an Australian.

Anyway, my United States success went on for quite a number of years, until I couldn't travel anymore because I had married and had a baby. I carried on working until one or two days before I gave birth. I managed to have my second child over the Christmas holidays. She was born on the 26th of January, so instead of going back to work on the 27th, I went back in February, taking two weeks off. It's very hard, I'll tell you, having babies and running a business. I was so vague, I'd have to sit half the day writing notes to myself just to organise my time.

Before having my first child, I had been travelling overseas at least four times a year, sometimes up to three months at a time, so I was hardly around at all. I decided that I couldn't keep this up, so I dropped out of the American and English markets but retained the Japanese contract. The Japanese are great people to do business with. In the United States they expect you to send them the garment and do every detail for them. They may put the garments straight into the showroom, whereas the Japanese plan about 18 months to two years in

Prue Acton with namesakes

advance. They launch it properly — they put in a whole department. In Tokyo I have a department with 15 employees and my own floor in a really beautiful building in the city. We have continuity there and can overcome any market changes in a product, because obviously timing is very vital in fashion. It doesn't matter how good your styling is, if it's not delivered at the right time, it's useless. By setting up a division, the Japanese have marketing people who can say, right, we can put this in at this time, and so on. In the United States they expect you to do such planning from Australia, and unless you're living in America 12 months of the year you can't do that, it's not possible. In Japan our contract has just been renewed for another four years, and has now been going for about 18 years. I'm with a different company but the agent is still the same, and I'm still with the same lingerie company as well. It's phenomenal, and wonderful.

The Japanese are tough, however. You only have to make one mistake and you're stuck with it. But I get a good income out of there and it's been long-term, rather than here today, gone tomorrow. You might get promised the world somewhere else but they don't deliver more than one or two seasons, whereas in Japan you know they won't drop you just because business is a little bit down. They'll keep with you and they are very good at marketing, looking at what something is, isolating its qualities and marketing the product. I had a different way of making clothes and I was promotable, so success came easily.

Australia is a highly affluent country with a small population, so we are ideal for product testing. If something sells here, it's going to sell anywhere from a marketing/business point of view. From a creative point of view, we have 15 million creative people, fine artists, writers, photographers, and film-makers who have a unique expression. We live in a particular part of the world which is not the Old World and is not the New World. I think this whole Pacific area is exciting, from California to Japan to China to Australia. The Pacific is truly where it's happening. Here we sit with all the world's influences at a time of communication breakthroughs. We are not stuck with the old, as they are in New York or Europe, we can think as a young country can. We can move fast if we unleash our entrepreneurial power from the clutches of taxation and bureaucracy which, for some stupid reason, Australians seem to love.

Everyone's saying we are perfectly situated to deal with China's emergence into the 20th century. That emergence is still happening, slowly, but they will be the power of the 21st century. We are on the same time zone, we're able to fly to China without jetlag, and we're able to talk to them in their own daylight hours, which is a great help. They have no animosity toward us as they do toward the Japanese, Americans, English and French, who invaded their country. They don't see us as having any imperialistic feelings, which we don't, so we are perfectly situated to deal with China's emergence into the 21st century.

As far as China and my business are concerned, I probably see myself in a consulting role, if anything. I do feel that I've had a very interesting career, and I'm probably coming to that second stage which most human beings seem to go through. You've been doing your own thing like crazy in the first part of your creative life, and then the next stage is that you start passing that information and that experience back to others. A few people have nibbled at me in that respect. One Japanese woman I know goes to China for two weeks every year and she said, 'Wouldn't you like to come and work in the factories? I'm training the workers.' Her Japanese company is training the Chinese to make clothes to Japanese standards, which are very high. So, little ideas are coming through and I'll be ready and able when the right one hits. I've no real ambition in that area, but I certainly would not turn down the opportunity to work with the Chinese.

I was brought up with a good dose of the constant work ethic. It took me years to overcome feeling guilty when my housekeeper brought me a cup of tea in the morning, because I was sitting and she was working. But hard work can be wonderful. I think we're harder workers than people in the East. They work long hours but they don't work hard. What I think we can learn from them is to be content and live more for the moment, without giving up our own knowledge.

Australia not only has unique flora, fauna, colour and light, but we are also world leaders in recreation. We give ourselves more holidays than anybody else and we love getting away at weekends. We tend to be a very casual society and the clothes and products we make reflect that lifestyle. I would say that we should push anything to do with leisure. In anything to do with a casual way of life we should be highly visual in the world, because that's both our way of life and the future way of life for the world. Ultimately, everybody wants to live in our climate, so they will be coming here more often for holidays and they'll want the products associated with that lifestyle, as the world has to work less. In Australia we are down to perhaps an average of 22 hours a week work, whereas only about 30 years ago it was more like 70. With four weeks of annual holidays, two weeks sick leave, and two weeks off for national holidays, we have dropped our working week by about two-thirds in the last few decades. So we are the world leaders in time off. Australian aborigines worked only two hours a day in their natural environment, and the rest of the time was spent in leisure — creative, artistic, religious, and social leisure. I can see, with technology, that we may again have to work only two hours a day.

As for the Americans, I reckon they're about 10 to 20 years ahead of us in everything they do. They're ahead in business, psychology, marketing, and taxation. I think we should be looking closely at their taxation systems. Now we're talking about capital gains taxes here, and America has already found out that when they raised their capital gains tax to 40 per cent, it wiped out business. That's frightening. How dumb of us not to look at the Americans and see what they're doing, because they have quite a changeable, volatile system and they do things before us, so we can learn from them. We can take the good and be careful not to take the bad.

When I closed down the American and United Kingdom operations but kept on with the Japanese market, my husband was doing much the same thing. He had started his own menswear business about the same time, and he also got some contracts in Japan and in America. I would go on ahead of him and then he would join me. We signed up with the same company in Japan at one stage. Ours were separate companies, although at one point I was a shareholder with my parents in his company. Later he had the company totally on his own and has kept it that way since the 1970s. We've been separated for two years now and are almost divorced.

I think to have a happy, supportive marriage and be a business person is wonderful, because you're not out there playing and raging, you have it all at home. Ideally, I'd like to have a good, steady relationship, probably living with somebody. I'm enjoying being single very much. I have my two kids living with me, a housekeeper, and a good support system — the female sort, of course. A lot of my friends are in the same position. They too have gone back into the workforce, so we're very supportive of each other. I know I can ring up any number of friends for help and they know they can do the same with me, so that's working well. I reckon my husband and I lived very well. We were together for about 17 years, so that's terrific. But I think you need a good support system, just as you need a good housekeeper. If you're working you either have a wife, or you have a home husband, or you have a housekeeper. I don't think it's possible to do a house-cleaning job, run an organisation, and run a business. Anyway, I hate house-work. It's one of the reasons I'd never give up work. I couldn't stand it.

When my parents wanted to retire completely, I bought their share out and now I run my own company. I employ a business consultant and an auditing accountant who's been with me for most of my career. I have a wonderful team of people. My marketing man in Sydney, Jim Myles, is like a brother — we're so close we think alike. Even on the phone we're on the same wavelength. And Betty Harrison is still with me after 18 years. I'm very lucky, I have very loyal staff. The tea lady has been here for 18 years, my production manager is into her 12th year, I think, and my accountant has been with me now for about nine years. I still have one designer who has been freelancing for me for 17 years. Some of these people are older — I've never been afraid to employ older people — some are younger, and some are the same age as I am.

Many of my Melbourne designers stayed with me a long time, say five or seven years, and that's wonderful, because it really takes me five years to train a designer. By then they're generally doing a wonderful job, but after about seven years people often get bored and need a change. That's my theory: it takes two years before you're getting anything out of a designer, or a factory for that matter. After five years you've reached the ultimate, and have a couple more years before you get bored.

That hasn't happened to me personally, because I've managed my own business. I always have something new, such as cosmetics, uniforms or shoes. During the 1970s I was making very big collections of shoes, 200 styles four or five times a year. We were marketing very strongly throughout the year and were a leader in Australia, making our second winter and our second summer lines into very important parts of our business. The turnover was growing by 30 to 40 per cent, year after year. I loved designing shoes, that was wonderful. I worked with Paragon. We did some beautiful shoes but then the quality went down, and I just won't have my name on inferior products. However I may well go into shoes again.

I did sheets for a while and then (Gough) Whitlam changed the tariff overnight and that was the end of that, because I unfortunately decided to have the sheets printed in Australia. That decision just wiped out the sheets project.

At about the same time we were also showing cosmetics, a line of knitwear, and my own prints were coming back from the textiles with all my own colours. Year after year we were introducing new fabrics onto the market which the market was following.

I have never opened a manufacturing plant for fashions, I have always sub-contracted, and I very rarely endorse a product because it has to be perfect. For instance, I wouldn't do cigarettes. I must know that the product is good and be happy with it, which is why I only do one endorsement every couple of years or so. I'm not overexposed. For the last three years I've been the official presenter for Vulcan Industries. The commercials I do engender a skill that I love perfecting. I did an hour session the other day, then they rewrote the script twice and said, 'Go for it'. I read the 30-second commercial in one take. So I'm learning another skill. Good!

In the late 1960s Angel Face put my name on some of their cosmetics. Then a couple of companies did some research and found out that I was a household name. I made my first advertising endorsement around that time also. It was for a sherry. In hindsight the ad was a bit worthless but it was an interesting experience. Then a couple of guys from Revlon said they wanted to start an Australian cosmetic company. They had money and wanted to call the product Prue Acton. My parents had heard all this about me being a household name, so they said look, instead of doing that, why don't we start our own cosmetics company? I said, I suppose so, if you want to. I let them set up a company, they got the finance together, we built our own factory, did all our own moulds, got the equipment and the whole caboodle together, which, now I think about it, was utter madness. We did it, though, with the help of our manager, who was a genius. He created the most wonderful products, which are still the best on the market. All this took longer than we expected. We didn't get paid, being a private company, so when we ran out of funds we went into receivership and sold the business to Hoechst six weeks later. But we paid every bill back on time and I was paid a lot of money for the takeover. Both the Revlon men left the company. I was sad to see the product manager, in particular, go. He decided that he couldn't work with another big company after working with Revlon, I suppose. But the company went on very well for about five years. It grew and grew, then started plateauing out, and Hoechst finally sold it to an Australian company. Before that we were Hoechst's fastest-growing and most profitable cosmetic line, then someone's ideas got too big and we decided to go into huge ranges of products. Suddenly, the profits weren't as good as they had been.

*Above, Prue Acton and members of the Japanese clothing industry in Tokyo.
Below, with Dudley Moore, Susan Anton, Allan Carr, and Olivia Newton-John
at Koala Blue*

I wasn't devastated by the eventual cash-flow problems of our cosmetics company, because again, I wasn't as deeply involved in that as my parents were. I was very young and I was excited by the challenge more than anything: what do we do? We had corporations from all over the world making approaches to us to buy the company, so I loved it. But my parents were horrified, of course, because in Australia you just don't go bankrupt. In the United States, fine, you are allowed to do so. In fact, I believe the whole attitude there is that the third time around is when businesses often make it big. That's why they are so successful — they're not afraid of failing — whereas in Australia we are afraid of failure. I didn't know enough at the time to know what failure was. In the same way that it never bothered me whether I succeeded or not, it also never worried me whether I failed or not.

After we sold the cosmetics company I worked for the next seven years as a cosmetics consultant. That was wonderful, I was flying around the world, spending a lot of time in Germany, and working with very interesting people from all over the world. Meanwhile my company was going along very nicely and I was being paid well by cosmetics. In fact we were a hot property in the 1970s. I didn't know this at the time but now I realise that to some women, a Prue Acton dress was just the ultimate thing you could have in your life. People have kept them. I've kept my first one, I'll never throw it out. But again, I didn't have any idea of all that then. Even after the mini-skirt was dropped and the midi came in, everybody except us lost money like crazy. We made that fashion into something very wearable and all our customers followed. We've been able to go with every trend and be the leaders of trends.

In the 1970s David Jones were actively promoting fashion. They had wonderful fashion parades in the evening in Sydney, they were spending hundreds of thousands of dollars, and all the designers were vying to win the Supreme Award. I won in 1973 and my husband also won it one year with his own company, which was great. I think it was good that we were in the same industry. We understood each other's problems. Not that we talked business. That was one thing I learnt from him, not to talk business after hours. All their lives my parents had talked business at night, because my mother was busy with the children part of the day. But it was the first thing my husband taught me: no business after hours. I think that kept me sane and it's a rule that I keep now with all my staff. We don't talk business on weekends or nights. It would have to be an absolute emergency to phone anyone on business.

I did my first uniform for the federal Government in 1972 for the Japanese Expo. Previously, I had always based the design of uniforms on my current best-seller. At the time, we were doing a sportswear dress which had a ribbed top and skirt attached. It had taken off in Tokyo, we were selling millions there and thousands here, although it was not doing well in America. For the Japanese Expo uniform I did a beautiful yellow version, with a digger's hat and a coat over the top. The girls were voted by the other girls as the best-dressed team, but of course when the outfit was previewed at the Governor General's office in Canberra, whoever was co-ordinating that part of the operation was disgusted. He said, 'You can't send these girls off looking like that, with short skirts, looking really young and jazzy'. The uniform simply didn't look like a normal pleated skirt with a blazer, a style which is still around. But I wouldn't change it. This particular gentleman was very upset. He said to my parents, 'I'm also in charge of the OBEs and your daughter will never, ever receive one while I'm in this office'. I never thought I'd get one anyway, and couldn't have cared less, could I? When I got the OBE in 1982, my mother laughed her head off.

Actually, I can think of two days in my life — although there have been more than that — when I really have felt wonderful. One was the day that I got my OBE. I knew I was getting it, so I couldn't be excited about it until it was actually announced. As I drove down to my country house that day, I remember sitting in the car just feeling so humble. How wonderful that I've had the opportunity, among 15 million people, to have been singled out by my peers for this honour of recognition. I felt so tiny, I felt like a grain of sand, and that was a wonderful moment. The second time was at the last Olympic Games. My outfits had won awards at other Olympic Games when I wasn't there, but this time being in Los Angeles was really important, because Australia is in the forefront of the world now and how we presented ourselves for the Games was vital. When the team walked into that arena and 100,000 people there rustled, oh, you could feel that people just loved that outfit. As they walked past, everyone kept saying, oh, I like this. That was a marvellous feeling because it worked theatrically, as it should.

Of course you can't please everyone. Someone said criticism should only come from your peers, but there are an awful lot of people in this country, especially journalists, who are only too quick to criticise. On a job like the Olympics uniforms, for one, they do not have the brief, they have no idea what the job is or what the specifications are, and you're working on a very tight brief. So I don't listen to criticism. It hurts, and you wonder and worry, am I wrong, but that job took two years from the day I thought of it, when the light went on. I knew someone else might do a good job, but I also knew what it had to look like and I was not going to let anybody else do it, because they might have mucked it up. I started to worry when all the criticism arose, but at the same time I knew I was not making a 1985 summer high fashion statement in Paris. This was a theatrical experience but the uniforms had to be practical and comfortable under hot conditions, as well as being visually successful. The impact was of the Australian bush's haze of colour, a softness and a gentleness which contrasted with, say, the Japanese team's white and red, their athletes standing so precisely in their sharp white boaters, their red blazers, and their white pants. In contrast, our team had this sort of haze, as if they were in the bush. I hadn't quite realised what I was doing when I added a soft wool hat to the outfit, but it was like you were looking through the mist, the blue haze. It succeeded perfectly. It was so lovely.

It was my third go on Olympic uniforms and I had worked before with Judy Patching, who has just retired. He was one of the most wonderful men I have ever met in my life. He said, 'Prue, I absolutely believe in you', and there was no way I could let him down. You can't let a man down who says I believe in you. He said, 'Prue, Los Angeles is young. We must appear young, we must appear casual, and we must be colourful and comfortable.' And he said, 'You can do it, you did it for Montreal, you can do it again'. Other designers came to him with boaters, blazers, and pleated skirts, and he chucked them out. Red, white and blue blazers and pleated skirts would have looked like the British team. Oh boy, would there have been some criticism about that one! It would have been terrible to look identical to the English team.

I would have loved to have had a chance at designing Qantas Airline's new uniforms, but I put in a very bad submission, because it was done in absolute haste. It was advertised in the local rag trade paper, which I don't read. I only read the New York one. I didn't know it was on so I only had a couple of days to prepare, and then I managed to be sick and I was very tired, because I was doing the Olympic uniform at the same time, so I couldn't have fitted Qantas in anyway. I missed out on being in the final eight Australian designers who submitted for it, and I was very sad about that. At the moment, Qantas are waiting to hear from Parisian designers. I think I should be given a chance to at least put in another submission. But whatever's going to be, will be.

I have to have challenges. Fashion is a challenge, because it's a creative, artistic expression, and it is also a market-oriented discipline which is changing all the time, especially in Australia, which is a very competitive market overloaded with designers and ideas. We have the ideas of the whole world, plus our own creative ideas. Although I've been selling in America and around the world for 18 years, for the first time journalists have been coming to us in the last couple of years. There are also a lot more buyers coming to us now. We'd like to have all the buyers start coming to us, although that may not happen. But we're not far from Hong Kong, so it may be that the Americans will decide to send their buyers to Hong Kong and then on to here.

Australia has an unusual fashion market, it's one that needs ideas, eats ideas. Overseas, you can make the same product year in year out, because the market is enormous. I have dresses that have been selling on the market there for five years. When I started that was true in Australia, but now it seems that we are down to only four or five weeks, maybe four or five months for the lifespan of a design, if it is an absolute winner. But what I'm interested in now is developing a Prue Acton handwriting that has a universal value. I want to go beyond being a trendsetter in Australia, responding to a local market's perceived requirements. I want my own collection which are my classics, this is a Prue Acton, the same as top world designers have. The Lagerfelds, the Chloes, the Kritzias, the Montanas, the Muglers, you can identify their style, because they stick to it once they've made it big on the market, even though they may have been big trendsetters, like Montana and Mugler were about six years ago. Now they are able to develop their own, recognisable handwriting and they are not chasing the new. Another designer, Jean Paul Gautier, is the world's trendsetter. He's the one the little designers around Chapel Street are all copying. Because the global market is so enormous, he will be able to choose his expression and keep with those products. In Australia, that's very hard to do. That is why I say my collections will become smaller. Those pieces will become more precise and internationally-oriented, not oriented purely to a domestic market. They'll be appreciated here as well because Australians appreciate world trends, but I will not be looking for big growth, I will be looking for a solid world market. That's my plan.

I'm also looking now to perhaps scaling down the size of my collection to what I do best in the ready-to-wear department. The collections used to be a couple of hundred pieces, but we are now down to about 100 pieces. Fashion goes across all products, so I'm looking to diversify further, as I've done with cosmetics, where the colours go straight from fashion to cosmetics. It's still a joy for me to sew because I'm a colourist, so that's where I'm eminently suitable, but there are other logical steps for a designer to take. Perfume is one because it expresses a lifestyle, how you feel about yourself, but there are also homewares and all sorts of other things that are logical next steps for me to take.

My other interests include writing, which I began when my youngest daughter was about five or six. I was looking for more personal challenges and so now I write a diary, some poetry, and if something worries me politically, I'll write letters to newspapers, although I haven't done much of that this year. I don't post most of these letters, but for a time I was getting them in the paper regularly. It took me a while to learn the art of writing letters that are precise and clear and punchy. Despite my name, editors turn down the letters if they're no good.

I ski in the winter, surf in the summer, read, write in my diary, and talk with friends. I read a lot of books on psychology, philosophy, and I'm reading more history now. I love talking to friends or going to Trotters Restaurant on Saturday morning. We solve the problems of the world, which is what holidays are about, changing my head-space really. Anytime I'm working, that's what I'm looking for: stimulating ideas and people, a fresh way of looking at the world. As soon as any-one says they have a problem and asks what we are going to do about it, I love it, the adrenaline rises. I like to turn anything that looks like a disadvantage into an advantage. I've had masses of such problems over the years, but in the long run they didn't turn out to be setbacks. They may have felt like it at the time but not later, because I always have a way of saying, okay, what are we going to do about it? With help from the people around me, we come up with something and off we go again. I think that's why I'm still in business. Nothing is too terrible. Solve it, fix it, or live with it. Okay, I made a mistake, let's not do it again.

One day I want to go and paint, so when I'm 100 I might be painting portraits. I feel at the moment I still have lots of energy and I plan a number of years ahead. I have an idea that say, in 10 years' time, I might be starting to do a lot more in terms of personal expression, perhaps through painting. I might start giving back some of the knowledge I have gained. Exactly how that will be I don't yet know.

People just write and say, we've decided it's you, please fly up to Canberra for three days and give us a lecture. Well, when do I run the business, when do I see my family? It doesn't matter how wonderful the offer is, I usually say no. Sometimes, though, I can turn a minus into a plus. For example, tonight I'll work with a communications expert on a video machine. He'll tutor me and we'll write a 10-minute speech for television which we'll practise in front of the video. Now, that's a skill I don't have. Although I can stand up in front of people and talk, it takes a fair bit out of me. So the training session this evening is the start of a learning process that one day may help me to speak better publicly.

Success has obviously had some fantastic plusses. I have had the opportunity to meet wonderful people all over the world, my name is an entrée to most places that I go, and I guess I've got a lot of confidence out of meeting all those people, because even where my name is not well-known, I'm still confident that I can go anywhere in the world and talk with anybody. That's the biggest plus, but the success I've had has also given me enough backing and resources to experiment and create unique products. I have a big design team and a lot of research goes into our product. That's been wonderful. In personal terms, it's rewarding to be well-known and have people admire what you've done. I'm not a starving artist sitting in a garret with a sewing machine, I have something other people want to have, that they love wearing and keep and have good feelings about, and in turn tell me about.

Whatever you do, you have to know that you're doing something better than someone else is doing it, and that it's something you love doing. You must have love and a vision of how you can create, or be associated with a product or service in a way that's better than someone else. If someone is making better jeans than I could make, then I won't go into making them. There's no point in just putting my name on the products. A lot of designers do simply bung their name on the bum and take a royalty, but I'm not interested in that. You have to feel in your heart that you can do a really good job. It's more than merely self-confidence to have a vision that if I'm going to get that raincoat to the public, why are they going to buy it from me and not from Joe Bloggs? I've answered that question all my life. For example, in cosmetics, I know I have a wonderful eye for colour. I'm also very lucky to live in a country where light is beautiful. We are a very colour-conscious country, and I think being Australian I have a unique expression of colour that you won't find anywhere else in the

world. Now I'm looking to go back into textile printing. I dropped out for a while because fashion has been a bit anti-print. Nevertheless, colour is what is important; the first thing Australians buy a product for is colour. Therefore, I would be crazy to go into a field where I'm not going to use what I do best, where I have a unique expression.

Every human being has a unique potential. Life is about every one of us developing our fullest potential and passing on that information through other humans, which in turn builds their knowledge. To me, civilisation is about cumulative knowledge. When people live together in huge cities like New York, okay, there are some terrible things about it, but out of that collection of humans the creative knowledge is enormous, unlimited. I think we are on the verge of another leap in the way humans are. In the Dark Ages we were virtually animals, there was no humanity and very little kindness. But as we communicate more and more, as more information is exchanged through books, television and the arts, the more we take in, the more we can express, the closer we can come to this perfection. I think there is something happening in our brains with this information exchange or explosion. I think we're past the technical era and into a communications era. That's the human breakthrough that we are about to have.

I think communication will make us more tolerant, and as we have more information, as we become more tolerant, I think we will reach our full humanness. I'm talking about tolerance where we let people be, and we are kind and not aggressive. I foresee that eventually we will work far more harmoniously, enabling the individual to express his/herself to the fullest. If everyone were doing that, I would say that we would be fulfilled and happy and begin to be able to solve the problems of distribution of wealth and food, home and learning, the lessons of creativity and health.

I'm an artist, yet I still want to find within myself my true form of expression, and set up an environment where I can work creatively within a team, because I know that the product of a number of minds is greater than my own. Creative work is my career ambition but goals in my personal life are also very important. I want to continue to give up some of my ways of being negative, which work against me. I want to listen more. I have started the process where I do listen to people. I'd like to make sure I always do that, but sometimes I go off on an ego trip or some negative way of responding. I would like to respond freshly to every moment of the day, to learn to relax and get myself in a good, creative frame of mind. I'd like to do that more at will rather than relying on holidays to get myself into that creative, open headspace, where I just love to be.

Years ago, a very good friend of mine said to me something about brainstorming. He said, 'Prue, do you know you can be in a brainstorm every moment of every day?' With that, my brain opened up. I felt as if I had access to every bit of wisdom that I'd ever come across, all my ancestors, all humankind. That open-brain feeling is something I experienced last year for many months, feeling really positive and refreshed. I'll work towards having that most of the time, because it would be bliss, it would be pure joy. Shirley MacLaine talks about being in that space. Last year, I spent seven months just living in a state of joy, just laughing and being happy, no matter what happened. If I had a headache, I'd say, 'I can sit here and be miserable or not miserable', and with that I would suddenly feel fine. Even though I still had a headache, I would feel happy. I'm very much looking forward to having what Shirley MacLaine describes: a positive, joyful approach to life, being in that state all the time.

John Newcombe

Sport teaches lessons on life, and those who learn well may win even more than fame and fortune from the playing of games. John Newcombe is one who not only has converted the lessons of sport into life-after-Wimbledon, but has done so with the same unburdened delivery that carried him to the top of the tennis mountain.

That he was a gifted athlete is something Newk admits without pride or guilt, but that he developed this gift, beginning at an astonishingly early age and despite barriers erected by older people who should have known better, was an early tip-off to the sort of man the boy would become. Newcombe mentions 'destiny' in recounting his three Wimbledon championships and his number one ranking in the world as both a singles and doubles player (plus a host of other major titles), but he's also well aware that such destinies are earned, not bestowed.

Behind the affable Aussie charm, which is just as engaging in person as on television, Newk has clear and strong ideas about what makes Newk tick. Putting 'know thyself' together with 'know what you want', he has engineered a life for himself, wife Angie, and their children, which must be any sportsman's post-playing-days dream. Having sold off much of the mini-empire he built up after retiring from tennis, Newcombe now works when and where he pleases, lives most of the year in his homeland, and enjoys all sorts of leisure activities with friends around the world. In other words, the man's got it made.

No wonder his six-storey headquarters in the Sydney suburb of Crows Nest exudes feelings of health, openness, and general good cheer. It's as if both office and workers have taken on their famous leader's own charisma, like a lesson learned, like a game won.

I was always keen on all types of sports. I had the gift of natural hand-eye coordination, so playing tennis or cricket or any game involving a ball was something that came very easily to me. My parents first noticed it when I was five. They were on holidays, playing tennis, and I went on the court and they couldn't believe how well I was able to hit the ball. I had been hitting around on the road at home with some of my friends. At seven, they took me to Vic Edward's Coaching School, which was about the biggest in Australia then. It seems strange today that the coaches said, 'Sorry, we don't take them until they're 10 years of age'. Nowadays they take them at three and four. My parents said, 'Well, can you have a look at him play? He hits the ball pretty well.' They grudgingly had a look at me and said, 'All right, we'll take him'. After I'd been there for a while various coaches said, 'Gee, this guy has real talent'.

At age 10 I started playing in tournaments. Frank Sedgman had just turned professional and (Lew) Hoad and (Ken) Rosewall were the teenage whiz kids, at 18 years of age. That's when the dream was set in my mind. At 10 I knew what I wanted to do, or knew what my destiny was. From that moment on I never doubted that I would arrive where I have arrived. Maybe not winning as much as I have won, but I never doubted that I was going to play Davis Cup and that I would win a Wimbledon Championship. For some reason I just believed it was my destiny to do that.

My father was a dentist and pretty consistent I guess. He was in the same surgery and had the same nurse for 35 years, in Lane Cove (a Sydney suburb). We were brought up at Longueville, which is a mile from Lane Cove, and I lived there until I got married. I went to a GPS school nearby. I had two sisters, one two-and-a-half years older than me and one younger by two-and-a-half years. It was a middle-class upbringing. I was an average student, passed all my exams, but there were other things that I thought were more important. School work was something that I had to do, so I got it done.

At preparatory school I played cricket, football, and tennis, and was in the athletics and swimming teams. I left Grammar Prep at St Ives with a reasonable academic record and a glowing sporting report. I was captain of the cricket team, in the first football team and so forth. Then I went to Shore, and the teachers read the report on me. Suddenly, I'm in the 13 and over cricket team and competitions are about to start, and I find out that I have to play Saturday afternoons and practice three times a week. On top of that, I was having a tennis lesson once a week, a tennis practice once a week, and I was playing tennis all weekend. My parents said, 'Hey, you can't do everything. If you are serious about your tennis, then you've got to do that, or if you just want to be casual about it, then you've got to do that.'

At this stage I was number one in the State and probably in Australia, but they didn't have Australian Championships for that age group at that time. So my parents said, 'It's up to you. Make up your own mind about what you want to do.'

There was no choice, really, because as much as I wanted to play other sports, I had decided what I wanted to be. So I had to notify the school that I was pulling out of the cricket team because I wanted to be a tennis champion, and that went over like a lead balloon. Because tennis wasn't that accepted you were supposed to play team sports, and how could you be so selfish and so ridiculous to say that you are going to be a tennis champion at 11 years of age?

So I went through a particularly unpleasant two years at Shore, because there were only one or two teachers there who understood. The chap who was headmaster then had been there forever. If you were on the rowing team or the first football team, you could do anything you wanted. Tennis, however, was just not accepted. In my second year at Shore the headmaster got so bad that I told my parents I might want to go to some other school. I decided to stay. Probably the only real reason I was able to do it was because most of my friends at the school were in the cricket or football team, and they didn't give me a hard time.

In my second year some of the teachers put me on report. That means you have a weekly time sheet, and after every period you have to get the teacher to initial it if you have been a good boy in that period. That's like you're one step away from going to reform school. I wasn't anywhere near that. I was a sportsperson, and the average kid in class. But at 11 o'clock every day I had to go down and see the headmaster, and he would grab me and twist my ear inside out and turn my head around. Obviously I was doing something they didn't believe was right, and they were trying to break my spirit.

After my first two years at Shore the headmaster retired, another headmaster came, and by that time I was getting more recognition in the newspapers. As I came through the junior ranks I won every tournament there was. The teachers started to realise that maybe the kid does have some talent, maybe he is going to become a champion. I wasn't unhapppy at school, because I had lots of friends. It was just the old English system, 'If you try to work outside the system, we're not going to allow you to, because we have to have everybody doing what we say'. Well, I went along with it, but they weren't going to bully me into not doing what I wanted to do.

If an obstacle is stopping me from getting to something that I don't really care about, I'd rather just ignore it. If it's stopping me from getting what I really want, then I have to find a way to remove it. I'd rather go around it but if I can't, I'll go through it.

In my last two years at school I was captain of the tennis team. I don't think they have ever had a captain of sport who was not in their final year of school. I initiated some new programs, new competitions, but in my last year I was not made a prefect. I think I'd be the only captain of sport who ever went through Shore without being made a prefect. They could say, 'Oh, he didn't have leadership qualities', but that has been disproven.

My father used to keep telling me to get into the commercial world, not to go into the professional world because there's more money in the commercial world, so I concentrated on accountancy at school. It was the best advice I could have gotten, because any kid should learn to do a profit and loss and balance sheet and how to manage money. You have to deal with that all your life, no matter what you're doing, so that was very good and my thoughts were in the direction: if I failed in tennis, I would go into accountancy or something in that field.

I was 16½ when I did my leaving. I got selected to play Junior Davis Cup matches in Miami, and went over with a guy from Newcastle and Ron Brandt. We didn't have a manager or anything — we were over there for a month by ourselves and played for Australia against other countries. That was about mid-January, and in February I got named to the official Australian team, which was going overseas with a manager on a seven-month trip. I was still 16 and the next youngest guy in the team was 21.

Ken Fletcher, Fred Stolle and Bob Hewitt were the other team members. We left in March and the first stop out of Australia was

Calcutta. At that time, there were eight million people living in Calcutta. Six million didn't live under a roof. We arrived about 5 o'clock in the morning, and that long drive from the airport into the city, seeing all the people sleeping in the street and the stench of the place, was a real eye-opener.

I had my 17th birthday in Paris in May during the French Championships. I reached the semi-finals of the Wimbledon doubles that year, playing with Ken Fletcher, which was a pretty good effort since I had just turned 17. We lost to Roy Emerson and Neil Fraser. I played my first singles match at Wimbledon, on Court One, against a chap who was about number nine in the world: Jan Linquist of Sweden. I lost the first two sets, won the next two, and had him down a break in the fifth set when he started lobbing every return of serve to me about 100 feet in the air. We finished up breaking even and breaking even again. I couldn't believe what was happening. He beat me 6-4 in the fifth, but coming from two sets down, and in my first match at Wimbledon almost beating this guy who was so much more experienced than I, it was obvious that I had some sort of future in that tournament. I was happy.

That was 1961. Another learning year followed, pretty much like 1961, but 1963 was a much more traumatic year for a lot of reasons. In 1963 we left Australia on tour and went to Malaysia first. I was kidding around with Tony Roche, wrestling, and I did some damage to my wrist. For about 10 weeks I couldn't play. I had broken a tendon sheath. As we travelled around, I went from having my arm in plaster in Italy, having injections, arriving in Berlin and trying unsuccessfully to play, to finally arriving in London and getting treatment from one of the Wimbledon masseurs. A very deep hand massage, up and down the arm, fixed it just in time for Wimbledon. I lost in the first round, to someone I should never have lost to, in a five-set match. It was my first tournament in about three months.

I had a pretty difficult time that first year. The manager of the team, Esca Stephens, was going to send me home at one stage. I was loose baggage. That was just the halfway point of the year, though. In August we went to Hamburg, and I met a German girl, went out with her one night, and came back and woke up my room-mate (Alan Davidson) and told him that I'd just gone out with the girl I was going to marry. Actually, our manager Esca was the one who introduced me to her in the clubhouse. She lived in Hamburg and was playing in the tournament. Suddenly there was a high point in the year.

I came back to Australia, started on the Australian circuit, and played very well. I won the South Australian Championships, beating Dennis Ralston in the finals, and suddenly got selected in the Davis Cup team in the final four, which was unexpected. It was Anderson, Fraser, Stolle and I. In the challenge round at the end of December against the Americans, McKinley and Ralston were selected to play singles for the United States. So that year was traumatic, the first half of it spent injured and being at a very low point at Wimbledon, then meeting someone who I did end up marrying, coming back to Australia, and performing well enough to suddenly get selected to play Davis Cup.

I wasn't really ready to play Davis Cup, but I had a suspicion from the way (coach) Harry Hopman was carrying on while we were practising that he had something on his mind. But 24 hours before the Cup is played they have a draw on the centre court. When I walked on the court for that ceremony I had not been told I was playing. Then they pulled my name out of the Cup, which was a bit of a traumatic experience — 24 hours to get ready against these guys who were much more experienced than I was in similar circumstances.

I performed very well in the matches. I lost to Ralston 7-5 in the fifth set, and I lost to McKinley in the final matches at the tie in four sets. But I had him in lots of trouble, and he was the Wimbledon champion. So I was sort of a hero after the Davis Cup, but in my own mind I knew I hadn't won. I wasn't that happy, because I lost in both my matches, and yet the Australian public and the media were treating me like a hero because I'd come back in each match. In the opening match of the tie, Ralston had me two sets down. I won the next two sets and then he had me 5-3, 40-love in the fifth set and I broke back and finally lost 7-5. It was like I had put up a great fight, and maybe that's what the Australian public wanted. Winning or losing wasn't as important as the fact that I'd given everything I had, and it was just that I was beaten. Maybe that was it, I don't know, but I got all this adulation which certainly didn't go to my head because I knew I hadn't won the matches.

I think the next year, 1964, was spent getting over that unbelievably emotional experience. I should have advanced more in my tennis prowess that year than I did, and Stolle replaced me in the Davis Cup team as the singles player.

Nothing really big happened in 1964, except that I kept writing letters to Angie, the girl I'd met in Hamburg, and saw her when I went over there. At the end of 1964, during the Australian Championships, there was a major moment. Roche and I played Stolle and Anderson, who were considered to be the number one pair in the world at that time, and Tony and I were 19 and 18 years of age respectively. They had us two sets to love in the final and we came back and beat them in five sets. That was one of the most joyous moments I had in tennis. We were good mates and we'd only been playing together for a year, and we'd cracked through with a Grand Slam win. Six months later, Tony and I won the Wimbledon doubles. That was the big start of our climb in doubles together. Ten years later we won Wimbledon for the fifth time together.

It was getting a bit tense on the personal side in 1965, because I was getting sick and tired of writing letters to Angie and only seeing her once a year. Something had to be done one way or another. I was in the Australian team, so I left Australia a couple of weeks early, stayed in Hamburg with her parents, and was there for about two weeks. Near to the end of the time I said I was sick of writing letters, so let's get engaged or perhaps it'll never happen. She said she wanted to do this and that, so I said, 'Well, we just have to decide. Why don't you go for a walk around the block and come back and tell me your decision?'

So she went for a walk around the block and came back and said okay. We got engaged in August of that year, and in September she came out to Australia and stayed with my parents. The idea was that we were going to get married the following year in Hamburg. When it came to January, 1966, she'd been in Australia for four months and was due to go back to Hamburg, and I was going off to the Caribbean circuit to play. I said, 'Isn't it a pity we're not going to see each other for four months? Pity you have to go home.' She said yes and I said, 'I guess we'll have to get married in Hamburg.' She said, 'Well, I don't really care', so I said, 'If you don't really care, let's do it now'. Three weeks later we got married. Then we went away together on a private tour.

Tony and I won the Wimbledon doubles again in 1966, but the thing of real note to me was that I hadn't been able to crack through in the singles. Once again, I'd lost in the round of 16. I'd played at Wimbledon six years by then and hadn't reached the quarter-finals.

By the end of 1966 I was in the top eight in the world in singles but I hadn't really smashed through the barrier. I went away in 1967 and started winning in a lot more tournaments in the first three months of the year, but at this stage I was starting to look very much to the future. I was married, we were probably going to have kids, I was 22,

Above, John Newcombe and Tony Roche with the visible signs of victory at Wimbledon. Below, the ultimate accolade, even Snoopy recognises Newcombe's moustache

and I still had the dream and the belief that I was going to arrive, but there were just a few doubts.

You start at the bottom of the mountain, and there's room for a hell of a lot of people. I call it the tennis mountain. As you go up to mid-way, a lot of those people who started have to fall off because there's not enough room, and as you get closer to the top there's room for, let's say, eight or ten people who have a chance to climb to the top of the mountain. I was in that group. The question was being asked, 'How badly do you want to arrive at the top?'

It was never really explained to me that way but I see it now, in analysing what was going on. Anyway, a guy had called me and said he was into sport psychology. He'd had the glasses on me and he believed I was not achieving as much as I could achieve. I spent about 18 hours with him, doing a lot of very simple things that I think helped. I believe very much in the mental side of things. This guy showed me ways to get more out of myself, just little things, and there was a lot of speaking about things you might have hang-ups about, that you purge out of your system just by talking about them. These were things to do with other players, psychological barriers, such as why you can't jump over that extra inch of bar, why you can't get that inch higher, when everybody knows that you can jump that high. I think it all played a part in the progress that was taking place.

In 1967 I was in Texas, and at that stage tennis was just starting to build up. There was a job being offered in Houston at a big racquet club that was being built. The job would have paid $30,000 a year, a lot of money at that time, and I was probably making about $12,000 a year in amateur tennis, not all of which was profit, because I had to pay a lot of expenses, air fares, etc. So I was seriously starting to think that future-wise, maybe that's what I should be doing. Anyhow, I won a series of tournaments, and then in April I won a major tournament in Texas. But I was developing terrible arm problems.

It was not the same injury of several years earlier — this was the elbow and the muscles above the elbow. I was in a lot of pain and I played the French championships, but lost in the third round or something and lost in the Spanish championships. Then I went to London and was having a bit of a downer, because I was in pain every time I played. Then a doctor gave me some pills to take. Whatever the reason, I suddenly won the tournament before Wimbledon, which was Queen's Club, and then won Wimbledon.

Three months before that the first seeds of doubt had begun creeping into me. Not serious seeds, but they were seeds, and it only needs little seeds to start mushrooms. All of a sudden, bang, I'd won Wimbledon and six weeks later, I'd won the United States Open. I was number one in the world, and it just happened like that. Maybe all the preparation, plus getting married and wanting to enlarge my goals, had an effect, I don't know. I do know I thought it was my destiny from the time I was 10, and the only real doubts I'd had about achieving it were three months before I'd achieved it.

I won the final in near-record time, as it turned out, but for the first two games I was really nervous. It was against Willy Bongert, the German, and it went 6-3, 6-2, 6-1. Wimbledon was amateur then because open tennis didn't come until the next year. I'd broken through the barrier, number one in amateur, but there were still (Rod) Laver and Rosewall, who were professionals and better players than I was then.

At that stage there was a lot of movement to make tennis open. It had been going on for eight years, but professionals were still not allowed to compete in any of the tournaments. A fellow called Lamar Hunt came on the scene with World Championship Tennis, and after the United States Open that year Tony and I agreed to sign up, among an eight-man crew of players, to play 20 tournaments a year at $20,000 per tournament. We signed a five-year agreement. As far as we were concerned, we were never going to be able to play Wimbledon again or any of the other big tournaments. December of that year would be our last year of the Davis Cup.

We could have stayed amateur and won more amateur championships, but we were offered a contract at a guaranteed minimum of $45,000 a year. As the top amateurs, we were probably bringing in around $15,000 a year, less our expenses — thus netting about $9,000, then paying tax on that — and we were number one in the world.

As it turned out, World Championship Tennis was a disaster for the first six months, and it was only Lamar Hunt's money that kept it going. Anyway, we played, and as luck would have it tennis went open. I think we were the catalyst to it. Hunt had signed six of the top twelve in the world, including Roche and me, while Emerson and Stolley had already signed the year before. Actually, Wimbledon were the first ones to go. Wimbledon said to the International Tennis Federation, 'Okay, we don't know what you're doing but we're going to have an open tournament'. So they went open and the rest of the world said, 'Gee, if Wimbledon is going to, we have to. Otherwise we'll be nothing.' So I didn't miss a chance to play at Wimbledon after all.

As an amateur you are only legally allowed to receive your expenses, but they would give us accommodation, so it would cost nothing to live. And you would always stay at the best hotels. I was getting $500 in addition, though under the rules only $250 a week was allowed. One tournament director down in South America was told, 'We know you paid this person more than you were supposed to'. He said, 'I only paid him what I was supposed to', so they said, 'Well, where did the other money come from?' He said, 'I made him a bet that he couldn't jump over a line and he was able to do it, to my amazement, so I had to pay him that extra money'. That was how stupid the whole thing was. It's the same thing with amateur athletics these days.

I was seeded about four or five at Wimbledon the next year. The one thing we weren't allowed to do, even though tennis went open, was play Davis Cup, because we were termed 'contract professionals'. The likes of (Arthur) Ashe and (Stan) Smith hadn't signed a contract with World Championship Tennis, but they were still making money and were allowed to play Davis Cup, while we weren't. For five years from 1967 we didn't play Davis Cup, although we played at Wimbledon. Well, that hurt the Davis Cup, it didn't hurt us. Still, Davis Cup is different from any other individual tournament. You are out representing your country, not yourself. It's a very emotional feeling.

At that stage my goal was probably to be able to hang in there with the top three. I don't think there was any particular goal to be number one. I believed in my own mind that Laver was number one and it was a matter of trying to knock him off the perch. But I couldn't see myself winning two Grand Slams like he did, in 1962 and 1968.

I'd played against Laver before he turned professional and was the last amateur to beat him, when I was 18. He had just won his first Grand Slam and everyone knew he was about to turn professional. I beat him in the quarter-finals of the South Australian Championships. After winning Wimbledon and the United States Open a few years later, I knew how good I was and how good I wasn't, so it was just a matter of improving my overall game. I really think any psychological barriers I'd had to achieving my full potential were gone at this point.

The biggest thing that happened in 1968 was the birth of my son in August. That was our first child, and a change of lifestyle — all of a sudden having not two but three of you.

I remember 1969 was a classic Wimbledon final, played with Laver. The year before, although we'd won the doubles, I'd lost to Ashe in the round of 16 in the singles. In fact, every time I ever got to the quarters of the singles at Wimbledon, I got to the finals. So it was just a matter of getting through to the first part.

I got through to the finals in 1969, played a very good match against Rod, and surprised a lot of people because I played a game which they didn't think I was going to play. Instead of playing power, I played touch and lobs. I had cracked the Wimbledon barrier back in 1967 — that was amateur — but I still hadn't cracked the barrier at open. That came in 1970, and I rate that as probably my best match for a lot of reasons. I played Ken Rosewall in the final at Wimbledon.

It was the first five-set final they'd had for a long, long time. Here I was playing Ken Rosewall in the final, when at 10 years of age I had been listening on the radio to him playing in the final. I stayed up until two o'clock in the morning, listening to that match. I'd listened to him on the radio playing Davis Cup, I'd watched him when I was 10 playing at White City against the Americans, and here I was against him in a Wimbledon final. I'm not saying that I was overawed by the fact that I was playing against Ken, because I'd played him lots of times before, but here I was in the red carpet event, at the pinnacle. On top of that, the Wimbledon crowd were determined to repay Rosewall for cheering against him in 1954, and here he was in the final again. The English media were all on his side, I was the young guy, I had more years left, this might be his last chance, and so on. He won the first set 8-6 and I won the next two, 6-3, 6-2. I was sort of steam-rolling him. I led 3-1 in the fourth and the crowd started to really get behind Rosewall. I would serve a double fault or miss a volley and they'd clap. And I went, gee, what have I done? I haven't done any-thing wrong, why are they against me, this isn't fair. I let the whole emotional thing disturb what I was about, which was winning a match. Suddenly, he won five games in a row to win the set 6-3. The tension was electric and the crowd were all excited. Rosewall was back in the match, he was psyched up. We changed ends and I said, I've got 60 seconds here to pull myself together. How badly do you want to win this match? And I thought, yes, I really want to win it badly. It was the first time that I'd been under such pressure and had to do what I'm going to explain now.

I had to go back inside myself, I had to reach right down inside and purge all the negative thoughts that were in there about the crowd. I had to push them out and then I had to go within myself, so that when I walked out on the court the only things I could see were another player at the end of the court and a tennis ball. Apart from that, I was

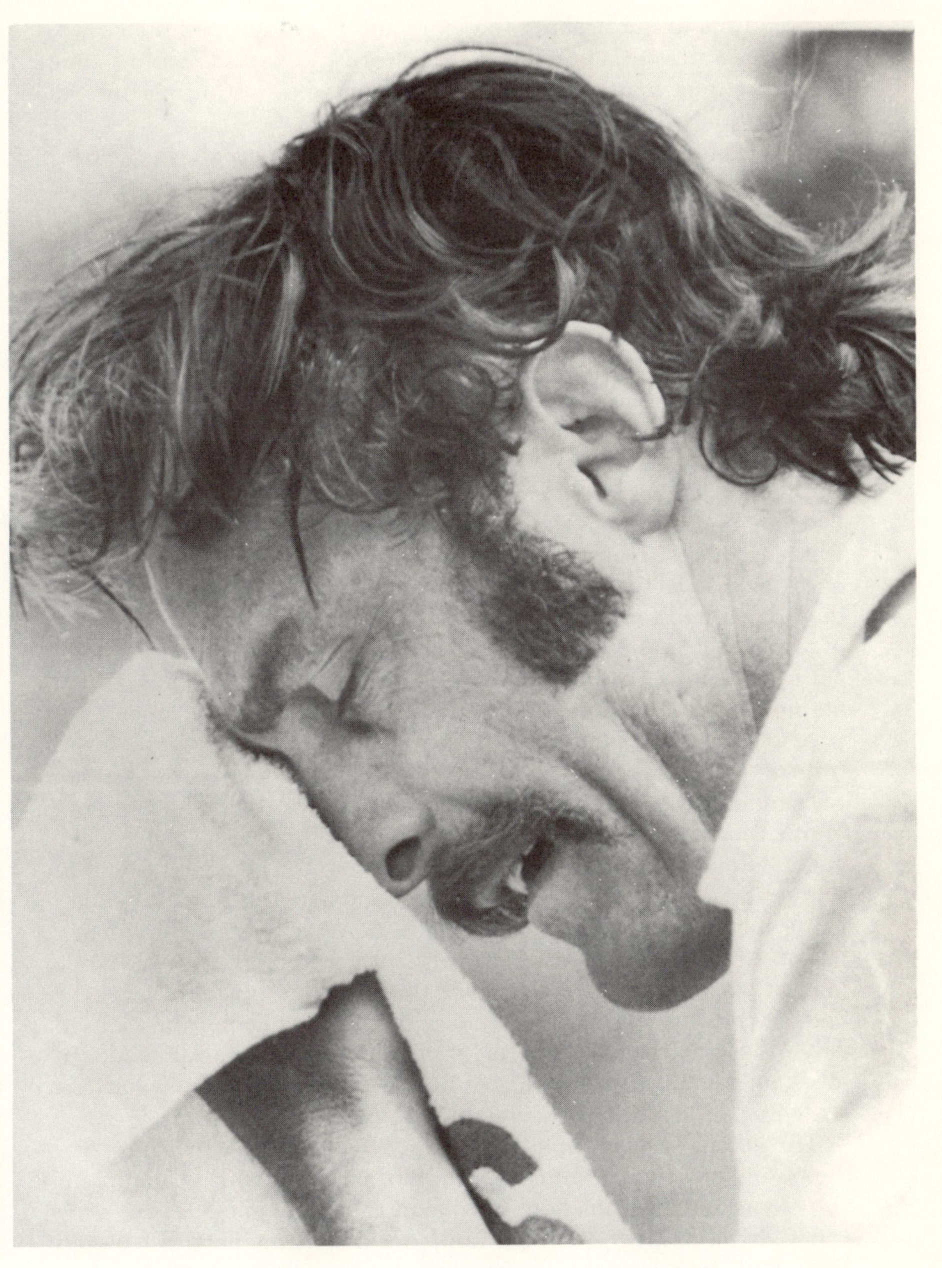

aware of the umpire calling the score and I was aware of the crowd, but I was not aware of them. In other words, I put myself into a zone where nothing mattered except the person who was hitting the ball and the ball itself.

I played a set of tennis as good as I can play, and ever have played. I won that set 6-1. It seemed that I knew everything Ken was going to do before he did it. That's why I rate that as my best match, because I rate that fifth set as the best set of tennis I've ever played. I was psychologically down and out and 90 per cent of the crowd was pulling for my opponent, so the easy thing to do was just feel sorry for myself. That is where you come down to the psychological side of sport and you have to learn how to go down inside of yourself, to dig out something. I use the word 'purge' because it's a strong word, and it's good. You have to purge all the negative things and put the positive back in.

A year later I won Wimbledon again by beating Smith in the final — another high point. The crowd were at least 50 per cent for me in that match, maybe a bit more. There was a point during the match where things didn't look very good. I was down two sets to one, and once again I had to do something similar to the year before. I had won the first set and was playing better than he was, until towards the end of the second set I dived for a ball and fell right on my solar plexus. I got up and continued playing, but from that moment on I just went off the border. I lost the set 7-5 and was down 4-2 in the third set. I felt tired and couldn't understand why I was so tired, because I was trained to play four, five, six hours.

I suddenly thought, my God, that fall! I'd had the wind knocked out of me, I hadn't thought enough about it, and I hadn't sucked in deep and regained my energy level. I thought, well, I've got about five to 10 minutes to revitalize my system. I'm going to lose this set but then I'm going to start the fourth set, and if I don't get myself into shape, revitalize myself, I'm gone. So I spent the next five to 10 minutes while that set ran its course, just breathing deeply and trying to recharge the batteries. By the end of the set I'd done that. In the fourth set, I led 5-4, 40-love before I lost a point on my serve. He got back to deuce in that game but that was the only game he won any points on. I won that set 6-4, and the fifth 6-3 or something.

Then there were a couple of funny years after that. The biggest disappointment I had in tennis came in 1972, because World Championship Tennis and Wimbledon were having a disagreement. I was in my last year of contract World Championship Tennis and had played there four years in a row, under the same conditions. Suddenly, they said I couldn't play at Wimbledon. Nobody had won Wimbledon three years in a row since (Fred) Perry in the 1930s. Here I was coming back to do history and they wouldn't let me play.

I did the television broadcast of the final, which was Smith, the guy I'd beaten the year before, winning against (Ilie) Nastase. But I don't like negative thoughts, they don't make me happy, so I don't entertain them. I'd rather find some reason to think that it was good that it happened.

In 1973 I decided I wasn't going to play any tournaments the first four or five months of the year. I was on the verge of saying enough is enough. I was not allowed back in the Davis Cup, so I went and played in Japan and India. Then I thought, I'll go across and play Rome and Paris, leading up to Wimbledon. I lost first round in the Italian, and I lost first round in the French. I was playing terribly. Obviously my heart wasn't in it. My wife was pregnant, we were going to have our third child, and I probably wondered what I was doing over there. Then I didn't play Wimbledon for the second year in a row, because all the players boycotted it.

The Yugoslavia Tennis Association wanted to suspend a player because he hadn't played Davis Cup. We said it wasn't right, so that fight went on for about two months, every tournament. The question came up for discussion and the officials passed it to the next tournament. Finally, they all passed it on to Wimbledon, saying, 'You've got to stand up to these players'. We had just formed the Players' Association, and the officials didn't want us to have it. They thought, we'll use Wimbledon, we'll split the players right down the middle. It turned out that 84 of the players who were in the Association and were entered at Wimbledon didn't play. There were only three turncoats. Strangely enough, the turncoats never did very well from then on.

Anyway, after Wimbledon my family and I went back to Texas and did a couple of weeks of tennis camp. I really was mulling over just what I wanted to do. I finally put it to Angie. I had never won World Championship Tennis and I said, 'I don't want to stop playing now, because I've just had a disastrous year and it would leave a bad taste in my mouth. It's four weeks to go before the United States Open starts. What I'd like to do is bear down and win that tournament, and then I'd like a nine-month campaign to win World Championship Tennis next May. But if I do that it's going to be very tough on the family, as well as tough on myself. It's going to require a lot of travel and a lot of dedication on my part. If you don't want me to do it, if you think that it's very important that I don't do it, then you should tell me. It will be a bitter pill to swallow but I don't mind.' She gave me the green light to go ahead and I started. I went back to grass roots, getting myself physically fit. I'd now made up my mind and I think that was a big difference. I had made a clear-cut decision, I wasn't going half-and-half.

So I entered the United States Open and received a 10 seeding. It had only been a little time earlier that I was number one, but that's where I had slipped to in that eight months. Anyway, I won the United States Open, and nine months later I won the World Championship Tennis in Dallas. So I'd achieved the goals I had set out to achieve, but I'd gone about it very single-mindedly and that was what had to be done. In May 1974 I was back as number one.

A young bloke that I'd beaten in the quarter-finals of the United States Open in 1973, named Jimmy Connors, was bursting onto the scene. After World Championship Tennis in May, my goals were finished. I played Wimbledon but it wasn't a goal-oriented effort, and I lost to Rosewall. I went to the United States Open and was a little bit more goal-oriented there. I got through to the semis and lost to Rosewall again. Jimmy Connors won both those events. So by the end of 1974 he was seeded one and I was seeded two, but we didn't play each other the whole year.

As far as I was concerned that was it. I'd had enough, I was ready to stop, so I came back in November. The Australian Championships were on over Christmas 1974, but I told them I wasn't playing. My saga was over. I didn't tell anyone I was retiring, I'd just had enough. About 10 days before the tournament the promoters rang me from Melbourne and said Connors was coming. They knew that he and I weren't seeing eye-to-eye at the time. There was a difference of opinion. I don't think it was anything personal, even though he was suing the Association of Tennis Professionals. He seemed to be running his own course. I'd been instrumental, with some other guys, in setting up the Association. I believed in a certain course and I guess his was another one. He just wasn't that popular with all the players at that time.

So the organisers said, 'He's coming, and does that change your mind?' I said, 'If he's in that tournament, you can enter me right now'. I had 10 days to get fit, because I hadn't done anything for about six weeks and was about eight pounds overweight. All of a sudden, I had another goal.

I started running a three-mile course, of which the last mile-and-a-half was up a very steep hill. I nicknamed that hill, 'Connors' Hill'. It was a very hot December and I used to run it at midday, every day. When the day was at its hottest and I was halfway up that hill and I wanted to stop, I just pictured in my mind that I was five-all in the fifth set and Connors was at the other end and I wanted him. And I just started burning it up the hill. I didn't play that much tennis, I was just concentrating on that hill.

When I got down to Melbourne, I barely beat a German bloke in five sets in the first round. But it was good because I knew I could play five sets after that. I got through to the quarters, which was on a Monday. Although I didn't know it, I was about to enter into a physical torture test. I beat Geoff Masters in the quarter-finals, 10-8 in the fifth set, from two sets to one down. I played a doubles set after that, then played Tony Roche the next day. Tony had me 5-2 in the fifth set and had seven match points, but I beat him 11-9 in the fifth set. Of the last 45 minutes of the match, I have no recollection. Normally in a match I can remember points, but it was as if I knew I had to reach a goal and I didn't know what I was doing, but I was going there. Everything was on automatic drive.

Mike Williamson, who was commentating for Channel 7, came down to do a courtside interview after the match. He asked me for the interview and he said later I was like a fighter who was punch-drunk. He said I looked at him but I wasn't seeing him. So he just walked away. I remember putting the towel over my head and all I wanted to do was cry. It was like I had been through an ordeal.

The next day I had to play Connors. I had a doubles match to play after the match with Tony, but I asked Tony if he'd mind if I pulled out because I was buggered and he said okay. There is a guy called Stan Nichols who used to be a Davis Cup trainer, and Stan's a great masseur. He can go in deep. He spent an hour-and-a-half to two hours after each of those matches, the quarters and the semis, just on my legs. He pushed all the fluid that had built up out of my legs, so that I had no stiffness. I woke up Wednesday morning and ran a mile, played Connors and beat him 7-6 in the fourth set. I served in the match at 5-3 in the fourth and he, in typical fashion, came back. We got to the tie-breaker and he had a set point to make it two sets all. I won it but I had some very, very serious doubts about what I would have had left in the fifth. I had dug as deeply as I could, I thought. Maybe I would have found something that I didn't know was there, but in my experience I was down as far as I could go.

It was the last big tournament I won. I played in 1976 a bit, then broke my leg skiing in 1977, so that made for an easy decision not to play. In the meantime I had started getting involved in a lot of businesses with different friends, in Asia and America and out here.

Back in 1968, when we first started travelling, I had become a partner in a tennis ranch over in Texas. Two other guys and I had bought a run-down dude ranch and we converted it into a tennis ranch. So that was our home away from home, the Ranch. I'm still an owner, but we haven't lived there for five years. We used to spend half the year there and half in Australia, so the kids went to school in Texas and here. Really, what we did was create two homes to accommodate my profession. It's called the John Newcombe Tennis Ranch. I used to do some camps there and some clinics, but just living there was the main reason for having it. I never had an office back here in Australia. I had an office in my house here which I worked out of, but I didn't have a secretary or anything like that, so I guess my business life emerged from Texas rather than Australia.

I don't think I could live anywhere else but Australia. I could live over there in the States when it was necessary to do that, but as soon as it became necessary for my eldest child to have a continual year at school in one place, rather than to split his time when he was 11, then there never was a question of whether we would live here or over there. Fortunately, my wife likes Australia better than anywhere else. This is my home. Unless I was in a situation where I couldn't feed my family in Australia but I could feed them living somewhere else, there wouldn't be a question of living anywhere else. You only have one life, so you may as well live where you think it is best.

I'm proud of being Australian, I'm proud of Australia. I don't stand up and say, this is the best place in the world to live. That's what I think but other people think that their country is best. We have a lot of faults, we have a lot of strengths. No matter where Australia is or is not going, I think the most important thing is that everyone does their own little bit and believes in their country. I've got certain beliefs but I'm not hung up on them. I know other people believe different things. They may be right, and I'm happy to listen.

I don't think there is any one way to make a country successful, except everybody pulling their weight and believing in their country. If I walk along the street and see someone throw bits of rubbish on the ground, I'm going to get really upset. I think that if you can drive along in your car and just throw a bit of paper out the window, that means you don't really care about your country. So it's down to such a small thing as that. Then you can take it up as high as you want to take it. Believe in your country; I think if we have that, and we all pull

together in the belief and have the freedom of speech and freedom of thought, we'll come out on top.

The business in Asia that I got involved in, when I began to think about retirement from tennis, was our own trading company for sporting goods, clothing, racquets and shoes, selling around South-East Asia with offices in Hong Kong and Singapore. The Ranch in Texas was still headquarters. There were some businesses in Hawaii, then I started tennis camps down here with Tony Roche, and I started opening some tennis shops which my brothers-in-law totally ran.

So now, just from doing the Tennis Ranch, I was suddenly sprung into the business world. I spent about three or four very hard years, travelling more than I was playing tennis. It was a tough time, because I was a cog in the wheel. I was involved in all these different businesses with different partners, and I was the centrepiece. I wasn't responsible for the day-to-day business, but I was involved in a wide diversity of things. Fortunately, I didn't get burnt by anything and some activities were reasonably successful, so it turned out well. Now I'm just about out of everything that we had then. I just decided I'd had enough.

I could be playing the 35s tennis circuit now but I'm not interested in getting into that. I played 35s at Wimbledon and in the United States. Some of the guys really enjoy it, but I have already spent half my life travelling around, staying in hotels and playing tennis tournaments. To me, there's more to life than that.

I'd tried it and done it. We were able to sell a couple of things and I'd had enough of travel. I thought it was time to settle down and spend more time in Australia, so that's been the objective which I've now achieved. I'm in Australia for about nine months of the year and travelling for the other three months, picking and choosing what I want to do. Not so much in the business field, though.

If I want to go skiing, I go skiing. I went on a car rally, from Bourke to Burketown, in which all the cars had to be at least 20 years old. I was talking just last night with Noel Fullerton, who runs the camels out of Alice Springs, about going on another safari with him and a couple of mates of mine from America. I enjoy going to Wimbledon every year and I connect that with business, doing television work and newspaper writing from there. I do about 10 weeks of television a year, what with Australian and American obligations, and whatever else comes along.

When I turn 50 years of age, my goal is to be able to look back on the 10 years from 40 to 50 and say I achieved something in that time in my family life and in my personal advancement. I'm not talking about business or money, I'm talking about knowledge of things that I don't know now, say the cultural field, or the fields that I haven't been involved in until now. I want to expand my own knowledge.

One of my current interests is junior tennis in Australia, which I've been very involved with for the past five-and-a-half years. It's a volunteer thing. I've been instrumental in putting a pretty good package together, which now is run by a Junior Development Board that I'm chairing. We have, approximately, a $1 million budget each year, and we're controlling all junior tennis in Australia, 18 and under. It's the official program of the Lawn Tennis Association. Our goal is to help get Australia back to where we were. You could run a business like Australian tennis was run back in the 1950s, but you couldn't run it like that as time went on. It had to change.

So there's that; also I'm president of the National Australia Day Council, which is a federal government-appointed body. That's another voluntary and goal-oriented interest which I have. We've been restructuring that whole organisation and have spent a lot of time on it. All day Monday I was chairing a meeting, and I met some really interesting people who I normally would not meet. The government has appointed people to that committee representing different walks of Australian life. I've been on it for three-and-a-half years, and I'm supposed to do it until 1989.

I really have about four months a year of work that is connected to making money, and the other eight months is for doing things that I want to do myself. You go out, you compete, you do as well as you possibly can, but the money shouldn't be the factor that is driving you. It should be the fact that you want to achieve, and that you have goals. Unfortunately, money takes over and you find top players today who probably have $5 million or $10 million in the bank who can be bought to go anywhere for $50,000 or $100,000. They still seem to put a priority on money rather than the sport. They're not thinking of it as a sport, they're thinking of it as a business, and unfortunately that doesn't leave you very happy.

You bring pressure on yourself, too, in those circumstances. For example, Pat Cash has brought pressure on himself by his actions, but you're going to get different personalities in all sports. In every decade there are people who are more volatile than others and act differently. There's nothing new to the game in having a (John) McEnroe, it's just that there is more publicity these days. (Pancho) Gonzales was as volatile as you'd want to get.

But the biggest pressure on tour is a form of loneliness. The hotel room, the four walls, the regimented routine of what time you wake up in the morning, when you eat breakfast, lunch and dinner, when you practice, and when your match is going to be played, then to your hotel room for sleep — that can be very lonely.

The best defence against that is if you can have a regular doubles partner who is a very good friend, and you get on well together. Anybody on tour can go chasing girls and hitting bars and all that, but you aren't going to be very successful if you do that all the time. If you have a good friend and you have both lost in the singles, you can go out and have a few drinks together and relax and get some of the pressure off. Apart from that, you've got someone there fighting who's got the same problems as you do. Tony and I were pretty good mates all through. We used to fight very hard against one another on the court, but that was all left on the court.

To succeed, you must first of all do your homework, whether that be training or whatever. Second, a very good knowledge of your own strengths and weaknesses is needed. That's true psychologically and in the case of sport, it's true physically as well. You can't get there unless you know yourself. And third, develop a firm belief that you can do what you want to do.

I've got things that I want to achieve and I'll go out and achieve them, but just because someone else hasn't achieved what I've achieved doesn't mean I'm better or worse or even different from them. They might not want to achieve that. They may even be happy in not achieving that. You can't say achievement is better than non-achievement, because the non-achiever may be happier inside himself than the achiever. In my opinion, it really comes down to how happy you are inside yourself.

In the run to the judge, that's what you are going to find, I think: how happy you are, your attitude to life, and how many friends you have are what count most. Real friends. Being number one or being the top achiever is not necessarily going to bring you happiness or friends.

STUMP JUMPING

The reality of stump-jumping

All the literature about how you can acquire success by following the rules misses the point, because it refers to a cliché. Success is not a cliché — it's a real, living thing. There is no single book of rules which will work. Everyone must formulate their own.

Success is unpredictable, highly individualistic and means different things to different people. To J. P. Getty it meant amassing power and money. He was pretty successful at that. Success to Mother Theresa means helping those in need and there's no disputing her success in that direction either.

Success is tangible and accessible, and increasing numbers of Australians are grasping it each year. On the basis of material success, in Australia today the ranks of millionaires are swelling every year. In art, literature and many other fields of endeavour, Australia boasts a growing number of success stories. We can only learn some important guidelines from the people inside *The Stump-Jumpers* — the rest is up to us.

So, if there is no clear path, how do we find our way? Well, we're not sure that we know, and even if we had the formula it might work for us and not for anyone else. It's a trial and error process of playing the game and learning what works for ourselves as individuals.

When Vera Randall started Knitwit she could have followed the rules and strategies used by any of the organisations she checked out either in Canada or the United States. Instead, she formulated her own game plan, carried it through and realised a greater success than anybody dreamed possible.

We tried to create '10 Golden Rules' that would encapsulate a gospel of success, but found it impossible to apply them to all the stump-jumpers we had interviewed.

What all these people have in common is that they are free-thinkers. Individualists.

For some people such as Rosemary Moore, success means self-discipline and endurance. For others, such as Paul Hogan, it means letting go and thinking laterally. Use the A-Z of stump-jumping attributes to find your individual strengths and weaknesses. We should build on our strengths and work on them, as Millie Phillips has done, for that is when we'll start winning. Most people fight their weaknesses, compensate for them and end up losers.

Next, we should find the game that suits our skills so that we're naturally winning. If you are leading from your weaknesses, change the rules and redefine the game so that you can begin to play from strength, as John Leard did with ANI. Ideally, if you're able, delegate your weaknesses.

Some stump-jumpers have achieved this by finding the perfect complementary partner, for instance Rosemary Moore and Diana Rose, or Paul Hogan and John Cornell. Both have created unified teams, in which each other's strengths compensate for and balance each other's weaknesses. If you can't delegate or share those weaknesses, then face up to them realistically and create the best environment possible to offer you the greatest prospect of success. Progress always involves risks. You can't squeeze an extra run with one foot still inside the bowling crease and your bat grounded at the other end.

Whatever our chosen field of endeavour, we will achieve nothing unless we have the guts to translate thought into action. How often have you come up with the 'great idea' — and that's just what it remains. Benjamin Franklin summed it up many years ago: 'Well done is better than well said'. If we really want to be stump-jumpers, we should try anything and everything.

The future stump-jumper is a skill-seeker — a person not so much after money or a particular job as looking for self-development. We live the most intensely and progressively through new experience, and it is only through new experience that learning grows. It doesn't matter what the task is — the goal should be to do it to the best of our capabilities and to learn from it.

Ralph Sarich is a prime example of a skill-seeker who deliberately set out to acquire skills, and then had the guts to throw security to the wind and have a go. In fact, Sarich's courage is all the more notable as the task he set himself had been, and, indeed, currently is being, attempted by individuals and companies with large resources all over the world.

Security means death to the stump-jumper. A would-be stump-jumper leaves mediocrity for others to settle into. The important thing is not to find, but to keep searching and stretching. As Oliver Wendell Holmes said: 'Man's mind, once strengthened by a new idea, never regains its original dimensions'.

There's nothing wrong with being sacked or having failed, if you've tried. To die as a stump-jumper is to settle into what you have. Steven Rich had carved a successful career with Hunter Douglas when he decided that what was missing was the challenge. So he resigned and undertook, successfully, new vistas and new challenges.

All the slogans: excellence, money, self-actualisation, freedom, etc., amount to the same thing and take you to the same place. They are labels to keep you rolling . . .

Success is not conformity. Conformists are replaceable. Conformity means acceptance of mediocrity. It is an acceptance of what we feel we should do, rather than what we want to do. Lang Hancock is probably one of the most celebrated non-conformists in Australia today. It was his refusal to accept the status quo that led to the repeal of the iron ore exportation ban, after many years of lobbying. This in turn led to the extraordinary mineral resources boom that Australia enjoyed in the 1960s. Sooner or later, everyone has to select. Destiny, as the saying goes, is not a matter of chance, it is a matter of choice.

The individuals inside *The Stump-Jumpers* haven't learnt their tricks from a book. They are 'real' people, mostly self-taught, who have learnt it their way. John Laws has developed his own style over the years, a unique and very personal style that has carried him to the top of his profession worldwide.

Learning normally means a process of acquiring someone else's conclusions. Whilst it may be true to *their* lives, it won't necessarily work for you or me.

In marketing, all around the world, the bulk of the marketplace copies the competition. We believe that the key rule and strategy in marketing should be: 'be different'. Be the individual that leaves the beaten track to blaze a new trail. Let the others follow.

This particular quality of being 'different' from the competition applies to every one of our stump-jumpers in one way or another. After all, it's the extension of true individualism. Whether it be Bob Ansett, with his complete approach to Budget Rent-A-Car, or Richard Holden, with his revolutionary marketing concept and strategy for Chloe wines, or Stefan Ackerie who has quite literally created a new wave and unparalleled success with his group of hairdressing salons, there is no disputing that the word 'unique' applies to the success they enjoy and the path they have taken to reach it.

Australia is only now finding the courage to be different. For too long we have been unquestioningly absorbing and imitating the United Kingdom and the United States. It is probably through the field of the arts in particular that Australia has begun to discover original values — the sort of values that the stump-jumpers inside this book display.

Australia sets less store on social conformity than most other countries in the world. Perhaps this is because of the great ethnic mix, coupled with the fact that many of the people who migrated to Australia chose this country because they didn't want to inherit predetermined values. Also, of course, they chose Australia because it is an open country replete with opportunity.

Several of the families of our stump-jumpers were migrants. To all of them, Australia is their adopted home. A home they have prospered in, and contributed to, a home where they are building their future.

Our pioneers were self-taught individualists who adapted to the local environment. We need a resurgence of that spirit on all levels.

There is a myth of success that runs along the lines of, 'If only I was like . . .' What these people should be asking is: 'Who am I?' Answering that question is a step towards directing skills into action. Imitating the successful brings imitation success. When Bob Ansett was so successful in storming the rental car market, with a perceived American style, the opposition brought in American managers. Ansett's answer was swift and characteristic. He reverted to Australian citizenship. Either way, it didn't help his competitor's market share.

Imitation will, however, bring plaudits from peers who see in this emulation a justification of their own lifestyle — the cliché of success. But the imitators both limit and cheat themselves, and ultimately the one person we can never fool or delude for very long is ourselves — and you will need your true self to be successful.

You can fake the mask of success, but it never stays intact for long. You will pay a price, whether it be exposure or corruption of your own integrity.

What we can learn from the personalities in *The Stump-Jumpers* are techniques and skills as applied to different crafts. We should all learn our own craft, then apply our own core individuality and strengths to it. To know the craft alone will not make us successful.

Fred Schepisi is a man of sensitivity and vision who infuses into all his projects an individuality that is unmistakable. Coupled with his skill as a craftsman in his chosen field, the resultant work is striking because of its integrity of concept and execution.

We gain inspiration from our stump-jumpers, as well as the courage to jump in and get our feet wet.

We tend to measure our own weaknesses against the strengths of others, but what short-sighted comparisons we are drawing. We don't know the mix and balance of the other person's relative weaknesses in the comparisons we are making, so any conclusions we come to are both worthless and debilitating. Stump-jumpers have confidence in themselves and in their strengths. John Newcombe demonstrated this when he decided to make his final comeback against the younger Jimmy Connors. He not only had courage, but he believed, against the odds, that he could win — and what a sweet victory it was.

Often, we judge ourselves by the dominant stereotype of the time, but the world shakers have mostly been the uncompromising individuals who are totally true to themselves and do not conform for conformity's sake. Conformists are unlikely to feel that they are failures, as they are now integrated into their peer groups, but they have lost their potential because they have corrupted their core individuality. As Andrew Jackson noted: 'One man with courage makes a majority'.

People sense conformity without realising what they are identifying. Conformists lost drive, self-motivation and stimulus, because they are cheating themselves of their potential.

Vince Lombardi, the American motivation guru, summed it up in this quotation: 'The difference between a successful person and others is not a lack of strength, not a lack of knowledge, but rather a lack of will'. That is the will to retain your core individualism, and to put thoughts into action. To take the decision to step on the roller-coaster of experience, building and desiring to achieve, regardless of upsets en route.

Keith Williams epitomises these qualities. His determination and vision can be seen in what he has already achieved, and the plans he has for Hamilton Island. When fire hit his administration centre on the island, he was in a plane en route for Sydney. The plane immediately returned to the island, and the very next day the process of reconstruction began, followed by an exhausting series of interviews through the media to reassure the public that Hamilton Island was still operating.

As Polonius said to Laertes: 'To thine own self be true', and it's as relevant and appropriate today as when Shakespeare penned those words in the 17th century. (The other piece of advice meted out by Polonius in the same speech: 'Never a borrower nor a lender be' is probably more contentious!) Ask Prue Acton. Her success has continued and grown over several years. In the highly critical world of fashion, imitative success is transient.

A conformist looks in the mirror and spends his whole time apologising, and trying to fit the mould of somebody they are not, nor ever will be. Perhaps the conformist's credo should be: 'Success is simply a matter of luck', to which the achiever might reply, 'Ask any failure'. As Louis Pasteur said, 'Chance favours the prepared mind'.

Probably the difference between the ordinary conformist and the extraordinary individual is that little extra. Individuals, such as those people inside *The Stump-Jumpers*, are committed to the path of experience, ever challenging themselves to succeed in new arenas. Trying to keep pace with their current projects is an impossibility for a book which cannot have the immediacy of newspaper, television or radio.

The real message that comes through their deeds may be encapsulated in a rather wry observation of Somerset Maugham. 'It is a funny thing about life: if you refuse to accept anything but the best, you very often get it!'

All the stump-jumpers inside this book are self-starters. They began with propsects no greater or smaller than you or I possess. It is up to us whether we really want to stump-jump in any particular way or not.

But you'd better hurry up!

'Things come to those who wait, but only the things left by those who hustle.' — Abraham Lincoln, perhaps one of the greatest individuals American has ever seen.

And now for more Australian quotations than you can poke a stick at, see how you rate against the stump-jumper's self-evaluation quiz. Good luck — we hope that we hear from you in the future.

The A-Z of stump-jumping

The attributes listed below are not necessarily the only ones common to our stump-jumpers, but they were the ones that were cited most frequently in the discussions.

Based on a content analysis of the personalities interviewed in this book and other stump-jumpers who have already been interviewed for Volume II, these 26 attributes were the dominant characteristics that filtered through to the surface. However, even where the personalities might agree on the category, in many cases they would dispute the interpretation. Some of them would disagree with various categories altogether, but we do think it's worthwhile to put these comments side-by-side in order to watch the beginnings of a pattern emerge. Following here are just some of the quotations from the book, and often the stump-jumpers demonstrated their capacity in a given area without specifically addressing that field as a topic.

Here, then, are some key quotes from the interviews that illustrate our 'A-Z of stump-jumping'.

Ambition — the desire to gain maximum yield from the field.

The path to achievement has to begin somewhere, and obviously a desire to change one's current circumstances is fundamental.

'You start at the bottom of the mountain,' notes Newcombe, 'and there's room for a hell of a lot of people. I call it the tennis mountain . . . The question is, how badly do you want to arrive at the top?'

Leard says of his early ambition to one day head ANI, 'After I'd been there about six months, being a sort of brash young man, I think I did say to somebody . . . "Within 15 years, I will be running this place". That became a bit of a joke which some people forgot about and some people remembered. But that's what happened . . .'

Flippantly, Laws pegs ambition as 'another reason to get out of bed in the morning', but in a more serious moment he says, 'Everybody likes power. Not too many people like to admit it, but I think it's a great driving force behind the designs of many men.'

Williams believes that ambition should be instilled from an early age in all children. 'We should be building up our heroes so that our children will realise there is something to aim for. Otherwise, they will be totally devoid of ambition,' he declares.

Backbone — the audacity to face the challenge.

Courage is one topic about which most of our experts have much to say, perhaps because it's a quality linked to the turning point in their lives.

'Our two kids were only little when we built and sold the house, which was a dream home for my wife . . .' Sarich recalls. 'We went to live in an old asbestos house in Morely . . . So I threw security out the door and my wife supported me.'

To others, backbone represents a stubbornness which borders on contrariness.

'The more people tell me I can't do something, the more I enjoy doing it,' Williams declares.

Moore's challenge came from her husband. 'Had he said, "Run along, Rosemary, you'll be fine", I probably wouldn't have continued. But because he doubted my ability to be successful, I felt challenged and said, "I *will* do it." '

Hogan remembers, '. . . as a kid I'd acquired a habit whereby if somebody said, "Someone should set fire to that building or someone should ride his bike through there", I tended to see it as a challenge and therefore do it.'

Rich sums it up beautifully: 'I think the seduction of challenge is both a human frailty and our greatest strength.'

Creativity — the ability to see many different ways of approaching the opportunity.

Everybody can be creative, not just artists. 'To create something is an instinct that's locked up inside every one of us. This creative urge is a part of us that needs fulfilling . . .' states Randall.

Sarich believes that creativity can be infused into most situations, particularly ideas. '. . . a person should start looking for different horizons, be creative in what they do, and listen to other people . . . You don't necessarily have to adopt (other people's) views, but sometimes what they say triggers a thought in one's own mind in some other direction,' he said. In fact, Sarich recognised the importance of creativity as a boy at school. Tired of being told what he should learn, he concluded: '. . . if I devoted the school hours to business, I could in turn employ mathematicians, if I wanted to, and be creative in ways that weren't taught at school. You could say that what I'm doing now is what I aimed at during my school years,' he remarked.

For designer Acton, you don't define creativity, you use it — every day. 'An idea that may have taken 12 months to create pops out and here it is, this is it. Then someone asks you to rationalise that product. Well, I can take you through all those steps and give you a rational answer, which sounds awfully good, but what a waste of time. I could be onto the next idea.'

Decisiveness — the strength to examine an opportunity from all sides reach a decision and implement it, whilst not being locked into parochialism.

'The first thing that's going to make you successful is to know how to make decisions,' says Holden. 'Know when you should decide and when you should ask for more information, because decision-making at the right time, given the right level and quality of data, is what makes you successful. Sitting at a desk is not in itself a factor at all.'

Some people make on-the-spot decisions, and others, including Sarich, like to mull it over. 'People often think that I make spur-of-the-moment decisions,' he says, 'but I rarely do. Because I try to anticipate what will happen, I usually have many options thought out for each commitment made.'

Acton agrees with Sarich: 'I try to never make a decision until I'm happy with the idea, which drives people insane. They think I'm not concise or decisive, whereas in fact, until I'm absolutely happy that that's the right decision, I won't make one.'

For Phillips, in her fickle world of investment, 'Decision-making comes easily to me. I have one speed, and that's fast. I know quickly whether or not I'm interested in a deal.'

Entrepreneurship — the readiness to take a calculated risk.

Ackerie, who wanted his own hairstyling show on television, recalls: 'I took the risk of having pilot tapes privately done to show them what I could do and how I would do it . . . next thing they accepted. Public response was almost unbelievable.'

Such examples of smark risk-taking are legion among these people. Says Phillips: 'To be an entrepreneur is largely a matter of driving by the seat of one's pants.' And: 'Mine was a creative exercise that grew out of itself, without any nurturing from outside. Perhaps that's pure entrepreneurship.'

Leard, who refers to himself as a 'corporate entrepreneur', believes, 'You've got to have the capacity to look around and look ahead.'

On a national level, Acton thinks, 'We are not stuck with the old, as they are in New York or Europe, we can think as a young country can. We can move fast if we unleash our entrepreneurial power from the clutches of taxation and bureaucracy . . .'

First Class — the competitive spirit to pursue quality
and perfection.

Williams has a private jet bought from King Hussein, Laws owns a collection of Rolls Royces. Whether in business or in private life, what they enjoy is also what they want to create: the best.

For Leard, 'I suppose it became a personal ambition of mine to run the company with the best gross record in the world . . . that was more important to me than all the money in the world.'

Schepisi is equally dramatic: '. . . I want to be the best at what I'm doing. If you ask me who is the best film-maker in the world, I can't tell you, because I think there are 20 of them and I want to be among those 20 . . . I want to look back and be proud of every effort.'

'Whatever you do, you have to know that you're doing something better than someone else is doing it . . .' Acton believes. 'If someone is making better jeans than I could make, then I won't go into making them . . . You have to feel in your heart that you can do a really good job.'

Goal-Setting — the forethought and planning to decide where
you want to go.

'To be successful you need to have a dream, make it a goal, then chase that goal for all you're worth,' counsels Moore. 'You cannot know the joy of arriving if you never aim to go anywhere.'

'. . . first of all, set some sort of goal,' is a lesson Randall learned the hard way. 'It might take years, as it did with me, to determine what it is. Then, determine whether it's realistic, whether you really want it or whether it's some sort of fantasy . . . Defining an objective, setting a goal, writing a plan and then working very hard, I've since discovered, is a classic business strategy.'

It's a strategy that works well in other areas of life, too. 'Most of my goals are business-related, but there are personal ones,' says Ansett. 'Two years ago I set myself a goal of running a marathon, which I achieved, and I have now decided that I'll do one every five years . . .'

'I wanted to become a pilot and became one,' Ackerie says. 'That was a major goal, but my goals now are my work and my children. I don't like goals that aren't realistic.'

Newcombe recounts how he ran himself into fitness in order to beat the then-rising star, Jimmy Connors, in a big tournament: 'When the day was at its hottest and I was halfway up that hill and I wanted to stop, I just pictured in my mind that I was five-all in the fifth set and Connors was at the other end and I wanted him. And I just started burning it up the hill.'

Hard Work — the sweat and effort to see it through.

If there are any qualities in our A-Z list on which our stump-jumpers would be in unanimous agreement, this is surely one.

Williams begins at the beginning of the topic, with: 'An old friend, Archie Spooner . . . said to me one day, "Keith, the most difficult part of any job is to take off your coat, roll up your sleeves, and say you've started." I often think today how true that is . . .'

Hancock sees the application of elbow grease as a natural trait for some people: '. . . you can't stop a wheel when it's spinning,' he states, 'and I've always bounced back from setbacks.'

Phillips, who no doubt works harder than almost any of her employees, says, 'I see myself as a worker, which is my own excuse for being a capitalist, because I don't sit back and collect money that others are slaving to earn for me.'

While he, too, endorses personal industry, Holden sounds a wise warning: 'Hard work isn't necessarily digging ditches and it isn't necessarily the Protestant work ethic.' By this, he means, 'Hard work as we are taught it is often a means of avoiding decision-making.'

Intuition — the sensitivity to recognise that little voice which
tells you the way to go.

That little voice, of course, comes from within, and what it says must be balanced against the words of trusted associates. For many of those in this book, intuition plus information is the right combination.

'As you grow and expand, you take on other people and you have to listen to their advice, but you should listen to your instincts as well,' Schepisi cautions.

'To be successful in business you need the right mix of instinct, reason and advice,' is the Phillips formula.

Moore's father was really talking about instinct when he advised his daughter about whether or not she should sell books: 'There are only two worthwhile considerations, your God and then your own opinion. Don't be directed by anyone else's opinion in life.'

'You have to back your judgement and instinct, both with regard to people and situations . . . ' Rich declares.

Like many artists, Acton is deeply instinctive. Yet she says, 'I call it non-instinct, I call it my computer. I believe if I put enough information into my computer, then it's only a matter of assessing that information, which I usually do in a brainstorming session or a creative moment.'

Joie de Vivre — the love of life and work that results in fulfilment through pure enjoyment of each task, regardless of the outcome. Also, the sense of humour that allows you to laugh at yourself, in times both good and bad.

What's the point if it's a grind? Again, our stump-jumpers are unanimous on the importance of this attitude.

'. . . if you hate your job, as I did for many years, it means you're throwing away a third of every day of your life,' is how Hogan looks at it. Now that he's in a job he likes, he notices that, '. . . there are entertainers who . . . take themselves and what they do too seriously. You've got to guard against that.'

Even in the rough-and-tumble arena of big business, Leard learned: 'A sense of humour is also important, being able to laugh at yourself . . . don't believe your own bullshit.'

Perhaps the key to *joie de vivre* is to be able to ignore the line on your personal ledger between 'have to' and 'want to'. For example:

'I've always subscribed to the theory that there isn't much point in being in something if you don't enjoy it.' — Laws.

'I just can't see a difference between work and play . . . to me, it's all there to be enjoyed and it's all precious.' — Randall.

'I don't think I worked very hard or long hours, because when you enjoy what you're doing it's not like that . . . It's only when you are not interested that the energy becomes hard to generate.' — Ackerie.

'. . . I suppppose most important is to love your work in a way that makes it not just work but a hobby, an entertainment, and an all-fulfilling experience.' — Phillips.

'I don't think I've missed out on a damn thing. I've always been able to make my hobby a business or vice versa . . . If you don't enjoy what you're doing, you shouldn't be doing it.' — Williams.

Knowledge — the perception to receive information and to learn from it.

Whether knowledge comes from book-learning, experience, practical knowhow, or reliance on intuition, it's a quality elemental to achievement.

'I'm an advocate of formal education,' says Sarich, 'but once this has been completed, a person should start looking for different horizons, be creative in what they do and listen to other people.'

'My formal education was very limited but I've never stopped learning,' Phillips notes. 'I suppose that there is a certain amount of knowledge which one can bring to one's work which makes it easier to succeed quickly. However, sometimes acquired knowledge, especially if it is very academic, is a stumbling block that has to be overcome before one can relax into creativity.'

'My father wanted me to go on to university and become a mathematics professor,' Hancock remembers, 'but luckily I elected to go back to the bush. For a few packets of lollies you can buy a professor to work for you, so I'm very glad I didn't waste my time at university.'

Concerning the value of practical knowledge, Williams is in accord with Phillips and Hancock. 'In the type of business that I'm in, you need to have the ability to look at something, assess its potential, imagine it in Australia, then alter it to suit our situation and the likes and dislikes of the average Australian,' he explains.

'I learnt . . . things by trial and error and pain, lots and lots of pain,' says Ackerie. He also offers an unusual insight into the usefulness at times of not knowing *too* much: 'Everybody tells you about the stump you can't jump, but because you're ignorant you just think you can do it.'

Despite being in a rather 'mental' line of work, Schepisi also sees the dangers of trying to be too smart. 'If something is intellectual, don't get so intellectually clever that you don't deliver the physical, emotional impact which is warranted by any specific scene,' he says of film-making. 'I guess I'll go on learning that forever.'

Expansion of their knowledge is something many of the stump-jumpers still seek. On one hand, Leard admits, 'I'm a bit of a Philistine on education . . . Education, as I see it, is basically trying to put on old head on young shoulders.' On the other hand, he insists that, 'I want to be more knowledgeable about the world.'

Newcombe likewise is high on 'personal advancement'. 'I'm not talking about business or money, I'm talking about knowledge of things that I don't know now, say the cultural field, the fields that I haven't been involved in until now. I want to expand my own knowledge.'

Leadership — the quality of generating confidence and loyalty
by inspiring and directing others through example,
whilst accepting responsibility for the whole.

With his usual no-bones-about-it style, Leard claims: 'I'm a great elitist. I believe in leadership — it's the top 15 per cent of the people who make it happen. If you lose them — that's what happened in Russia, Stalin chopped their heads off — the country will suffer from it, as Russia still does.'

Ansett, another proven leader, believes that '. . . leadership is probably the single most important factor' in a successful enterprise. 'You have to . . . lead by example, rather than by instruction.'

Rich adds, 'If you can set that direction, then you can be one of the few in the world who doesn't have to follow. You can get yourself into a leadership position.'

Phillips, who points out that leadership by a woman is a somewhat more difficult task than by a man, especially in the past, also reveals: 'I hold meetings with line managers and we talk about pursuing common goals . . . it's important to me that I have a consensus from the line managers that they feel entirely comfortable with our objectives . . . The hardest thing a senior executive has to learn, I think, is to keep from meddling and getting too close to the day-to-day running of affairs.'

'Today, management is very responsible for the bad things they do to their staff,' Ackerie believes. 'Management must give their staff a clear direction. If the management is unfair . . . (the staff) can't succeed and the minute they don't succeed they feel awful. When they feel awful they don't succeed, it's a Catch 22 . . .'

In that vein, Sarich opines, 'There are no hard and fast formulas — you can't say this is what you should do — it's a matter of getting a feel for what the employees want. It's impossible to know every employee, but you have to get to know enough of them to get a feel of what the general impression is of the company they work for. We try to make them feel that it's their company and try to break down the employer-employee barriers.'

When that happens, hopefully the result will be an entire company that leads within its industry. Acton reflects, 'We made . . . fashion into something very wearable and all our customers followed. We've been able to go with every trend and be the leaders of trends.'

Finally, Hancock draws this thumbnail sketch of the ideal leader: 'I'd take a little bit of character from Sir Joh Bjelke-Petersen, I'd take a pinch of Lee Kuan Yew for political effectiveness, a bit of commercial nouse from D. K. Ludwig, and the scientific brain of Dr Edward Teller. Then you'd have the cream of the world.'

Money-Raising Skills — the pragmatism to evaluate what you are doing and to sell the concept successfully to investors.

Many of the people included in this book have commented on how hard it has been to raise money inside Australia. Hancock is one of the most obvious examples; after struggling with reluctant Australian investors, he finally had to go overseas for risk capital to develop his iron ore mines. Phillips has also had difficulties raising money, but in the early days her problems in that respect were often related to being a woman in business.

A once-precocious entrepreneur, Leard recalls: 'In my younger years, I ran into the problem of, "You're too young to do this job, you're too young to get support for this." . . . Some grey-headed bloke who looked as though he'd been thrashed by life was more likely to get a loan or get money for his company than some young bloke who looked as though he was still wet behind the ears. I suppose that was the greatest of things I've overcome.'

Ansett, who has much to say on the subject of money-raising, sums up his feelings with, 'If an entrepreneur comes up with a great idea, he must then find the funds to be able to produce a product or offer a service, and that's very hard to do in Australia.'

Non-Conformity — the freedom to be your own person.

Whilst Australia does not have a monopoly on stump-jumping, it's a nation build on non-conformity — which is perhaps the most typical quality of a stump-jumper.

Schepisi says: '. . . I now appreciate that Australia offers the world virility, in the real sense of the word. It's a feeling that there are no real rules, that if you believe there's a way of getting or achieving something you just go out and do it, not allowing yourself to be hindered by the way it should be done.'

On a more personal level, Ackerie reveals, 'I've never been one to follow what London or New York or Paris says, I've been one to do what is best for you.' In his work, he laments, 'For years I was forced into that mould, I resented it and was so happy when I could break out.'

Leard, who broke many of the corporate rules, says, 'I suppose I'm non-conformist and unorthodox in my approach. I have always been regarded as a rebel.'

On his phenomenal success with his own production company, Hogan says, 'We broke some rules, including changing channels when everybody told us that if you change channels, you die.'

A non-conformist refuses to accept the status quo. Williams relates how, 'I went to the Lands Department and they threw me out the door. They said, "Don't be silly, nobody has ever done that". I kept coming back and coming back, until finally a new section of the Act came about.'

Organised Mind — the commonsense and will to discipline
yourself, your time, and your resources.

At the risk of waxing platitudinous, 'get your head together' is one important thing we suspect these achievers have learnt.

For instance, Leard declares: 'I'm a great believer in self-discipline. I've been enormously self-disciplined and I think that's one of the reasons I've been successful. I'm my own harshest critic.'

Referring to an American survey, Moore says, '. . . the results showed that only one single quality was common to all achievers. Some of them had courage, some didn't; some showed tenacity, some didn't; some had stamina, some didn't. But what do you think was the one trait they all shared? It was *self-discipline.*' She deduces, 'Self-discipline is a major contributor to success. With it, you can make yourself do the things that need to be done, though you don't really want to do them at all.'

At another of his many critical moments in big championships, Newcombe displayed just that quality, and he describes it stirringly: 'I had to go back inside myself, I had to reach right down inside and purge all the negative thoughts that were in there about the crowd. I had to push them out and then I had to go within myself, so that when I walked out on the court the only things I could see were another player at the end of the court and a tennis ball . . . In other words, I put myself into a zone where nothing mattered except the person who was hitting the ball and the ball itself.'

Talk about the final word!

Personality — the personal style that seduces because it's authentic.

Ackerie passes on some words of wisdom in this regard: 'My grand-father said, "Do good and throw it in the sea. You never know when you're going to drown and it will save you." I find it is easier to leave people feeling good than otherwise. It requires more effort but it is still easier.'

'. . . if you are in an entertainment industry, you have to be a bit grand, have a bit of pizzazz, a bit of sparkle,' Laws believes.

Of course, even outside the field of entertainment, people's personalities count. 'In job interviews it's important to select the right people,' Sarich says. '. . . it's not good enough for us to merely select, for example, a brilliant engineer — he must have a personality that is compatible with others.'

Projecting a pleasing personality goes beyond the internal workings of a business, too. 'I must always be in touch with the public and I do this in many ways,' Ansett says, 'such as working in the rental office regularly, serving customers, and answering every letter that comes to me . . .'

In this book, Hogan is one of the prime examples of the importance of personality. It's a quality that speaks for itself rather than of itself, and as such it defies description. But it is vital.

Quick-Thinking — the alertness to recognise and seize
opportunities as they present themselves.

'. . . did you ever hear the saying that opportunity knocks and you should listen?' asks Moore. 'It's not true. Opportunity doesn't knock at all. Usually, it rushes past you in the dark and if you put out your hand, you feel the wind. Most times, that's as close as it will ever come. You do the rest.'

'Maybe the difference between the successful man and the unsuccessful man is the unsuccessful man had the opportunity right in front of him and he didn't see it or he didn't take it,' is Leard's analysis.

Timing is a critical factor in the grasping of opportunity. Whereas Moore notes the importance of seizing it quickly or missing out, Acton believes in preparation. 'I futurise . . . In this way, opportunity walks in at my gate. I recognise it, because I've already done the pre-plans for a number of eventualities,' she says.

Schepisi draws a graphic situational picture of how quick-thinking works on a film set. 'When you're on the floor, the adrenaline pumps through to get you thinking fast, there's humour and tension and pressure.'

Resilience — the natural tenacity and determination to bounce
back from adversity.

'You need to be tenacious in this world to get anywhere,' says Williams.
'You've got to decide that you are going to get the job done and go out
and do it. If the game gets tough, you kick it into shape and make it
work.'

'Character is the resolve to keep going long after the desire to do so
has passed,' Moore states.

'There's a story that is supposedly true about a guy who bought a
gold mine,' Ackerie recounts. 'He dug and dug, found nothing, and
finally sold the mine. The bloke who came in dug another two feet and
found the greatest gold reef in the history of mining. Motivators are
full of these stories . . . a lot of people quit just before they make it.'

How one deals with setbacks is at the core of the ability to be
resilient.

'Sometimes I see it as a form of enforced rest,' Laws says, 'but it
really just represents a nuisance. I don't ever think of it as more than
that.'

Says Randall: 'I've made mistakes but I don't dwell on them. I don't
catalogue them . . . but I can remember after things went wrong that
I said, "Well, you won't do that one again." . . . I think it was Robert
Townsend who said, "Problems are opportunities to choose between
solutions". I love that.'

On the international front, Acton makes an important point: 'In the
United States . . . I believe the whole attitude there is that the third
time around is when businesses often make it big. That's why they're
so successful — they're not afraid of failing . . .'

Self-Confidence — the inner conviction that what you believe in
is right.

If you don't believe you can jump a stump, you're going to knock your
shins. To wit:

'I think right from the time I was a kid I had confidence in my own
ability . . .' — Leard.

'At 10 I knew what I wanted to do, or knew what my destiny was.
From that moment on, I never doubted that I would arrive where I
have arrived.' — Newcombe.

'Self-confidence is a prerequisite to making decent decisions. If
you're not confident in yourself, you'll make excuses to cover your lack
of self-confidence. You cannot give what you don't have a surplus of.

Nothing sets me apart from my peers, except that I'm not afraid of failure.' — Holden.

'. . . you don't do anything unless you have confidence in yourself, and generally I was very confident that I could do better than what I had seen other people do and I was prepared to gamble on my ability to do just that.' — Sarich.

'If you wish to succeed, you should have a single-minded confidence in yourself and your ability to deal with most situations, because no matter what you do in life, whether it's in a profession or in business or in school, it's never smooth sailing.' — Ansett.

Teamwork — the ability to delegate wisely and to orchestrate the parts into a harmonious entity.

Schepisi's description of teamwork is a parable in itself: 'Do you like jazz? Have you ever seen Gil Evans? His is a philosophy on life that I like to sit and watch. His group has 17 individuals . . . yet there is complete freedom and complete cohesion. I think that's how life should be and how art or films should be made. Everybody should have . . . freedom of expression and yet be able to meld and become a greater element in combination with others.'

Ansett's variation on that theme has been elemental to Budget's success: 'The first thing I wanted to do was to create a team involvement . . . an environment that encouraged winning . . . although you should top it off by making it as much fun as possible.'

Another highly effective team that has been assembled by Sarich, who offers this philosophy: 'Above all, if we employ somebody we respect their intelligence, and therefore encourage their contribution to how the company should be run . . . we try to create a pleasant environment first. Then, as I said, we encourage people to have an input . . .'

Undivided Loyalty — the integrity and fairness to stick by your friends, partners and colleagues regardless of circumstances.

In order to survive on the lonely rigours of the professional tennis circuit, Newcombe found that, 'If you have a good friend . . . you've got someone there fighting who's got the same problems as you do.'

'. . . I just do not like letting people down who have put their faith in me,' Sarich says simply.

Ackerie echoes that thought: 'My formula for success is to be honest and fair, to yourself and to the people . . . you must always honour what you say you are going to do.'

'I think the great satisfaction you get out of business is the people that you associate with,' says Williams. 'There are too many people who will try to become the high and mighty overnight and they forget about the people who helped along the way.'

'Forget yourself, and work for the things you believe in: your product, your company, your manager, your family, or your country,' says Moore. 'Then, and only then, can other things come through for you.'

Vision — the clear sight to conceptualise what really can be.

Although it is a fine line between dream and vision, the true stump-jumper is able to make that distinction. Some of Hancock's biggest and best visions may still be unrealised, but he continues to fight for their fruition — and to exercise a sense of proportion in doing so.

Hogan credits his partner John Cornell with the vision that brought them both fame and prosperity. 'Cornell was different,' he says. 'He'd always thought from the word go that Hogan could last as long as he wanted to last . . . after a while, I saw that the faith he had in the show was justified.'

'. . . for the better Australians there is no wall,' Schepisi says, 'they have an open vision, and when they come up against an obstacle they do a bit of lateral thinking to work out a way around it. They'll challenge, they'll come up with an entirely different idea or approach to get where they're going.'

Well-Being — the intelligent self-management of one's body
and resources.

All but one of the people in this book is a non-smoker. Many of them set aside time in their daily routines for exercise, though work commitments often do battle with their good intentions. Hogan keeps in terrific shape through sports and activities with his children, Williams often goes sculling with his son in the morning, Randall learned to scuba dive from her young son, Ackerie, an accomplished sportsman, has a personal goal of becoming Australia's top off-shore speedboat racer, and Leard played 20 sports and weighs about the same as he did in high school.

But even out of such a health-conscious group as these stump-jumpers, it's Newcombe who probably wins hands down. 'I really have about four months a year of work that is connected to making money,' he says, 'and the other eight months is for doing things that I want to do myself.' One thing he definitely likes to do is stay healthy.

X-Factor — the one factor outside the stump-jumper's control, based on the luck of being in the right place at the right time. (True stump-jumpers seem to attract this.)

In 1952, Hancock flew over the Hamersley Ranges in thick, low-lying clouds. He recalls, '. . . I'd left it later than usual to get out . . . the clouds got lower and lower. I didn't have the instruments or the power to get up through the top of them, so I had to follow them down and I found a creek flowing through one of the gorges.' Was that pure chance or was there something that made him recognise the iron ore he then discovered? Hancock believes it was the latter case — and no doubt, he's right.

By the same token, when Williams bought a piece of land that was on the top of a hill and had no access, all his friends said, ' "You're a fool" . . . but by sheer luck, about six months later some fellow bought all the land up the side of the hill right to the boundary of my property. He put in a complete sub-division and a road.' Again, was that luck, or was it the X-Factor?

Schepisi lost out on an opportunity to direct a film called 'The Consultant', but along came 'Iceman'. Another time, he'd laboured months on the film 'Raggedy Man' and on the day that the project fell through for him, he signed up to direct 'Barbarosa'. 'It's the luck of the draw,' he claims.

Was Hogan lucky to be 'discovered' by the television studios when he was working as a rigger on the Harbour Bridge?

'. . . am I lucky?' Laws asks of his success in radio. 'Why am I lucky? I don't think I'm lucky. I was in the right place at the right time, but so were a lot of other people . . . But it seems like when opportunity knocks, a lot of people are putting the garbage out or are in the bath.'

Yabber Mastery — the persuasion of the thinker's gift-of-the-gab.

That the communications skills of these people are well-honed must be evident in the interviews themselves, yet often they've worked hard to develop those abilities. A few cases in point: Williams's long verbal struggle to establish the Ski Gardens in Queensland; Hancock's search for venture capital; and, of course, Laws's virtuoso performances on the radio every day.

'The last great initiative I took was to talk the government into backing the tourist campaign,' Hogan says.

Such expertise in negotiation has become a science with Sarich, who examines each issue from everybody's point of view, anticipating the questions and providing answers in advance. 'People in business usually can't understand technology well enough to weigh its potential and viability,' he says. '. . . it's natural that they are very guarded, very sceptical. It's up to the technologist to put across the argument properly, to convince them that a project is worthwhile. The manner in which you approach that task is the key. People must first of all trust you and trust your motives.'

Says Leard, 'I've always been a great believer in softly, softly. Talk about it and do it behind the scenes.'

Zest — the contagious enthusiasm and optimism that
excite others around you.

Even as a young 'gopher' in an advertising agency, Schepisi remembers, 'I was very enthusiastic and used to drive them mad asking them to give me opportunities.'

Ansett, a master of injecting zest into his entire organisation, says, 'You always have your ups and downs, and the key to me is to be able to deal with the down periods with confidence, enthusiasm and cheerfulness, and not reflect any noticeable despair.' He believes, '. . . an entrepreneur has to bring great energy and enthusiasm to the development of a business, and must infuse the organisation with a similar energy. I think energy is the number one thing — the energy quota, rather than the intellectual quota, is paramount.

The stump-jumper's self-evaluation quiz

The stump-jumper's analogy has us all starting off in a field littered with stumps. It's the application of the 26 characteristics listed below that will decide what kind of yield we can realise from the field.

Nobody is strong in all 26. The name of the game is to find the ones you are particularly good at and work with them in stump-jumping your way to your own goals.

To see how you rate as a potential stump-jumper, score yourself from 0-10 points in each of the 26 categories depending upon your assessment of your relative strength in each area.

Obviously this is a highly subjective quiz, and it is up to you to be honest and critically fair in the evaluation of your abilities as a stump-jumper.

We recommend that you rate yourself once and then have somebody else, close enough to you to have insight into your strengths and weaknesses, to rate you independently. The results can be intriguing . . .

Place a ruler over the scoring values in the table, or have a friend or partner write in your scores for you.

We have provided several scoring columns so that you can try this quiz on your associates, and evaluate your abilities as a team.

If you find that you consistently fall into a stump-jumper score and your circumstances tell you that this is unlikely, don't worry! At least you have a high rating on that key stump-jumper attribute — self confidence!

As you progress with your field and your motivation changes, try re-evaluating your score every six months or so to monitor your growth.

Ambition: *the desire to gain maximum yield from the field.*

Backbone: *the audacity to face the challenge.*

Creativity: *the ability to see many different ways of approaching the opportunity.*

Decisiveness: *the strength to examine an opportunity from all sides, reach a decision and implement it, whilst not being locked into a rigid parochialism.*

Entrepreneurship: *the readiness to take a calculated risk.*

First-Class: *the competitive spirit to pursue quality and perfection.*

Goal-Setting: *the forethought and planning to decide where you want to go.*

Hard Work: *the sweat and effort to see it through.*

Intuition: *the sensitivity to recognise that little voice which tells you the way to go.*

Joie de Vivre: *the love of life and work that results in fulfilment through pure enjoyment of each task, regardless of the outcome. Also, the sense of humour that allows you to laugh at yourself, in times both good and bad.*

Knowledge: *the perception to receive information and to learn from it.*

Leadership: *the quality of generating confidence and loyalty, by inspiring and directing others through example whilst accepting responsibility for the whole.*

Money-Raising Skills: *the pragmatism to evaluate what you are doing and to sell the concept successfully to investors.*

Non-Conformity: *the freedom to be your own person.*

Organised Mind: *the commonsense and will to discipline yourself, your time, and your resources.*

Personality: *the personal style that seduces because it's authentic.*

Quick-Thinking: *the alertness to recognise and seize opportunities as they present themselves.*

Resilience: *the natural tenacity and determination to bounce back from adversity.*

Self-Confidence: *the inner conviction that what you believe in is right.*

Teamwork: *the ability to delegate wisely and to orchestrate the parts into a harmonious entity.*

Undivided Loyalty: *the integrity and fairness to stick by your friends, partners and colleagues regardless of circumstances.*

Vision: *the clear sight to conceptualise what really can be.*

Well-Being: *the intelligent self-management of one's body and resources.*

X-Factor: *the one factor outside the stump-jumper's control, based on the luck of being in the right place at the right time.(True stump-jumpers attract this.)*

Yabber-Mastery: *the persuasion of the thinker's gift-of-the-gab.*

Zest: *the contagious enthusiasm and optimism that excites others around you.*

	Multiple Value	Your Score Out of 10	Total	Your Score Out of 10	Total	Your Score Out of 10	Total
A	4 x						
B	2 x						
C	1 x						
D	1 x						
E	2 x						
F	1 x						
G	1 x						
H	4 x						
I	1 x						
J	5 x						
K	1 x						
L	1 x						
M	1 x						
N	5 x						
O	2 x						
P	1 x						
Q	1 x						
R	2 x						
S	4 x						
T	1 x						
U	1 x						
V	2 x						
W	1 x						
X	3 x						
Y	1 x						
Z	1 x						
	50	Grand Total:					

Explanation of the scoring system: Each stump-jumper characteristic has been given a value which is multiplied by your score out of 10. Whilst all the characteristics are important in varying degrees, the top scoring categories reflect their relative importance based on the frequency of display by the personalities interviewed.

We have broken up the attributes into three groups for scoring purposes.

The Essentials: Ambition, Hardwork, Self-Confidence, Joie de Vivre and Non-Conformity.

The ambition to want to stump-jump in the first place, the hard work required to succeed, the self-confidence to believe that you will achieve, the joie de vivre without which both the undertaking and yourself would suffer, and the non-conformity to do it in your own way. These are the essential characteristics most common to the stump-jumpers.

Ambition, hard work and self-confidence are all attributes one would expect to be 'core' to a stump-jumper. Each scores 4 points.

Joie de vivre and non-conformity come as more of a surprise. Every single one of the stump-jumpers expressed the opinion that you must enjoy what you are doing. Non-conformity is a particularly Australian characteristic, and indeed, is the one other attribute that linked all the individuals. Score 5 points for these 2 categories.

The Required: Backbone, Resilience, Vision, Entrepreneurship and X-factor. A stump-jumper requires guts, elasticity, clear sight, the courage and confidence to take a calculated risk, and lastly, but not least, a dash of luck.

Backbone, resilience, vision and entrepreneurship each score 2 points.

The X-factor is peculiarly relevant to stump-jumpers in the 'lucky country', and many of the personalities have enjoyed this added edge. The score for this category is 3 points.

The Optional: All the other attributes are important, but no stump-jumper is uniformly strong across the board in all these categories. A stump-jumper may have to exhibit many of these characteristics, but can often delegate weaker areas to other team members. Score 1 point for these characteristics.

How You Rate

0-100 points — Stump-Bumper:
In deference to both your body, and the stumps, you should carefully select a field of endeavour that offers you the greatest joie de vivre.

101-200 points — Stump-Stumbler:
Your legs must be pretty battered by now. You must make the decision of whether you wish to cross the Simpson and put in the work required to progress in stump-jumping, or to give your legs a break (metaphorically-speaking) and be content with your lot in life.

201-350 points — Stump-Hopper:
You're well on your way, but you need more spring in your approach. Try practising on smaller stumps to gain confidence and increase your skills. You're on the first leg of the triple jump to stump-jumping.

351-450 points — Stump-Skipper:
You are only inches away from clearing the stump. Those extra inches may seem like feet (battered ones if you've progressed from stump-bumping), but with resilience and hard work you will succeed in besting that wretched stump.

451 plus — Stump-Jumper:
You obviously could have articulated these conclusions if you weren't too busy harvesting. If we haven't already heard from you, or contacted you, please get in touch with us for an interview in the next volume of *'The Stump-Jumpers'*.

Acknowledgements

When a project spans as long a period as *The Stump-Jumpers*, the list of people who have contributed to its realisation become legion. My appreciation goes out to all those who have contributed, many of whom are mentioned below.

Firstly, I would like to thank all the Stump-Jumpers inside this volume (and those who have already contributed to Volume 2), in particular for their generosity of time and spirit, and most especially those who gave me additional time, insight and support over and above the interview itself.

TAA and Pan Am who assisted with travel. Conventional plaudits apart, the calibre of service of these airlines can be measured against the fact that I was able to step off long and frequent flights straight into interviews without finding myself physically exhausted — or underfed!

My deep gratitude to all those friends around the world, who helped me in keeping the hotel bills to a minimum: Stephen and Rosie French; John and Margie Young; the recently married Mr and Mrs Jabez Jacobs; Stefan Ensler and partner; Julian and Polly Coles (also recently married — is this a trend?); the Brooklyn Monster Magnates, brothers Phil and Angelo Melito; and Lesley and Bill Veale for their premises that provided welcome rest and relaxation mid-craziness. Special thanks also for their active support, encouragement, and faith to Tony and Ann Lawrence, Jim Walpole, Sue Maitland, Phil Jarratt, Neil Jamieson, Brian Agnew, Jim Wells, Caty Young, Franziska Liebermann, James Fraser, Noelle Morgan, Dick and Dora Manclark, and, for his guidance, to Jock Young. Also, Haydon Lawrence and Nicholas Dingwall who contributed through their recent, vital and refreshing approach. Many people helped with suggestions of nominees for Stump-Jumpers, but I would like to single out Libby Escolme-Schmidt in particular for her kindness and assistance in the focusing of potential women Stump-Jumper candidates; and, for the part he played in providing an initial stimulus in pursuing this project, my thanks to Warwick Hamill.

Then, of course, the team who worked so hard in developing *The Stump-Jumpers*, spear-headed by Steve Bunk and Barbara Wuthrich for their forbearance, co-operation, hard work, input, and cheerfulness. It would have been a stump-jumping feat of magnificence to have completed this book without the assistance at all hours and computer back-up provided by David Davis of Dasys. Thanks also go to all those who helped in providing photographs, especially John Smith, Photographic Editor of a major Sydney newspaper, and to Pascual Locanto who burnt the midnight oil to produce such fine work. My indebtedness to Madeleine Behrens and family for putting up with interminable brain-storming sessions, and endless discussions whilst producing 'a la carte' hospitality - and finally, Constant Behrens, who has helped by prodding and stretching the concept of 'Stump-Jumping' into the reality of a book, plus . . .